Child Labour

Books in ABC-CLIO's World History Companion Series:

Capitalism, Larry Allen

Child Labour, Sandy Hobbs, Jim McKechnie, and Michael Lavalette

The Industrial Revolution, Peter N. Stearns and John H. Hinshaw

Utopian Movements, Daniel W. Hollis III

Child Labour
A World History Companion

Sandy Hobbs, Jim McKechnie,
and Michael Lavalette

ABC-CLIO

Santa Barbara, California
Denver, Colorado
Oxford, England

British Library Cataloguing in Publication Data

Hobbs, Sandy.
    Child labour : a world history companion
    1. Children - Employment   2. Children - Employment - History
    3. Children - Employment - Law and legislation   4. Children -
    Employment - Psychological aspects   5. Children - Employment -
    Social aspects
    I. Title II. Lavalette, Michael III. McKechnie, Jim
  331.3'1

ISBN 1 85109 346 X

ABC-CLIO Ltd.,
Old Clarendon Ironworks,
OXFORD OX2 6AT, ENGLAND

Printed and Bound in Great Britain by
MPG Books Limited, Bodmin, Cornwall

Contents

Entries by Category, ix
Preface, xiii
Introduction, xv

Child Labour: A World History Companion

Abbott, Grace, 1
Accidents, 1
Addams, Jane, 2
Adler, Felix, 2
Adolescence, 3
Advocacy, 4
Africa, 4
Agriculture, 5
Alcohol and Drugs, 7
Algeria, 7
America, Central, 9
America, Latin, 9
America, South, 9
American Academy of Political and
    Social Science, 10
American Federation of Labor, 10
Anthracite Coal Strike, 10
Anthropology, 11
Anti-Slavery International, 11
Apparel Industry Task Force, 12
Apprenticeship, 12
Argentina, 13
Asia, 13

Bal Mazdoor Union, 15
Bangladesh, 15

Belgium, 16
Beveridge, Albert J., 17
Bhima Sangha, 19
Blincoe, Robert, 19
Bonded Labour Liberation Front, 19
Boy Slaves, 19
Boy Soldiers, 20
Brazil, 21
Bruce, Rev. Charles Lang, 23
Burkina Faso, 23
Burston School Strike, 23
Business Ethic, 24

Camel Jockeys, 25
Cameroon, 26
Canada, 27
Capitalism, 27
Career, 29
Caribbean, 29
Carpet Manufacture, 30
Causes of Child Labour, 31
Centuries of Childhood, 31
Child Markets, 32
Child Migrants Trust, 33
Child Slaves, 34
Child Workers in Nepal, 34

Contents

Children's Bureau, 35
Children's Rights, 37
Chile, 39
Chimney Sweeping, 39
China, 40
Cinema, 41
Coal Breakers, 43
Colombia, 44
Concerned for Working Children, The, 46
Confederacao Nacional de Accao sobre Trabalho Infantil, 46
Construction Industry, 47
Consumerism, 47
Convention on the Rights of the Child, 49
Costs and Benefits, 50
Cultural Traditions, 51

Defence for Children International, 55
Definition of Child Labour, 55
Defoe, Daniel, 57
Delinquency, 58
Delivery, Milk, 59
Delivery, Newspaper, 60
Denmark, 60
Dickens, Charles, 61
Dinwiddie, Courtenay, 62
Division of Labour, 62
Domestic Service, 63
Drawboys, 65
Dundee Factory Boy, 65

Education, Universal, 69
Educational Achievement, 70
Egypt, 72
Elimination of Child Labour, 72
Engels, Friedrich, 74
Entertainment Industry, 76
Ergonomics, 76
Ethnicity, 77
Europe, 78
Europe, Council of, 79
Europe, Eastern, 81
European Union, 81
Exploitation, 83

Factory Acts, 85
Factory Inspectors, 86
Fair Labor Standards Act, 87

Fair Trade, 88
Family Relations, 88
Family Wage, 89
Feminism, 91
Fishing, 92
Folks, Homer, 94
France, 94

Garment Industry, 97
Gender Differences, 98
Gender Stereotypes, 101
General Federation of Women's Clubs, 102
Germany, 102
Glass-Making Industry, 103
Global March against Child Labor, 103
Globalization, 105
Gompers, Samuel, 106
Great Depression, The, 106
Greece, 107
Greenberger, Ellen, 108
Guatemala, 108

Half-time Working, 111
Hammond, J. L., and Hammond, Barbara, 111
Harkin Bill, 112
Harvesting, 112
Health, 113
Herding, 114
Hine, Lewis Wickes, 114
History of Childhood, 115
Hotel and Catering Industry, 116
Household Labour, 118

Immigrant Children, 121
India, 122
Indonesia, 123
Industrial Revolution, 125
Industrial Society Thesis, 126
Industrial Workers of the World, 127
International Confederation of Free Trade Unions, 128
International Financial Institutions, 129
International Labour Organisation, 130
International Meeting of Working Children, 131
International Monetary Fund, 132
International Working Group on Child Labour, 133

International Year of the Child, 133
Italy, 134

Japan, 135
Jordan, 135

Keating-Owen Bill, 137
Kenya, 137
Kielburger, Craig, 138
Knights of Labor, The Order of, 138

Labour Codes and Policy of the U.S.S.R., 139
Lawrence Mill Workers' Strike, 140
Legislation, 141
Legislation, International, 142
Leisure, 143
Liberationism, 143
Lindsay, Samuel McCune, 144
Livingstone, David, 145
Lovejoy, Owen R., 145
Low Pay Network, 146

Malawi, 149
Malaysia, 150
Malta, 150
Malthusianism, 151
Market Economics, 151
Marxism, 152
Masih, Iqbal, 153
McKelway, Alexander J., 154
Meknes, 156
Mexico, 156
Middle East, 158
Migrant Workers, 158
Mining, 160
Modelling, 162
Morocco, 163
Mother Jones, 163
Movement of Working Children and Adolescents from Working-Class Christian Families, 164
Multinational Companies, 164
Murphy, Edgar G., 165
Myanmar, 165

Nardinelli Thesis, The, 167
National Child Labor Committee, 168
National Committee for the Rights of the Child, 169
National Consumers League, 170

National Movement of Street Children, 171
Navy, 171
NCH-Action for Children, 171
Nepal, 172
Netherlands, 173
New England Association of Farmers, Mechanics, and Other Working Men, 174
New Zealand, 174
Newsies, 174
Nicaragua, 176
Nigeria, 176
Nongovernmental Organizations, 177

Oastler, Richard, 179
Operation Child Watch, 180
Organisation for Economic Cooperation and Development, 180
Organizations of Working Children, 180
Outwork, 182
Owen, Robert, 182

Pakistan, 183
Palmer-Owen Bill, 184
Parents, 184
Parliamentary Committees and Commissions, 186
Paterson 10-Hour Mill Strikes, 186
Pauper Apprentices, 187
Permanent Conference for the Abolition of Child Labor, 188
Peru, 188
Philippines, 189
Pinchbeck, Ivy, 190
Pornography, 191
Portugal, 191
Post-Fordism, 192
Poverty, 193
Prison, 194
Product Labelling, 194
Pro-employment Arguments, 195
Projects, 196
Prostitution, 197
Protectionism, 198
Proto-industrialization, 200
Psychology, Developmental, 200

Religion, 203
Retail Trade, 203

Contents

Rights Discourse, 203
Romania, 205
Rugmark, 205
Runaways, 205
Russia, 206

Saturday Evening Post, 207
Save the Children Fund, 207
Scandinavia, 208
Scavenging, 208
Self-employment, 208
Service Sector, 210
Shaftesbury, Lord, 210
Social Class, 211
Social Construction of Childhood, 212
Socialization, 214
Somalia, 215
South Africa, 216
Spain, 216
Sports, 217
Stabilization and Structural Adjustment
    Programs, 218
Steinberg, Laurence, 219
Stop Child Labour, 220
Street Children, 220
Sweated Labour, 222

Tanzania, 225
Thailand, 225
Thompson, E. P., 227
Tourism, 227

Trade Unions, 228
Traditional Societies, 229
Training, 229
Transition Debate, 230
Triangle Shirtwaist Factory Fire, 232
Turkey, 232

Unfree Labour, 235
United Arab Emirates, 236
United Kingdom, 236
United Nations International Children's
    Emergency Fund, 238
United States of America, 238

Van Houten, Samuel, 241
Vietnam, 241
Voices of Children, 242

Wages, 245
Water Babies, The, 246
Welfare, Child, 246
Work Ethic, 247
Work Values, 247
Workhouses, 248
World Bank, 250

Young Caregivers, 253

Zetkin, Clara Eissner, 255
Zimand, Gertrude Folks, 255
Zimbabwe, 255

Appendix: Web Sites, 257
Glossary, 259
Acronyms, 265
Chronology, 267
Bibliography, 273
Index, 285
About the Authors, 293

Entries by Category

The Jobs Children Do and the Industries They Work In
Agriculture
Boy Soldiers
Camel Jockeys
Carpet Manufacture
Chimney Sweeping
Cinema
Coal Breakers
Construction Industry
Delivery, Milk
Delivery, Newspaper
Domestic Service
Drawboys
Entertainment Industry
Fishing
Garment Industry
Glass-Making Industry
Harvesting
Herding
Hotel and Catering Industry
Household Labour
Mining
Modelling
Navy
Newsies
Outwork
Pornography
Prostitution
Retail Trade
Scavenging
Service Sector

Sports
Street Children
Tourism
Young Caregivers

Child Workers and Former Child Workers
Blincoe, Robert
Dickens, Charles
Dundee Factory Boy
Livingstone, David
Masih, Iqbal

Countries and Regions of the World
Africa
Algeria
America, Central
America, Latin
America, South
Argentina
Asia
Bangladesh
Belgium
Brazil
Burkina Faso
Cameroon
Canada
Caribbean
Chile
China
Colombia
Denmark

Entries by Category

Egypt
Europe
Europe, Eastern
France
Germany
Greece
Guatemala
India
Indonesia
Italy
Japan
Jordan
Kenya
Malawi
Malaysia
Malta
Mexico
Middle East
Morocco
Myanmar
Nepal
Netherlands
New Zealand
Nicaragua
Nigeria
Pakistan
Peru
Philippines
Portugal
Romania
Russia
Scandinavia
Somalia
South Africa
Spain
Tanzania
Thailand
Turkey
United Arab Emirates
United Kingdom
United States of America
Vietnam
Zimbabwe

Problems Associated with Children Working
Accidents
Alcohol and Drugs
Apprenticeship
Business Ethic
Career

Child Markets
Consumerism
Cultural Traditions
Delinquency
Educational Achievement
Ethnicity
Family Relations
Family Wage
Gender Differences
Gender Stereotypes
Health
Immigrant Children
Leisure
Migrant Workers
Parents
Pauper Apprentices
Prison
Religion
Runaways
Self-employment
Sweated Labour
Training
Unfree Labour
Welfare, Child
Work Ethic
Workhouses

Economic and Technological Context
Capitalism
Defoe, Daniel
Division of Labour
Globalization
Great Depression, The
Industrial Revolution
International Financial Institutions
International Monetary Fund
Multinational Companies
Organisation for Economic Cooperation and Development
Post-Fordism
Poverty
Proto-industrialization
Stabilization and Structural Adjustment Programmes
Traditional Societies
Wages
World Bank

Attempts to Understand Children Working
Adolescence

Anthropology
Causes of Child Labour
Centuries of Childhood
Costs and Benefits
Definition of Child Labour
Greenberger, Ellen
Hammond, J. L., and Hammond, Barbara
History of Childhood
Nardinelli Thesis, The
Pinchbeck, Ivy
Psychology, Developmental
Social Class
Social Construction of Childhood
Socialization
Steinberg, Laurence
Thompson, E. P.
Transition Debate
Work Values

Child Labour Strategies
Advocacy
Children's Rights
Elimination of Child Labour
Engels, Friedrich
Ergonomics
Exploitation
Feminism
Half-time Working
Industrial Society Thesis
Liberationism
Malthusianism
Market Economics
Marxism
Pro-employment Arguments
Protectionism
Rights Discourse
Saturday Evening Post
Voices of Children

Organizations Concerned with Child Workers
American Academy of Political and Social Science
American Federation of Labor
Anti-Slavery International
Apparel Industry Task Force
Bal Mazdoor Union
Bonded Labour Liberation Front
Child Migrants Trust
Child Workers in Nepal

Children's Bureau
Concerned for Working Children, The
Confederacao Nacional de Accao sobre Trabalho Infantil
Defence for Children International
Europe, Council of
European Union
General Federation of Women's Clubs
Industrial Workers of the World
International Confederation of Free Trade Unions
International Labour Organisation
International Working Group on Child Labour
Knights of Labor, The Order of
Low Pay Network
Movement of Working Children and Adolescents from Working-Class Christian Families
National Child Labor Committee
National Committee for the Rights of the Child
National Consumers League
National Movement of Street Children
NCH-Action for Children
New England Association of Farmers, Mechanics, and Other Working Men
Nongovernmental Organizations
Permanent Conference for the Abolition of Child Labour
Save the Children Fund
Stop Child Labour
Trade Unions
United Nations International Children's Emergency Fund

People Who Have Worked on Behalf of Working Children
Abbott, Grace
Addams, Jane
Adler, Felix
Beveridge, Albert J.
Bruce, Rev. Charles Lang
Dinwiddie, Courtenay
Folks, Homer
Gompers, Samuel
Hine, Lewis Wickes
Kielburger, Craig
Lindsay, Samuel McCune
Lovejoy, Owen R.
McKelway, Alexander J.

Entries by Category

Mother Jones
Murphy, Edgar G.
Oastler, Richard
Owen, Robert
Shaftesbury, Lord
Van Houten, Samuel
Zetkin, Clara
Zimand, Gertrude Folks

Ways People Have Tried to Control Child Labour
Convention on the Rights of the Child
Education, Universal
Factory Acts
Factory Inspectors
Fair Labor Standards Act
Fair Trade
Half-time Working
Harkin Bill
Keating-Owen Bill
Labour Codes and Policy of the U.S.S.R.
Legislation
Legislation, International
Operation Child Watch
Palmer-Owen Bill
Parliamentary Committees and Commissions

Product Labelling
Projects
Rugmark

Specific Incidents
Anthracite Coal Strike
Boy Slaves
Burston School Strike
Child Slaves
International Year of the Child
Lawrence Mill Workers' Strike
Meknes
Paterson 10-Hour Mill Strikes
Triangle Shirtwaist Factory Fire
Water Babies

Organizations of Child Workers
Bal Mazdoor Union
Bhima Sangha
Global March against Child Labor
International Meeting of Working Children
Movement of Working Children and Adolescents from Working-Class Christian Families
National Movement of Street Children
Organizations of Working Children

Preface

Some readers skip prefaces, preferring to go straight to the heart of the book. However, we believe that a few words of introduction can be useful, and the reader may get much more out of a book if certain things about it are explained.

First, we must say something about the people with whom this book deals: children. Opinions differ as to when someone stops being a child. Our definition of a child is fairly broad. This book therefore covers people who also might be described as adolescents or young people, as well as younger children.

Secondly, we should make clear our usage of the word *labour*. Labour is work, some say. Others wish to distinguish between work and labour. Some readers may have a fairly narrow picture of what child labour involves, thinking mainly of children in factories or mines. We have adopted a much broader view, ranging from acting and modelling through carpet weaving and caring for others, to selling newspapers and delivering milk.

Thirdly, there is the question of time. It seems that children have worked throughout history. However, in early times it was so much taken for granted that there are few records of child labour and few comments upon it. It is with the beginnings of the industrial revolution, which started in England in the eighteenth century, that child labour became a matter of public debate. For that reason, there are few references in this book to events before the eighteenth century.

Readers may notice a certain imbalance in the treatment of different countries in this book. We have covered the histories of two countries, the United States and the United Kingdom, in great detail. Other countries are addressed in a single entry. This is not a bias created by a combination of American publishers and British authors. The United Kingdom was the first country to undergo the industrial revolution, so it experienced first what came to other countries later. The United States is the greatest industrial power in the world. Thus many of the events and experiences that are described as occurring in these two countries have been mirrored in other countries; some have not yet been experienced elsewhere.

Outside of the United Kingdom and the United States, we have been selective in our coverage. Countries such as India and Brazil could not possibly be omitted from such a book, because child labour is known to exist there on a huge scale. In many such countries, national and international bodies have investigated child labour in some depth, so we have had reasonably adequate sources on which to draw for our descriptions. Information about other countries has been harder to find, either because there is a lack of awareness of any problem or because the governments of those countries do not divulge information about it. In some cases we have managed to describe child labour despite the silence of a government, because of the hard work and ingenuity of individual investigators.

It is doubtful that anyone could say for certain that child labour is entirely absent from any country in the world. Thus, the fact that we have not included an entry for a particular country should not be taken to mean that there is no child labour there.

It has not been possible to include a large amount of detail about every country. If we had tried to do so, the reader might have found much of the information repetitive. We have included any particularly distinctive or unusual features of child labour in a particular country. Most entries focusing on a particular country begin with basic geographical, economic, and historical facts. These facts are meant to serve as a background against which readers may interpret the information about child labour that makes up the bulk of the entry on a given country; the specific character of child labour in a particular country is often influenced by such factors. On the other hand, we must make clear that the descriptions of the countries are not definitive by any stretch of the imagination. If a fuller picture of the country is required, other reference works should be consulted.

Acknowledgments

Compiling this book has helped us to appreciate the efforts of the many researchers and activists who have attempted to increase public awareness of child labour.

We are grateful to a number of colleagues with whom we have worked to try and increase our understanding of child labour, including Sandra Lindsay, Margaret A. Lynch, Les Obre, and Niamh Stack.

It was of great benefit to us to be associated with the International Working Group on Child Labour. We received much friendly assistance from members of the secretariat in Amsterdam: Clare Feinstein, Caroline Gorissen, Stan Meuwese, and Julie Niebuhr.

Our most heartfelt thanks go to the many children who answered our questions during our research.

Introduction

Child labour is a broad, complicated, and controversial subject about which many books and articles have been written. However, if you consult and compare any two of them, you will probably find that the subject has been approached in quite different ways. For example, Clark Nardinelli's *Child Labor and the Industrial Revolution* depicts children working in the historical past; in contrast, *Child Labour: Targeting the Intolerable*, published by the International Labour Organisation, is concerned with understanding children's work in the world today with a view to finding the best ways of eliminating the worst forms of child labour. Some people write about particular circumstances in which children work—for example, Peter Cross's *Kashmiri Carpet Children: Exploited Village Weavers*. Others write about the benefits of children working; one need go no further than the title of W. N. Stephen's *Our Children Should Be Working* to know the author's point of view. Then consider *Boy Soldiers* by A. W. Cockerill and *Young Carers and Their Families* by Saul Becker and his colleagues. These activities are not presented as child labour, although there is good reason for considering them as such.

The present volume differs from most previous publications on child labour in that it adopts a very broad approach. This is not to say that it contains everything known about the subject. We have sifted through a wide range of materials and have selected those that we believed most valuable for presenting a clear picture of what is involved in children's working. We also try to explain why the subject has aroused the passions of so many in the past and why it is still important today.

A number of themes run through this book, and it may be helpful to specify some of the more important ones and indicate how they are related to particular entries.

The Work Children Do

Children perform a wide variety of jobs. Some of these are activities we take for granted in our society, such as the home delivery of newspapers and the provision of service to customers in a shop. These are usually thought of as light jobs, unlike the work done by children who dig coal or weave carpets. Some jobs seem timeless; children have probably guarded animals and helped with the harvest throughout history. Some jobs are associated with a particular period or place: For example, drawboys and drawgirls performed particular tasks for hand loom weavers making complicated patterns. Technology changed, and the job disappeared. Some work has an apparently high status, such as performing on stage or screen. Other work places the child clearly among the most disadvantaged in society. Children scavenging on garbage dumps on the outskirts of big cities fall into this category, as do those who beg in the streets. It can never be said that a job has no dangers attached to it. However, some jobs place children at great risk, as was the case with children in nineteenth-century Britain who climbed chimneys in order to clean them. Today the same is true of prostitutes and fighting soldiers; both of these jobs unfortunately exist in many countries.

It is reasonable to ask not just what jobs children do but also how many children are engaged in these jobs. It is often difficult to answer the question precisely. In traditional agricultural communities, it is probably safe to assume that most children work as soon as they are old enough. In modern industrial societies, it is usually assumed that education is the first priority for children. However, school and work may be in conflict with each other. Children may drop out of school in order to work. Others may still attend school but spend so much time in a part-time job that their school work suffers. Some work may be illegal and hence not recorded. When that is the case, official statistics underestimate the extent of child employment. However, it is often possible to form a general picture even without precise figures. For example, it is clear that carpet weaving is widespread in India and Pakistan, although no one can be sure of exactly how many children are involved. To know that it is common may be enough. But on balance, it is preferable to try to obtain precise figures, particularly if there is a dispute about the scale of an activity.

An experience of the authors of this book may help illustrate this point. In 1991 we published the results of a study that suggested that most teenagers in Britain had a job at some time while still at school. Other small projects indicated the same picture. Government ministers, confronted with these findings, cast doubt on whether they gave a true picture. They argued that children's work did not take place on such a large scale. Four years later, the results of a study carried out by a government department confirmed the general picture of widespread working that the government had previously wished to deny. There is now general agreement on the scale of children's working, thanks to the existence of systematically collected information.

Although statistics are important, it is also worth remembering the individual children who make up the statistics. It is in the nature of things that the great majority of working children will remain anonymous to most of us. Only in exceptional circumstances do we learn the personal details of their lives. Occasionally, someone who becomes famous in later life turns out to have been a child worker: Explorer and missionary David Livingstone and novelist Charles Dickens are examples. From the history of the British industrial revolution, we know of Robert Blincoe, because his life was used as propaganda in the battle against bad working conditions. We are uncertain of the identity of the "Dundee factory boy" from around the same period, but his autobiography gives a vivid picture of what his working life was like. Among child workers of the modern world, the tragic figure of the Pakistani carpet weaver Iqbal Masih is by far the best known.

Children's Work throughout the World
When we look at child labour in different countries, we find over and over again that precise figures are lacking. However, in many cases the scale of working is clear from simple observation. A review of some of the places listed in the book will allow a fairly accurate general picture to be painted of patterns of child labour across the world.

One of the most visible forms of child labour in big cities in many countries is that performed by street children. This applies to countries such as Brazil in South America, Kenya in Africa, and India in Asia. The numbers of street children are increasing in the former communist countries of Eastern Europe. However, in those same large cities, many child workers are hidden from public view, such as the children who help out in small workshops and garages in Cairo, Egypt, or those who scavenge in the garbage dumps outside Lima, Peru.

Most of the countries of Latin America, Africa, and Asia have similar economic problems. They have been agricultural communities in the past, but the pressures to industrialize are great. Child workers are found both in traditional work and in modern industrial production. Children fish in Indonesia, for example, and herd animals in Zimbabwe. They also work in the coal mines of Colombia and the garment factories of Morocco.

Those of us who live in the economically more advanced countries of the world cannot regard ourselves as cut off from the problems of child labour in these poorer countries. In "Eastern" countries such as India, Pakistan, and Morocco, children weave carpets for sale in the "Western" countries. Affluent Westerners travel to many countries in Asia and Latin America as well as to southern European countries such as Spain, Portugal, and Greece. There, as tourists, they come into even more direct contact with child labour, since tourism is a major employer of children.

Western countries have their own child labour problems, although on the whole the scale is smaller in North America and western Europe than elsewhere in the world. A good deal of the work performed by Western children is part time and does not interfere with their attending school.

Problems of Child Employment

The tone of what we have written so far suggests that child labour is a social problem. There are many reasons why this is so; but before mentioning some of them, let us make clear that people do not always see it as harmful for children to work. The factory owners during the industrial revolution defended themselves by claiming that the children were better off working for them than if they were elsewhere. Similar arguments are put forward today.

Some writers today suggest that we should not see work as inherently bad for children but rather as an activity that involves both costs and benefits. For example, work may interfere with schooling, which would be a cost, but the child may learn skills in the job, which would be a benefit.

On the other hand, some aspects of work give obvious cause for concern. The early factories were unhealthy places, as are many microenvironments in which children work today, particularly in Africa, Asia, and Latin America. Farms may seem healthy environments, but there are dangers from pesticides and machinery. Health and safety are major concerns among those interested in child labour.

The financial circumstances in which children have worked in the past and continue to work are also alarming. There are several conditions not unlike slavery, including bonded labour, where the child is required to work in order to pay off a debt incurred by his or her parents to the employer.

Most children in Western countries do not face such extreme conditions, but that does not mean that their work can be regarded as problem free. Does work reduce opportunities for leisure? Does work create barriers between parents and children? Do young workers have greater than average access to alcohol and drugs? Are working children more likely to be drawn into committing crime? What values and attitudes do children pick up at work—respect for good working practices, or cynicism?

Work cannot be divorced from other aspects of social life. Does work help foster gender stereotypes? Are girls paid less than boys? Are members of ethnic minorities discriminated against? Does work encourage too great a concern with buying fashionable consumer goods, or is it the desire for these goods that causes some children to work in the first place?

The Historical Context of Child Labour

Daniel Defoe, in recounting his travels around Britain in the early eighteenth century, described children working in a tone that made it clear that he approved. Children have always worked, particularly in rural communities; but with the industrial revolution, first in Britain and then elsewhere in the world, came a different kind of work. Children either worked as members of a family group to earn a family wage, or more commonly, they worked apart from their parents, in factories, mills, and mines. It was this kind of working situation that gave rise to some of the greatest criticism.

Gradually child labour became less and less common in industrialized countries, partly because of reformers' efforts to outlaw certain kinds of work, partly because of laws to make education compulsory, and partly because technological advances made children less suitable as employees.

However, what happened in England in the past has parallels in other parts of the world today. Many poorer countries have been forced by pressure from international financial institutions such as the International Monetary Fund to introduce so-called structural adjustment programs. The primary aim of such programs is to stabilize the economy of the country; but the main outcomes are that more poor families find it necessary to rely on the earnings of their children and that small business enterprises seek out cheap labour, including children.

Understanding Work by Children

Why do children work? There is no simple, universally accepted explanation—which is not surprising, if one realizes that people have different opinions about what a child is and what work is. Historians have focused on explaining the large numbers of children who went to work in the early years of the Industrial Revolution. Some, such as J. L. and Barbara Hammond and E. P. Thompson, see these children as victims of the selfishness of others. Others,

like Clark Nardinelli, suggest that child labour often might have been a rational decision on the part of the children and their parents, given the choices open to them at the time.

Anthropologists and sociologists have concentrated on child labour in more modern times. They stress how important it is not to look at working children in isolation from other aspects of society. The idea of what is "natural" for a child may depend heavily on what we have come to believe because of the traditions of the society in which we have been raised. Many "child" workers are actually going through the stage of life we call adolescence, and their desire to work may be linked with their desire to become an adult.

Psychologists began to study child labour relatively late. It is the nature of their work that they concentrate on children here and now. Trying to cast aside preconceptions, psychologists such as Ellen Greenberger and Laurence Steinberg have stressed the necessity of looking both at possible costs and possible benefits to the young worker. On the whole, they have found clearer evidence of costs than of benefits among American teenagers, but psychological research still has a long way to go.

What Is to Be Done?

Many people who are interested in child labour are not content merely to try to understand it; they believe that action is necessary. For a minority, today, child employment is a good thing. Child employment advocates wish to encourage more children in countries such as Great Britain and the United States to work. Some writers see the economic forces encouraging children to work as virtually inevitable. If this is so, the best that can be done is to encourage children to get all that they can out of their work. However, most people who write about child labour in the world today see more problems than benefits. They wish action to be taken that will remove abuses. There are varying views on what should be done. Some stress the need to protect children. Others wish to extend children's rights, which include the child's right to choose whether he or she should work.

Some of these variations arise, of course, from deep-seated differences of opinion—not just about child labour but about the whole nature of society. It is hardly likely that a Marxist and an exponent of the market economy will agree on child labour if they disagree on so much else.

Working on Behalf of Child Workers

Many different groups have concerned themselves with child labour. These include large international institutions such as the European Union and the International Labour Organisation (ILO) as well as nongovernmental organizations at both the international level and national level that are concerned with children's problems generally. The Save the Children Fund and the British society, NCH-Action for Children, are examples. Workers' organizations such as the American Federation of Labor and the International Confederation of Free Trade Unions look after the interests of children as well as those of adults. A number of national bodies focus specifically on child labour, such as the Concerned for Working Children in India and the National Child Labor Committee in the United States.

Many individuals have devoted much of their lives to working children. These include nineteenth-century pioneers such as Richard Oastler and Lord Shaftesbury in England and Samuel Van Houten in the Netherlands. Similar figures in the United States include the photographer Lewis W. Hine, the clergyman Rev. Charles Bruce, and trade unionists such as Samuel Gompers and Mother Jones.

What is the most effective action to take on behalf of working children? As we have seen, opinions vary; but we can say with certainty that many different approaches have been adopted. International bodies such as the ILO and the United Nations have formulated policies that they then attempt to persuade the countries of the world to follow. Individual countries have passed laws to restrict child labour. In England there were the Factory Acts and other laws aimed at encouraging simultaneous work and education in the Half-Time system. Many of these laws were ineffective, often because no steps were taken to fund a system of inspection and enforcement. This same problem occurred also in other countries that developed child labour laws. In the United States, there have been constant debates about the relative merits of state and federal laws.

A country's legislation may be aimed not only at child labour in that particular country but also at child labour elsewhere. Examples of such laws might be those banning imported goods that have been manufactured with the use of unacceptable forms of child labour, as is the case with the so-called Harkin Bill passed in the United States. Not everyone approves of this approach. People in other countries resent such interference. An alternative internationalist approach involves product labelling, whereby goods may be certified as produced in acceptable conditions. The consumer may then be persuaded to show preference for such goods. However, this practice too can be interpreted as interference from abroad. There are no easy roads toward solving child labour problems.

Concrete Cases

In addition to discussing broad economic and historical forces, it is also worth considering specific events to obtain a more rounded picture. Examples are strikes in which child workers played a part and tragedies such as the Triangle Shirtwaist Fire. A number of books and films have focused on such cases in order to highlight the plight of working children. That approach is not always effective at helping the children, however. The Meknes case is one where the well-intentioned efforts of television reporters left child workers worse off in the end.

Children Take Action

Our final theme is one of the most fascinating, partly because it is not possible to tell yet how big a phenomenon it will become and how successful it will turn out to be. In a number of countries around the world, organizations *of* child workers are being formed as distinct from adult organizations *for* child workers. Often adults help set up these groups; but once the groups are formed, the children themselves formulate policies. There also have been efforts to coordinate child worker groups from different countries. Such efforts could be temporary and short lived or the start of an important international development. This is only one of the many puzzles about child labour that have yet to be resolved.

Finally, here are some further points that may help you in using this book.

The word that is spelled "labor" in the United States is "labour" in Britain and other countries where English is used. We have used the British spelling except when we are quoting text or citing titles in which the American spelling has been used. In those cases, we have followed the spelling of the original authors. For similar word pairs, such as behavior/behaviour and program/programme, we have adopted the same policy.

A glossary and list of acronyms have been included to explain some of the words and sets of initials that occur in the main text. If you seek an explanation of a word in the glossary and it is not there, this may be because there is a full entry on the topic in the main text, so it is worthwhile checking for that.

At the end of most entries we have listed one or more references that may be consulted if you need more information than we have included. These references are in a shortened form, giving only author's name, title, and date of publication. Titles in quotation marks are either articles in periodicals or chapters in books. Other titles are books. Full publication details may be found in the bibliography at the end of the book, where works are listed in alphabetical order by the authors' surnames. When a work has more than one author or editor, the work is listed under the first author's surname.

Child Labour

Abbott, Grace

Grace Abbott (1878–1939) was an American social worker who devoted her life to the protection of immigrants and children. She was an active member of the Illinois child labour movement and became the director of the Child Labor Division of the United States Department of Labor Children's Bureau in 1916. She served as chief of the United States Children's Bureau from 1921 to 1934.

See also Children's Bureau.

Accidents

When the issue of child employment comes to the attention of the media, it is usually because of some sensational issue, such as flagrant exploitation or injury of children while at work. That cases of acci-

Grace Abbott, 1930 (Library of Congress)

dental injury occur is not in doubt. However, problems arise when we try to estimate the number of accidents. The main problem arises from the fact that in many countries accident figures relating to child workers are not collected. Even in cases where figures are collected, there might be problems with the reliability of data sources.

Some research into children's accidental injury at work has taken place in the industrialized countries of Europe and North America. In Britain a number of studies throughout the 1990s have estimated that between 20 and 30 percent of children who work sustain some form of accidental injury. These injuries range from minor cuts, bruises, and burns to major accidents involving broken limbs, and in some cases, fatalities. Research in the United States has produced similar results, highlighting the potential risks in specific forms of employment. The agricultural sector has been seen as an example of a hazardous area of employment where accidental injury is associated with machinery. Employment in agriculture also has been associated with health hazards related to the use of toxic pesticides and developmental problems arising from the impact of physically demanding work on children whose physical growth is still incomplete.

Given that it is possible to identify the risk of accidental injury among children who work in the economically developed countries of North America and western Europe, it is not surprising to find that the magnitude of the problem is greater in economically less developed countries. This partly reflects the fact that more children work in these countries. Many of them work full time and are employed in a wide range of jobs, many relying on outdated machinery and engaging in work practices that have been aban-

1

doned in economically more advanced countries.

Although specific data on the level of accidental injury in these countries is lacking, the range of hazardous jobs children do has been highlighted by the International Labour Organisation. In India, children work in the ceramic and glass factories, with molten glass and hot furnaces. In other Asian countries, such as Burma and Indonesia, children work in deep-sea fishing. This activity involves diving to considerable depths without protective equipment, often resulting in drownings, ruptured eardrums, or illnesses resulting from decompression. In Pakistan, children are found working in the construction industry, including brick making. Other children are involved in metalworking and slate production, which entail working with dangerous machinery and using inappropriate and unsafe hand tools.

We need more detailed and systematic information about the forms and causes of accidental injury among working children. Methods of gathering such information would include risk assessments of the jobs children do as well as evaluations of whether children are at greater risk due to their attitudes toward risk taking and their stage of development.

See also Agriculture; Health; Italy.

References Brooks, Daniel R., Davis, Letitia K., and Gallagher, Susan S., "Work Related Injuries among Massachusetts Children: A Study Based on Emergency Department Data" (1993); Hobbs, Sandy, and McKechnie, Jim, Child Employment in Britain: A Social and Psychological Analysis (1997); International Labour Organisation, Child Labour: Targeting the Intolerable (1996); McKechnie, Jim, Hobbs, Sandy, Lindsay, Sandra, and Lynch, Margaret A., "Working Children: The Health and Safety Issue" (1998); National Institute for Occupational Safety and Health, Child Labor Research Needs: Recommendations from the NIOSH Child Labor Working Team (1997); National Research Council Institute of Medicine, Protecting Youth at Work (1998); Wilk, Valerie A., "Health Hazards to Children in Agriculture" (1993).

Addams, Jane

Jane Addams (1860–1935) was a noted American social worker and humanitarian. She founded the Hull House social welfare center in Chicago, cofounded the American Civil Liberties Union, and was awarded the Nobel Peace Prize in 1931. She became a member of the National Child Labor Committee when it was formed in 1904. After the Beveridge bill failed to gain national support, she was partly responsible for the development of a new strategy in the battle against child labour. Addams was convinced that in order for the regulation of working children to be accepted, the population at large would have to be made aware of the conditions under which children worked. This conviction resulted in the proposal that the Bureau of Labor should be asked to undertake a complete review of the working conditions of women and children. President Theodore Roosevelt adopted this policy when the Beveridge bill failed, but it was not until 1907 that Congress authorized and made funds available for the study to be carried out.

Addams was attacked for her views on child labour by the National Civic Federation, a business-oriented group that had the support of the National Association of Manufacturers. She was labeled a "radical" and linked to "socialism." In 1912 Addams was approached to head the United States Children's Bureau, but she did not accept the position. She remained in the National Child Labor Committee and argued for the view that federal legislation was needed to combat child labour.

See also Beveridge, Albert J.; Children's Bureau; National Child Labor Committee.

Adler, Felix

A professor at Columbia University, Felix Adler (1851–1933) was founder and head of the Ethical Cultural Movement in the United States. He also founded the kindergarten movement. Initially a member of the New York Child Labor Committee, he played a major role alongside Edgar Murphy in forming the National Child Labor Committee in 1904. He played a prominent part in that organization for many years afterward. He served as chairman of the committee from 1904 to 1921.

See also National Child Labor Committee.

Adolescence

An examination of specific cases of child labour makes clear that many working children are adolescents. In recent years, academics have spent an increasing amount of time studying this period of development.

The notion of "adolescence" is both old and new. It is old in the sense that the ancient Greeks talked about this period of development. Plato associated it with the development of reason, and Aristotle's writings treated it as the beginning of self-determination. However, our contemporary ideas on adolescence are more commonly viewed as having emerged in the early twentieth century. Developmental psychologist J. W. Santrock labels this the "inventionist view" of adolescents. This approach considers the concept of adolescence a sociohistorical creation. Changes in the economic and social structure of society in the early twentieth century resulted in the emergence of the concept of adolescence as we currently know it.

That culture plays a part in defining adolescence was a position put forward by cultural anthropologist Margaret Mead. She contrasted the notion of adolescence in different parts of the world and argued that cultural variation in this period of development was apparent. Although details of Margaret Mead's work have been challenged, it does support the inventionist view.

If our culture plays a part in defining adolescents, then what are the dominant views related to this period? A common position is to consider adolescence as a period of transition when the individual is no longer a child but is not yet an adult. Psychologist Erik Erikson talks about the period of adolescence as one in which we resolve our identities, defining who we are and who we will become. Occupation and sexuality are two key areas in which identity resolution occurs.

The commonsense view depicts adolescence as a period of "storm and stress." This interpretation partly reflects the early theory of adolescence proposed by psychologist Calvin S. Hall in 1904, and partly reflects the popular media's construction of adolescence. As researchers have shown, the reality is somewhat different. For the majority of adolescents this period in development is not marked by major psychological upheaval. Rather it is simply one more stage in the developmental process, with its own tasks and challenges. In that sense, adolescence as a developmental stage is no more stressful than any other stage.

In moving beyond the stereotype of adolescence as a "problem period," researchers have focused instead on identifying the specific developmental tasks faced by this age group. Psychologists Philip Newman and Barbara Newman proposed a number of different tasks for this period of life. These include dealing with physical maturation and changing cognitive abilities, tackling changing emotional relationships, adapting to new peer group relations, and developing heterosexual relations. They go on to argue that older adolescents face additional challenges of establishing autonomy from their parents, establishing their sex role identity, internalizing moral principles and values, and establishing a career choice. Many of these tasks appear to fit with the idea of adolescence as a period of transition. The resolution of these tasks results in the creation of adults. Across a wide range of theories and writings, the idea of adolescence as a period where one defines one's identity and establishes one's autonomy from others constantly reappears.

It is in this context of adolescence interpreted as a period of change that the literature on employment takes on particular importance. One of the dominant perspectives to emerge about the importance of work is that it can facilitate the process of development. This developmental view of child employment emphasizes the positive contribution of work to the establishment of autonomy and identity. This view has not gone unchallenged. Recently, psychologists Sandy Hobbs and Jim McKechnie drew attention to the suggestion that work might actually present more problems for adolescent development instead of aiding it. If there is a poor fit between the demands of a job and the individual's developmental stage, work might have a negative effect on development.

See also Costs and Benefits.

References Heaven, Patrick C. L., *Contemporary Adolescence* (1994); Hobbs, Sandy, and McKechnie, Jim, *Child Employment in Britain: A Social and Psychological Analysis* (1997); Mead, Margaret, *Growing Up in New Guinea: A Comparative Study of Primitive Education* (1975); Newman, Philip, and Newman, Barbara, *Adolescent Development* (1986); Santrock, J. W., *Adolescence* (1996).

Advocacy

Advocacy is the work of an advocate—that is, someone who speaks out in support of or who acts in behalf of an individual or a group. With regard to child labour, a range of organizations advocate working children's rights or interests (for example, Anti-Slavery International, Defence for Children International, Save the Children Fund, and UNICEF). However, the notion of child advocacy is also tied up with debates over liberationist and protectionist conceptions of children and of children's rights. Liberationists stress the need for children to be free to make their own decisions. Protectionists stress the need for adults to take care of children's needs.

Most organizations' advocacy of children's rights, whatever this may mean, is linked to their interpretation of and understanding of the social world. This means that for some organizations advocacy will be something done by adults, based on their interpretations of what is best for children in specific situations. For example, the Stop Child Labour group in the United Kingdom is overwhelmingly made up of adult socialist activists who view child labour as gross exploitation of children occurring under capitalism.

Their aim is to stop all manifestations of child labour, in the interests of children and other workers. Anti-Slavery International is an organization, again staffed by adults, committed to abolishing human rights abuses. Their purpose is to research child labour (among other issues) and to influence national governments and international bodies in an attempt to combat this activity. Politically these two organizations are quite far apart, but they are linked by the fact that they both claim to advocate what's best for children, on the basis of their general worldview.

However, these types of perspectives have been criticized by a number of children's rights activists, who suggest that many advocacy organizations have failed to find out what children themselves want or feel about certain issues. In general terms, the International Working Group on Child Labour took this position. They claimed on the basis of their discussions with children that children want to work and therefore should be allowed to. Again, however, the majority of people involved in that organization were adults and were advocating their position on behalf of children.

Finally, a number of children's organizations—that is, organizations made up of and representing children—advocate positions on child labour and related issues. A small number of organizations of working children exist to represent child labourers and promote their interests with regard to wage rates and conditions of employment.

See also Children's Rights; Organizations of Working Children; Stop Child Labour; Voices of Children.

Africa

Children work in all African countries. In most, it is regarded as healthy and normal for children to perform routine domestic tasks and help with activities essential to the family's livelihood. However, many children throughout the continent are engaged in forms of labour that governments and other bodies are seeking to eliminate or restrict. Although the type of work varies with the many different social and economic circumstances in which children grow up, certain forms are particularly common.

Children are often found to be employed in agriculture, particularly in the southern African countries. In many cases patterns of living and working created during the colonial era survive today. African families in the past were moved into reserve areas where the only form of livelihood was to work on large farms. The farmers typically rely on child labour, particularly for harvesting.

Mining is a field of employment that is regarded as particularly hazardous for children. The work is often physically arduous, shifts are long, and the children often come into contact with toxic chemicals.

Small-scale craft and manufacturing enterprises throughout Africa typically employ children. Nationally, the young workers are referred to as apprentices. However, in practice, instruction is usually haphazard, and the children concerned have few rights. They are poorly paid, and the "apprenticeship" is merely a cover for harsher forms of child labour.

Many African children are engaged in domestic, restaurant, and shop work. These are sometimes seen as less objectionable forms of child employment than manufacturing, mining, or agriculture. However, most of the children receive little pay and have few educational opportunities, and some are ill treated by their employers.

Street children are a common feature of African cities. They engage in a range of activities, from peddling and performing small chores to begging and petty theft.

Most of Africa at one time was under the control of European countries. Although the era of formal colonial power has ended, the development of African countries is still linked to the former colonial powers through the workings of the global economy. Children grow up in Africa today under the influence of a variety of conflicting forces: traditional African society, with its heavy emphasis on family ties; colonialism, which has transformed local economies and undermined traditional values; and the world economy, which continues to expand the influence of wealthy and powerful countries.

See also Algeria; Burkina Faso; Cameroon; Egypt; Kenya; Malawi; Morocco; Nigeria; Somalia; South Africa; Tanzania; Zimbabwe.

References Bekombo, Manga, "The Child in Africa: Socialisation, Education, and Work" (1981); Bonnet, Michel, "Child Labour in Africa" (1993); Ojwang, J. B., *Child Labour in Africa* (1996).

Age of the Child
See Definition of Child Labour.

Agriculture
Children's agricultural work is the most widespread and long-standing form of children's work. In many traditional, precapitalist or preindustrial societies, children have a role to play at key points in the agricultural calendar. At harvest time, in particular, all family members participate in gathering the crops. In this context children begin to work at an early age, either directly helping in the growing of crops or aiding the process by fetching and carrying implements and food or water; by herding goats, sheep, or cattle; and by feeding, watering, and milking livestock. In these types of societies, production and harvesting are under the direct control of the family or kin network. It often has been assumed that a child's participation in the agricultural family economy involved a positive recognition of his or her progress both in age and in ability.

With the development of capitalist agriculture, the relationships of labour fundamentally were altered. Food, animals, and crops began to be produced primarily for profit rather than for direct consumption by the families of the people who produce it. The rise of capitalist agriculture saw the spread and intensification of market relations, with two major consequences. First, small commodity producers (peasants,

5

Young Alex Reiber topping sugar beets near Sterling, Colorado, ca. 1910–1920 (Lewis Hine, Library of Congress)

semipeasants, and small farmers) faced a squeeze on their standard of living and labouring activities from large capitalist farmers. This process continues today, and many peasant and small farmers face immense hardship in rural locations across the globe because they exist in a world determined by global rates of profit and production. The consequence is to increase and intensify the level of exploitation needed in order for them to compete with large agribusinesses. Essentially this means that families have to work longer and

harder for smaller returns and have to employ the labour of all their family members for longer and more intensive periods. Children in rural and peasant sectors of the world economy remain a vulnerable and exploited source of labour as a consequence.

Secondly, large agribusinesses also have periods of peak demand for labour and children still remain an important source of the labour reserve during these periods. In the United States and western Europe, the heart of the advanced capitalist economic system, children are still found working on farms. They are engaged in thinning plants, picking various crops, and sorting vegetables by size and quality on the back of harvesting machines. They are involved in feeding, cleaning, rearing, and moving animals; and they are hired to perform a range of fixing, cleaning, and sorting tasks on the farm.

A number of studies conducted in the United Kingdom and the United States have suggested that the farm is a very unsafe place for children to work. R. B. Taylor's study *Sweat Shops in the Sun* examines the plight of child workers on American farms. Taylor estimates that when he undertook his research in the early 1970s, about a quarter of all workers on farms in the United States were boys and girls, many of whom were working illegally. He dismisses any idealized conception that farm work is a healthy activity, carried on in a vigorous, outdoor world, free from exploitation or harm. He argues that agricultural work for children in agribusinesses is exceptionally hard. He records a number of instances when children were covered by pesticides carried on the wind from adjacent fields that were being sprayed as the children worked, with potentially horrific long-term health consequences. Alec Fyfe, in his book *Child Labour*, argues that children in Great Britain continue to be hurt in accidents on the farm. Children often drive tractors, hang on to trailers, and work around an array of farm machines. Fyfe suggests that the recorded increase in farm accidents during the summer months is in some part accounted for by accidents to children.

See also Harvesting; Herding; Sweated Labour
References Fyfe, Alec, *Child Labour* (1989); Taylor, R. B., *Sweat Shops in the Sun* (1973).

Alcohol and Drugs

Research on the consequences of employment for drug and alcohol use have tended to focus on the industrialized, developed economies. Ellen Greenberger, one of the pioneers of research on adolescent part-

time workers, argues that their work experience can be shown to be associated with increased use of cigarettes, alcohol, and marijuana.

Such conclusions were reinforced by Steinberg and Dornbusch, who related the specific variable of long working hours to alcohol and drug consumption. They suggested a number of explanations for this relationship. First, increased disposable income allows the adolescent to engage in this behavior. Second, the use of alcohol and drugs is a response to the stress of work; working long hours increases the stress. A third possibility is that having a job brings adolescents into contact with older workers who introduce them to a range of illicit activities.

There is now a general consensus that there is a link between alcohol consumption and part-time work among adolescents. Jeylan Mortimer and her colleagues believe that there is compelling evidence to support this link; but they are less convinced of a link with other drug use. It is possible that the findings of such studies undertaken in economically developed countries would not translate to other cultural contexts. In cases where children are working full-time due to family poverty, it is unlikely that they would have disposable income for such uses.

See also Greenberger, Ellen.
References Mortimer, Jeylan T., Finch, Michael D., Ryu, Seongryeol, Shanahan, Michael J., and Call, Kathleen T., "The Effects of Work Intensity on Adolescent Mental Health, Achievement and Behavioral Adjustment: New Evidence from a Prospective Study" (1996); Steinberg, Laurence, and Dornbusch, S. M., "Negative Correlates of Part-Time Employment during Adolescence: Replication and Elaboration" (1991).

Algeria

Algeria, which has an estimated population of more than 25 million, lies on the North African coast of the Mediterranean Sea. It achieved its independence in 1962, after more than 100 years of rule by France. The country has substantial reserves of oil and natural gas. Child labour exists on a

Two children making a rug in Algeria ca. 1910–1920 (Merl LaVoy, Library of Congress)

large scale in Algeria, although statistical evidence is lacking. Children make up a growing proportion of the street traders who operate on a large scale in the towns. A very wide range of goods are on sale, from food to electrical appliances. How-ever, although street trade is the most visi-ble form of child labour, it is not necessar-ily the most serious. Many children work in domestic service or in small craft enter-prises. The most difficult form of child labour to investigate in Algeria takes place within the family home or in the small family business.

References Schlemmer, Bernard, *L'enfant Exploite: Oppression, Mise au Travail, Proletarisation* (1996).

America, Central
Central America comprises the seven countries that make up the narrow isthmus joining the continents of North America and South America. All but one of these countries is Spanish speaking, having belonged at one time to the Spanish Empire. Because of Spanish linguistic ties, *Central America* is also often defined as including Mexico, even though geographically that country is part of North America. Compared to Mexico, which has a population of around 90 million and a land area of well over 700,000 square miles, the Central American countries are small, together equalling less than a third of the population of Mexico and only a little over a third of its area. Of the five countries that gained their independence from Spain in 1821, Guatemala, with around 10 million, has the largest population, followed by El Salvador (5.5 million), Honduras (5 million), Nicaragua (4 million), and Costa Rica (3 million). Panama (population 2.5 million) achieved its independence from Colombia in 1903. Belize (population over 200,000), formerly known as British Honduras, became independent from Great Britain in 1981. The extent and character of child labour in all of these countries is about the same, since the countries share a similar status of economic underdevelopment.

See also America, South; Guatemala; Mexico; Nicaragua.

America, Latin
The phrase *Latin America* is often applied in reference to South and Central America because the dominant language in most countries there is either Spanish or Portuguese. Both languages derive mainly from Latin, as Spain and Portugal both came under the influence of the Latin-speaking Roman Empire.

See also America, Central; America, South.

America, South
In most South American countries, children make up a substantial proportion of the population. Although there is a failure of governments throughout South America to produce meaningful statistics on child labour, circumstantial evidence suggests that it exists on a large scale and is probably increasing. It is believed to be somewhat more common in rural areas than in urban ones. Generally speaking, governments proclaim their responsibility for the welfare of the children in their respective countries. However, in practice, governments frequently follow economic policies that are harmful to children. In some cases, the governments do so under pressure from international financial institutions. Whatever governments do for child workers is carried out in a paternalistic way. There is little recognition of children's right to speak or take action on their own behalf. One of the most scandalous aspects of official policy is the extent to which harassment of street children by members of the police force is condoned.

Because of bad living and working conditions in rural areas, there is a high rate of migration into towns. The migrants, including their children, are drawn to urban areas because they believe that such places provide a better quality of life. However, few migrants to towns achieve substantial improvement in their economic circumstances. Many children exchange work on a farm, where they were at least a member of a family group, for casual work in a town, which might necessitate a rupture in family ties.

Educational provision in many countries is limited and in some cases of poor quality. One outcome of this state of affairs is that any child faced with a choice between school and work might well find work more appealing. Similarly, parents might prefer that their children work rather than attend school because they cannot be sure that school will benefit the child's long-

9

term job prospects and earning capacity.

See also America, Central; Argentina; Brazil; Chile; Colombia; Peru.

References Garate, Martin, and Salazar, Maria Cristina, *International Working Group on Child Labour Regional Report: Latin America* (1996).

America, United States of
See United States of America.

American Academy of Political and Social Science
The American Academy of Political and Social Science treated the issue of child labour as important from a very early period. The Academy devoted a complete session of its 1902 annual meeting, held in Philadelphia, to what it termed "the child labor problem." The proceedings of the session were later published in the Academy's *Annals*. The Academy also published the proceedings of the annual conference of the National Child Labor Committee for a number of years.

See also National Child Labor Committee.

American Federation of Labor
From its beginning, the movement to abolish child labour in America received the support of the trade unions. It is not clear whether this was due to self-interest or humanitarian principles. In the early 1880s, labour unions were forming and focusing on the issue of child labour. Organized labour approached the issue by making demands for shorter hours for children. Some have argued that the motivation behind such demands was that once shorter hours for children had been achieved, the union would be in a position to tackle the working hours of adults. Unions also believed that child workers depressed adult wages, which helps explain their willingness to adopt strong positions on child labour. In 1836, the National Trades Union Convention called for a minimum age for factory workers.

The Knights of Labor were calling for federal legislation on child workers as early as 1880.

Formed by Samuel Gompers in 1881, the American Federation of Labor (AFL) brought craft unions together to increase their bargaining position and strength against capital. It also attempted to maintain craftsmen's pay differentials—the superior rates they enjoyed in comparison to nonskilled workers. In its earliest days, it organized only skilled workers, and many locals restricted membership on the basis of colour, race, and gender.

The AFL was at the forefront of union activity on the issue of child labour. At its first annual conference in 1881, the AFL adopted a resolution calling upon individual states to introduce legislation barring the employment of children under 14 years of age. In 1897, the AFL shifted its position slightly and began to advocate federal rather than state legislation to tackle this issue.

The union's commitment to resolving the issue of child labour did waver at certain points in time. For example, AFL boss Samuel Gompers argued for a time against federal child labour regulations, believing they would set a precedent for excessive federal intervention in labour regulation. However, by 1915 the AFL's position had firmed up in favour of action at the federal level. The union ardently supported the unsuccessful Palmer-Owen Bill.

See also Gompers, Samuel; Knights of Labor, The Order of; Palmer-Owen Bill.

Anthracite Coal Strike
This strike by miners in 1902 helped to focus attention on the numbers of children employed in Pennsylvania mines and the extent to which those young workers were exploited. The miners used the issue of child labour to justify their demands. They argued that the poor wages they were paid by the mining companies reinforced the child labour problem, since it became economically essential for mining families to send their children to work. The publicity

created by the strike evoked a wave of indignation against the practice of employing children in the mining industry.

Anthropology

The field of anthropology comprises two very different areas of study: physical anthropology, which is concerned with diversity in the physique of different human groups; and social anthropology, which is concerned with the various sorts of social relations that can be found in different societies. It is the latter that has most to contribute to an understanding of child labour. Social anthropology in its present form began to emerge in the nineteenth century. As Europe came into closer contact with other parts of the world through trade and colonization, speculations arose about the differences between European societies and others. Attempts were made to distinguish between so-called primitive societies and those at a supposedly higher stage of civilization. Although these ideas about cultural variation were products of cultural bias and lacked adequate scientific support, they played a role in the development of social anthropology as a distinctive field of study.

One of the strengths of the social anthropological approach to understanding human society is that professional practitioners generally spend a considerable period of time in face-to-face contact with members of the community that they are studying. As a result, social anthropology deals not only with the directly observable and measurable features of human relations but also with evidence of how the people themselves perceive their relationships. Dutch anthropologist Olga Nieuwenhuys carried out a study of the everyday life of poor children in a coastal village in Kerala, southern India. Contrary to the view that increased school provision would help reduce child labour in economically underdeveloped countries, she found that expanded schooling led to an increase in the drudgery experienced by the children. To cover the costs of school clothes and study materials, the children had to continue working while they were going to school. One benefit that she discovered from the increased school attendance was that children seemed to be more capable of asserting themselves and expressing their needs. The authoritarian nature of past parent-child relationships was being undermined.

Although anthropologists frequently study the role of children in communities, studies of the sort just described are less common than might be expected given how frequently children work in most societies. Nevertheless, anthropology has contributed to our understanding of child labour and has the potential to do so even more in the future. Olga Nieuwenhuys argues that in the past, "child labor" was overwhelmingly associated with factories of Western-style economies. Anthropologists have demonstrated the rich diversity of children's work. They also have shown how some views of child labour and of the methods by which its evils might be combated have been deeply colored by assumptions based on Western ideals of family relationships. By focusing on the concrete realities of children's lives, especially the lives of poor children, anthropology can contribute to an understanding of children's place in communities. It does so by taking into account how children actually contribute to society through work, the value of which is often underestimated; and by examining how some children negotiate a reassessment of the value of their efforts.

See also Adolescence; Psychology, Developmental.

References Nieuwenhuys, Olga, "To Read and Not to Eat: South Indian Children between Secondary School and Work" (1993); idem, "The Paradox of Child Labor and Anthropology" (1996); Schildkrout, Enid, "The Employment of Children in Kano (Nigeria)" (1981).

Anti-Slavery International

Formed in 1839 as the Anti-Slavery Society for the Protection of Human Rights, this organization recently changed its name to Anti-Slavery International. The Anti-Slavery Society had its roots in the movement for the abolition of slavery in the British empire, but was also always concerned with questions of slavery and various forms of exploitation in countries outside Britain's direct jurisdiction. In Britain and its colonies, legal restrictions on, and the eventual abolition of, slavery and various forms of "apprenticed" indentured labour were implemented between 1807 and 1838. Anti-Slavery International is a nongovernmental organization (NGO) that works for the eradication of slavery and servile forced labour (including child labour) and on behalf of indigenous peoples whose identities and ways of life are threatened. The organization pursues its aims in a number of ways, using all available means to publicize abuses of human rights and to put pressure on recalcitrant states. It undertakes research, publishes reports, and sends delegations to countries where human rights violations are reported. It also lobbies national governments and the United Nations. Anti-Slavery International has "consultative status" with the United Nations Economic and Social Council.

Anti-Slavery International in 1978 began publishing an influential series of pamphlets on child labour. The first dealt with conditions in the Moroccan carpet industry. Others have described child labour in a number of countries in Europe and Asia (for example, Italy, Portugal, and India). The organization's position is not one of total opposition to child employment, as its founders and members believe that an occasional job can provide an excellent introduction to post-school life. However, most of the work described in its reports is unfortunately damaging to children's social, economic, and physical development.

See also Global March against Child Labor.

References Anti-Slavery Society, *Child Labour in Morocco's Carpet Industry* (1978); Valcarenghi, Marina, *Child Labour in Italy: A General Review* (1981); Whittaker, Alan (ed.), *Children in Bondage: Slaves of the Subcontinent* (no date); Williams, Suzanne, *Child Workers in Portugal* (no date).

Apparel Industry Task Force

Legislation is a weapon commonly used in tackling child labour issues. Some laws prohibit child labour altogether; others specify the circumstances under which children may be allowed to work. However, all legislation, current and past, can be effective only if it is enforced. Much of the present-day discussion about child labour highlights the lack of inspectorates to monitor and enforce legislation relating to this issue. New York State has attempted to respond to this matter by creating the Apparel Industry Task Force. New York has a long history of garment production, which traditionally has been linked to child labour.

See also Garment Industry; Triangle Shirtwaist Factory Fire; United States of America.

Apprentices, Pauper
See Pauper Apprentices.

Apprenticeship
Traditionally apprenticeships were undertaken by young boys, as a means of gaining entry to a craft guild. Skilled craftsmen would take on one or two apprentices and train them in the arts of their labour. Very often the craftsman would be paid to train the apprentice, who would be indentured to the craftsman until some future date. Only after seven or eight years would the apprentice be in a position to be accepted by the guild as a fully trained craftsman. The length of the apprenticeship was, in part, a consequence of the guilds' attempt to control the labour market, to ensure that the craft did not become too common and cheapened as a consequence.

With the development of capitalism, particularly after the industrial revolution, apprenticeship underwent a number of important changes. First, in a number of employment sectors, the apprenticeship in effect became a means of tying young children to an employer for a number of years, with little training being given and few skills for future use being imparted to the child. In Great Britain, in the eigh-

Be it remembered, it is this Day agreed by and between SAMUEL GREG, of *Styal*, in the County of *Chester*, of the one Part, and *Peter and Sarah Stockton* of

Heel in the County of Stafford — of the other Part, as follows: That the said *Sarah Stockton* shall serve the said SAMUEL GREG, in his Cotton-Mills, in *Styal*, in the County of *Chester*, as a just and honest Servant, *Twelve* Hours in each of the six working Days, and to be at *her* own Liberty at all other Times ; the Commencement of the Hours to be fixed from Time to Time by the said SAMUEL GREG, for the Term of *Eight* Years at the Wages of *Nine Pence* *per Week the first Year and One Shilling a Week the Remaining part of the Term also Mr Greg Engages to fill the Said Sarah Stockton With meat Drink, Washing and Lodging For the above Term Sufficient for one in her Station* And that if the said *Sarah Stockton* shall absent *herself* from the Service of the said SAMUEL GREG, in the said working Hours, during the Term, without his Consent first obtained, that the said SAMUEL GREG, may abate the Wages in a double Proportion for such Absence; and the said SAMUEL GREG shall be at Liberty, during the Term, to discharge the Servant from his Service, for Misbehaviour, or Want of Employ.

As Witness their Hands, this — *Tenth* — Day of *October* —179*6* *Sarah Stockton her Mark* *Peter Stockton his Mark* *Witness Matt Fardner*

Sarah Stockton is to be allowed One week in Every Year to go See her Friends —

An apprenticeship contract from late eighteenth-century England (Library of Congress)

teenth and early nineteenth centuries, "pauper apprentices"—that is, children of the destitute, would be indentured to mill owners or farmers from the age of 6 or 7 years until their twenty-first birthday. Legally they could not leave until their term of indenture was fulfilled.

Secondly, in other areas, such as hairdressing and various engineering trades, the apprenticeship remained (and still does today) the training route that young adults take in order to obtain a recognized skill and a place within the labour market. The apprenticeship gradually evolved into a paid work activity and training scheme for young people after completion of their general schooling.

Argentina

Argentina occupies most of the southeastern part of South America. It became a Spanish colony in the sixteenth century and achieved its independence in 1816. It has a population of around 32 million.

The capital, Buenos Aires, and its suburbs have a population of more than 10 million. It is common for girls in the city areas to work in domestic service. Both boys and girls engage in street trading. Boys work in the building industry and as cleaners in the commercial sector.

The high level of child labour that exists in some rural areas has been well known since extensive surveys were undertaken in the 1970s. In the cotton-growing area of Chaco, almost 40 percent of children between 6 and 9 years of age have been found to be working, and the proportion rises to around 100 percent by the age of 14 years. Figures obtained in the tobacco-growing area of Corrientes have been almost as high.

In other areas the extent of child labour is difficult to estimate because the children work as members of family teams, picking tea and stripping sugarcane, for example.

References Mendelievich, Elias (ed.), *Children at Work* (1979).

Asia

Asia is the largest and most heavily populated continent. It contains the world's highest mountains as well as land that is frequently flooded. Politically and economically it is equally diverse, containing the world's largest communist country (China), two countries close in style to "Western" democracies (Israel and Japan), and economically underdeveloped countries such as Bangladesh. Because of this variety, it is doubtful whether there is much value in attempting to generalize about Asia. However, *Asia* is often understood as including the countries of the Indian subcontinent and of Southeast Asia, which share a number of common characteristics.

Southeast Asia is characterized by countries with large rural populations predominantly working in agriculture, and in most cases very poor. There is a tendency for the populations of these countries to move to large cities in search of a better life, where they often merge with the urban poor. Both in the countryside and in town, child labour is widespread. Compared with the countries of North America and Europe, infant mortality is high and literacy rates are low. Almost invariably, women suffer worse conditions of life than men. Almost all Asian countries are striving for economic development; but where economic growth has been achieved, it has not necessarily been accompanied by equivalent improvements in standards of living. This is illustrated by the many cases in which successful exporting industries rely heavily on poorly paid child workers.

See also Bangladesh; China; India; Indonesia; Middle East; Myanmar; Nepal; Pakistan; Philippines; Thailand; Vietnam.

References Concerned for Working Children,

Bal Mazdoor Union

The Bal Mazdoor Union (BMU) is an organization of Indian child workers that was formed in the early 1990s as the result of the maltreatment of child porters in a market in Delhi. Although it took a specific incident to bring the union to fruition, the idea had been discussed for some time by children participating in the Butterflies, a voluntary organization concerned with child welfare. The BMU views itself as a means by which children can have their voices heard on issues relating to their basic rights. The union seeks to educate children about their rights both as children and as workers.

The structure of this body was based on the model of traditional adult trade unions, as the BMU sought recognition as a union in its own right. However, the attempt to gain legal recognition was unsuccessful. The reason given was that children under 15 years of age could not be union members. BMU members believe this violates Article 15 of the Convention of the Rights of the Child, which states that children have the right of association. Attempts to appeal the decision have to date been unsuccessful.

See also India; Organizations of Working Children.

Bangladesh

When the British government granted independence to its territories in the Indian subcontinent in 1947, they were partitioned into two countries, India and Pakistan. Pakistan was made up of two areas a thousand miles apart, entirely separated from each other by India. These two regions had in common the fact that their populations were largely made up of adherents of the Islamic religion. In 1971, the eastern part declared itself an independent republic and adopted the name Bangladesh. It has a population of more than 120 million.

It is an exceedingly poor country, with average earnings equivalent to less than 250 U.S. dollars per year. Large parts of the country are flat and low lying. These areas are very fertile but unfortunately are subject to frequent flooding. Thus the many Bangladeshis who rely on agriculture for a living experience regular crop failure. As the population increases, there are two substantial effects. One is migration to the cities. The other is that small independent farmers fail to sustain themselves and their families. In order to survive, they bond themselves and their children as labourers to *zamindars* (large landowners). The extent of child labour in Bangladesh is believed to be very large, but since many of the children are employed in unregulated and informally organized work, there is limited statistical evidence.

The range of work undertaken by Bangladeshi children is wide, but five categories are particularly worth noting. One is weaving, a traditional craft in which the master weaver employs a *shagrid* (helper), generally a boy between 9 and 14 years of age. *Shagrid*s work long hours in unhealthy environments, sometimes without payment on the pretext that they are too young to handle money. A second category are the children of *mahtas* (sweepers), a poor, low-status group, subject to many social prejudices. They earn a living in menial ways, such as by cleaning public toilets. Some of these children supplement their family income by selling drugs and locally brewed alcoholic drinks. A third distinctive group of child workers are those employed on "tempos," which are three-wheeled vehicles widely used as buses in Bangladesh. Young boys are employed to solicit customers and to give out information about the routes. They also clean the vehicles and take tickets. Ticket collecting involves them standing on a precariously narrow step at the back of the tempo. Accidents, including fatal ones, are common, due to the rapid movement of the vehicles and the numerous potholes in the roads. The work is illegal, and the tempo boys are uninsured.

The fourth notable category of child labour is to be found in the relatively recently developed garment industry. The production of clothes for export grew rapidly in the 1980s, and it is estimated that more than half of the predominantly female workforce is under 16 years of age. They work long hours in unhealthy conditions for low wages.

Fifthly, there are the children who work in the construction industry. It is estimated that about a third of all construction workers are children. They are commonly employed in stone breaking. Hired by site subcontractors on weekly contracts, they earn minimal wages for their piecework; and they are expected to provide their own tools, such as hammers, umbrellas for protection from the sun, gloves, and watering cans. A basic hammer costs about 80 taka, the equivalent of two days' wages. The workday is long, starting at 7 A.M. and ending about 10 P.M.

See also Asia.

References Cadman, Eileen, *No Time to Play: Child Workers in the Global Economy* (1996); Cain, Mead, and Khorshed Alam Mozumber, A. B. M. "Labour Market Structure and Reproductive Behaviour in Rural South Asia" (1981); Concerned for Working Children, The, *Child Labour in Bangladesh* (1995); Lee-Wright, Peter, *Child Slaves* (1990); Sadeque, Shah Ahmed, *Tempo Boy: Child Labour on the Buses of Bangladesh* (1992).

Belgium

The Kingdom of Belgium is situated in northwestern Europe, between France and the Netherlands, with which it shares strong cultural links. Constitutionally, Belgium is a federation of three regions. The northern part of the country predominantly speaks Flemish, a language closely related to Dutch, the language of the Netherlands. The southern, Walloon region is predominantly French speaking. The country's third region is the capital, Brussels. The population of Belgium is just over 10 million, of whom almost a million live in the capital.

Belgium was second only to Great Britain in its participation in the industrial revolution. Like British children, children in Belgium played a large role in the process of industrialization. In the nineteenth century, children worked in virtually every sector of the economy. In agriculture, children between 8 and 14 years of age worked as members of weeding gangs, pulling weeds from the fields under the direction of adult gang leaders. As rural craftsmen found themselves competing with new machine-based production, many of them reacted by bringing younger and younger members of their families into the production process. Children as young as 6 or 7 years were to be found making rope, spinning flax, and plaiting straw for baskets, chairs, and hats. Children under 10 years of age were not permitted officially to work in coal mines, but it is doubtful that employers routinely verified the ages of their young employees. Children also worked in the newly developed mills and factories, constituting between a quarter and a third of the workforce in some of these establishments. A government inquiry into child labour across a wide range of industries published in 1848 found almost 20 percent of workers were younger than 16 years. Working hours for children in industry were generally the same as for adults, typically at least ten hours per day and sometimes as many as sixteen. The conditions of work were generally unhealthy. The worst environments were those in matchstick factories, where young children worked in poorly ventilated rooms, dipping matchsticks into a phosphorus mixture that was harmful to their bones.

Despite its early participation in the industrial revolution, Belgium was one of the last European countries to introduce laws on child labour. In 1842, King Leopold announced a bill for the protection of children working in factories. It was not until 1848 that this bill was actually introduced in Parliament. It would have prohibited work by all children under 10 years of age and would have restricted work hours for those under 15 years of age to six and a half hours per day. However, Belgian industrialists were a particularly powerful force in their country's politics. They argued that the proposed law would harm Belgium's competitiveness in international markets. As a result, the bill was not passed. However, in 1886—a year of economic crisis— riots broke out across the country as working people fought to improve their conditions. Another investigation was held into working conditions, and the outcome this time was a law passed in 1889. This law prohibited children under 12 years of age from working in industry, outlawed night work for children, and restricted the number of work hours per day. Domestic labour and agriculture were not covered by this law, and even in industry the law was easily circumvented by employers' registering children as apprentices rather than as workers.

The Belgian Labour Law of 16 March 1971 includes among other provisions a ban on the employment of school-age children, except in certain artistic activities. Young people under 18 years of age may not work for more than ten hours a day and are excluded entirely from working in certain situations, such as mining.

A particularly vivid portrayal of child labour in nineteenth-century Belgium is to be found in the 1992 film *Daens*, a Belgian-French-Dutch coproduction directed by Stijn Coninx. Based on a true story, the film stars Jan Decleir as Father Adolf Daens, a Roman Catholic priest who campaigned for improved pay and working conditions in Belgian factories.

References De Herdt, Rene, "Child Labour in Belgium, 1800–1914" (1996).

Beveridge, Albert J.

Although a number of bodies in the United States, including trade union groups, had been calling for national legislation to tackle child labour, the first attempt to introduce such legislation in 1906 was made by Albert J. Beveridge, U.S. senator from Indiana. Beveridge had a number of reasons for wishing to introduce such legislation. He was in part motivated by humanitarian concern regarding the working conditions that children had to endure. He also was influenced by the desire to help his own political advancement, and by racist views that held that child labour was contributing to the racial degeneracy of the country. In this latter respect, his outlook was similar to that of Alexander McKelway, secretary of the National Child Labor Committee (NCLC).

Beveridge's legislation targeted what he perceived as the national evil of child labour by prohibiting the interstate movement of goods produced by children under 14 years of age. Enforcement of the law would be the responsibility of federal district attorneys, and stiff penalties would be imposed to ensure compliance with the law. It is worth noting that child labour in agriculture was excluded from Beveridge's bill. This reflected the belief that the exploitation of children took place only in factories and mills. In contrast, working on farms was viewed as not only acceptable but even beneficial to children.

To ensure the success of his legislation, Beveridge understandably turned to the NCLC for its support. However, rather than helping the NCLC, his proposed bill created a major problem for the Committee. The NCLC had been set up to advance state legislation on this subject, and many NCLC members were not convinced that federal legislation was viable or desirable. The Committee's initial reaction to Beveridge's approach was to seek clarification from NCLC members about how they should react.

In early December, Beveridge introduced the bill to the Senate. At the same time, Herbert Parsons, congressman from

Albert J. Beveridge (Library of Congress)

New York, introduced an identical bill to the House of Representatives. The NCLC still had not decided on its position regarding the bill. However, after discussion within its board, the NCLC agreed to support the bill. The decision was by no means unanimous. Some of the board's trustees had opposed this move, believing that it undermined the work of the NCLC, which they thought should focus on state legislation. The logic of this argument appears to have been that since conditions varied between states, legislation had to be specifically targeted to the situation in each state. For example, some Committee members felt that Beveridge's bill would not go far enough in tackling the problem of child labour in the Southern states. Some members felt so strongly about this that they resigned from the NCLC. Edgar Murphy, a leading figure in the founding of the NCLC, resigned from the Committee, arguing that the NCLC was in breach of its original promise to seek state legislation on this issue. Murphy,

who was from the South, believed that Beveridge's bill would hamper attempts to improve the lot of children in the Southern states. After resigning, he lobbied against Beveridge's bill and openly raised money to fight against federal legislation on this issue.

In throwing its weight behind Beveridge's bill, the NCLC sent Alexander McKelway to Washington to lobby for its passage. This was not forthcoming. Some trade unions were suspicious about federal legislation on labour issues, and President Theodore Roosevelt had doubts about whether the bill would be constitutional. Roosevelt realized that the bill did not have unanimous support, and he therefore adopted a different strategy, asking Congress to set up a national investigation into the working conditions of women and children in the United States. This review was authorized in 1907.

Beveridge was dismissive of Roosevelt's initiative, arguing that the time for collecting information had passed and that action was needed urgently. He continued to push his bill forward and adopted political strategies to achieve his ends. On 23 January 1907, the Senate opened debate on a child labour law for the District of Columbia. Beveridge tabled his federal bill as an amendment to that measure. In doing so Beveridge took the floor of the Senate for a total of three days—23, 28, and 29 January. To highlight the plight of child workers, he read descriptions of their working conditions that had been supplied to him by the NCLC. Although his actions met with public support, the bill was voted down.

Beveridge's failure, along with the resignation of Murphy from the NCLC, created a crisis within the Committee. The board met once again to review its support of the proposed federal legislation. This time, after much heated debate, the board withdrew its support for federal legislation. Beveridge's bill had not only failed but had caused deep divisions within the NCLC. The Committee resolved to return to the fray but once again to place the emphasis on state legislation.

See also McKelway, Alexander J.; Murphy, Edgar G.; National Child Labor Committee.
References Trattner, Walter I., *Crusade for the Children* (1970).

Bhima Sangha

Based in India, Bhima Sangha is an independent organization of working children. The formation of this organization was facilitated by The Concerned for Working Children, an adult nongovernmental organization. Launched in 1989, Bhima Sangha is mainly active in South India and has a membership of 13,000 young workers. The aim of the organization is to represent the views of working children and to take these into the political forum. Priorities and issues are established by the children themselves, and they have had an important input into the local and international debate. At the local level Bhima Sangha has highlighted working children's views and made presentations to local and national politicians. At the international level, representatives of Bhima Sangha have attended the First International Meeting of Working Children and have participated in conferences on child labour in Amsterdam, Trondheim, and Oslo.

See also India; International Meeting of Working Children; Voices of Children.

Blincoe, Robert

A Memoir of Robert Blincoe played a prominent part in the agitation that took place in England in the first half of the nineteenth century for reform of the laws governing the running of factories. Blincoe was born in London around 1792. In 1799 he was sent as a pauper apprentice to a mill near Nottingham and later was transferred to another mill in Derbyshire. The author of the account of Blincoe's early life was John Brown, who first published it in 1828 in *The Lion*, a radical magazine. John Doherty, a trade union leader who was also a printer, published Blincoe's story in book form in 1832. He gave the book the full title:

A Memoir of Robert Blincoe,
An Orphan Boy,
Sent from the Workhouse of St.
Pancras, London,
At Seven Years of Age, to Endure the
Horrors of a Cotton-Mill,
Through His Infancy and Youth,
With a Minute Detail of His Sufferings,
Being the First Memoir of the Kind
Published.

Blincoe was in later life a successful manufacturer and dealer.

See also Pauper Apprentices; Dundee Factory Boy.
References Brown, John, *A Memoir of Robert Blincoe* (1977).

Bonded Labour

See Unfree Labour.

Bonded Labour Liberation Front

One of the major organizations in Pakistan working to improve conditions for child workers is the Bonded Labour Liberation Front. Founded in 1988 by Elisan Ullah Khan, the Front works in several ways to help both child workers and adult bonded labourers, who are often at risk of physical attack because of the hostility of many employers. The Front obtains the release of workers by petitioning the courts. It also provides protection, shelter, and education for those it has succeeded in freeing. Despite its many successes, the Front is working against overwhelming odds because of the scale of the exploitation that takes place in the country.

See also Masih, Iqbal; Pakistan; Unfree Labour.
References Anti-Slavery International, *"This Menace of Bonded Labour": Debt Bondage in Pakistan* (1996).

Boy Slaves

A rare example of a Hollywood movie devoted to the subject of child labour, *Boy Slaves* was made by RKO Radio Pictures in 1939. It was an indictment of the turpentine farms found in parts of the southern United States, where boys were kept in a virtually permanent state of indebtedness to their employers. The foreword to the film states that although the love and defence of children is a primary instinct, there are isolated communities in the United States where children labour "from sunup to sundown" because their employers put a love of money before humanity. Although the film was commended by Eleanor Roosevelt as "almost as exciting as *Jesse James*," others at the time commented on its melodramatic incidents and its preaching. With only one minor star in the cast list, Anne Shirley, the film was moderately successful in cinemas as part of double-feature programmes. This was the only film directed by P. J. Wolfson, who was better known as a producer and writer of films on more lighthearted subjects.

Boy Soldiers

There is evidence from ancient and medieval times that children served as soldiers and took part in fighting. That tradition continued into modern times. According to A. W. Cockerill, the youngest soldier ever to enlist officially in the British Army was Drummer James Wade, who did so on his seventh birthday. The role of drummer was a common one for boys. It was also dangerous, as the beat of the drum accompanied infantry into battle and the drummer was a conspicuous target for enemy fire. Both the British and the American Armies in the American Revolutionary War contained large numbers of boy soldiers. General George Washington complained of being sent boys unable to bear arms. In the nineteenth century, several boys won the Victoria Cross, the highest award for bravery in the British Army.

In the twentieth century, countries such as the United States and Great Britain have set higher age limits for participation in combat, but it has not been unknown for younger males to lie about their ages in order to be recruited. In contrast to this enthusiasm for the military life shown by

some young people, there are parts of the world today where it is the practice of participants in guerrilla warfare to kidnap children and force them to fight as soldiers. This has been done in recent times, for example, by the so-called Lord's Resistance Army in Uganda. Governments too are guilty of the forcible conscription of children into their armies. It is reported that in Sudan, high school students are sent into war zones after only three weeks of training.

It is not always clear in what circumstances children join armies. When it was reported in December 1997 that official Cambodian government forces fighting Khmer Rouge rebels included children as young as 8 years, a military spokesman acknowledged the existence of child soldiers but claimed that they were deserters from the Khmer Rouge Army.

Quite apart from the obvious dangers of taking part in battle, child soldiers are also at risk from disease because of the unhealthy conditions in which they often live. Three hundred children who had volunteered to join the government forces of Congo-Kinshasa died from cholera and dysentery at a camp in 1998.

The Convention on the Rights of the Child adopted by the United Nations in 1989 treats a child as a person below the age of 18 years. However, Article 38, which deals with the participation of children in armed conflict, does not call for them to be excluded entirely from warfare. It requires states to take "all feasible measures to ensure that persons who have not attained the age of fifteen years do not take a direct part in hostilities." States should also "refrain from recruiting any person who has not attained the age of fifteen years into their armed forces." This aspect of the Convention had been a matter of contention when it was being drawn up; and when ratifying it, Colombia, Ecuador, and Spain all expressed the view that the age limits set for taking part in fighting were too low.

In the face of an alarming increase in the use of children in military conflict,

UNICEF is campaigning to have children treated as "zones of peace." Technological advances have made it easier to use children in warfare: Whereas a child wielding a sword or an axe is unlikely to be a match for an adult soldier, a child may be trained to be as effective as an adult in the use of a rifle. Another impetus for children's participation in armed forces has been severe social disruption in which many children have been orphaned or abandoned; under these conditions, the children may see the army as the only substitute for a family. The army provides the child with food and clothing and his or her fellow soldiers offer comradeship. In parts of Myanmar, the country formerly known as Burma, where ethnic minorities are fighting the central military government, some parents even send their children to join the army, because they believe living conditions are better there.

The Swedish organization Radda Barnen publishes a regular newsletter on child soldiers, *Children of War*, which reports on countries where children are alleged to be members of either government or opposition forces in an armed conflict. A recent listing included 32 countries in which children under 18 years of age were taking part in fighting. In 24 of these countries, child soldiers were only 14 years old, or younger. Among the many reports of disease and death, *Children of War* is sometimes able to report more favourable developments. For example, in 1998, Radda Barnen confirmed the truth of claims being made in Sudan by the opposition group, the Sudan People's Liberation Movement, that they had started to demobilize their child soldiers. The programme would include reeducation and reintegration of the former soldiers into the civilian community. Save the Children, the British equivalent of Radda Barnen, is involved in a child soldier rehabilitation programme in Liberia.

See also Convention on the Rights of the Child; Navy.

References Cockerill, A. W. *Sons of the Brave: The Story of Boy Soldiers* (1984); Wessells, Mike, "Child Soldiers" (1997).

Brazil

The Federal Republic of Brazil, which has an estimated population of over 150 million, is the largest country in South America. The capital is the specially built city, Brasilia, which has over two million inhabitants. However, the largest cities are Sao Paulo (around ten million) and Rio de Janeiro (around seven million). Brazil was colonized by Portugal in the sixteenth century and became independent in 1822. Brazil has rich and varied mineral deposits ranging from iron ore to gold and diamonds. Its agricultural industry exports coffee, soybeans, meat, and fruit.

Although education is free and compulsory, many children attend school little or not at all. It has been estimated that more than two-thirds of adult workers started work before the age of 14. Thus child employment is a major feature of Brazilian society. Public concern naturally focuses on its more extreme and hazardous forms.

Around two-thirds of the population live in cities and large towns. Over a third of the population are under 16 years of age. It follows that many Brazilian children live in urban areas—often not in the cities themselves but in favelas, shantytowns built by rural people who migrated from the countryside in search of work. This is because rural poverty is so extreme. In rural areas, children as young as 5 years old may be found working with their parents. Migration to the cities does not bring a release from work for such children. Many urban children live on the streets, more or less cut off from their parents and therefore fending for themselves.

The shoe industry is one of Brazil's main export industries. In 1993 alone, the United States imported $1.4 billion in footwear from Brazil. One of the main regions for this employment is Franca, in Sao Paulo. The industry is dominated by subcontract labour. In 1993, a study revealed that 7,000 people were employed in this part of the industry, of which 1,300 were children under the age of 14. The working days were long and the conditions inadequate: Most production sites

Children working in cotton fields in Brazil, 1975 (OAS)

were small, poorly ventilated outlets. The buildings were dark, and doors and windows were often covered to hide the fact that the company was employing illegal child labour. The facilities were not highly mechanized, and most tasks were performed by hand, at workbenches. Children were employed to spread glue, fit fastenings, cut thread, polish soles, and stitch shoes by hand.

Children also are used on sugarcane plantations throughout Brazil. Most children work alongside their families and get around the law by either falsifying papers or ignoring child labour laws. A recent study, for example, suggested that 90 percent of child workers on the plantations are unregistered. Conditions on the plantations are extremely poor. Children work between 12 and 14 hours a day, excluding travel time (many children are transported on planters' vehicles as far as 12 miles to get to their work sites). For the privilege of being transported to work, the workers are

charged by the plantation owner. The work is repetitive and physically demanding, and tired bodies lead to accidents with the sharp machetes; 85 percent of all injuries on the plantations are knife wounds. The sun can be intense, and the heat is made worse by plantation owners who burn the stubble soon after cutting. As a result the atmosphere is full of smoke and toxic fumes that are being burned off.

In Brazil's tea plantation industry, children can be found working from the age of 7. They work as part of a family work unit, and thus detection is often difficult. The tea bushes are low, and the work is often backbreaking for adults, so picking is thought the ideal job for children and their "nimble fingers." Workers are paid depending on the amount they pick, the rates are exceptionally low, and tea pickers live in desperate poverty.

There is an official agency known as FUNABEM (the Portuguese acronym for "National Foundation for Child Welfare"). This body has responsibility for dealing with the many problems faced by street children, but Brazilian observers have described it as ineffective. More hope is seen in attempts to develop self-help skills among children, which are supported by some priests.

In 1980, *Pixote*, a film vividly depicting the life of Brazilian street children, was released. The leading roles, including that of Pixote, the central character, were played by real street children. It is perhaps symbolic of the problems faced by these children and those who try to help them that despite the success of the film in publicizing the dreadful conditions on the streets, the leading actor returned to life on the street and died in 1987. Suspected of robbery, he was ambushed and shot by the military authorities.

See also National Movement of Street Children; Street Children.

References Cadman, Eileen, *No Time to Play: Child Workers in the Global Economy* (1996); Di Robilant, Andrea, and Moorehead, Caroline, "Street Children: Brazil" (1989); Ennew, Judith, and Milne, Brian, *The Next Generation: Lives of Third World Children* (1989); Lee-Wright, Peter, *Child Slaves* (1990); Rosemberg, Fulvia, and Andrade, Leandro Feitosa, "Ruthless Rhetoric: Child and Youth Prostitution in Brazil" (1999).

Britain
See United Kingdom.

Bruce, Rev. Charles Lang
During the 1800s, an awareness gradually developed among Americans of the number of children working in a wide range of settings. The number of children seeking employment increased in the latter part of the century, with increasing numbers of immigrants to the United States. Toward the end of this century, activists started to speak out about the worst excesses of child labour. The Rev. Charles Lang Bruce was one such activist. In 1872 he raised the issue of child workers with particular reference to children working in factories in New York City.

References Trattner, Walter, *Crusade for the Children* (1970).

Burkina Faso
Formerly known as Upper Volta, this landlocked West African republic has an estimated population of more than nine million. Formerly part of the French empire, it achieved full independence in 1960. Children in Burkina Faso typically begin to work around the age of 10. They are to be found in all of the principal economic activities of the country: cattle and sheepherding, growing of cereal crops, mining, and small-scale manufacturing. Children, predominantly girls, also engage in domestic labour.

One distinctive form of child labour is associated with the Quranic schools. Students are sent to live with Quranic masters for periods of five to nine years, during which they are taught to read the Islamic holy book, the Quran; to recite various prayers and perform religious rituals; and to write in Arabic. Their parents pay no fees; in exchange for their tuition, the boys work on the master's farm. In some cases, they are also sent to beg. Begging is an acceptable local occupation, because giving money to beggars is considered a religious virtue. The proportions of time children spend in study and at work vary with the seasons. In the schools surveyed by Mahir Saul, around a quarter to a third of all farm labour was performed by the students.

See also Africa; International Labour Organisation; Religion.

References Saul, Mahir, "The Quranic School Farm and Child Labour in Upper Volta" (1984); Schlemmer, Bernard (ed.), *L'enfant Exploité: Oppression, Mise au Travail, Proletarisation* (1996).

Burma
See Myanmar.

Burston School Strike
The Burston School Strike is the name given to a series of events that took place in

the county of Norfolk, England, in the early part of the twentieth century. The central figures were two teachers, Mr and Mrs Tom Higdon. They were employed at two rural schools in the county, Wood Dalling (1902–1911) and Burston (1911–1914). In both places, they came into conflict with local farmers and with the school managers. They were dismissed from both of their posts, but at Burston they received strong support from the pupils and their parents. With assistance from people throughout Britain they built and ran a rival school, to which many parents in the village sent their children. The Higdons were dedicated Christian socialists who tended to sympathize with the local farm labourers against the powerful local farm owners. Tom Higdon assisted in the formation of branches of the Labourers' Union in both villages and helped to have farm labourers elected to the local parish councils.

One major point of dispute between the Higdons and the farmers was that children were expected to work when they should have been attending school. On one occasion Tom Higdon was charged with assaulting a farmer who had enraged him by frequently taking children out of school to work. On the day of the assault, one boy had had his meal on the school premises but was then called away by the farmer to lead a drill horse. What had particularly annoyed Tom Higdon was the fact that the boy was working in a field directly opposite the school and could be seen by the other children. Even today, there are frequently conflicts in rural communities between the requirements of schooling and the desire of farmers to utilize children as an extra, seasonal supply of labour.

References Edwards, B., *The Burston School Strike* (1974).

Business Ethic

The *business ethic* is a phrase describing the outlook of those who hope to succeed in business. Although there is no single, precise definition of this outlook, it is normally thought of as including a belief in the market as a way of determining value; a preference for taking initiative rather than merely following instructions; a sensitivity to the needs of the prospective customer; a sense of competitiveness; a respect for the value of money; and a dedication to hard work. In this last respect, it is close in meaning to the phrase *work ethic*. One of the arguments in favour of children's work in industrialized countries such as the United States and Britain is that it provides an opportunity for children to acquire the business ethic. Children's work therefore is seen as preparing children for adult life and as enhancing their chances of later success in business. However, these results are contingent on the nature of the work that children perform. Many jobs that children are given are repetitive in nature and provide few opportunities to learn useful skills and productive attitudes.

See also Saturday Evening Post; Work Ethic.

Camel Jockeys

Camel racing is an extremely popular sport in the United Arab Emirates. Camels were formerly an important mode of transport for the local people. However, the production of oil in the past thirty years has led to the creation of a rich elite in the country who treat camel racing as an expensive hobby. The wealth of the camel owners has allowed large-scale investment in the breeding of camels. An Embryo Research Station for Racing Camels was established in 1989. An individual camel might be sold for as much as 3 million U.S. dollars.

The use of children of ages 6 years and younger as jockeys in the camel races has given rise to considerable criticism, for three main reasons. The first is that in the races the children are at risk of death or serious injury. The second is that they are treated very badly. Training methods are often harsh, and children are

Bangladeshi children were rescued from India where they were sold for use as camel jockeys, 1998 (Dsikan Krishnan, Associated Press)

frequently beaten. They are fed poorly to keep their weight low. They are not given access to education while they are employed, and they are abandoned without help when they become too heavy to be useful as riders. Former camel jockeys are either deported by the authorities or scrape together a living in the underground community of illegal immigrants. The third objection is that these children are brought from other countries, such as Bangladesh, by trafficking. Their parents are sometimes paid small sums of money and led to believe that they can expect a much better standard of living than is available to them at home. In other cases, the children may be abducted without parental consent. In either circumstance, the result is that these very young children are taken from their parents to an entirely different society with a different language.

In 1993, Sheik Zayed, president of the United Arab Emirates, decreed that children should not be used as camel jockeys. The Camel Jockey Association has rules forbidding the use of riders younger than 14 years or weighing less than 45 kilos. However, journalists have produced evidence of 6-year-old children weighing less than 20 kilos taking part in races. Anti-Slavery International has played a prominent role in campaigning for an end to the use of young children as camel jockeys.

See also Anti-Slavery International; Sports; United Arab Emirates.

Cameroon

The Republic of Cameroon is situated in West Africa between Nigeria and Congo. It became an independent state in 1960, after many years of rule by Germany and then by France. In 1961, the British-run territory of South Cameroons voted in a plebiscite to become a part of the new republic. The Cameroon economy is predominantly agricultural, but there is also substantial oil production. Cameroon has a population of around 12 million, almost half of whom are 15 years old or younger. The 1990s were marked by economic cri-

sis and political unrest. A structural adjustment programme introduced in the late 1980s has brought considerable hardship to much of the population.

The law forbids children under 14 years of age to work. However, there are more than two hundred ethnic groups in the country with varying notions of when and how the transition from childhood to adulthood takes place. Child labour is acknowledged to be at a very high level, but accurate statistics are not available. In most communities young children are expected to undertake simple household duties. In some northern areas where the tradition of child labour is strong, enrolment rates at primary schools are particularly low. Girls are particularly likely to become involved in housework. Historically, it has been common for a boy to start to learn the trade of his father. However, traditional arts and crafts are on the decline. As a consequence, there are fewer boys entering apprenticeships. In contrast, children in rural areas are often withdrawn from school to perform seasonal agricultural tasks.

Most of the children who are engaged in domestic work in urban areas have come from rural families. In many cases they have come to their employers through intermediaries, some of whom earn substantial fees for setting up employment contracts. The nature of the contracts varies. Sometimes they involve direct payment to children for the work they have done. In other cases, it is the parent who receives the payment and who thus has control over how the child's earnings are to be spent. Parents often see the intermediaries as performing a useful function of seeking out suitable employers for their children. However, the system does not always produce satisfactory results. It is common for ill-treated child workers to become runaways.

Another form of urban child labour is apprenticeship in small industrial concerns such as metalworking, carpentry, and brickmaking. This type of work is on the increase. In actuality, however, the child apprentices receive little professional training. In the main, their conditions of work are exploitative, arduous, and hazardous to their health. The loss of fingers and eyes is common.

Street children are a very visible part of the life of cities such as Yaounde, the capital. Some of them are employed to sell goods, either on their own or as assistants to their parents. However, others have little or no contact with their parents. Some street children are involved in begging or in prostitution.

See also Africa; International Labour Organisation; Stabilization and Structural Adjustment Programmes.

References Amin, Aloysius Ajab, "The Socio-Economic Impact of Child Labour in Cameroon" (1994).

Canada

Canada occupies the whole of continental North America north of the United States (apart from Alaska). It has a total landmass of almost 4 million square miles and a total population of around 30 million people. Its official languages are English and French, a legacy of the role played by the British and the French in colonizing the area. It has a federal constitution and is a member of the British commonwealth. The influence of French culture is particularly strong in the province of Quebec, which is now constitutionally recognized as a "distinct society."

It is common in Canada for high school students to work part time, and the proportion working appears to be on the increase. An estimate of 50 percent of high school students having jobs was made in 1993, compared to a figure of 37 percent in 1976. High school dropout rates have been associated with child labour in four Canadian provinces that have the most successful economies—namely, Alberta, British Columbia, Ontario, and Quebec. Jobs such as cleaning and door-to-door sales are common among child workers.

One in six families in Canada are immigrant families. The children in these families are particularly likely to be drawn into employment. The Christian Children's Fund of Canada has identified garment manufacture, amusement park operation, agriculture, cleaning, construction, and exotic dancing as areas of work in which immigrant children are to be found.

References Knight, Sheilagh, *Child Labour in Canada: A Look at Our Children* (1995).

Capitalism

Capitalism is commonly defined as a market-based social and economic system in which individuals are free to own private property and the means of production in order to maximize profit by employing the labour of others. Resource allocation is determined via the price system. In other words, all commodities, including labour, find their natural price through the relative strength of supply and demand in the market. Scarce resources, which at any particular time could be skilled labour, gold, or, indeed, any commodity, command high prices. However, such high prices encourage investment in this area and a greater supply of this particular good to meet the demand. Thus capitalism is expansive and constantly produces greater amounts and improved quality of goods. For this reason, capitalism has brought greater wealth to human society than was ever imaginable in precapitalist society.

For critics of capitalism, the above outline is only half the picture, however. German sociologist Max Weber defined capitalism as a system organized in accordance with principles of rationality; and he was not necessarily implying that he supported the system. By outlining the rationalizing tendencies of capitalism, Weber was noting the way in which formal law, bookkeeping, the division of labour and industrial organization were structured around visible and logical principles. But such processes, he argued, gave rise to an ever increasing and ever less accountable bureaucracy. As a consequence, life became darker and more hopeless, and individuals were constrained by an "iron cage."

For Karl Marx, capitalism was a class-divided system based on what he called the "anarchy" of production. Marx portrayed the system as one in which a relatively small minority of the population—which he called the "bourgeoisie"—owned or controlled the physical means of production, including the land, factories, machinery, raw materials, offices, and so on, but could not produce anything without the labour of others. On the other hand, the vast majority of the population, which Marx referred to as the proletariat, or working class, had no means of surviving except by entering the labour market and working for a wage in the factories and offices of the bourgeoisie.

The complex and specialized division of labour that capitalism establishes means that no producer is able to survive on the output of his or her own production alone. Instead they must sell their own products and in turn purchase the products of others. Producers, therefore, are interdependent. Whether commodities will sell is something that can only be discovered after they have been manufactured. In this sense, production in capitalist societies is always a risk-taking exercise.

Although it may appear from these definitions that capital and labour are equivalents, interdependent on one another, with the one providing the means of production and the other the labour to work with machines and tools on natural resources to produce commodities, the reality is somewhat different. The bourgeoisie's ownership and control of the means of production give it enormous power to exploit the labour activity of the vast majority within society. In contrast, there is no mechanism forcing the bourgeoisie to pay wages equivalent to the wealth or value created by the labourers they employ.

The competition between capitalists drives the system forward, and in this sense, capitalism is dynamic. This dynamism has two consequences. First, capitalism is increasingly bringing new areas under its domain. A system that started in western Europe is now truly global. Secondly, capitalism is constantly changing what is produced and how it is produced. Therefore, the world of work and the labour tasks we perform are subject to constant change. The job of a miner, an engineer, or an office worker is radically different today from what it was twenty or thirty years ago. The source of such dynamism is that each "unit of capital," whether it be an individual, a national corporation, a multinational company, or even a state, must try to produce more goods at a cheaper price than their major competitors. But essentially there are only two ways in which they can do this. One is by increasing the exploitation of their workforce; for example, by lowering wages or lengthening the average workday. However, wages cannot be reduced below subsistence levels; and if the workday is overextended, workers become fatigued and inefficient.

The other way of achieving cheaper production is by reinvesting greater sums in machinery and technology and constantly revolutionizing the forces of production. But this process leads to problems. The very fact of competition means that production in general does not take place in a rational, planned manner. Instead, historically, the system has lurched from periods of boom into periods of severe crisis. Secondly, the boom and slump cycle shows the inefficiencies of the market system. The system generates overproduction, and during those periods of overproduction, goods cannot be sold or even offered on the market. Generally, when boom turns to slump, products are left to rot, and resources, including labour, are left idle. As firms get larger and technological advances improve and become more expensive, there will be fewer workers creating surplus value, working with larger and more expensive machines. The drive toward innovation, in order to undercut competitors, means that machines become redundant and are discarded before they are exhausted or have been paid for. The result is that there is a tendency for the general rate of profit to fall. The costs of entering the productive process to buy the newest machines and factories are excessive, and the surplus value created by the relatively few workers is proportionately small.

Historically, the search for the cheapest labour to work in fields, factories, and mines has resulted in the labour of children. In recent years there has been a growing debate over the role of capitalism in the exploitation of child labour. For many writers, child labour is caused by economic backwardness. By this argument, there is not enough capitalism, and child labour is a precapitalist practice that will be eradicated by further development. This line of thinking comes through in many of the International Labour Organisation's publications about child labour from the 1970s and early 1980s. Such explanations also appear in the writings of sociologists committed to the Industrial Society Thesis and in those of optimistic nineteenth-century historians. Both groups, in general terms, suggest that the full development of capitalist social relations in modern industrial societies has led to the eradication of child labour. For other writers, such as Friedrich Engels and Clara Zetkin—or more recently, historian E. P. Thompson—child labour has become worse with the commodification of labour. Child labour is a central feature of the inequalities and class relations that characterize modern capitalist societies.

See also Division of Labour; Engels, Friedrich; Industrial Society Thesis, Marxism; Stop Child Labour; Thompson, E. P.; Zetkin, Clara.
References Lavalette, Michael, *Child Employment in the Capitalist Labour Market* (1994).

Career

The notion of a career suggests a linear development of increasing job specialization and progress during an individual's working life. However, this model is an idealization. The economic context in which most people work involves increased flexibility at work, and both unemployment and job restructuring. Thus the idea of a career is perhaps less straightforward than it may have been in the past. Instead "career development" is used to refer to a process of individual growth and learning in relation to the world of work. People are seen as making decisions at key points in their lives based on their experiences, knowledge, and desires. They need to take account of the existing economic conditions and employer needs. The notion of career development suggests that we acquire a range of transferable work-related skills in a range of settings, and that many such skills are acquired prior to formal entry to the adult labour market. Hence there has been some discussion regarding the usefulness of the career enhancement skills obtained from child labour. Some psychologists in the United States have suggested that one of the benefits of part-time employment for children is that it teaches children about the world of work, appropriate behaviour during employment, and how to handle relationships with other employees and employers. Part-time work performed by children that provides these benefits can be viewed as an appropriate part of their early career development.

See also Costs and Benefits.
References Stevens, C. J., Putchell, L. A., Ryu, S., and Mortimer, J. T., "Adolescent Work and Boys' and Girls' Orientations to the Future" (1992).

Caribbean

The islands of the Caribbean Sea were the first parts of the American continent to become known to Europeans after the voyages of Christopher Columbus. Over the centuries that followed, the various Caribbean islands came under the control of European countries such as Spain, France, the Netherlands, and Great Britain, and later also of the United States. The islands today have a variety of social, economic, and political regimes. Child labour appears to exist throughout the Caribbean, but it is better documented on some islands than on others.

The largest single island, Cuba, with a population of about 11 million, has been a communist state under the leadership of Fidel Castro since 1959, although there are signs of a softening in the government's economic policies since it lost the support of the Soviet Union following the collapse of communism in Eastern Europe. The Castro government from the start put a heavy emphasis on basic education. For example, in Castro's first ten years in power, the number of children in primary schools more than doubled. The Cuban government's policy has been effective in raising literacy rates. It also probably has led to a decline in child labour, since when children attend school, they are not available for work. However, to solve its current economic problems, the Cuban government has been rebuilding its tourism industry, which had been very vigorous under the previous regime. One unintended consequence of this policy has been more visible child employment again in the tourist areas.

Jamaica is an island of more than 2.5 million inhabitants situated southeast of Cuba. Ruled first by Spain and later by Britain, it achieved independence in 1962. Jamaica has a large tourism industry and exports minerals, bananas, and sugar. It provides one example of the pattern of child labour in the Caribbean.

Jamaican family structures are particularly fluid, with as many as three-quarters of children being born out of wedlock. High adult unemployment contributes to a situation where many children are brought up in households without an adult male breadwinner. Accordingly, children are expected to fend for themselves and to contribute to the household income at an early age. Children often drop out of school around the age of 10 or 12 years, to earn money by working. Domestic service and agriculture are the main sources of employment. According to anthropologist Judith Ennew, because of these circumstances Jamaican children learn independence and self-reliance early in life.

References Ennew, Judith, "Family Structure, Unemployment, and Child Labour in Jamaica" (1982); Ennew, Judith, and Milne, Brian, *The Next Generation: Lives of Third World Children* (1989).

Caregiving
See Young Caregivers.

Carpet Manufacture
Over the past few decades there has been increasing interest in the conditions of children involved in carpet making. The media and nongovernmental organizations (NGOs) have on a number of occasions shown the distressing conditions under which these children work. The most well-known child carpet maker is probably Iqbal Masih, who became a prominent spokesperson for working children in Pakistan until his death.

The majority of carpets made by children are for export, and the main market is in the countries of western Europe, particularly Germany. The carpets are made in Pakistan, Nepal, the People's Republic of China, Morocco, Egypt, Iran, Afghanistan, and India.

It is important to consider in detail what is involved in this work. Although a loom is used, the carpets are not woven but are tied by hand. Each carpet consists of thousands of pieces of knotted wool or silk. The value of the carpet is measured by the number of knots per square inch. The child workers have to choose the appropriate colour of thread, knot it in place, and trim it. A number of children work at a single loom, following a pattern shouted out by a foreman. Each child is responsible for about half a metre of carpet. The child workers are paid different rates, depending on their level of skill and speed. One recent research paper noted that an average wage was the equivalent of 38 cents per day in U.S. currency. In another example, a 13-year-old carpet maker typically received 28 U.S. dollars for one carpet. It takes three to four months to make a single carpet. However, in addition to the child carpet makers who receive very low pay, there are some who are not paid at all because they are slave or bonded labourers. Working hours are long: Some researchers have described children carrying out this task for 10 to 15 hours per day.

Children employed in this sector are also working in hazardous conditions. The looms are housed in cramped buildings with little work space. The children work sitting in uncomfortable positions and in poorly ventilated spaces. Sitting for long hours and having to concentrate on a complex task proves extremely tiring, and accidents often occur when the children are cutting threads. Damage to eyesight is another common consequence of working in poorly lit environments. Additional health problems may arise from skin contact with the dyes used in the wool.

It is difficult to estimate the number of children that are currently involved in such work. If we take India as an example, then we find estimates for the number of children in this sector ranging from 50,000 to 1,050,000. The International Labour Organisation in 1996 estimated that the figure was closer to 130,000. Researcher Mohini Gulrajani has asserted that the informal nature of carpet making makes it difficult to get an accurate figure, but suggested that the number of children employed in this type of work is between 100,000 and 300,000. Since this figure applies to India alone and there are a number of other countries where children are employed in this way, the total number of child carpet weavers worldwide must be regarded as significant.

Within the carpet making sector, it is common for employers to offer a particular justification for using children. It has been proposed that children are particularly suited to this task since their small dexterous fingers allow them to knot the carpet threads more effectively. This so called "nimble fingers" justification has been questioned by many. Gulrajani argues that children are employed in this sector because of cost; they are a source of cheap labour, which helps manufacturers keep production costs low. Gulrajani suggests that in India carpet making can only exist because of cheap child labour.

Carpet making is only one form of employment in which children around the world are gravely disadvantaged. However, nongovernmental organizations have been able to draw attention to the wider issue of child employment by using carpet making as an evocative example. The example arouses strong emotions because poorly paid (or unpaid) children are producing carpets that are exported to the rich countries of the world and sold at exorbitant prices.

The high public profile of the industry has led to a number of initiatives to tackle child employment in this sector. Product labels such as "Rugmark" have been developed as a means of signalling to potential buyers that carpets carrying such trademarks were made without the exploitation of children.

See also Masih, Iqbal; Product Labelling; Rugmark.

References Anti-Slavery Society, *Child Labour in Morocco's Carpet Industry* (1978); Cross, Peter, *Kashmiri Carpet Children: Exploited Village Weavers* (no date); Gulrajani, Mohini, "Child Labour and the Export Sector in the Third World: A Case Study of the Indian Carpet Industry" (1994).

Catering
See Hotel and Catering Industry.

Causes of Child Labour
It is often assumed that the amount of child labour in a country is determined by the nature and extent of poverty in that country. Studies that have been undertaken in various countries around the world, particularly those that are relatively underdeveloped economically, do show that child labour and poverty are intimately linked. However, it is also clear that the specific circumstances of child labour in particular countries, or parts of countries, is influenced by many other factors. Cultural traditions also play a part.

See also Cultural Traditions; Poverty.

Centuries of Childhood
First published in French in 1960 and in

English in 1962, *Centuries of Childhood*, by French historian Philippe Aries, has been a seminal work in establishing how modern childhood has been constructed through social processes. The book has three interlocking themes: the development of education; changes to the family form; and the discovery of childhood. In the book, Aries asserted that the concept of childhood is relatively recent, having been "discovered" toward the end of the thirteenth century in France. By this he did not mean that no distinctions were made between people of different ages prior to this period. Rather, he meant that the stages of human development were defined differently than our modern definitions of developmental periods, and that the pattern of age stratification that existed then was different from what we see today.

To justify his claim, Aries drew on several pieces of evidence that he thought proved that in premodern times children were integrated into the community as small adults and not distinctively as children. The material gathered by Aries includes evidence relating to the development of education, to changing sexual attitudes, and to the history of children's dress, games, and pastimes. Pictorial evidence presented in the book suggests that artists were unable to depict a child "except as a man on a smaller scale." The most detailed source used by Aries is the diary of the court physician, Heroard, in which is depicted the daily life of the future King Louis XIII of France. This diary clearly portrays a childhood quite distinct from that of a child today. Aries concluded that childhood as we view it today was first hinted at during the thirteenth century and did not fully develop until the sixteenth and seventeenth centuries.

Several powerful criticisms have been leveled at Aries's work. Critics have questioned the sources that Aries used as well as the conclusions he drew from this evidence. For example, Aries made significant use of pictorial evidence; yet in doing so, he seemed to have assumed that art directly mirrors social life. The miniature adult paintings he discussed actually had a social role: Many were used as tools for negotiating arranged marriages between powerful families that sought to maximize their influence by forming strategic alliances. Accordingly, they were painted in such a way as to suggest how the subjects would look in future, how significant they would be, and what wealth they would have at their disposal. Similar limitations exist with each of the sources Aries used. Furthermore, each of the sources draws on the experiences of children from wealthy and powerful groups within society. Critics complained that the children of the poor were absent from the picture drawn by Aries. *Centuries of Childhood* contains no comparative discussion of the different lives led by young people from different social classes and no significant discussion of the extent to which a child's role was determined by prevailing conceptions of gender.

Yet despite the criticisms directed at Aries's methods, sources, and conclusions, there is a general consensus among sociologists of childhood that Aries's work is a useful starting point for understanding the experiences of children from a historical perspective. When attempting to understand child labour in its historical context, the position put forward by Aries may be helpful, even though he did not deal with the issue directly himself. Aries has encouraged commentators to question assumptions about childhood that might otherwise have been taken for granted.

See also History of Childhood; Social Construction of Childhood.

References Aries, Philippe, *Centuries of Childhood* (tr. ed. 1973; orig. ed. 1960); Pollock, Linda, *Forgotten Children* (1983).

Child Markets

In England during the period known as "proto-industrial," which prepared the way for the industrial revolution, it was not uncommon in the weaving and spinning trades for entire families to be employed in the production of goods for sale in the marketplace. Very young children would be given work tasks to perform or would start what was referred to as an "apprenticeship" with their parents. In periods of very brisk trade the absorption of the entire family in productive tasks meant that there was occasionally a need to hire other child workers either to take part in productive activity or to help with domestic tasks. In the weaving trade in London, the demand for casual child employees led to the establishment of a Child Market in Bethnal Green. According to historian Ivy Pinchbeck, between 50 and 300 children would congregate at Bethnal Green every Monday and Tuesday between 6 A.M. and 8 A.M., looking for employment in weavers' cottages. The children would be hired for a few days or a week. They were casual employees and were quite different from indentured apprentices, who entered into contracts with their masters. The children available via the child market were normally between the ages of 7 and 10, since children over the age of 10 were thought too expensive. Boys were hired to undertake subsidiary tasks within the production process, such as winding material or helping at the loom, and would be supervised by the male weaver. Girls were taken on to nurse young children, clean the home, or cook meals under the supervision of the woman of the house, who would be working at the loom. The Child Market gradually disappeared in the middle of the nineteenth century, with the decline of the hand loom weavers and the growth of weaving in the factory setting.

See also Drawboys; Industrial Revolution; Proto-industrialization.

References Pinchbeck, Ivy, *Women Workers and the Industrial Revolution* (1981).

Child Migrants Trust

The Child Migrants Trust is a British organization dedicated to helping people who were sent away to British colonies, such as Australia, Canada, New Zealand, and Rhodesia, as children. It was founded by a social worker, Margaret Humphreys, who came across cases of child migrants being seriously mistreated. Britain seems to have "exported" destitute children over quite a long period of time, dating back as far as the seventeenth century, when some were sent to the colony of Virginia. Within a fifty-year period beginning in 1880, around 100,000 children were sent to Canada. The work of the Child Migrants Trust focuses on those who were sent abroad during the middle decades of the twentieth century, during which time Australia was the main destination. Most of the children involved had been placed in the care of charities or public bodies because their parents were unable to look after them.

The organizations that undertook child migration schemes included some of the largest and best known children's charities in Britain, including Dr Barnardo's, the Salvation Army, and the National Children's Home, as well as charities associated with the main churches. Sending the children to other countries seemed a satisfactory way of dealing with them. First, the countries concerned were former British colonies that were keen at the time to increase the proportion of their populations who had British backgrounds. The Archbishop of Perth, Western Australia, in welcoming some of these migrants in 1938, expressed an openly racist standpoint when he referred to them as people "from our own stock" who would be a defence against the menace of the teeming millions of neighbouring Asiatic races.

Secondly, the prospects for such children looked poor in Britain. They would exchange the slums of Britain for a healthy outdoor life in their new homelands. One charity that was seeking donations to help migration ran an advertisement in which a boy standing sadly on an unattractive street was compared with children playing happily in the Australian sunshine. Indeed, one of the organizations involved, the Child Emigration Society, had been set up in 1909 with the particular goal of promoting juvenile migration to the colonies of the British Empire. It was founded by

Kingsley Fairbridge, who, contrasting his own adolescence in Rhodesia with the lives of children in the London slums in the early twentieth century, said, "Children's lives wasting while the Empire cries out for more."

Thirdly, for some charitable organizations, the cost of sending quite young children abroad was seen as being offset by the fact that they would no longer be a financial burden on the British organizations that had taken on responsibility for them.

Unfortunately, in the implementation of this policy, the rights of the children and their parents were often overlooked. Most parents were unaware that their children had been sent to another country and believed their children had been adopted or fostered by British families. Many children were not consulted about their futures, and those who were consulted were not given adequate information on which to make a reasoned choice. Many were wrongly told that their parents were dead. They were not provided with adequate documentation that could establish their family backgrounds. Some children were separated from brothers or sisters.

The British organizations responsible for child migration appear to have assumed that they had no responsibility for the welfare of the children once they arrived at their destinations. Although some of the migrant children seem to have been treated well in the countries to which they were sent, too often this was not the case. Many of the organizations who received them believed the children had an obligation to work in order to repay the cost of their food and lodging. One client of the Child Migrants Trust explained that he had been compelled to become apprenticed to a local fitter because the institution he had been sent to stated that he "owed" it two years' work in payment for having been allowed to attend high school. Bindoon Boys' Town, one of the best known children's homes in Australia, was largely built with the labour of the boys sent there as migrants. Since little was done to monitor the care of the children, it

is perhaps not surprising that the Child Migrants Trust has uncovered many cases in which children were malnourished, beaten, and abused in various other ways by those who were supposed to care for them.

Paradoxically, one group of children were the accidental beneficiaries of racism. Because in Rhodesia heavy work was seen as inappropriate for Europeans, children sent there seem to have had much better experiences of life in their new countries than the majority who went to Australia and Canada.

References Humphreys, Margaret, *Empty Cradles* (1994); Sherington, Geoffrey, and Jeffery, Chris, *Fairbridge: Empire and Child Migration* (1998).

Child Slaves

An influential documentary film made with the backing of the British Broadcasting Corporation, *Child Slaves* was directed by Peter Lee-Wright. It graphically depicted child labour in several countries of the world, notably Bangladesh, Brazil, India, Malaysia, Mexico, Philippines, Portugal, Thailand, and Turkey. In demonstrating the broad scale of child labour, the film was particularly effective. Peter Lee-Wright also wrote a book covering the same subject matter, giving documentation that could not be included in the film.

References Lee-Wright, Peter, *Child Slaves* (1990).

Child Workers in Nepal

Child Workers in Nepal (CWIN) was established in 1987 with the aim of protecting and promoting the rights of children in Nepal. It is mainly active in Kathmandu and Pokhara districts but also operates in at least ten other areas. This group has spearheaded the local movement for children's rights and supports the United Nations Convention on the Rights of the Child. CWIN has worked to rescue and rehabilitate children at risk from bonded labour and to end trafficking in and selling of children. It provides support for street children and has a literacy programme that operates in a number of regions. Its magazine, *Voices of Child Workers*, is published in English. In 1997, on National Social Service Day, CWIN was awarded the country's prestigious "Tulsi Mehar Award" in recognition of its work.

See also Convention on the Rights of the Child; Nepal; Unfree Labour.

Children's Bureau

April 1912 was a significant time for child labour reformists in the United States. It was then that the United States Children's Bureau was established. This represented a major shift in the government's position on child labour. For the first time it was being recognized that a specific body needed to be created with the responsibility of ensuring that children were protected and that relevant research was carried out.

The notion of a bureau for children had first been proposed in 1903. Those behind the idea argued that there was need for a federal agency whose task would be to collect and circulate information relating to children and their needs. The plan received support from many important quarters, including the National Child Labor Committee (NCLC) and activists such as Florence Kelley and President Theodore Roosevelt. A bill was drafted to allow for the creation of such a body and was brought before the Senate in January 1906. The bill was debated at length, since it was in the interests of those in favour of child employment to prevent the creation of such an organization; in the end, however, it was passed.

When the Children's Bureau was finally established, its first head was Julia Lathrop, an attorney and a leader in the area of children's welfare. The Bureau was housed within the Department of Commerce and Labor and was provided with a modest budget. It is important to note that the aim of the Bureau was not an administrative one; in fact, it had no administrative

Julia Clifford Lathrop, first director of the Children's Bureau (Library of Congress)

power. Its purpose was to carry out research and disseminate information on "all matters pertaining to the welfare of children and child life among all classes of our people." Nonetheless, it was perceived by many activists as an important resource because it had the power to consider children's status across the United States, whereas previous bodies had operated in individual states only. The creation of the Children's Bureau meant that organizations such as the NCLC no longer had to use their own resources to carry out research on child labour.

Julia Lathrop oversaw the development of the Children's Bureau as it evolved into a key institution in what has been termed the United States's "semi–welfare state." Its primary objectives were to reduce infant and maternal mortality, improve child health, advocate care for children with special needs, and abolish child labour. It proposed what was termed a "whole child" philosophy based on the idea that every child had the right to a protected childhood, free from oppression, exploitation, poverty, ill health, and want. In this regard, however, it was perceived as trying to make all children conform to the experience of white, middle-class children.

With regard to child labour, the Bureau's initial task was to assess the position of children at work across the United States. In 1915 it produced a 1,131-page report, *Child Labor Legislation in the United States*, which detailed existing child labour laws in each state. The report showed that there were wide variations in law and practice from state to state. This finding led the Bureau to advocate a federal child labour law. To this end, the Child Labor Division was set up within the Bureau in 1917, with 67 dedicated staff members. The head of this new unit was Grace Abbott.

Relations between the Bureau and the NCLC were not always harmonious. This was ironic, given the role of the NCLC in drafting the bill that created the Bureau. Relations between the two bodies became strained when the Children's Bureau was put in charge of enforcing the Keating-Owen Bill.

The NCLC and the Bureau began to clash over issues relating to work permits and factory inspection. The NCLC felt that the Bureau was too willing to cooperate with the new factory inspectorate. Julia Lathrop also started to argue that the Bureau needed to be able to show its independence and should not be seen to be too reliant on the NCLC. Although relations between the two bodies remained strained, the NCLC was instrumental in arguing for increased funding for the Bureau to allow it to carry out its policing of the legislation. In the end, however, the legislation failed to stand up to legal challenges.

When the Fair Labor Standards Act was passed in 1938, the Children's Bureau was put in charge of administering the Act. This was the first federal legislation to tackle child labour. The Bureau turned to the individual states' labour departments to work out a system of inspection and enforcement. The Bureau became the central body for establishing which forms of employment were hazardous, and it passed many hazardous work orders.

The next challenge to the Bureau came during World War II, when pressure was exerted to release children into the labour force. The Bureau responded by setting up a Commission on Children in Wartime. The aim of this body was not to prevent children from working but rather to protect their welfare during this time.

There were those who saw the Bureau's work generally as evidence of "creeping socialism" in the United States. In 1946, the Bureau was dismembered and its functions redistributed to a number of different government bodies. In the field of child labour its lasting legacy is the fact that the Child Labor Division produced a substantial number of reports listing the extent of child labour exploitation. These portrayed a bleak picture of long hours of arduous labour for little financial reward. Furthermore, child labour was traditionally viewed as something that occurred in mills, factories, and mines; but the reports were central to extending the definition of exploitative labour beyond these areas. This it did by focusing on farm work, street selling, and an array of before and after school jobs. The Bureau had failed in its attempt to establish a federal law on child labour, due to the opposition that came from various sources. These sources included traditionalists who argued against state interference in family matters; those who advocated the rights of states to make their own laws; and business interests keen to maintain child employment in mills, factories, mines, and agribusinesses.

See also Abbott, Grace; Fair Labor Standards Act; Keating-Owen Bill; National Child Labor Committee; National Consumers League; Protectionism.

References Lindenmeyer, K., *A Right to Childhood: The U.S. Children's Bureau and Child Welfare, 1912–1946* (1997); Sumner, H. L., and Merritt, E. A., *Child Labor Legislation in the United States* (1915).

Children's Rights

Recent years have witnessed an increasing interest in children's rights. The focus on rights has had the effect of moving the academic debate about the standing of children in society toward a position where children, as social actors, are treated seriously as subjects shaping their own social lives rather than as passive objects to be studied by adults. It has also pushed practitioners in legal, welfare, and educational settings to address the issue of children's participation and empowerment in institutional processes that affect them. For example, there have been demands that children have the right to avoid physical punishment in the home and at school, a right that immediately confronts and questions dominant and traditional child rearing. Similarly, there have been demands for children's rights in a range of institutional settings—for example, in children's homes, in schools, and in the criminal justice system. These demands clearly acknowledge that as much as any expert caregiver or educator, children have opinions about how the institution should be run and should have the opportunity to make significant choices on these issues. In this regard the claim for rights amounts to a series of political demands that challenge orthodox prescriptions regarding child rearing and traditional perceptions of children and their abilities. Conventional ways of thinking about the place of children in society are challenged by people who advocate children's rights. In place of convention, these individuals put forward a reform platform aimed at prioritizing children's needs and promoting the idea that children are a group whose voices should be heard and whose opinions should be taken seriously.

However, those who proclaim the rights of children do not constitute a unified political force. The demand for rights has been utilized in a number of different ways and with a variety of implications that often are contradictory. Within what observers refer to as the "children's rights movement," the discussion of "rights" reflects the input of two contrasting perspectives for change. First, the focus on rights has been given great impetus by the increased interest in this issue within the international political community in the last quarter of the twentieth century. The year 1979 was designated the International Year of the Child; and in that year, a United Nations Convention on the Rights of the Child was proposed. The Convention was eventually adopted by the U.N. General Assembly, in 1989. Most member states of the United Nations, including Britain, have ratified the Convention. The United States is one of the few that have not done so.

The Convention sets forth basic standards for the treatment, protection, and participation of children in society and makes a claim for children's equality with other children and with adults, even as it acknowledges that childhood is uniquely valuable in its own right. The Convention thus embodies claims for a mixture of protective, welfare, moral, and political rights, encapsulated by what has been termed the three p's of children's rights: provision, protection, and participation.

There are several issues worth considering in this regard. First, the Convention makes certain assumptions about upholding children's rights. It aims to balance and promote the "best interests of the child" within existing institutions. By so doing, it makes assumptions about the best location for child rearing and protection (within families) and about both appropriate and inappropriate activities for children to undertake (education as opposed to labour); and it stresses the view that children should have the right to a protected childhood. The variety of rights promoted in this way often pull in different directions. For example, the commitment to liberty and equality for children often clashes with concerns discussed by adult professionals and state officials in terms of protecting children's best interests.

Secondly, the Convention requires states to become agents of progressive social legislation and change. Yet states are not neutral entities pursuing the abstractly determined best interests of all their citizens. States exist, operate, and organize within particular socioeconomic structures and pursue interests and objectives aimed at maintaining social relations and optimizing state economic priorities. For a variety of reasons and in certain situations, this may include a reform agenda; but the priorities of states are always broadly socioeconomic. The primary consequence of the reconsideration of children's rights by academics, politicians, and legal and welfare practitioners has been to transfer responsibility for children from the exclusive domain of the family into a wider public sphere. Other adults with positions of statutory responsibility—such as the police, the courts, teachers, social workers, and doctors—have the power to contribute to, or to impose, decisionmaking on children's lives. The children themselves in most cases do not have equal power.

Thirdly, Conventions and international proclamations may become mere idealized social policy blueprints that avoid the difficult questions of how the broad goals might be reached in specific, existing circumstances. For example, the Convention on the Rights of the Child has been signed by many countries that are at present subject to stabilization and structural adjustment programmes, required by the major international financial institutions—the World Bank and the International Monetary Fund. These programmes require governments to cut public expenditures on education and welfare in order to achieve the economic priorities of the financial institutions. Thus these states undermine their ability to fulfil both the letter and spirit of the Convention.

Finally, as Judith Ennew notes, the Convention was drafted with "a particular type of childhood in mind." In essence, the assumption underlying it is that modern, Western childhood is the best basis on which to develop a number of values aimed at increasing children's liberty and equality.

The issue of rights has not simply been framed in terms of the possibilities and limits contained within the Convention. For some writers, the recognition that childhood is a social construct that devalues children as social, political, and economic actors and ascribes an inferior status to their actions, activities, and abilities has meant that the banner of children's rights has been raised to counter all manifestations of their oppression. This is the second perspective for change within the rights debate. As Bob Franklin argues, childhood is a cocoon that can "stifle and oppress as well as comfort." The "radical" rights of children are proclaimed as a mechanism to free children from childhood and guarantee them equal citizenship rights with adults. The liberation of children from childhood includes demands that children, of whatever age, should be free to make all decisions about their lives that adults normally would make. For these writers, this includes the rights to vote, to work, and to own property—in essence, full modern citizenship rights should be made available to the socially excluded child. Franklin recognizes that rights can sometimes best be met by protective and welfare measures (as indeed adult rights are often guaranteed in this way), but he argues that children's rights should be extended to include "liberty rights."

In other words, this radical approach to children's rights is, on the one hand, a philosophical commitment to children's liberation, and on the other hand, a mechanism through which that liberation is supposed to be achieved. Here there are two general issues that need to be considered. First, as noted above, this approach ignores the nature of the state, the vehicle that is expected to deliver the rights. Second, the rights discourse overlooks the full range of social divisions in society. Further, as has become evident with regard to equal opportunity movements in the areas of gender and race, the adoption of legally enshrined rights and policies does not automatically lead to changes in social practices.

In addition, an abstract commitment to rights in general is always vulnerable to counterclaims. For example, the right of children to work cannot be separated from the right of employers to exploit children as a cheap source of labour. This is not to dismiss claims for rights but to argue that we must be aware of the context of the demand and its consequences.

Finally, there is the question of how rights should be obtained. Ironically, among liberationists committed to the perspective that children are active social agents capable of shaping and reforming their world, there is an apparent consensus that children's rights will be secured by adult legislators and adult advocates.

See also Advocacy; Convention on the Rights of the Child; Liberationism; Protectionism; Rights Discourse; Social Construction of Childhood; Stabilization and Structural Adjustment Programmes.

References Ennew, Judith, "Outside Childhood: Street Children's Rights" (1995); Franklin, Annie, and Franklin, Bob, "Growing Pains: The Developing Children's Rights Movement in the U.K." (1996); Franklin, Bob (ed.), *The Handbook of Children's Rights* (1995); Holt, John, *Escape from Childhood* (1975); Landsdown, G. "Children's Right to Participation: A Critique" (1995).

Chile

The Republic of Chile is situated along the Pacific coast of South America. It has a population of around 14 million people. Bounded by the Andes mountains to the east, it is an unusually shaped country, extending around 2,800 miles from north to south but averaging only around 100 miles from east to west. Chile was colonized by Spain in the sixteenth century and obtained its independence in the early nineteenth century. Today Chile is a parliamentary democracy, although for almost twenty years it was governed by a military dictator following the overthrow of a democratically elected government in September 1973. Chile has a well-developed agriculture and considerable mineral resources. Minerals and agricultural produce are among its main exports.

Chilean law permits children to work from the age of 14, provided they have met minimum educational requirements and have the permission of their family. However, this applies only to formal contracts of employment. The only effective control on informal work and self-employment is the law on compulsory schooling. However, this law has been widely flouted. The 1970s saw a substantial rise in child employment, largely due to declining family income caused in part by adult unemployment. Children began to work to supplement family incomes, and some became the primary breadwinners. Some working children have been found to be as young as 9 or 10 years. Both boys and girls are engaged in agricultural work. In urban areas, boys work predominantly in the commercial and manufacturing sectors, whereas girls are generally employed in service industries.

See also America, South.

References de la Luz Silva, Maria, "Urban Poverty and Child Work: Elements for the Analysis of Child Work in Chile" (1981).

Chimney Sweeping

In Britain, in the seventeenth and eighteenth centuries, an unusual form of child labour emerged—the child chimney sweeper. In the homes of the rich, the children of the poor, often as young as 6 or 7 years, would be sent up chimneys to clean the flues or to fight fires. The children would be under the guidance of a chimney sweeper, who might employ several children to perform such tasks. The chimney sweeps were often brutal and exacting, forcing the children to work long hours and pushing them to the very extremes of their physical capabilities. The children would climb inside the intricate chimneys, dragging brushes behind them to clean the soot clinging to the chimney walls. The work was exhausting, hot, and extremely dirty. Soot would enter the children's lungs and eyes and would cling to their skin. The skin on their elbows and knees would be scratched and abraded by the rough surfaces, often resulting in infection when mixed with soot. Many children's knee and ankle joints were permanently deformed as a consequence of the irregular distribution of their body weight while climbing in narrow spaces. Often the intricate design of chimneys meant that children would have to strip their clothes off to squeeze through the flues. As John and Barbara Hammond noted, some flues that children swept were only seven inches square.

Even more dangerous was the practice of sending the children up flues to fight fires. The children would be sent into the chimney cavity to face the terrifying prospect of putting out a fire that would be in varying stages of development. The heat was intense, and the fire-fighting equipment was primitive. Not surprisingly, such fires often claimed the children's lives.

Despite these horrors, chimney climbing was not controlled in Britain until after the Chimney Sweepers Act passed in 1875. The first attempt to control and regulate the practice of chimney climbing was introduced in Parliament in 1760. Yet each time a bill was introduced, it was defeated by legislators who refused to acknowledge that the practice was harmful to children, despite the substantial evidence available.

This episode has been important to recent debates surrounding the history of child labour regulation in Britain. Some historians maintain that child labour was regulated as soon as legislators became aware of the plight of child workers. They argue that in the cottage industries and early factories, child labour exploitation took extreme forms because legislators were ignorant of what was occurring. The cottages and factories were in distant and inaccessible locations, far from the seat of government in London. As the argument goes, when the legislators became aware of what was actually happening and the degradation of child labour that was taking place, they acted to control and regulate the various practices. In essence, this argument suggests that legislators are enlightened individuals who act in the best interests of the entire community at all times and do not pursue their own or group interests. The history of the nineteenth and twentieth centuries is one of enlightened progress toward a humanitarian and just society. The case of the chimney sweepers calls such assumptions into question. The chimney sweepers were not employed in far-off locations, hidden in cottages and factories, but were crawling around the arteries of the great mansions and houses of the legislators themselves. Further, many of the arguments used against general child labour regulation could not easily be applied to this case. As John and Barbara Hammond noted, even the most vivid imagination could not discover any dangers from foreign competition. The plight of the chimney boys is perhaps one of the more distasteful examples of child labour exploitation in British history.

See also Shaftesbury, Lord.

References Hammond, J. L., and Hammond, Barbara, *Lord Shaftesbury* (1939); Hammond, J. L., and Hammond, Barbara, *The Town Labourer, 1760–1832* (1967).

China

The People's Republic of China was founded in 1949, when the Communist Party, under the leadership of Mao Tse-tung, established control over the whole of mainland China. The Communists' rivals, the Kuomintang, with whom they had fought a bitter civil war, remained in control on the island of Taiwan, in which an independent Republic of China was set up that continues to function today. Mainland China has a population of around 1,200 million people. A reduction in the growth of the population has been a long-term goal of the government. China has many large cities, including the capital, Beijing (formerly called Peking), and Shanghai, both of which have well over 10 million inhabitants.

In the early years of the Communist government, efforts were made to increase the number of primary schools in rural areas. This programme came into conflict with the traditional practice of employing children in agriculture. However, in more recent times, when the government has tried to accelerate China's economic growth with a view toward the country's becoming an important part of the world economy, child labour has come to be seen as a "rational strategy in overcoming rural-urban disparities," in the words of Irving Epstein. Thus, although the government continues to encourage better school provision, in many poor villages throughout the country the long-term economic benefits of receiving an education are not clear to parents, so they continue to encourage their children to work. The government permits schools in some rural areas to charge parents fees for their children's education, which acts as a further disincentive. In some areas, children working in the fields are as young as 8 years.

The Chinese Compulsory Education Law passed in 1986 makes it illegal for children of 16 years and younger to work. The following year another law was passed forbidding employers to take on children who had not completed minimum compulsory schooling. However, many foreign observers believe that these laws are not being strictly enforced. Official figures acknowledge that children make up between 10 percent and 20 percent of the workforce in some enterprises.

As part of its drive for growth, the government has set up Special Economic Zones. Unfortunately, evidence indicates that in these zones the exploitation of children is rampant. Many of the factories make consumer goods for export, including children's toys popular on the American and European markets. Reports published in the West have described one factory in which workers hand-painted dolls without wearing masks to protect them from the noxious fumes coming from the paint. In another, women workers, some as young as 12 years, slept in dark and damp dormitories, two or three to a bed. In a third factory, seasonal increases in demand led the management to require girls to work two 24-hour shifts each month. It is unclear how many children have been victims of fires and explo-

sions in Chinese factories, but eleven child workers died in one district in one year alone.

A number of Chinese enterprises employing children have been built up with the aid of foreign investment. However, there is no sign that investors feel any personal responsibility for the conditions under which these children work.

References Epstein, Irving, "Child Labor and Basic Education Provision in China" (1993).

Christianity
See Religion.

Cinema
Child actors have played an important part in the film industry throughout its history. Some major stars, such as Elizabeth Taylor, began their careers as child performers. However, clearly not all children appearing in films could expect to maintain their popularity when they grew older. The careers of three performers, Shirley Temple, Mary Pickford, and Jackie Coogan, illustrate various experiences of children working in motion picture production.

Shirley Temple (born 1928) is probably the most outstanding example of a commercially important child star. Appearing in a short film for the first time when she was less than 4 years old, she was signed to a contract by the Fox company (later Twentieth Century Fox) and soon became one of its major assets. Her name appears in the list of top ten box office stars every year between 1934 and 1939, and for four of those years she was at the very top of the list. However, as she entered her teens, she lost her appeal to film audiences, and Fox terminated her contract. She made a few films for other companies with limited success, and entered television in the 1950s. Later, she made a more radical change in career, becoming involved in politics. She became a prominent spokesperson for the Republican Party. Later, as Shirley Temple Black, she became United States Ambas-

Shirley Temple in The Littlest Rebel, *1935 (Archive Photos)*

sador, first to the United Nations and then to Ghana. She is thus an example of a child actor who could not maintain her success in the movie business but was able to achieve success in other fields of activity.

One of the first successful child actresses in movies was Mary Pickford (1893–1979). Unlike Shirley Temple, she had a successful career also as an adult actress. She had begun as a stage performer and was 16 years old when she signed her first film contract with the Biograph company, earning $40 a week. Biograph at that time did not identify its performers by name, for fear of their demanding higher salaries. Mary Pickford was billed as "Little Mary" or "The Girl with the Golden Curls." Astute in business matters, she soon realized she was not earning a salary in line with her commercial value to the studio. She made a series of moves from one company to another. In 1916, seven years after her first contract, she signed with the Famous Players Company for $10,000 plus bonuses. She was by then an adult, but cinema audiences still thought of her as a child. She continued playing children until she was actually 27 years old. She later formed The Mary Pickford Company, and along with three of the major creative talents in the Hollywood at that time—D. W. Griffith the director, Charlie Chaplin, and her husband, actor Douglas Fairbanks—was one of the founders of the United Artists Corporation. A major star throughout the 1920s, she made few talking pictures. However, she may be regarded as a child actor who survived to achieve success as an adult performer.

Mary Pickford had to fight to receive fair payment from the studios. However, company executives are not the only adults with whom children who work in the cinema may have problems. In 1939, the California state assembly introduced the Child Actors Bill, widely known once it was passed as the Coogan Act. It provided for half of a child actor's earnings to be set aside in a trust fund or some other type of savings account, which would be open to scrutiny by the court. Since 1927 the courts had had the authority to approve child actors' contracts, and the new Act could be seen as an extension of that power.

The name "Coogan Act" was attached to this piece of legislation because it arose from a case involving Jackie Coogan (born in 1914), who had been a very successful child star, his most famous film being *The Kid* (1921), in which he starred with Charlie Chaplin. Coogan's earnings were paid to a company called Jackie Coogan Productions, Inc., run by his parents. In 1935, Coogan reached the age of 21 and expected to take over direct control of his earnings. However, his father died in a car crash that year, and Jackie, who was about to marry actress Betty Grable, found himself denied access to the company's funds. He sued his mother and stepfather for his childhood earnings. The couple made a case that under the common law of the United States, which had been inherited from English common law, the earnings of a minor were the property of his or her parents. In the final settlement of that case Coogan received $126,000, although his earnings were said to have been around $4 million. The case drew attention to the possibility of a conflict of interest between a child actor and his or her parents. Coogan himself continued as an actor, but his success as an adult did not match what he had experienced as a child. One of his biggest adult successes was in the role of Uncle Fester in the television series *The Addams Family*. Although acting is widely regarded as one of the most glamorous forms of child employment, it is clearly not a sphere of activity that can be regarded as problem free.

In 1991, the organization A Minor Consideration was founded by former child actor Paul Petersen. This body counsels former child actors and lobbies for stricter control of the conditions under which children perform.

The cinema industry has not found child labour a particularly attractive subject for films. *Boy Slaves* (1939) seems to be the only Hollywood film devoted to the subject, although there have been more recent films on the subject made in other countries. These include *Pixote* (Brazil, 1980) and *Daens* (Belgium, 1992). Both films garnered considerable international attention, but they cannot be said to have had much influence on public policy on child labour. Documentary films made primarily for television, such as *Child Slaves*, may have made a bigger impact on public opinion.

See also Belgium; *Boy Slaves*; Brazil; *Child Slaves*; Entertainment Industry; Modelling.

References Greenfield, Lauren, *Fast Forward: Growing Up in the Shadow of Hollywood* (1997); Zierold, Norman J., *The Child Stars* (1965).

Coal Breakers

Coal breaking formed an integral part of traditional coal production, which involved the manual removal of waste, stone, and slate from coal deposits. In the United States, in the nineteenth century, many hundreds of boys as young as 10 years worked as coal breakers in treacherous conditions. The work involved sitting in rows placed over chutes through which the coal speedily passed. For eleven hours a day, the boys had to constantly bend down

Coal breakers at work in South Pittston, Pennsylvania, 1911 (Lewis Hine, Library of Congress)

and reach into the fast-moving coal with their bare hands to examine it and remove any foreign materials while completely enveloped by clouds of coal dust. The results of these conditions were rounded shoulders, narrow chests, and a multitude of serious injuries and deaths. In addition, a foreman or "breaker boss" was on hand to constantly supervise and to beat those who were not thought to be working hard enough.

See also Mining.

Colombia

The Republic of Colombia is situated in northwestern South America, with coasts on both the Caribbean Sea and the Pacific Ocean. Conquered by Spain in the sixteenth century, it won its independence in the nineteenth century. The population is around 35 million. Because of its varied climate, many different crops are grown in Colombia, with coffee being a major export. Colombia also has large supplies of coal, gas, and hydroelectric power. In recent years the politics and economy of the country have been greatly affected by the operation of left-wing guerrilla forces and by the existence of powerful drug exporting gangs.

Thanks to the research of Cecilia Munoz Vila and her colleagues, the history of child labour in Colombia is unusually well understood. Child labour has been a feature of Colombian society since the time when it was a Spanish colony. In keeping with their traditionally important role in the economy, children also fought in Colombia's war of independence. In more modern times, census data show increasing numbers of boys and girls engaged both in manufacture and in agriculture. Children play a particularly large role in the informal sector of the economy. Political concern about issues of child labour has varied. Laws were passed in the early 1920s and early 1950s, but at other times

Children old enough to carry a single brick are put to work in brickworks on the outskirts of Bogota, Colombia, 1980 (AP/Wide World Photos)

child labour seemed to have been forgotten. More recently, international attention has raised the profile of child labour in Colombia. The use of children in mining has been particularly criticized. The International Confederation of Free Trade Unions recently reported that a large part of Colombia's exported coal is produced in small, informal, and marginal operations. It is illegal for children to work in the mines in Colombia, but enforcement of child labour legislation is not a priority for the government.

Colombian government estimates put the number of child miners in the country at around 5,000. However, child welfare organizations believe this is a gross underestimate. Ecocarbon, the state coal mining company, has recently undertaken pilot projects to move young miners into lighter work that they can combine with school attendance.

See also America, South; Mining.

References Cadman, Eileen, *No Time to Play: Child Workers in the Global Economy* (1996); Munoz Vila, Cecilia, "The Working Child in Colombia since 1800" (1996).

Concerned for Working Children, The

The Concerned for Working Children (CWC) organization is an example of the many nongovernmental organizations that exist in present-day India. It was officially formed in 1985 as a registered society. The main aim of the CWC is to work toward the eradication of child labour in India.

The CWC is based in Bangalore and has its roots in the adult Bangalore Labor Union, which began work in urbanized sectors in 1978. Union officials found that a number of working children were attending their meetings, and it became evident that such children lacked any representation in the labour market. However, when the union attempted to intervene, it found that most employers simply sacked the children and left them without work. Rather than improving the conditions of working children, the union's efforts created financial hardship for them and their families, as their work was a necessity.

The union encouraged the working children to outline how the law should be changed to benefit them. The net result of this process emerged in the form of the 1985 CWC draft child labour bill. The Indian government was influenced in part by this when it introduced the 1986 Child Labor (Prohibition and Regulation) Act.

The CWC was formed when the Bang-

alore Labor Union realized it could not fully represent the needs of working children. The aim of the CWC was to adopt a proactive position in terms of the issues facing child workers. To achieve this, the CWC has established a number of projects to create "time and space for children to grow." For example, on the outskirts of Bangalore, they run Namma Mane (Our House), a shelter for street and working children.

One of the emerging aims of the CWC has been to develop ways to provide working children with a voice. To this end they were involved in the formation of Bhima Sangha, an organization of working children.

Although the CWC has been active in fieldwork, it also has recognized the need for better information on working children and their conditions. A number of other nongovernmental organizations that shared this view joined the CWC in establishing the Centre for Applied Research and Documentation. The Centre draws together relevant data on programmes and issues facing working children and acts as an information resource to promote the needs of working children.

The CWC is one of many nongovernmental organizations in India. Although its primary objective is the eradication of child labour, it has recognized that this goal will not be achieved overnight. That recognition has led to the development of a more pragmatic, short-term goal—to encourage child workers to air their views and have their voices heard in the battle to improve the reality of their everyday lives.

See also Bhima Sangha; India; Nongovernmental Organizations.

Confederacao Nacional de Accao sobre Trabalho Infantil

The leading organization in Portugal dealing with problems of child labour, founded in 1994. The organization's Portuguese name translates as "National Confederation for Action on Child Labor"; but it is more commonly rendered in English by the Portuguese acronym CNASTI.

A number of Christian organizations, parents' groups, and trade unions support CNASTI's activities. CNASTI's main office is located in Braga, in the north of the country, where some of the more serious forms of child labour are to be found. CNASTI ran a campaign called Time To Grow Up, with the slogan "School is the best place for children," the aims of which included increasing the effectiveness of the labour inspectorate in Portugal. CNASTI also was responsible for the first meeting of working children to take place in Portugal. In 1998, CNASTI organized an international conference on child labour in Europe in the northern Portuguese city of Porto.

See also Portugal.

Construction Industry

Across the globe, many children can be found working on building sites in the construction industry. Children can be found mixing cement, carrying bricks, unloading trucks, and running errands on site for various groups of employees.

The construction industry (or substantial sections of it) is notorious the world over for utilizing the "black economy" and for hiring labour on daily contracts, using uninsured workers, and exploiting migrants. In some countries, children form part of this supply of marginal workers. Such marginal workers are utilized especially when the trade union presence on sites is weak or nonexistent, itself a consequence of the difficulties of organizing workers who are constantly changing work locations and who are particularly vulnerable to the slightest shift in the economic climate.

In many countries the constant movement of workers from site to site and the predominance of labour subcontracting make it difficult if not impossible to regulate working conditions. Construction is one of the most dangerous industries for workers. Death and injury commonly result from the use of machines, tools, and materials, and even from scaffolding as the height of new buildings increases.

See also Accidents.

Consumerism

The stereotypical reason for children's being drawn into the labour force is poverty. Children work in order to survive. Although this picture may explain child employment in the history of developed countries, it cannot be presumed to be the sole explanation. Modern aspects of child employment both in developed countries and in developing ones require us to look at other causes.

One such cause is consumerism. In other words, children work in order to be able to purchase goods. That children and adolescents are thought of as major consumers is self-evident when we look at the mass media. A wide range of consumer goods, from fashion to music and computer technology, are targeted at this group of consumers. In many cases children's ownership of such goods comes through their parents, who either directly purchase the goods or provide an allowance from which the children can buy what they desire.

From an international perspective, the persistence of child employment in the developed as well as the developing countries testifies to the fact that poverty is not the sole explanation for children's working. Jo Boyden, an anthropologist, has suggested that children from relatively well-off families in the developed and developing countries work in order to obtain access to luxury items.

Ben White, a rural sociologist particularly concerned with the problems of the developing economies, has argued that in many poor countries children turn to employment to earn money so that they can buy goods that are increasingly seen as "essential." White links this trend in consumption to globalization. White argues that children are an increasingly significant market segment for various kinds of mass-produced consumer goods. Media and

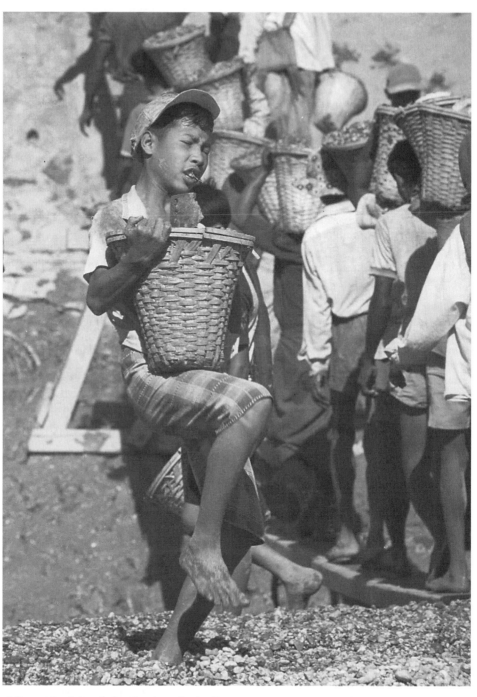

A Burmese boy hoists a basket of sand onto his shoulder at a construction site in Rangoon, Burma, 1998 (Thaksina Khaiakew, Associated Press)

peer pressures make it increasingly important for children not just to have sufficient food and clothes, but to have certain *kinds* of clothes and other possessions, to consume certain kinds of food and drink, and to engage in certain kinds of leisure activities.

It is possible to demonstrate that children's income is not always linked to the purchasing of basic items. In a recent report for the International Working Group on Child Labour, it was noted that some children in Egypt were working in order to provide their families access to television.

However, it is in the developed countries that we tend to see the most obvious links between child employment and consumerism. Research evidence indicates that few children here work because their families are poor. The children typically are allowed to keep most of their earned income and to dispose of it at their own discretion. The majority of children who work spend their income on clothes, compact discs, computer ancillaries, and other goods. When children in the developed economies were asked why they work, a dominant response is "for the money." They perceive the ability to purchase goods as an important justification for working.

Increased consumption of luxury goods among children has raised doubts in some quarters about the values that children are learning in these circumstances. American scholar Jerald G. Bachman has argued that children are experiencing a form of "premature affluence." By this he means that their part-time income constitutes disposable income. At no other time in your life can you simply spend all of your earned income on consumption goods. Other demands on your income emerge in the form of domestic responsibilities, food, and housing costs. Ellen Greenberger and Laurence Steinberg have also suggested that employment driven by the desire to have income for goods creates an extremely instrumental attitude toward work. This means that one works simply for the money, with personal satisfaction or career aspirations being less important.

However, not all researchers in the United States have drawn such negative conclusions. Some academic researchers in this field have suggested that we need to look more closely at spending patterns. They argue that these patterns change as adolescents move through school. Initially spending is dominated by consumer goods. However, as they move into their later years at high school, part of their earnings are put into savings for future education. In addition, these researchers found that different spending patterns emerged between rural and urban workers. Rural workers were less likely to spend money on their immediate wants than were their urban peers.

What is evident is that consumerism must be considered as one of the forces motivating children to work. In addition, parents might be encouraging their children to work so that they will be able to purchase goods.

See also Globalization; International Working Group on Child Labour.

References Bachman, Jerald G. "Premature Affluence: Do High School Students Earn Too Much?" (1983); Boyden, Jo, *The Relationship between Education and Child Work* (1994); McKechnie, Jim, and Hobbs, Sandy, *Working Children: Reconsidering the Debates* (1998); Nieuwenhuys, Olga, "Global Childhood and the Politics of Contempt" (1998); Shanahan, Michael J., Elder, G. H., Burchinal, M., and Conger, R. D. "Adolescent Earnings and Relationships with Parents" (1996); White, Ben, "Children, Work, and 'Child Labour': Changing Responses to the Employment of Children" (1994).

Convention on the Rights of the Child

The Convention on the Rights of the Child was adopted by the General Assembly of the United Nations on 20 November 1989. Article 1 defines a child as a person "below the age of eighteen years unless, under the law applicable to the child, majority is attained earlier." The issue of child labour is dealt with primarily in Article 32. Section 1 of Article 32 refers to the "right of the child to be protected from economic exploitation and from performing any work that is likely to be hazardous or interfere with the child's education, or to be harmful to the child's health or physical, mental, spiritual, moral or social development." Section 2 deals with the requirement of state parties to take legislative, administrative, social, and educational steps to ensure implementation of this article. In particular this will require states to:

(a) provide for a minimum age or minimum ages for admission to employment;
(b) provide for appropriate regulation of the hours and conditions of employment;
(c) provide for appropriate penalties or other sanctions to ensure the effective enforcement of the present article.

The United Kingdom appears to have been the only country to express reservations about Article 32 when ratifying the convention. However, these reservations concerned the relatively technical point that British legislation on employment distinguished between two categories of people under 18 years of age: "children," by which is meant those people who are less than 16 years of age, and "young persons," who are those aged 16 to 18 years.

Other articles also have a bearing on child labour. Article 34 refers to the protection of children from "all forms of sexual exploitation and sexual abuse," including prostitution. Article 35 refers to measures to prevent "the abduction of, the sale of or traffic in children for any purpose or in any form." Article 36 is even broader, dealing with the protection of the child from "all other forms of exploitation prejudicial to any aspects of the child's welfare." Article 38 requires states to limit the participation of children in armed conflict.

See also Children's Rights.

Costs and Benefits

The dominant image of child employment that appears in the mass media highlights the potentially exploitative nature of the relationship between adult employers and child employees. This emphasis is found particularly in examples of child employment that emanate from the poorer countries of the world. There are, however, examples of similarly exploitative practices occurring in developed countries. Such stories tend to draw us toward consideration of the costs of child employment. This contrasts with many adult assumptions about children's work experience, especially in the West.

As Ellen Greenberger and Laurence Steinberg pointed out in their book *When Teenagers Work*, the dominant view of child employment in the developed economies is that it is a positive experience. This view is partly based upon the assumption that compulsory education and legislative frameworks prevent the worst excesses of child employment. Greenberger and Steinberg were not convinced that this stereotyped view of children's work was valid. Their research started to draw attention to the fact that work could be "good" or "bad"—that is, it may have costs and benefits for the individual. Over time, two opposing perspectives have emerged, the zero sum model and the developmental model. The former emphasizes the negative effect of work, particularly on education. The latter views work as "character building," since it facilitates the transmission of knowledge and skills and develops an adult perspective.

It is not surprising that the subject of education has figured prominently in debates about the positive and negative influences of work. Scholars now generally acknowledge that in some circumstances work may have educational benefits, and in others it may exact costs. The number of hours worked appears to play a significant role in the balance between these two outcomes.

The developmental model draws attention to the contribution that work can make to a range of psychological functions. For some theorists adolescence is associated with the development of autonomy. Researchers such as Sheila Cole have linked part-time work to the individual's gaining a sense of independence. Others have linked work experience to the development of a sense of control. The ability to earn an income often reduces the level of children's dependence, or their sense of dependence, on their parents. However, adolescents might not in all cases be given a degree of autonomy in the disposal of their own earned income. Although work may create a sense of independence for the adolescent, it may also create tensions for parents who are trying to balance control over their child with the need to encourage independence. Work may antagonize a potentially difficult reconfiguration of the parent-child relationship.

One of the assumed benefits of work is that it introduces adolescents to the world of work. If this is the case, one could argue that those adolescents who leave school with work experience should be more employable than those who do not have such experience. The research evidence tends to support this idea, showing that adolescents with work experience are less likely to be unemployed and that they earn more in the early years of their work. However, this benefit does not continue over the long term. Those with better educational success achieve greater long-term occupational success.

Greenberger has argued that in evaluating the impact of work, it is necessary to consider its effects on a wide range of behaviour. She argues that there is evidence linking part-time work to increased use of cigarettes, alcohol, and marijuana. Writers such as Jeylan Mortimer are less pessimistic about the impact of work, but they do find compelling evidence linking part-time employment with alcohol consumption.

The picture that emerges is potentially confusing. Some studies suggest that work may be beneficial, and others highlight the costs. The reality is that certain key variables will influence the balance between the costs and benefits of work. Greenberger and Steinberg argue that the key factor is the number of hours committed to employment. As adolescents increase the number of hours worked, the delicate balance between costs and benefits is disrupted and the costs outweigh the benefits. The watershed in terms of hours worked appears to lie in the range of 15–20 hours per week.

More recently, Jeylan Mortimer and Michael Finch have suggested that although hours worked may be important, other factors are equally relevant if not more so. For these researchers the type of employment and the quality of work experience are crucial to determining the outcome of work.

It is worth noting that all of the above studies have been carried out in the United States. It is likely that differences between countries are great enough to prevent easy generalizations. Nevertheless, the issues raised by researchers in the United States about the impact of work should help those trying to understand the balance of costs and benefits in their own societies, whether economically developed or underdeveloped.

See also Education, Universal; Educational Achievement.

References Greenberger, Ellen, and Steinberg, Laurence, *When Teenagers Work: The Psychological and Social Costs of Adolescent Employment* (1986); Marsh, H. W. "Employment During High School: Character Building or a Subversion of Academic Goals?" (1991); Mortimer, Jeylan T., and Finch, Michael D. (eds.) *Adolescents, Work, and Family: An Intergenerational Developmental Analysis* (1996).

Crime
See Delinquency.

Cuba
See Caribbean.

Cultural Traditions
Although poverty is widely regarded as the major central factor helping to create child labour, there is little doubt that certain traditional cultural values also play a part.

Cultural Traditions

First, there are traditional conceptions of childhood. These may be particularly strong in rural, agricultural communities but may also influence the treatment of children in changing economic and social circumstances. A striking example is to be found among the Tonga people of Zimbabwe, where boys as young as 10 traditionally might own and work land and cattle. In agricultural societies, families are the basic productive unit, and the child "naturally" contributes to production in various direct and indirect ways early in life. In addition, in many societies, work is regarded as an important educational process. In parts of Nigeria, for example, responsibility training for children involves their participation in domestic work from the age of 4 years. Children can become involved in nonwaged work that forms part of a network of reciprocal social obligations. To see childhood as "naturally" a time for education rather than work is to fail to take account of the fact that education may be defined in many different ways, some of which overlap with the concept of work. Domestic labour is widely considered a private matter; hence the lack of legislation and control. There is also a tradition of fostering children out to richer relatives or prominent figures, which generally involves them in domestic labour. This is viewed by the underclasses as a route to social mobility.

Secondly, there are traditional notions of gender roles. In some countries or parts of countries, distinct differences exist between boys and girls with respect to work. For example, a survey of the matchstick industry in Tamil Nadu, India, found that 90 percent of the children employed were girls. In many countries, girls have traditionally been taught sewing, cooking, and other "female" skills, whereas boys would be apprenticed to small craftsmen. These different practices obviously arose from different conceptions of the adult roles boys and girls would eventually play. However, these traditions also might have made it easier for families in countries that are becoming more industrialized to take for granted the newer forms of child employment, such as factory work, where the personal relationship between master and apprentice no longer holds. Traditional values may interact with other factors. It is common in Morocco, for example, for quite young girls to be employed as maids in households. This is a "traditional" practice that many people take for granted, despite the vulnerability of young children separated from their families. However, the "little maids" often come from very poor rural communities, and their work is seen by them and by their families as a way of escaping grinding poverty.

In societies where male children are more valued than female ones, it is not surprising that poor families may traditionally have found it acceptable to "sell off" girls for work. Although both boys and girls face this possibility, traditional attitudes toward girls place them at greater risk. The fact that girls will be expected eventually to marry might also lead them into work. In India, girls work to earn a dowry. For Moslem girls in Nigeria, street trading is an accepted way of meeting potential suitors.

Where employers have a choice between girls and boys as employees, they appear sometimes to favour girls because they are more likely to be docile. This too may be regarded as a result of traditional values, in that girls have been trained to act in a more subservient fashion.

Thirdly, there is ethnicity. In many countries there are substantial differences in the extent of employment among different ethnic groups. In South Africa, working children are predominantly from black and so-called coloured communities, in part a legacy of longstanding social and economic relations between white and other groups in that country. In India, caste influences whether a child is working. Also in India, it is reported that the children of Moslems and tribal peoples are more likely to work. Similar differences are reported in, for example, Brazil, where blacks work more; Ecuador, where non-Spanish-speaking

Many children, like this girl making matches near Tamil Nadu, India, in 1996, work an average of 8–9 hours each day for less than 1 dollar per day and do not attend school (Srinivas Kuruganti, Archive Photos)

children work more; and Canada, where the children of parents of non-European descent work more.

Traditional religious values may also give rise to particular child labour practices. For example, in parts of Nigeria, children at Quranic schools traditionally spend time begging, since the giving of alms is regarded as a religious duty.

See also Burkina Faso; Causes of Child Labour; Ethnicity; Gender Stereotypes; Kenya; Morocco; Poverty; Religion; South Africa.

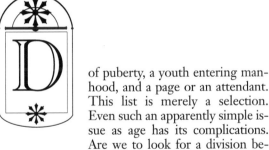

Defence for Children International

Defence for Children International (DCI) is an organization set up in Geneva, Switzerland, with national sections in some 40 countries, including the United States. It works to promote the rights of children worldwide and to monitor the United Nations Convention on the Rights of the Child. In 1994, with the International Society for the Prevention of Child Abuse and Neglect, DCI jointly founded the International Working Group on Child Labour. DCI's quarterly magazine, *International Children's Rights Monitor,* frequently carries articles dealing with child labour in many parts of the world.

See also International Working Group on Child Labour.

Definition of Child Labour

The phrase *child labour* might seem straightforward and easily defined. However, both component words have uncertainties attached to them. When does an individual stop being a child: at the age of 15 years, or at 18 years? Or is childhood defined also by characteristics other than age? For example, does someone attending school remain a child until he or she graduates? Is adolescence a stage of childhood, or should "children" and "adolescents" be considered separately? Is "labour" determined by the activities undertaken or is it any inherently economic activity? Are "labour" and "work" the same thing, or is "labour" perhaps arduous in a way that "work" is not?

The meanings of words constantly change. At different times in the development of the English language the word *child* has been employed to refer variously to a newborn infant, a female toddler, a young person of either sex before the age of puberty, a youth entering manhood, and a page or an attendant. This list is merely a selection. Even such an apparently simple issue as age has its complications.

Are we to look for a division between childhood and adulthood, or is there a tripartite split among child, adolescent, and adult? Whatever we decide, we find difficulty in reaching a decision on the age groups included in each category. Some might argue that it depends on the individual, on how mature that person is. This may well be a sound argument, but it makes drawing the line harder. Some research defines *child* arbitrarily as someone who has not yet reached the legally set minimum age for leaving school. This definition is relatively precise, but it also might give rise to the objection that few nowadays would refer to fifteen-year-olds as "children." In addition, when a country changes its laws on the minimum age for compulsory schooling, individuals of a particular age might well be recategorized from "not a child" to "child" by mere administrative fiat.

The Convention on the Rights of the Child adopted by the General Assembly of the United Nations in 1989 defines a child as a person "below the age of eighteen years unless, under the law applicable to the child, majority is attained earlier." The International Labour Organisation, which is affiliated with the United Nations, has designated 15 years as an appropriate minimum age for entering the labour force, and 18 years as the minimum age if the work is hazardous. This sort of distinction corresponds roughly to the categories of "child" and "young person" made in Britain. Thus, the work of those whom the United Nations regard as "children" is differentiated on grounds of age both by national and by international bodies. For some purposes, "young person" and "adolescent" may be regarded as interchangeable ideas, although adolescence may also be defined as a stage of biological, psychological, and social development.

Turning to the meanings of the word *work*, we would draw attention to two in particular. Work may refer to "what a person has to do, employment"; it may also refer to "any action requiring effort." There is also a use of the term *work* in which its meaning is seen as a contrast to something else called *play*. The work-play dichotomy is generally employed to contrast something that is imposed and onerous (work) with something that is freely chosen and enjoyable (play). Some writers have developed this contrast further in discussing parents' attitudes toward children's games. They suggest that children get intrinsic pleasure from playing games. However, if parents take too obvious an interest in their child's performance in competitive games by giving a lot of advice and direction and by reacting strongly to victory and defeat, this may interfere with the child's enjoyment. By imposing extrinsic rewards and sanctions, the adults are said by these writers to "turn play into work." This issue is also important; but in discussions of child labour, the area of childhood activity that is generally referred to as *work* is economic activity. Either the child is paid for the activity undertaken or the child is contributing to a process, such as manufacture or selling, which has an economic value.

Some cases are straightforward. For example, a child enters into a contract with an employer and receives money in return for services rendered in a factory, farm, shop, or restaurant. But what if the parent receives the money and the child is left with nothing? What if the employer is the child's parent? What if the child assists a parent in work but receives no monetary reward? This last example holds true in many agricultural communities throughout the world.

Just as some commentators wish to emphasize the work-play distinction, so others wish to draw a line between *work* and *labour*. It is a good idea to remind ourselves here that we are dealing with a particular language, English. Those who speak other languages sometimes have difficulty finding an appropriate way of translating *work* and *labour* differently. This may be taken as a strong signal that the work-labour distinction is not clear cut.

The entry on child labour in the *Encyclopaedia of the Social Sciences* drew a distinction between child work and child labour that was to prove very influential. According to its author, Raymond G. Fuller, of the State Charities Aid Association of New York, *child labour* refers both to an economic practice and to "the attendant social evil." He saw the industrial revolution in England as being a critical period. Earlier, the "economic practice" had been taken for granted; but during the industrial revolution, the "social evil" was discovered. To understand why Fuller called child labour a social evil, one must consider three circumstances: first, the character of the actual jobs; secondly, the dangers to which the work exposes the children; and thirdly, the "desirable opportunities" of which children are deprived through their being employed. However, Fuller stressed that to oppose child labour was not to argue that all work is bad for children. He contrasted child labour with child work, which he characterized as "not deadening, but enlivening and self-developing work." Such work, which involves "purpose, plan and freedom" is primarily developmental, not economic. He concluded this discussion by labelling children's work "a social good" and child labour "a social evil."

A number of other writers in English, such as Alex Fyfe, have adopted similar terminology. When the International Working Group on Child Labour (IWGCL) began its activities, it adopted Fuller's distinction. However, it is significant that by the time it produced its final report, that terminology had been put aside. This was in part because it was a distinction that did not translate easily across borders of countries and languages. It was also in part because the IWGCL took account of the work of scholars in the field who were subjecting the terminological distinction to critical analysis.

A major objection to the child work–child labour dichotomy is that it may encourage those who use it to take it for granted that it is easy to distinguish between work and labour. A consideration of children working in different conditions in different countries undermines this assumption. An activity may be harmless to children in one situation but may be harmful in another. A job may be harmful to a younger child but harmless to an older one. A job may have both good and bad features. A job may be objectionable but nevertheless preferable to the only alternates that are realistically available. Accordingly, it is proposed that the work–labour distinction be abandoned in favor of dispassionate analysis of the character of the work undertaken by particular children in particular settings.

There is no watertight definition of *child labour*. The onus is on all who use the phrase to attempt to make clear how they are employing it. Similarly, those who read about child labor should be on their guard and question whether any given writer is using the phrase in a coherent and consistent way.

See also Leisure.
References Fuller, Raymond G., "Child Labor" (1930); Fyfe, Alec, *Child Labour* (1989); McKechnie, Jim, and Hobbs, Sandy (eds.), *Working Children: Reconsidering the Debates* (1998); Myers, William E., "Considering Child Labour: Changing Terms, Issues, and Actors at the International Level" (1999); White, Ben, "Defining the Intolerable: Child Work, Global Standards, and Cultural Relativism" (1999).

Defoe, Daniel

Daniel Defoe (1660–1731) is perhaps best known as author of the novels *Moll Flanders*, *Roxana*, and most famous of all, *Robinson Crusoe*. However, Defoe was also an active journalist and commentator on the dramatic social, economic, and political changes taking place in England during his lifetime. In the period after the English Civil War (1644–1648), Great Britain saw the establishment of a capitalist economic system and the creation of a constitutional monarchy. In his *Tour through the Whole Island of Great Britain*, published between 1724 and 1726, Daniel Defoe presents his observations on life in the British Isles in the early eighteenth century. As well as earning his living by writing, Defoe was a merchant, and in his accounts of many of the places he visited he included descriptions of the dominant trades. Defoe's references to working children in this book make it an important source for historians of child labour in proto-industrial Britain.

A number of Defoe's references to child labour were made in passing and were not particularly stressed. For example, describing an area in the west of England where "the whole country" was involved in cloth manufacture, he mentioned that "the spinning is generally the work of women and children." Similarly, his account of Linlithgow, a town in Scotland, states that in the bleaching season "a thousand women and children, and not less," were to be found tending and managing the business. At another point in his description of Scotland, he mentions another kind of child worker, the "shoe-blacker," which appears to have been the equivalent of the shoe shine boy found in modern cities. The point he was making was that although such children often used foul language in England, their peers in southwest Scotland did not. To the modern reader, what is particularly of interest is that the reference to shoe-blacking is so casual that Defoe must have assumed his readers would be familiar with this sort of activity. He passed no judgment on the job.

However, when he gave a fuller account of children engaged in employment, his approval of their being put to work seems clear. Halifax, in the north of England, was a centre of cloth manufacture. Defoe referred to "an infinite number of cottages" where workmen were employed. In these cottages women and children also were "always busy, carding, spinning, etc." Thus, everyone worked, "from the youngest to the ancient"; and "hardly anything above 4 years old, but its hands are sufficient to itself." Defoe's tone here is enthusiastic. Describing weaving in Taunton, in the west of England, Defoe quoted an informant, apparently with approval: "There is not a child in the town nor any village round it, of above five years old but, if it is not neglected by its parents, and untaught, could earn its own bread." Defoe appears to have been suggesting that in his view, the parents who did not put their children to work were guilty of neglect.

However, some recent historians have questioned others' heavy reliance on Defoe's reports. Hugh Cunningham, who has written several works on the history of childhood generally and on child labour in particular, has asked a pertinent question: "If child labour was as common as is often assumed, why did Defoe think it noteworthy and not simply the norm?" Cunningham suggests that opportunities for children to work were shaped by the regional employment structure, and in many parts of Britain there were not enough jobs available for children. Defoe notes the instances of child labour, Cunningham suggests, precisely because they were not common.

See also Proto-industrialization.

References Cunningham, Hugh, "The Employment and Unemployment of Children in England c. 1680–1851" (1990); Defoe, Daniel, *A Tour Through the Whole Island of Great Britain* (1971).

Delinquency

There is evidence that a strong common-sense assumption exists whereby work is seen as a deterrent to delinquent behaviour. As long ago as 1646, a statute of the state of Virginia demonstrated this point. The statute supported the idea of children working because it led to their education in profitable trades but also kept them from idleness and indolence. The reason for avoiding these was that they left children open to corruption.

Such views have been at the root of a number of attempts in the United States, Britain, and elsewhere to support the employment of youths. These views are based upon some basic assumptions. First, having a job occupies the child's time and reduces the time available for the child to get involved in delinquent acts. Second, working provides the child with an income and allows him or her to buy goods that the child might have considered acquiring through illegal means. The third assumption is that through work adolescents are integrated into society. They acquire the appropriate value and attitude systems that enable them to feel that they are part of society.

Such assumptions need to be tested; but to date, research has been limited and inconclusive—in part, due to the difficulty of defining "delinquent behaviour." Some researchers have argued that instead of reducing the likelihood of delinquency, employment might increase it. This view, put forward by researchers such as Ellen Greenberger and Laurence Steinberg, suggests that work may provide children a number of opportunities where illegal activity may flourish. For example, earnings from employment might facilitate children's participation in illegal activities like drug and alcohol consumption. Similarly, employment may lead to the acquisition of negative work values according to which theft, petty pilfering, and vandalism are acceptable behaviour. Adolescents are socialized into accepting such values as the norm. Finally, work may lead to the heightened awareness of material desires at the same time as it fails to provide an adequate wage to fulfil such desires. In these circumstances one might be led to think of illegal behaviour as a way to satisfy what might be perceived as legitimate rewards.

Some research exists to demonstrate that the latter relationships do exist. However, more study is needed in this area. It is possible that work both causes and prevents delinquent behaviour; but at present we do not know under what circumstances these alternative outcomes emerge. One could hypothesize that the nature and quality of the work experience would be one variable that would need to be considered in some detail. For example, an interesting job that leaves room for initiative and imagination might bring an individual a sense of deep satisfaction. Repetitive work with little social contact might lead the worker to look for excitement when the workday is over, with the consequent risk of involvement in delinquent activities.

See also Greenberger, Ellen; Pro-employment Arguments; Runaways; Steinberg, Laurence; Street Children.

References Greenberger, Ellen, and Steinberg, Laurence, *When Teenagers Work: The Psychological and Social Costs of Adolescent Employment* (1986).

Delivery, Milk

Today, in certain advanced economies, the delivery of fresh milk to people's homes is an important job undertaken by children. In Britain, for example, home milk delivery is quite normal and this form of employment is often listed as one of the two jobs most commonly undertaken by children. The job is often portrayed as healthy and an appropriate task for children; but closer inspection throws this idealization into question. For instance, people expect their milk to be delivered before they have their breakfast, but this requires children going to work before most people get up in the morning. There have been recorded instances of children starting milk delivery at 3 A.M. and 4 A.M. This is problematic on at least three counts: First, it is illegal. British law forbids the employment of children before 7 A.M. Second, there is concern that the child workers are not getting an appropriate amount of sleep. This raises the possibility that they will not be fully awake at school. Third, the children work until about 8 A.M. and then have to attend school (typically between 9 A.M. and 3:30 P.M.). The combined work and school hours of many milk delivery workers is greater than the working day of many adults in Britain.

Milk delivery work has long been associated with child labour, but the form of that labour has altered over the years.

Originally, milk was sold to consumers by employees of the dairy farmers who had produced it. Girls (usually) would walk from farms into urban locations carrying milk churns (or pails) on shoulder yokes and sell the milk on the streets or around the doors, distributing the milk to containers provided by consumers. These girls were called "milkmaids" and were a familiar part of everyday life in big cities in Britain.

The growing distance between farms and urban centres and the expansion of cities and towns eventually led to horses and carts being used to distribute milk. The development of railways meant that milk could be sent longer distances from rural areas to the cities where most consumers lived. Gradually the need for milk to be clean and safe, which had been a concern of medical authorities for a considerable time, came to be widely accepted. The requirement for milk to be pasteurized meant that distribution became more organized. It became more common for farmers to sell their milk to large wholesalers and distributors rather than directly to consumers. In Britain, for example, milk was purchased for a time by a quasi-governmental agency, the Milk Marketing Board, and then resold to recognized distributors. In this way the quality of milk sold on the market could be assured. Milk was also bottled and sealed, which made it possible for door-to-door delivery to expand and for fresh, pasteurized milk to be delivered to homes early each morning. This service was particularly valued in an era in which it was uncommon for ordinary households to have refrigerators. The work of milk bottle delivery was seen as suitable employment for boys. Although the proportion of milk sold by this method has declined, the role of children in delivery has remained substantial. In 1998, the British government issued new regulations on child employment that distinguished between "light" (acceptable) work and "heavy" (unacceptable) work and proposed that milk delivery should be placed in the latter category. Milk distributors protested against this interpretation of the character of the job.

References Jefferys, James B., *Retail Trading in Britain, 1850–1950* (1954); Judge, Roy, *The Jack in the Green* (1979).

Delivery, Newspaper

Newspaper delivery or sales has long been identified as an appropriate children's job, one that is light, harmless, and healthy and that can be easily combined with schooling. In the United States, in the early twentieth century, newspaper selling among boys was promoted by a number of newspaper companies as the embodiment of the business ethic. It was believed to show initiative, hard work, and entrepreneurial drive.

The job takes a number of forms. In many advanced economies, children deliver newspapers to readers' homes. Although this is often viewed as the most appropriate form of employment because children are working on "safe" suburban streets, this idealization can be questioned by a range of evidence that suggests this form of delivery work is potentially problematic. The main areas of concern are as follows: First, the weights that children may be carrying are excessive. In 1988, for example, a study in Britain suggested that some children could be carrying up to 68 pounds in their newspaper sacks. This weight was substantially greater than what negotiated agreements in the postal service allowed adult workers to carry. There was some concern at the time that such weights may have harmful long-term consequences on the children's physiques. Furthermore, children are often carrying such weights on inappropriately designed bicycles that do not have a front basket that carries and distributes the weight of the load. The second area of concern relates to the starting time of such jobs. Most people expect their newspapers to be delivered in the morning before they go to work or have breakfast. This requires young workers to be at their job early, when most adults are still in bed. Such an early start may breach national child employment laws and guidelines.

However, children are also involved in other forms of newspaper sales. Evening papers and first editions of the following day's morning newspapers are often sold on street corners and around bars, restaurants, and clubs late in the evening. Again, the weights carried by children can be excessive, but this form of selling also involves other potential concerns. First, there is uncertainty with regard to sales. The route and demand for papers is not predictable; thus, children sell either until their papers are sold out or until they are exhausted or have sold enough to satisfy their employer. On some occasions children's wages are commission based—that is, what they are paid is directly related to the number of copies they have sold. Thus, they must sell substantial numbers of papers to make money, which is an inducement to encourage children to work until they have sold all, or most, of their stock. All of this means that children can work until quite late at night. The resultant concern is that late working or lack of sleep can affect school performance. Finally, selling in this form means that children are walking city streets at night, carrying significant amounts of money. This too is often seen as a potential threat to the children's well-being.

See also Newsies; *Saturday Evening Post*.

Denmark

The Kingdom of Denmark is situated in northern Europe, south of Norway and Sweden and north of Germany. It has a population of more than 5 million, almost a quarter of whom live in the capital of Copenhagen or its suburbs. Although Denmark exports substantial amounts of agricultural products, only a small proportion of the working population is employed in this area of the economy.

Denmark's first child employment legislation dates from 1873. The laws have been revised over the intervening years. Current laws have been shaped by the need to implement the European Union's Directive on the Employment of Children and Young People, issued in 1994. In 1993, 113,000 people under the age of 18 years were employed in Denmark; but the government believes that the figure has fallen since then, in part because of new legislation. However, according to a report published in 1994, about 500,000 children between the ages of 10 and 17 were working in Denmark. Nearly half of these children were reported to have a steady or occasional job, whereas the rest said they would like to have one. Ten thousand children were reported to be working more than 15 hours per week. Added to the hours spent at school, this figure exceeds the maximum official working hours for young persons in many member states of the European Union. Many employers do not observe regulations for working hours or health and safety standards at the workplace. According to the report, quite a number of young workers have to handle dangerous machinery, substances, and materials, and 30,000 have been reported as having sustained injuries at work. Asked to give their reasons for working, most young people say that they want to be financially independent from their parents.

According to the government, child workers are mainly found in newspaper delivery, shop work, agriculture, and the hotel and catering trade. The minimum age for employment was recently raised from 10 to 13 years (other than if licensed to appear in films, television, or theatre). Only light work may be undertaken, and hours of employment are strictly limited. At the age of 15 years, a young person who has completed the minimum compulsory education may legally take a full-time job, provided it does not involve dangerous machines, hazardous substances, or the possibility of strain. Local Tax and Customs officials are expected to liaise with the Working Environment Service to ensure that there are no breaches of the law. The Danish government's action plan "Clean Working Environment 2005" places particular emphasis on the health and safety of children and young people at work.

See also European Union; Scandinavia.

References Frederiksen, Lisa, "Child and Youth Employment in Denmark: Comments on Children's Work from Their Own Perspective" (1999).

Developmental Psychology

See Psychology, Developmental.

Dickens, Charles

One of the most highly respected novelists in the English language, Charles Dickens (1812–1870) made many comments in his books on the social conditions of the England of his day. He made frequent use of his own experience, particularly in his novel *David Copperfield*, a slightly fictionalized autobiography. When Charles was 12 years old, his father, John Dickens, who worked as a clerk, was imprisoned for debt. The boy himself had to earn a living, working in a blacking warehouse situated near the River Thames in London. He worked 10 hours a day, covering, sealing, and labelling pots of paste-blacking. This experience left a profoundly negative impression on him and served as the basis for a number of vignettes in his novels—particularly Chapter Eleven of *David Copperfield*, aptly titled "I begin life on my own account, and don't like it."

In the novel, David Copperfield started work at the age of 10, even younger than Dickens himself, in the warehouse of the firm "Murdstone & Grinby": "It was a crazy old house with a wharf of its own, abutting on the water when the tide was in, and on the mud when the tide was out, and literally overrun with rats."

Murdstone & Grinby's business was the supply of wines and spirits to ships—perhaps a little higher class than blacking. David had to inspect, wash, cork, label, and pack the bottles, not unlike Dickens's real-life duties. David Copperfield is presented as being more upset by his companions at work than by the actual labour. Having described the senior boy, Mick Walker, the son of a bargeman, and his closest associate, who because of his pale complexion was known only by the nickname Mealy Potatoes, David Copperfield recalls the depth of despair into which he sank when working with them:

> No words can express the secret agony of my soul as I sunk into this companionship; compared these henceforth everyday associates with those of my happier childhood . . . and felt my hopes of growing up to be a learned and distinguished man crushed in my bosom. The deep remembrance of the sense I had of being utterly without hope now; of the shame I felt in my position; of the misery it was to my young heart to believe that day by day what I had learned, and thought, and delighted in, and raised my fancy and my emulation up by, would pass away from me little by little, never to be brought back any more, cannot be written. As often as Mick Walker went away in the course of that afternoon, I mingled my tears with the water in which I was washing the bottles; and sobbed as if there were a flaw in my own breast, and it were in danger of bursting.

The feelings expressed are strong, but the specific nature of the unhappiness needs to be stressed. David Copperfield, like Charles Dickens, came from a family that was genteel, or as we would say today, middle class. Although his family was not rich, he believed he could realistically aspire to become a "learned" man. To work rather than go to school might reduce his chance of becoming learned; but what seems to have been the most telling part of the experience was that his workmates came from a poorer social class than he and did not have the same aspirations. *David Copperfield* thus provides us with a view of child labour as experienced by a middle-class boy fallen on hard times. This account, however, tells us little about how poorer, working-class children saw their work. For that, a valuable source is *Chapters in the Life of a Dundee Factory Boy*, first published, as it happens, in 1850—he same year as *David Copperfield*.

David Copperfield, like Dickens himself, escaped from his apparently desperate circumstances to become a learned and distinguished figure in society.

See also Dundee Factory Boy.
References Ackroyd, Peter, *Dickens* (1990); Dickens, Charles, *David Copperfield* (1850).

Dinwiddie, Courtenay

Courtenay Dinwiddie was appointed secretary of the National Child Labor Committee in 1930 and served in the position until his death in 1943. An enthusiastic worker, he exerted a considerable stabilizing influence upon the Committee throughout his term in office.

See also National Child Labor Committee.

Division of Labour

The phrase *division of labour* has four possible definitions. First, it may refer to the technical division of the labour process—in other words, the splitting of a job into various components—and to the employment tasks that are thus created. For example, the job of building a house would involve architects, planners, brick builders, electricians, plumbers, painters, and other skilled labourers. The whole job has been divided into discrete skills and specialties. Scottish classical economist Adam Smith used the phrase in this sense, describing the extreme specialization of tasks involved in pin production. He argued that by breaking tasks down into minute operations, each of which could be repeatedly performed by an increasingly unskilled worker, labour costs would be reduced and productivity increased. The deskilling that accompanies this form of the division of labour makes it easier, in some sectors, for children to be employed to replace adult labour. This process is sometimes known as "substitutionism." In the early days of the industrial revolution, in Europe and North America, there was a tendency in some sectors to substitute child for adult labour as a consequence of the deskilling inherent in the technical division of labour, a process that can still be witnessed in parts of the newly industrializing sectors of the world economy today.

The second possible definition of the phrase refers to the social division of labour throughout society as a whole. Karl Marx used the phrase in this sense, describing the occupational divisions that shape society as a whole. According to Marx, the social division of labour meant that people had particular locations or sites within the occupational structure and that each saw the others as competitors for a job rather than as coworkers in the social process of production. The consequence was a society within which workers were alienated from each other and from the product of their labour—a society within which oppression and class division dominated. Within this interpretation of the division of labour, children could be viewed as an oppressed social group whose activities are shaped and restricted as a consequence of the social division of labour.

The third form of the division of labour is the sexual division of labour. This refers to the way in which society traditionally ascribes certain roles and labour activities to people on the grounds of their sex. There are particular jobs that are overwhelmingly populated by women and others that are the domain of men. Women workers are said to find their careers thwarted by a "glass ceiling"; thus, they are underrepresented in managerial and executive positions. The sexual division of labour also assumes the domination of women in the provision of domestic labour—in other words, unpaid work around the home, such as cleaning, cooking, and child rearing.

The sexual division of labour also operates within the child labour market. There are tasks that are overwhelmingly done by boys and others that are the domain of girls (for example, baby-sitting is dominated by girls, and milk delivery, by boys). The sexual division of labour reflects socially constructed assumptions about girls' and boys' abilities and future social roles. It is not based on biological or psychological needs or capabilities but on wider social or cultural interpretations of gender roles.

The fourth division of labour is international. In the economic organization of the world as a whole, certain forms of production may be more commonly carried out in some countries than in others. This influences the types of work children in a particular country undertake.

See also Capitalism; Gender Differences; Globalization; Marxism.

Domestic Service

In most societies, children perform duties around the family home. These duties might be regarded as work, although they are also regarded as part of the child's education. When the child is working for his or her own family, the work is not usually classified as child labour. The phrase *domestic service* usually implies that the child is employed in a household other than that of its own immediate family. In the past this type of work has been treated by governments and others as relatively unproblematic. For example, when attempts are made to compile national statistics on the extent of child labour, domestic service has been omitted. This may be partly because of the difficulty of taking a census of domestic workers; but it is no doubt also because whereas the hardships suffered by a child working in a factory or in a field can be readily imagined, a house may seem a relatively comfortable working environment. In many countries, the laws regulating work by children are framed in such a way as not to cover the employment of children in a household. However, more recently, a number of bodies have stressed that children employed in household duties are at risk in a variety of ways. This is particularly the case when the child boards at the house where he or she also works. Cut off from their own families, such children have no protection from their employers, who might make them work long hours or assign them onerous tasks, might feed them poorly, and might inflict physical

Girl in domestic service in Dakar, Senegal, 1996 (International Labour Office)

punishment. In some societies, domestic servants have very low status, and employers believe that their rights over their servants are extensive. Even if a country's labour laws cover domestic work, which is not always the case, the responsible authorities are not usually keen to intrude into private households.

See also Kenya; Morocco.

References Blagbrough, Jonathan, and Glynn, Edmund, "Child Domestic Workers: Characteristics of the Modern Slave and Approaches to Ending Such Exploitation" (1999); Camacho, Agnes Zenaida V., "Family, Child Labour, and Migration: Child Domestic Workers in Metro Manila" (1999).

Drawboys

The production of textiles played a major part early in the industrial revolution in Britain. Technical advances meant that production eventually took place in factories, where machinery was driven by water or steam power. However, many different kinds of textiles initially were produced by hand loom weavers, working either alone or in family groups or small workshops. Simple forms of weaving did not require a high level of skill. Because of this, simple weaving was a way of earning money that was open even to old people and children. Even adult males would undertake weaving to supplement their earnings from another occupation.

Many weavers working in more sophisticated and complicated parts of the industry learned their trade as apprentices, but this was by no means the only way in which children took part in hand loom weaving. Some of the more complex woven patterns required techniques in which the weaver had the use of an assistant. These were usually called "drawboys," although children of both sexes undertook the work. The drawboy sat under the loom, and at a signal, drew down a number of cords, which raised the threads of warp, under which shuttles of coloured weft were driven, thus helping to create the pattern of the cloth. One feature of this way of working was that if a mistake was made, neither the drawboy nor the weaver could tell until they saw that there was an error in the pattern. Since the weaver was paid by the piece and the agents buying the goods would inspect them before paying, errors could be costly. Drawboys also were expected to awaken the weavers in the morning and to clean and prepare their looms for use.

The job of drawboy has been described as the depth of boredom, since the child could not see the results of his or her actions. The weavers generally believed that they had the right to punish children, and some did so severely. However, there are a number of accounts by former drawboys that mention good as well as bad aspects of the work.

The hand loom weavers were self-employed and did not always feel the need to follow regular working routines. The jocular phrase "Saint Monday" referred to the common practice of extending Sunday's day of rest into Monday. If the weaver took a day off work, it was a holiday for the drawboy as well. When the looms were in use, there were various ways of passing the time. Conversation was possible, as the loom was not particularly noisy. Some parents insisted that their children should benefit from Bible reading while they worked. David Gilmour, a former drawboy in Paisley, Scotland—one of the major centres of high-quality weaving in Britain—recalled in his memoirs that singing was "a never failing solace to many weavers and boys."

Gilmour also traced the decline of the job of drawboy. In 1818 there were in Paisley between 6,000 and 7,000 looms, "and of these no fewer than 4,000 to 5,000 required the assistance of a drawboy." When he wrote in 1876, new machinery and steam power had led to a reduction in the number of weavers to 750, "and there is not one drawboy in town."

Spending a few years as a drawboy did not necessarily mean that an individual would become a weaver. As the child grew older, if he was a boy, the parents might seek an apprenticeship for him, and he might well find himself pursuing another trade.

References Clark, Sylvia, *Paisley: A History* (1988); Gilmour, David, *Reminiscences of the Pen' Folk, Paisley Weavers of Other Days, Etc.* (1879); Murray, Norman, *The Scottish Hand Loom Weavers, 1790–1850: A Social History* (1978).

Drugs

See Alcohol and Drugs.

Dundee Factory Boy

Chapters in the Life of a Dundee Factory Boy was first published in Dundee, Scotland, in

1850. The work was anonymous, but the factory boy of the title is referred to in the text as Frank Forrest. Since the book was published by a local man, James Myles, it is sometimes assumed that Myles was the author. However, Myles was one of four brothers, and the "Frank Forrest" in the book was reportedly an only child. Thus if Myles did indeed write the book, it was at least in part imaginative rather than the "autobiography" the book is claimed to be in the dedication to Richard Oastler. If it is not an autobiography, the author, whoever he might be, shows a deep understanding of the day-to-day reality of the working life of a factory boy.

The hero was born in a small rural village in Scotland, where his father was a shoemaker. His father was found guilty in court of "culpable homicide"—in other words, he was found responsible for the death of another person but not to the extent of meriting the more serious charge of murder. The father was transported to Australia (a form of punishment commonly used in Britain at that time), so Frank Forrest's mother took him to the city of Dundee to earn a living. Much of the book is devoted to his years working in a spinning mill.

The book gives descriptions in telling detail that convey something of the experience of a young worker. The hours were long:

When I went to a spinning mill I was about seven years of age. I had to get out of bed every morning at five o'clock, commence work at half past five, drop at nine for breakfast, begin again at half-past nine, work until two, which was the dinner hour, start again at half-past two, and continue until half-past seven at night.
However, although these hours were long, they only nominally made up the working day.
. . . In reality there were no regular hours, masters and managers did with us as they liked.
The working conditions were unhealthy.

About a week after I became a mill boy, I was seized with a strong, heavy sickness that few escape on first becoming factory workers. The cause of the illness, which is known by the name of the "mill fever," is the pestiferous atmosphere produced by so many breathing in a confined space, together with the heat and the exhalations of grease and oil. . . . This fever does not often lay the patient up. It is slow, dull, and painfully wearisome in its operation. It produces a sallow and debilitated look, destroys rosy cheeks, and unless the constitution be very strong, leaves its pale impress for life.

Such information might have been obtained from inquiries into working conditions. However, other passages describe aspects of work that clearly arise from deeply felt personal experience.

At that time mill-masters did not employ men for rousing their hands in the morning. . . . I wish I knew the benevolent person who first conceived and carried into execution the plan of warning them each morning. . . . The plan at once removed a load of anxiety and pain off the minds of the young, as the terror of sleeping in [oversleeping] kept them in a nightly state of unhappiness. . . . We had no clock in the house, and my mother used to rise at all hours of the night, and sit until she heard the Cowgate clock strike an hour. Often has she sat from a little past three until five, when she would waken me and return to her bed.

Eventually, Frank Forrest found other work, and when the book ends, he is on the point of leaving for Australia, where he anticipates a happy reunion with his father. The book closes with a clear statement of why it was written.

My purpose has been, to develop as far as I could, the evils of the long hours system, and the necessity there was for Legislative interference in the factory branch of industry. The old system, with all its horrors, is, I hope, for ever blasted with the detestation of the wise and the good, and its cruel reign will surely never be imposed on the young females and helpless children of our country. God grant that my anticipations may be fully realized.

See also Blincoe, Robert; Dickens, Charles; Oastler, Richard.

References Anonymous, *Chapters in the Life of a Dundee Factory Boy* (1951); Burnett, John, Vincent, David, and Mayall, David (eds.), *The Autobiography of the Working Class*, Volume 1 (1984); Vincent, David, *Bread, Knowledge, and Freedom: A Study of Nineteenth-Century Working Class Autobiography* (1981).

Education, Universal

The United Nations Convention on the Rights of the Child establishes, in Article 28, that children have the right to education. As a minimum, countries should ensure that primary education is available and free to all.

Article 28 reflects the general belief that childhood is a period of human development in which education should take priority. In developed economies such as those of the United States and Britain, it is possible to trace the fairly steady development and expansion of the educational system from the nineteenth century through to the present. The expansion of education, and the redefinition of childhood as a period during which education dominates instead of work, was accompanied by legislative changes. Such changes were relatively slow. For example, it was only in the middle of the twentieth century that Britain increased the compulsory school-leaving age to 16 years.

The idea of compulsory, universal education for all children has been accepted by most countries. However, the capacity of governments to ensure the effective delivery of education varies, as does their capacity to enforce legislation on minimum school-leaving ages.

For many activists concerned about child employment, the idea of universal education is closely linked to the eradication of exploitative forms of child labour. The argument is relatively straightforward: If children are at school, they cannot be employed.

The International Labour Organisation (ILO) believes that historically, compulsory education has been one of the most effective methods of eliminating child labour. Compulsory education removes children from the supply side of the employment equation, and in particular, from full-time employment. It is acknowledged that children may combine education and work; but ILO members believe that part-time forms of work are less likely to be exploitative of children.

The United Nations International Children's Emergency Fund (UNICEF) also has supported this interpretation, arguing in its fiftieth anniversary report of 1997 that a key strategy in tackling child labour is the implementation of compulsory education free of charge. Although this approach appears to offer a relatively simple solution, the reality is somewhat more complex.

It could be argued that this view is based upon a misreading of the historical facts in developed economies. In countries such as Britain and the Netherlands, it is not certain that education removed children from work. It could be suggested that other pressures removed children from work and education became a means of occupying children who were no longer needed, or wanted, in the labour market.

Even if we were to accept the central role that some wish to ascribe to education in solving the child labour problem, the reality is that many countries do not have the resources to fund an effective, free, compulsory educational system. Jo Boyden, a leading writer on child labour, identified a number of problems with the role of education in this context.

Boyden asserted that many families in developing countries need their children's economic contribution for basic survival. Children must either work and contribute to the family income or they must take the adults' places in domestic duties, such as child care provision, so that the adults can work. In such circumstances, families cannot afford to let children attend school. In that sense, education carries an opportunity cost in the form of lost income to the family. Boyden also challenged the simplistic view that education is the solution to all child labour problems. She did this by showing that in some circumstances education actually caused children to work instead of stopping them from doing so. This occurred for two reasons: First, the child had to work in order to be able to afford to go to school. The costs of school might include special activity fees even where basic academic instruction is free. Other costs are in purchasing books and supplies, transport to and from school, and school uniforms.

Second, children sometimes end up working because they opt out of school, perceiving it as irrelevant to their lives. If parents cannot see the direct benefit of schooling to their lives, then why should their children commit time and energy to it? For example, if the education system emphasizes academic skills but at the same time there are few white-collar jobs available, what value does education have for the majority?

This latter point expands the debate about the role of education. In effect, it starts to draw attention to the extent to which we think of education in narrow, "academic" terms. It would be possible to think of work as having the potential to provide some form of educational experience as well. By correlating the two, it is possible to think of different ways of conceptualizing education.

Although, as we have already noted, the ILO and UNICEF view education as a means of tackling child labour, we need to be careful and not jump to the conclusion that universal education will keep children from working. Evidence from the developed economies would suggest that this is not the case. What may happen is that the pattern of work changes to one where children combine full-time education with part-time work. In this context we need to be aware that such employment may in some circumstances undermine educational attainment.

Compulsory education can, and has, played a role in changing the nature of child labour. If it is to continue to do this in the developing countries, resources must be provided to increase the availability of practical, relevant, and child-centred education provision. However, we must also acknowledge that education by itself will not solve all of the problems. We must also pursue other measures to alleviate poverty and reform labour markets, if we hope to help the world's poorest families.

See also Educational Achievement; International Labour Organisation; United Nations International Children's Emergency Fund.

References Bellamy, Carol, *The State of the World's Children, 1997* (1997); Boyden, Jo, *The Relationship between Education and Child Work* (1994); Boyden, Jo, Ling, Birgitta, and Myers, William, *What Works for Working Children* (1998); International Labour Organisation, *Child Labour: Targeting the Intolerable* (1996); Nieuwenhuys, Olga, "To Read and Not to Eat: South Indian Children between Secondary School and Work" (1993).

Educational Achievement

The relationship between child employment and educational achievement has only recently become a subject for systematic research. This reflects the fact that not until the twentieth century did school come to be viewed as an alternative to work for children. Research in the developed economies of Europe and the United States has shown that it is normal for children to combine part-time work with full-time education. If it is common for children to combine these two activities, then the nature of the relationship between the two becomes of interest. Can it be argued that work has a positive or a negative effect on educational achievement?

In Britain, research by Emrys Davies, published in 1972, suggested that there was a negative relationship between part-time employment and educational achievement. Davies suggested that working had a detrimental effect on a range of school variables including attendance, industry, behaviour, and intention to leave school at an early age. Throughout the 1980s, research in the United States seemed to support this interpretation. The work of Ellen Greenberger and Laurence Steinberg was at the forefront of such investigations. Their findings indicated that children's work did have a negative effect on their educational achievement. However, they argued that it was not simply a question of whether someone worked or not. The key variable was the amount of time they committed to this activity. The results from a number of studies showed that school students who worked 15 to 20 hours per week were more likely to have a poorer academic performance.

Researchers in other developed economies have started only recently to consider this factor. Sandy Hobbs and Jim McKechnie have carried out their research in Britain. Their results are similar to those of Greenberger and Steinberg in that a relationship between the number of hours worked and academic performance emerged. In McKechnie and Hobbs's studies, students working more than 10 hours per week were more likely to have a poorer academic performance. It appears that the underlying relationship between education and work may transfer across cultures, but the actual number of hours at which the relationship emerges will vary.

The above discussion might lead one to conclude that a linear relationship exists between part-time work and education. However, research indicates that a more complex, nonlinear relationship exists. Researchers in Britain and America have shown that students who work 5 or fewer hours per week have better academic records than those who work excessive hours and those who do not work at all. Such findings suggest that we need to consider the possibility that a negative stereotype of the relationship between part-time work and education has tended to dominate. It appears that work might also have a positive effect on education. Some early studies have shown that those who had jobs performed better in academic tests on consumer behaviour and economics; but these studies have tended to be overshadowed by the more recent focus on the negative consequences of work.

It could be argued that work contributes to the individual's development and may result in the attainment of skills that are transferable to school. It is also possible that work can contribute to the individual's sociocognitive development, providing the adolescent with a greater awareness and understanding of social relationships and of other people's roles and views. It could be argued that such gains could have positive effects on adjustment and accommodation to the demands of the educational system. At a more basic level, gaining some experience of work may also motivate students to achieve academically. Most jobs that are available to adolescents require low levels of skill and are relatively repetitive and boring. Adolescents' experiences in such jobs might heighten their awareness of the need to obtain higher education in order to achieve more rewarding jobs. Hence, a more balanced interpretation seems appropriate, in which part-time work is viewed both as a potential cost and benefit to education. The goal of research then would be to identify when work is beneficial and when it is not.

In attempting to understand when work is beneficial and when it is not, researchers will have to widen their concerns beyond the number of hours worked. Jeylan Mortimer and Michael Finch have argued that the quality of the employment experience has been largely neglected in discussions about the links between work and education. It is naive to assume that all jobs are equal in effect, since jobs vary in terms of task demands, skill levels, and opportunities for training. Such qualitative variations need to be considered alongside the number of hours worked. Some researchers in the United States, for example Karen S. Markel and Michael R. Frone, have started to look at the interrelations between the quantity and quality of employment and its impact on education.

So far we have worked on the assumption that a causal relationship exists between work and education. That is, as students work more, their educational performance suffers. In this case work causes the poorer academic performance. One should be cautious in assuming that this is always the correct interpretation. It is possible that students who are performing badly in school or who are disenchanted with the school system opt out and commit themselves to the world of part-time work. In this case it is the experience of school that is causing the student to seek work. Steinberg and his colleagues in the United States have been addressing the question of the causal relationship between work and school and have concluded that both processes are operative.

Research into the relationship between work and education is in its infancy, and the subject requires further study for at least two reasons: First, the debate about the link between work and educational achievement has still not been resolved. Although some studies show that work affects educational performance, others have failed to support such findings. A recent analysis by Jeylan Mortimer and Monica Johnson shows the complex nature of the relationship. Second, it is apparent that many children will continue to combine work and education, especially those in developing economies. It is important that we understand the implications of the experiences of these children.

See also Costs and Benefits; Education, Universal.

References Bachman, Jerald G., and Schulenberg, John, "How Part-Time Work Intensity Relates to Drug Use, Problem Behavior, Time Use, and Satisfaction among High School Seniors: Are These Consequences or Merely Correlates?" (1993); Frone, Michael R., "Developmental Consequences of Youth Employment" (1999); Hobbs, Sandy, and McKechnie, Jim, Child Employment in Britain: A Social and Psychological Analysis (1997); Markel, Karen S., and Frone, Michael R., "Job Characteristics, Work-School Conflict, and School Outcomes among Adolescents: Testing a Structural Model" (1998); Mortimer, Jeylan, and Johnson, Monica, "Adolescents' Part-Time Work and Educational Achievement" (1998); Steinberg, Laurence, and Dornbusch, Sanford M., "Negative Correlates of Part-Time Employment during Adolescence: Replication and Elaboration" (1991); Steinberg, Laurence, Fegley, Suzanne, and Dornbusch, Sanford M., "Negative Impact of Part-Time Work on Adolescent Adjustment: Evidence from a Longitudinal Study" (1993).

Egypt

Egypt occupies the northeastern part of the continent of Africa. A powerful state for almost three thousand years, it fell consecutively to the Greek, Roman, Byzantine, and Ottoman empires. The modern state of Egypt dates from the declaration of the republic in 1953. Much of the territory is desert, and the economy of the country has always been dependent on the river Nile. The population is estimated at more than 55 million, of which 90 percent are Moslems.

Legal restrictions on child employment in Egypt vary with the type of work. The law does not prohibit children from working in agriculture. Typically children earn around a third of an adult wage. Work by children is particularly widespread in agriculture. This is so much taken for granted that children picking cotton is regarded as a suitable subject for picture postcards.

In some industries, work is permitted from the age of 12. Working children have been estimated to make up around 11 percent of the country's labour force. However, this may well be an underestimation, since there are high dropout rates from school in some areas. The Egyptian Ministry of Labor has set up a Child Labor Unit that works in conjunction with the International Labour Organisation's International Program for the Elimination of Child Labor. There are also nongovernmental organizations dealing with the issue, most notably the Al-Jeel Center for Youth and Social Studies. The Center has made a particular study of children working in the Masr Al-Qadeema district of Old Cairo. There children are to be found working both in traditional industries, such as tanneries and potteries, as well as in garages and small workshops.

See also Africa; Middle East.

References Abdalla, Ahmed, Child Labour in Egypt (1995).

Elimination of Child Labour

Among the writings of those who are concerned with the issue of child labour, a

A young machinist in Egypt, 1989 (J. Maillard, International Labour Office)

number of positions can be identified regarding what should be done about the employment of children. One common stance that is often taken up by writers in the mass media is the position that all children should be removed from work. Supporters of this view point to international law to support their view. The International Labour Organisation's Convention 138 focuses on the Minimum Age for Admission to Employment.

The abolitionists' view of child labour is readily supported by horror stories of children being sold into slavery or bonded labour. In addition, they can point to examples of children working in extremely hazardous conditions. It is self-evident that no one could support such working conditions for anyone, be they adult or child; but are such conditions representative of all working children's experience? If all of these extreme forms of labour were eliminated, it would still leave a number of other forms of employment that we find children in around the world. Are these to be abolished as well?

Some have suggested that the way out of this dilemma is to draw a distinction between child labour and child work. The former is deemed unacceptable, whereas the latter indicates forms of employment that are acceptable. The difficulty then becomes one of distinguishing between child labour and child work. Attempts to draw such a distinction have resulted in a number of problems. One problem is that it leaves some organizations with a dual goal—the elimination of child labour and the protection of child workers. This difficulty is most clearly seen in the ILO's major initiative on child labour, the International Program on the Elimination of Child Labor (IPEC). Although it calls for the eventual elimination of child labour, the ILO recognizes that this must be a long-term goal. Until its end goal is achieved, the ILO's transitional aim is to protect working children.

This position is clearly advocated in the ILO's recent publication *Child Labour: Targeting the Intolerable*, where it is clear that the most hazardous forms of employment are to be tackled first. The implication of such a position appears to be that once these intolerable forms of work are eliminated, the ILO will move on to eliminate other forms of employment and take children out of all work.

Ben White has questioned this position. For him, there is another issue underlying this discussion. If we were to eliminate all hazardous forms of work and to put in place adequate protection for children in all other types of employment, are we entitled to abolish children's right to earn money? Any attempt to answer such a question would ultimately take us into a discussion of children's position in society and the rights that they have.

Although discussion of this topic is currently at the forefront of debates about child labour, it is not new. Raymond Fuller was the director of research and publicity in the early stages of the National Child Labor Committee. In his book *Child Labor and the Constitution*, published in 1923, Fuller indicated that although he supported child labour legislation, he was opposed to prohibitory child labour laws. He argued that this implied that you could treat children en masse and that there was something inherently wrong with working for pay.

See also Definition of Child Labour; International Labour Organisation.

References International Labour Organisation, *Child Labour: Targeting the Intolerable* (1996); White, Ben, "Children, Work, and 'Child Labour': Changing Responses to the Employment of Children" (1994).

Engels, Friedrich

A friend and lifelong collaborator of Karl Marx, Friedrich Engels (1820–1895), also known as Frederick Engels, was a socialist who wrote widely about a range of subjects. He was born in Germany but moved to England in 1842 to work in his family business in Manchester. While there, he witnessed the living and working conditions of the industrial working class, and this became the subject of his first book,

The Condition of the Working Class in England. This work not only documents how people lived but also outlines Engels's argument about how this state of affairs could and should be changed. Child labour features widely in the book, as Engels describes how the newly developing factories of the industrial revolution often utilized the cheap labour of very young children and pauper apprentices to replace that of adults, who would have demanded a higher wage.

Engels noted that because of the use of steam and water power, the labour involved in spinning and weaving involved flexibility of fingers rather than muscular strength.

Men are, therefore, not only not needed for it but actually, by reason of the greater muscular development of the hand, less fit for it than women and children, and are, therefore, naturally almost superseded by them. . . . Of 419,560 factory operatives of the British Empire in 1839, 192,887, or nearly half, were under eighteen years of age, and 242,296 of the female sex, of whom 112,192 were less than eighteen years old.

He cited the Factories' Inquiry Commission of 1833 as noting one case where a child of 2 years was employed. Examples of children working as young as 5 or 6 were not uncommon, but usually children began work when they reached 8 or 9 years old. The working days lasted as long as 14 to 16 hours. The Commissioners also reported that supervisors flogged the children and otherwise treated them badly.

Noting the use of children from workhouses as so-called apprentices in the factories, Engels wrote:

They were lodged, fed and, clothed in common, and were, of course, completely the slaves of their masters, by whom they were treated with the utmost recklessness and barbarity. . . . Gradually the increasing competition of free work people crowded out the whole apprentice system.

Meanwhile, children worked at great danger to their health and physical safety. Engels cited testimony by medical experts to the harmful effects of factory conditions on the development of children's legs and spinal columns. Describing conditions in the stocking-weaving industry, he explained that young children typically worked shifts of 10 to 12 hours in small, enclosed rooms: "It is not uncommon for them to faint at their work, to become too feeble for the most ordinary household occupation, and so near-sighted as to be obliged to wear glasses during childhood." Engels listed many horrific accidents:

12 June [1843] a boy died in Manchester of lock-jaw, caused by his hand being crushed between wheels. 16 June, a youth in Saddleworth seized by a wheel and carried away with it; died horribly mangled. . . . 24 July, a girl in Oldham died, carried around fifty times by a strap; no bone unbroken. 27 July, a girl in Manchester seized by the blower (the first machine that receives the raw cotton) and died of injuries received.

Children employed in the mines also suffered. Some transported the ore or coal loosened by the miner to the main transport path or opened and shut the ventilation doors:

For watching the doors the smallest children are usually employed, who thus pass twelve hours daily, in the dark, alone, sitting usually in damp passages without even having work enough to save them from the stupefying, brutalizing tedium of doing nothing. The transport of coal and iron-stone, on the other hand, is very hard labor, the stuff being shoved in large tubs, without wheels, over the uneven floor of the mine; often over moist clay, or through water, and frequently up steep inclines and through paths so low-roofed that the workers are forced to creep on hands and knees; . . . therefore, older children and half-grown girls are employed.

Engels saw the Factory Act of 1833 as a modest advance. Among its provisions were the prohibition of most kinds of work for children younger than 9 years and of night work for all children, and the provision of two hours' schooling per day for children younger than 14 years. Engels bitterly attacked those manufacturers who had opposed the Act and noted that it was not as effective as it should have been: "Many employers disregard the law, shorten the meal times, work children longer than is permitted, and risk prosecution, knowing that the possible fines are trifling in comparison with the certain profits derivable from the offence."

See also Industrial Revolution; Marxism.

References Engels, Friedrich, *The Condition of the Working Class in England* (1987).

England

See United Kingdom.

Entertainment Industry

To many children, and indeed to their parents, the attractions of being employed in the entertainment industry are so great that it is hardly considered "work." Children are employed as singers, dancers, musicians, and actors in many countries and in many media, from street performance to the stage, cinema, and television.

Countries that have laws restricting child labour generally make exceptions for work in the entertainment industry. This is partly because the appeal of performing is acknowledged and partly because certain roles are deemed best played by children. For example, if a film or television script has a child as a character, it will be seen as inevitable that a child should be hired to perform the part.

Legislation in this case merely limits the hours of work and stipulates healthy and safe working conditions. For long-running stage plays, it is not unusual for two children to be cast in the same part, thus allowing each to take part in alternate performances. This reduces the number of hours per week that each spends on stage. Similarly, when making a film for cinema

or television, companies sometimes employ twins to share a single role. Legislation also makes provision for the child performer to have a certain number of hours of education per day. The most convenient way of achieving this is often the hiring of a personal tutor.

Despite legal safeguards, there continue to be fears about potential long-term harm to the child performer. Success as a child does not necessarily lead to success as an adult performer, and the former child performer may find it difficult to adjust to other types of work if he or she is unable to continue a career as a performer.

There are also fears that working in the entertainment industry is likely to introduce the young person to certain forms of adult lifestyle with which he or she is unready to cope. Early access to cigarettes, alcohol, or drugs is the most obvious example.

See also Cinema; Leisure; Modelling; Sports.

Ergonomics

Ergonomics is the study of machine design and the work environment with the purpose of appropriately constructing tools and machines to work in tune with the mechanics of the human body. There are three aspects to ergonomics. The first involves the design of machines in ways that avoid placing unnecessary stresses or pressures on the human frame—for example, ensuring that computer screens and keyboards are at the appropriate height and that typing desks and chairs are shaped and sized so as to enable users to avoid back strain, eye damage, or any form of repetitive strain injury. The second aspect involves the placement of levers so that the human body and the machine work together for maximum effect; for example, the positioning of levers on metal pressing machines so that people need not place their arms across their bodies in order to work the machine. The third aspect of ergonomics involves the maximization of efficiency within space and time. The goal is to ensure that work tasks continue without interruptions caused by inappropriate machine design—for example, that workers do not have to walk significant distances between one part of their task and another. Thus, ergonomics is only partly concerned with designing work tools to avoid injury or stress to the human body. It is also an attempt to construct implements in such a way that the labour task is tightly defined and controlled and that the worker's ability to control or decide how work should be performed is limited. In other words, the concerns addressed by ergonomics are both economic and mechanical.

With regard to child labour, machine design is of considerable importance. Machines generally are built to be operated by an adult, not by a child. This means they can put an undue strain on children's bodies, providing an inefficient utilization of their labour. In addition, safety equipment and shields might be rendered ineffective when machines are operated by children. Since the early nineteenth century, a number of writers have noted the crippling effects of factory labour on children as a consequence of their operating inappropriate machines. For example, Lord Shaftesbury in England complained that heavy working and use of machinery was causing ill health and deformity among child factory workers in the first half of the nineteenth century. But such concerns are not merely historical. Today children can be found working in factories across the globe, at machines that were designed to be operated by adults. In Britain, in 1995, a factory making cardboard boxes was caught employing children in operating precisely such a machine, and in hazardous conditions: To enable child workers to place the cardboard in the cutting machine, the safety shield had been removed. In many countries children are involved in work-related accidents that leave them crippled or debilitated, with permanent damage to limbs and fingers.

See also Accidents; Health.

Ethnicity

The word *ethnicity* is often used by sociologists in place of *race* because the latter word has come to be viewed as problematic on a number of levels. In particular, the usage of *race* to categorize human beings invokes the existence of discrete, permanent, biological subspecies of humans—an idea that all leading biologists and geneticists reject. There are no discrete human races but only the single human race.

Many people in Britain and the United States see ethnicity as something that only certain (usually nonwhite) minorities have. This is a "minus one" definition of ethnicity, which assumes that white North American and European culture is the standard or norm from which others deviate in various ways. More useful is the notion of ethnicity as encompassing more than one of the following features: common language, religion, social customs, history, and geographical or national origin. In this sense, everyone has an ethnic identity. One form of ethnicity may dominate in a particular country and others may be minority ethnicities, but everyone, to some measure, can be defined by ethnicity.

The problem is that people from the majority ethnic group may find it difficult to see themselves as having a shared ethnic identity. They will be aware of divisions in their ethnic group that are created by gender, disability, sexuality, social class, and intergenerational conflict. Yet this knowledge of the limits of ethnic cohesion among the majority does not often lead to an ability to see similar limits in the minority ethnic groups.

Paul Gilroy has suggested that ethnicity often is seen wrongly as a fixed cultural "essence." Minority ethnic groups can be attributed a very static ethnic identity in which it is assumed that all members of the group will speak a certain language and have certain dietary habits, religious practices, and marriage and family customs. However, ethnicity is neither fixed (since all cultures are constantly changing) nor invariably at the forefront of the consciousness of minorities.

One particular note of caution must be sounded about the term *ethnicity*. Ethnic labels are prone to mutation and change. The religious label *Moslem* was rarely used as an ethnic identifier until the 1980s, when the fundamentalist Islamic regime came to power in Iran and issued a challenge to Western governments and cultures. When the adjective *Bengali* is used in Britain, it usually refers to the predominantly Sylheti Moslem group whose national origins are in Bangladesh, rather than to the mainly Hindu population from the Indian state of Bengal. Before 1971 and the war between East and West Pakistan, this group was referred to as Pakistani. West Indians are now called African Caribbeans; but the diversity of cultures, religions, and languages on their islands of origin indicates that the convenient labels we use may obscure as much as they reveal about particular groups.

The question that has garnered the most interest from observers of child labour vis-à-vis ethnicity is to what extent child employment patterns vary by ethnic group within particular societies. Two lines of thinking have emerged regarding this issue. Some writers have suggested that particular minority ethnic groups have traditions of family business strategies that make it more likely for their children to be working in the family concerns. When considering this hypothesis, we must be aware of three underlying factors: First, one reason why families set up independent businesses might be because their general experience in the labour market is one of discrimination. In other words, family businesses among minority ethnic communities might be a response to oppression. Secondly, it may be that this notion reflects "commonsense" understandings (and misunderstandings) of the reality of particular ethnic groupings and their labour market activity. In other words, there may be a stereotype among the majority ethnic community that members of a particular minority group own small shops in which they employ all their family members in long, arduous labour; but the reality might be quite different. Some members of this community might own small shops or businesses but the majority may well participate in the general labour market. Finally, particular occupational groups among the majority ethnic community also might employ their children and family members in their businesses (farmers, for example), but this might be treated differently from child labour among minorities, and might be viewed as less problematic within mainstream society.

A second general hypothesis suggests that children from minority ethnic communities are more likely to face discrimination in the labour market, and as a consequence, are less likely to work. *Ethnicity* might be a more positive expression of human difference than *race*, but it is nevertheless tied in with notions of oppression and discrimination. A number of studies conducted in Britain have suggested that children of minority ethnic communities are more likely to face discrimination in the labour market (and less likely to find steady work) than are children of the majority ethnic grouping.

See also Cultural Traditions.

Europe

It may be claimed that since the industrial revolution was initially a European phenomenon, and since "child labour" was a concept developed during the industrial revolution, Europe has to be a special focus for anyone attempting to understand child labour. According to historian Hugh Cunningham, by the 1830s it had come to be thought that the more industrialized a country was, the more extensive would be its use of child labour. Campaigns against child labour are a comparatively recent phenomenon going against the previously unchallenged assumptions that children's labour is both necessary and desirable. The history of child labour in Europe and Europeans' experiences in combating it may therefore be relevant today both to developed and to developing countries.

The experience of combating child labour in Europe has informed much of general opinion today about how to combat child labour, primarily through a mixture of prohibiting legislation and the provision of universal and compulsory education. The worst forms of exploitation of children in work situations in Europe were undoubtedly curbed by these means. However, caution should be exercised in holding up legislation and education as the primary solutions to child labour. Increases in household income, the provision of increasingly comprehensive social benefits, and the need for a more highly skilled labour force as demanded by technological advances in production processes also contributed to the relative decline in child labour in European countries during the first half of the twentieth century. Child labour became less prevalent as the pattern of work by children gradually changed, from full time and permanent to more casual and part time. This reflects a noticeable trend in the adult workforce as the twentieth century draws to a close. The increasing "casualization" of labour in Europe during the 1980s and 1990s has led to much employment, of adults but also of children, becoming increasingly part time and subcontracted and perhaps less permanent than at any time since the reconstruction of Europe after World War II.

Because the lessons of history may be relevant to the situation of developing countries today, it is perhaps appropriate to highlight the following questions (especially in relation to the experience of Britain). Can child labour be fought effectively without the mobilization and articulation of public pressure on a large scale? In this respect, the example of Belgium provides us with a useful contrast to the British situation. Belgium experienced an industrialization of a rapidity and intensity second only to that in the United Kingdom. Yet Belgium took much longer to abolish child labour. It has been argued that this was because Belgium did not develop an effective public movement against child labour.

According to a 1989 labour force survey, there are thought to be almost 2 million fifteen-year-olds at work in the countries of the European Union. More than a third of this number are involved in work in the service sector, a rapidly expanding recruitment ground for underage and illegal workers.

See also Belgium; Denmark; Europe, Council of; Europe, Eastern; European Union; France; Germany; Italy; Malta; Netherlands; Portugal; Romania; Russia; Scandinavia; Spain; Turkey; United Kingdom.

References Cunningham, Hugh, "The Employment and Unemployment of Children in England, c. 1680–1851" (1990).

Europe, Council of

On 5 May 1949, ten countries signed the Statute of the Council of Europe. The aim of the signatory governments was to achieve closer unity in their "devotion to the spiritual and moral values that are the common heritage of their peoples and the true source of individual freedom, political liberty and the rule of law, principles that form the basis of all genuine democracy." At present, the member states in the Council of Europe are Andorra, Austria, Belgium, Bulgaria, Cyprus, Czech Republic, Denmark, Estonia, Finland, France, Germany, Greece, Hungary, Iceland, Ireland, Italy, Liechtenstein, Lithuania, Luxembourg, Malta, Netherlands, Norway, Poland, Portugal, Romania, San Marino, Slovakia, Slovenia, Spain, Sweden, Turkey, and United Kingdom.

The Council of Europe has two major institutions, the Committee of Ministers and the Parliamentary Assembly. The Council has produced over 100 treaties, of which the most important concerning child labour are described below.

The first treaty is the European Convention for the Protection of Human Rights and Fundamental Freedoms, of 1950. One of the most significant innovations established by this Convention is the creation "of machinery and procedures that especially enable the individual victim to institute proceedings on his own behalf . . . [to obtain] redress in respect of the violation of one of the rights protected by the Convention." Under the Convention, the Commission of Human Rights was established to examine all complaints for admissibility, to attempt friendly settlements, and to set out the merits of each case. At this stage, the case is forwarded either to the Committee of Ministers, which can judge whether a violation of the Convention has occurred and what measures should be taken; or to the Commission or appropriate member state party, which can refer the issue to the Court of Human Rights.

The Commission of Human Rights has the right to receive petitions from any person, nongovernmental organization, or group of individuals claiming to be the victim of a violation of the rights set forth in this Convention. *Any person* refers in particular to minors, groups of children, or NGOs representing children's rights. Therefore, even if children are not allowed to go to court within their own national legislation, they can still directly petition the Commission. In theory the European Court of Human Rights could be a strong political weapon in the fight against child labour. Children and NGOs acting on their behalf have the right to petition their own state if it violates one of the articles stipulated in the Convention. If the state in question accepts the ruling of the Court, then that decision is binding. However, although the Convention applies equally to children and adults, there are not many specific provisions for children in this document. For the Convention to assist in the fight against child labour, it would have to be expanded with more specific regulations concerning working children that would then have to be enforceable.

In the economic field, one of the noticeable achievements of the Council of Europe has been the European Social Charter, drafted between 1955 and 1958, signed in 1961, and enacted in 1965. Article 7 of the Social Charter deals with the right of children and young persons to protection.

Member states are expected to ensure the following conditions:

1. to provide that the minimum age of admission to employment shall be 15 years, subject to the exceptions for children employed in prescribed light work without harm to their health, morals or education;
2. to provide that a higher minimum age of admission to employment shall be fixed with respect to prescribed occupations regarded as dangerous or unhealthy;
3. to provide that persons who are still subject to compulsory education shall not be employed in such work as would deprive them of the full benefit of their education;
4. to provide that the working hours of persons under 16 years of age shall be limited in accordance with the needs of their development, and particularly with their need for vocational training;
5. to recognize the right of young workers and apprentices to a fair wage or other appropriate allowances;
6. to provide that the time spent by young persons in vocational training during the normal working hours with the consent of the employer shall be treated as forming part of the working day;
7. to provide that employed persons under 18 years of age shall be entitled to not less than three weeks annual holiday with pay;
8. to provide that persons under 18 years of age shall not be employed in night work with the exception of certain occupations provided for by national laws or regulations;
9. to provide that persons under 18 years of age employed in occupations prescribed by national laws or regulations shall be subject to regular medical control;
10. to ensure special protection against physical and moral dangers to which children and young persons are exposed, and particularly against those resulting directly or indirectly from their work.

This article is vague in the sense that it does not clearly define phrases such as *light work, dangerous or unhealthy work, need of development,* and *fair wages.* It is left to the member states to decide how to interpret these expressions.

See also Europe; European Union.

Europe, Eastern
After World War II, during which the United States and the Soviet Union were leading members of the alliance against Nazi Germany, the Soviet Union exerted its influence to create communist governments in Eastern Europe. The countries with communist governments included Albania, Bulgaria, Czechoslovakia, Hungary, Poland, Romania, Yugoslavia, and the eastern part of Germany. The Soviet government attempted to control both the internal and external policies of the countries in this "Soviet bloc," but its attempts met with resistance. For example, Yugoslavia asserted its independence in the late 1940s; Albania aligned itself with Chinese communism rather than the Russian form; and there were anti-Soviet uprisings in Hungary (1956) and Czechoslovakia (1968). Gradually, Soviet influence in particular East European countries loosened. When communism collapsed in Russia, it was inevitable that the same would happen in these other countries. Each of the former communist countries in Europe now has a government that accepts the capitalist system of free market economics.

The collapse of communism in this part of the world has led to social, political, and economic upheaval. This is most obvious in the case of national boundaries. For example, countries such as Estonia, Latvia, and Lithuania have regained their independence from Russia; East Germany has reunited with West Germany; and Yugoslavia has fragmented into several independent states.

The new economic circumstances have led to the rapid growth of private enterprise and to many businesses being run without adequate government regulation. In several countries it is reported that small, unregulated enterprises make sub-stantial use of child labour. Faced with large social and economic problems, few of the governments are able to devote much energy to the control of child employment. Social and economic dislocation has created new armies of children living and working on the streets of cities such as Moscow, St. Petersburg, Bucharest, and Budapest.

See also Germany; Romania; Russia.

European Union
The European Union (EU) is the most recent form of a series of organizations known previously as the European Economic Community and the European Community. It currently consists of twelve member states that cooperate in matters not only of economics but also in foreign affairs and the law. Current members are Belgium, Denmark, Finland, France, Germany, Greece, Ireland, Italy, Luxembourg, the Netherlands, Portugal, Spain, Sweden, and the United Kingdom; and a number of other countries are seeking to join, including some from the former communist bloc in Eastern Europe.

The EU is one of the most densely populated and urbanized areas in the world, with over 300 million inhabitants, representing about 6.5 percent of the world's population. Population in the EU is not divided evenly among member states. The Netherlands has 441 inhabitants per square kilometre, whereas Ireland has only 50 inhabitants per square kilometre. The areas with the highest population density are highly urbanized industrial regions or administrative centres. Over 80 percent of the total population in the Netherlands and in the United Kingdom live in towns. The population of the EU overall is aging; that is, the number of older people is increasing compared to the number of young people. The average household in the EU consists of fewer members than before. The number of one-person households is rising.

The Directive of the Council of the European Union on the Protection of Young

People at Work was passed in 1994 to come into force on 22 June 1996. The Directive begins with the statement of purpose, "Member States shall take the necessary measures to prohibit work by children." However, a close reading of the text shows that there are various limitations placed on this apparently simple and straightforward goal. Although the Directive addresses the work of young people, it makes key distinctions based on age and education. In the Directive, a *young person* is someone under 18 years of age, whereas an *adolescent* is a young person not classed as a child. Full-time work cannot take place before the end of compulsory schooling, and not until a young person reaches the age of 15.

Although children are prohibited from working by the Directive, allowance is made for "light work." This is essentially defined by exclusion, in that it is work not likely to be harmful to the safety, health, and development of the child or detrimental to the child's schooling or vocational training. In making a judgment on whether work is "light," both the nature of the tasks and the conditions under which they are performed are relevant. Occasional or short-term work is permitted in a "family undertaking," provided it is not harmful to the child. It is envisaged that national legislation specifying light work may cover children as young as 13 years of age. During the school term, up to 12 hours per week may be worked; between terms, up to 35 hours per week. On a school day, the maximum permitted work time is 2 hours, and on other days the maximum is 7 hours.

The Directive further limits working hours in terms of the time of day, periods of rest between shifts, and rest breaks during shifts. Work by children before 6 A.M. and after 8 P.M. is excluded. There should be 14 consecutive hours of rest in any 24-hour period, and two days' rest in every week, preferably consecutive days. If a day's work lasts over four and a half hours, there must be a 30-minute rest break. For adolescents, limitations are rather less restrictive.

One of the purposes of the Directive, as laid out in Article 1, is to ensure that young people are protected against economic exploitation. However, unlike the need to be protected against other dangers such as threats to health, safety, and development, this goal is not referred to or expanded upon elsewhere in the directive. No minimum rates of pay are mentioned, for example. Employers are obliged to establish in advance whether work is hazardous, and they must arrange for appropriate health and safety information and training. The lack of reference to the economic relationship between employer and child worker suggests that exploitation is not in practice treated as seriously in the Directive as are other goals.

The Directive specifies that a member state may choose to permit domestic service in a private household if such service is occasional or short term. This is presumably in acknowledgment that such practices are common and may be deeply embedded in a society.

It is worth pointing out that the limitations placed on the work of adolescents, as opposed to children, are explicitly stated to be open to suspension by individual states. The grounds mentioned represent a wide variety of cultural assumptions and practices. They range from work for the armed forces and police to work in cultural and sporting activities, in hospitals, on ships and fishing boats, and in agriculture and tourism.

The Directive is almost exclusively abstract and conceptual. The methods of implementation are left open. Article 4.1 states only that "Member States shall adopt the measures necessary to prohibit work by children." Although the Commission monitors the activities of individual states, it is clear that there is a good deal of scope for interpretation by governments, most notably on the meaning of *light work*. One of the few explicit constraints placed on how a particular country interprets the Directive is the Non-Reducing Clause, which states that the Directive cannot be used as grounds for reducing the general level of protection that already exists in a particular country. Only time will tell whether this Directive has a significant impact on the work of children in the member states of the European Union.

See also Belgium; Denmark; Europe; Europe, Council of; Greece; Italy; Portugal; Spain; Stop Child Labour; United Kingdom.

Exploitation

In sociological and economic analysis, the word *exploitation* is used to describe certain types of employer-employee relationships. However, the term is often used in different ways. For some, *exploitation* refers to the abuse of labour. This could mean that the working conditions are particularly bad—for example, that the hours are excessive, the health and safety environment poor, or machinery badly maintained and dangerous. Alternatively, *exploitation* may be a reference to the fact that the remuneration is not adequate by generally accepted criteria. Pay, for example, may be below legally established minimum wage rates; or it may be regarded as unfair based on other criteria, such as the average wage paid for the particular kind of work. A common slogan used by workers during pay disputes with employers in the past has been "A fair day's work for a fair day's pay." The problem with such terms is that they are subjective. What one person considers a fair day's wage, another may regard as inadequate. For some, a working day of 10 hours is appropriate; for others, the workday should be no more than 8 hours long. A second definition of exploitation, and of labour exploitation in particular, comes from Marxist interpretations of the world. For Marx, *exploitation* refers to the social processes, relationships, and mechanisms whereby surplus produce is taken from the direct producer by the dominant class to ensure that they can live a more or less leisured existence. Exploitation, therefore, has taken on various forms at different moments in history—slavery in the ancient world, political relations of obligation under feudalism, and wage labour under capitalism. The key factor in this interpretation is that most wage labour performed in modern capitalist societies is exploitative, since it is the mechanism whereby the wealth made by the vast majority is transferred to and owned by a small minority of capitalists.

Whatever the definition of *exploitation* employed, it seems likely that child workers will be found to be exploited at least as much as adults and frequently more so. Children are generally paid less than adults; and although this to some extent may be attributable to their more limited skills or lower rates of production, the latter is more often assumed than actually demonstrated. There are many cases where children are given distinctive jobs, jobs never carried out by adults; for example, some of the ancillary work in mining and the more delicate aspects of carpet making. It is striking that these forms of work are often cited among the least acceptable forms of child labour. The exploitative nature of such work makes the boundaries between the different meanings of exploitation insignificant.

See also Accidents; Capitalism; Elimination of Child Labour; Health.

Factory Acts

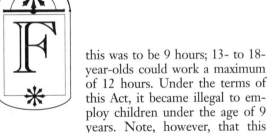

The Factory Acts are a series of parliamentary acts passed during the nineteenth century in Britain to deal with the issue of child labour and with other industrial problems. The traditional view of the industrial revolution in Britain is that it created a system that relied upon children as a main source of labour, most widely and notoriously in the textile industry.

Opponents of child labour took the view that legislation was needed to tackle the problem. It is worth noting that the aim of this legislation was to regulate and control the circumstances under which children worked, not to abolish their participation in the workforce.

The legislation that emerged later became known as the Factory Acts. Most discussions of the Factory Acts start by looking at the 1833 Act. However, this act was preceded by the 1802 Act. The 1802 Act was called "The Factory Health and Morals Act, 1802," and was targeted at apprentices in the cotton and woolen mills. The Act laid down regulations that apprentices must receive tutoring in literacy and arithmetic for the first four years of their apprenticeship, that on Sundays they should receive instruction in the Christian religion, and that they should receive two complete suits of clothes. The Act also stated that male and female apprentices should have separate sleeping quarters and that they should work no more than 12 hours per day. These working hours had to fall between 6 A.M. and 9 P.M.

The 1833 Act established criteria for a normal working day in one industry, textile manufacturing. The Act did this in two ways. First, it stated that the working day must fall between 5:30 A.M. and 8:30 P.M.; night employment was prohibited. Second, it specified the maximum length of the working day. For 9- to 13-year-olds, this was to be 9 hours; 13- to 18-year-olds could work a maximum of 12 hours. Under the terms of this Act, it became illegal to employ children under the age of 9 years. Note, however, that this regulation applied only to textile factories.

Subsequent Acts tended to focus upon redefining the normal working week and the age groups covered by the legislation. The 1844 Act reduced the working day for 8- to 13-year-olds to six and a half hours per day. These hours could be worked in the morning or the afternoon, and this helped to established the half-time system. At the same time, the Act required the tightening of regulations on the provision of certificates of age, the reporting of accidental injury, and the maintenance of an employment register with all employees listed, and of school attendance certificates for child employees.

The 1844 Act still left young persons between 13 and 18 years of age with a 12-hour working day. Agitation grew among reformers for the introduction of the 10-hour working day. The 1847 Act effectively did this by stating the maximum number of hours that could be worked in a week.

The steady accumulation of factory legislation did lead to some anomalies emerging between the Acts. For example, the 1844 Act specified that the working day must fall between 5:30 A.M. and 8:30 P.M. The 1847 Act specified that employees should work a 10-hour day but did not specify for young people when these hours should be worked. Employers started to manipulate the system by using the "relay system" of employment. Machinery was kept operating continually by workers employed at different times during the full working day. The 1850 Act sought to combat this practice by redefining the working day. In summer this would be from 6 A.M.

to 6 P.M., and in winter, from 7 A.M. to 7 P.M., with one and a half hours scheduled for meal breaks.

The Factory Acts up until this time had been targeted at employment in the textile industry. The 1867 Factory Extension Act extended the regulations to children and young persons employed in any manufacturing establishment that employed 50 or more workers.

The remaining two Acts were passed in 1874 and 1891 and introduced relatively minor changes. The 1874 Act reduced the working day by half an hour; however, the reduction applied only to textile factories and reflected the establishment of an effective trade union movement in this industry. In addition, the 1874 Act changed the minimum age of employment from 8 years to 10 years. The 1891 Act introduced tighter regulations on safety barriers on machinery and raised the minimum age at which a child could work, from 10 to 11 years.

What was the effect of this legislation on children's work in factories? The traditional interpretation is that the Factory Acts, enforced by factory inspectors and with social reformers continually amending the Acts throughout the nineteenth century, led to the reduction of child labour. It did this by making it less economically viable for manufacturers to employ children. In order to obey the law, employers had to have certificates of age and of education and had to keep logs on accidental injury, all of which reduced their profits. The regulation therefore led to the reduction of child labour.

A reduction did take place; but one might well question the extent to which the Factory Acts were responsible for it. Clark Nardinelli, an economic historian, has suggested that child labour levels may have fallen because of supply and demand factors. In economics the availability of a resource is influenced by the interaction of the availability of that resource (supply) with the extent to which people want that resource (demand). The demand for child labour fell, according to Nardinelli, because of technological change.

Two examples of such technological change can be given. Firstly, the move from water to steam power allowed for the relocation of manufacturing centres. With water power, many factories were placed in the countryside, close to fast-flowing rivers. In such places the available adult labour force was limited, and children were employed as an alternative. Steam power allowed factories to locate closer to urban centres and a larger pool of adult male and female employees, reducing their need for children. Secondly, improvements in technology, such as the self-acting spinning mule, reduced the demand for children. The invention of the self-acting spinning mule reduced the incidence of thread breakage during spinning; children traditionally had been employed to fix such breakages.

On the supply side, Nardinelli suggests that children were removed from the labour force because the nineteenth century was a period during which real incomes grew. According to this argument, children worked because of family poverty; therefore, as the real income of the adults in the family increased, the need for children to contribute to the family income declined. Children were removed from employment as it became more possible for families to invest in children as a future resource, through education.

That such different interpretations exist simply shows us that it is difficult to isolate one factor in any discussion about the reduction of child labour during the nineteenth century. Yet we should not lose sight of the extent to which the Factory Acts embodied and reflected a changing set of attitudes toward the use of children in the labour force.

See also Factory Inspectors; Family Wage; Half-Time Working.

References Nardinelli, Clark, *Child Labor and the Industrial Revolution* (1990).

Factory Inspectors

The 1833 Factory Act in Britain introduced restrictions on the use of children within textile factories. To ensure that factories complied with legislation regulating working hours and the minimum working age, the government appointed four factory inspectors.

The inspectors produced reports of their visits to individual factories, and these are valuable sources of information about child labour throughout the nineteenth century in Britain. For example, the Report of the Inspectors of Factories for 1878–1890 provides information on the number of children employed in textile manufacturing. It shows that during the period 1835–1838, when the inspectors started to enforce the legislation, the number of child employees in textile factories fell from 56,000 to 33,000.

Such figures might lead us to believe that the inspectors were effective in implementing the legislation. However, we should be cautious in this interpretation because there is also evidence that employers were willing to cheat. Since children had to be at least 9 years old to work in a textile factory, they needed proof of their age. It was not uncommon for false certificates to be obtained. Employers and parents alike were involved in such practices, since both gained from having the child employed.

One inspector's report from 1850 is interesting because it shows the lengths to which employers went to deceive the inspectors. When a particular factory was being inspected, no underage children were in evidence. However, the inspectors' suspicions had been aroused because one of the owners had witnessed their arrival at the factory and had run ahead of them. A return visit, prompted by an anonymous letter, revealed that underage children had been hiding in the rest rooms.

Such examples demonstrate the importance of the factory inspectors in enforcing the legislation, and resonate with modern-day discussions. Many today believe that legislation on child labour will be effective only if resources are made available for inspectors.

It is a frequent complaint made by organizations throughout the world that in many countries the legislation on child employment is ineffective either because too few inspectors are appointed or because poor rates of pay leave them open to bribery.

See also Apparel Industry Task Force; Factory Acts.

References Nardinelli, Clark, *Child Labor and the Industrial Revolution* (1990).

Fair Labor Standards Act

This United States federal act is also referred to as the Black-Connery Wages and Hours Bill. In the early 1900s, several attempts to introduce federal legislation to control child labour in the United States failed because they were deemed unconstitutional. The 1930s saw the efforts of interested parties being focused on introducing amendments to the Constitution to allow child labour legislation. These attempts also proved fruitless, and an alternative strategy emerged. President Franklin D. Roosevelt, although he favoured child labour regulation, also wanted to enact minimum-wage and maximum-hours legislation. The strategy he adopted combined all these elements together. The Fair Labor Standards Act, passed in 1938, produced the first success at introducing federal legislation on child labour. Child labour was defined as "the employment of children under sixteen, or the employment of children under eighteen in occupations designated as hazardous by the Children's Bureau." Although activist groups such as the National Child Labor Committee would have preferred to see a separate act on child labour, they did support this Act.

The Act is considered a milestone in American legislation on child labour, but it had several weaknesses: Firstly, children who worked in agriculture were exempted from the regulations when they were not legally required to be at school. In other words, if a state's legislation did not require children to be at school, they could be employed in farm work. And during the summer months, when many children normally required to be in school could legally be employed in agriculture, the legislation also did not apply to them. Another weakness emerged in that some firms who employed children to handle but not to produce goods were able to escape the law. Employers of "newsboys" also escaped the legislation, since the children worked on the street and not in factories. The Act did bring limited success, however. It is estimated that in 1938, 850,000 children under 16 years of age were working and that only 6 percent of them were in jobs covered by the Act.

The Fair Labor Standards Act was an important step in the right direction, and it was the first child labour legislation in the United States to withstand legal challenges to its validity. In 1941, the U.S. Supreme Court upheld the legality of the Act, thereby clearly establishing the power of Congress to legislate to protect employed children.

See also Legislation; National Child Labor Committee.

Fair Trade

Various nongovernmental organizations have committed themselves to fair-trade principles and agreements. Bodies such as Oxfam, Cathoaid, and Traidcraft, for example, argue that many multinational corporations have exploited the resources and labour of many developing countries for their own direct benefit. The natural resources of countries, their foodstuffs and various raw materials have been extracted, using cheap local labour, and transported to the economically advanced economies, where they are sold at prices that provide the companies with very high rates of profit.

The aims of fair trade organizations are primarily twofold: first, to draw attention to the exploitation of labour in the developing economies, the rates of pay and conditions workers face, and the use and abuse of child labour (either directly or indirectly) by multinational corporations; and

secondly, to provide goods for sale in the advanced economies that are purchased directly from producers in the poorer countries of the world. Profits are directed back to the producers, with the aim of supporting sustainable development. For example, tea, coffee, jelly, cereals, and various crafts are sold in this way.

The fair trade position on child labour reflects the complexities of dealing with the issue in the modern world. Advocates of fair trade argue that the employment of children in many economically underdeveloped countries is a direct consequence of family poverty. Hence, to stop consumers from purchasing goods made by children or to impede the use of child labour will actually only make children's situation worse in the short term. They argue that child labour can be effectively dealt with only when poverty is addressed; hence, sustainable development is the long-term solution to poverty, exploitation, and child labour.

See also Multinational Companies; Product Labelling; Rugmark.

References Durai, Jayanti, *Helping Business to Help Stop Child Labour* (no date).

Family Relations

Parent-child relations and the dynamic relations within families have always been an attractive area of study for social scientists, who have studied the changing relationships between parents and their offspring as children move through childhood and adolescence. Issues such as parent-child conflict are often discussed, but such conflict is only one part of the complex interplay of dynamic family relationships.

During the 1980s a number of researchers in the United States started to consider the impact of part-time work on family relations. Sheila Cole found that children who work spend less time with their families. However, we cannot assume that a reduction in time spent with family members of necessity will have a negative effect; quantity does not equate with quality in relationships.

Research findings suggest two opposing interpretations of the impact of part-time work on parent-child relations. Authors such as Laurence Steinberg and Sanford M. Dornbusch argue that employment removes children from important parental contact. Wendy D. Manning also believes that work affects the quality of relations. For Manning, work leads to greater conflict between children and their parents over household chores, money, and school, among other commonly contested areas.

One might well argue that independence and autonomy fostered by employment are at the root of such conflict. Parents may feel uncomfortable with their child's increasing independence, at the same time as the working adolescent wants more independence from his or her parents. Such an argument would have to be developed to accommodate for parents and children who adjust successfully to the impact of employment on their relationship.

That some parents and children do adjust to the impact of work on their relationship is supported by the work of Jeylan T. Mortimer and Michael J. Shanahan, who have a different view of the impact of work on such relations. Mortimer and Shanahan found no negative effects when they compared parent-child relations among groups of working and nonworking adolescents. On the contrary, they found evidence that father-son relations improved due to this type of employment experience.

Such outcomes may emerge if the adolescent views work in a positive light and if the parents accept and encourage employment as making a positive contribution to their child's development.

This discussion of parents and their children who work part time is based on research conducted in economically developed countries and does not necessarily apply to family relations in countries where it is common for children to work full time. In such circumstances the child's economic contribution to the family can be essential to the family's survival. There is some suggestion that children who perceive their work as contributing to the family gain a degree of self-worth from this realization. One must also note that parents' differential treatment of children may create problems. For example, if parents encourage one child to work and one to attend school, this might have an impact on family relations. In rural society, children's earnings are more likely to go to the family, providing adolescents with a sense of worth and leading parents to acknowledge the important role of the child in the family.

See also Adolescence; Costs and Benefits.

References Cole, Sheila, "Send Our Children to Work?" (1980); Manning, Wendy D., "Parenting Employed Teenagers" (1990); Mortimer, Jeylan T., and Shanahan, M. J. "Adolescent Work Experience and Family Relationships" (1994); Shanahan, M. J., Elder, G. H., Burchinal, M., and Conger, R. D., "Adolescent Earnings and Relationships with Parents: The Work-Family Nexus in Urban and Rural Ecologies" (1996); Steinberg, Laurence, *Adolescence* (1993).

Family Wage

There are two significant meanings attached to the concept of a "family wage." The first refers to payment for work that emerged in the early stages of the development of capitalism and the creation of a free wage labour force. There was a degree of social conflict over the mechanisms of paying wages to workers. In the earliest era, that of "proto-industrialization," piece-rate wages would be paid to the artisan, craft worker, or head of family on completion of the work task and they would distribute wages to those workers who had taken part in the production process. In essence, the skilled worker became a subcontractor of labour. Payment from the trader or merchant was a return on the labour of all those who had taken part in the work, and it was generally in the family's interests to try and ensure that as much of this money remained within the family as possible, although non–family members would be hired if the family could not fulfil its labour needs. The entire family—men, women, and children—

would take part in the production process, and the wage payment became in essence a family wage rather than an individual wage. This form of payment was common in the cottage industries in the proto-industrial period, and in mining, well into the nineteenth century. Indeed, even in the economically advanced countries there were still instances of this form of payment existing in the factory setting well into the twentieth century. In economically underdeveloped countries it is not uncommon today in the less well-regulated sectors of the economy.

The question of a family wage also relates to a set of debates about wages and family form in the mid-nineteenth century. In Britain, for example, the overall effect of the industrial revolution and urbanization was to undermine the family workforce. Employers now hired individuals, not families or skilled workers who would subcontract the subsidiary tasks to other workers. Men, women, and children were sucked into the labour market as individual wage earners, each hired by employers to do specific tasks. In many industries the consequence was overstock in the labour market—that is, a surplus of potential workers—and hence, lower wages. This had a detrimental impact on working-class families, which increasingly struggled to earn enough to meet their needs. A vicious circle formed. Inadequate income forced even very young children into the labour market and compelled all family members to work longer hours. This created even greater problems for family life, which according to Friedrich Engels in *The Condition of the Working Class in England*, began to disappear in certain working-class districts. However, such problems also affected the employers of the time. Long hours, poor nutritional standards, inadequate sanitation, and poor living accommodation affected both the health and the productivity of labour.

These pressures on employers and employees alike started a process that saw the re-creation of the working-class family. For the working class, reestablishing the family meant agitating for a family wage. This was to be a wage earned by a man, but large enough to support women and children in the home. The consequences were, it was hoped, that children and women would be removed from the workplace, women could concentrate on domestic labour (washing, cleaning, cooking, and child rearing), and children would be spared the "vice of the factory." For employers, the family wage would reinforce family values and create a stable institution where labour reproduction and socialization could be generated. Patrick M. Horan and Peggy G. Hargis, in their study of children's work and schooling in the United States in the late nineteenth century, found a positive relationship between a family's resources and the participation of its children in schooling and a negative relationship between family resources and the children's involvement in work.

The events surrounding the demand for a family wage are fiercely debated. Some feminist historians, such as Heidi Hartmann, suggest that the creation of the family wage reflected a "patriarchal agreement" between two sets of men, employers and employees. She suggests that men saw it as in their interests to expel women from the labour market and force them into the isolated world of the family home. Such a process brought benefits to capitalism as a system, since the production and socialization of new generations of workers were carried out by women for free, with no associated costs for employers. Working-class men became confirmed as the most powerful individuals within the family and found their lifestyle improved by the free domestic labour provided by women.

In contrast, Marxist historians, such as Lindsay German, have argued that although both the working class and the employing class supported the restoration of the family, they did so for different reasons. In working-class communities, the demand was supported both by women and by men who thought it would improve the material living standard of the entire family. The attraction of the demand was that it seemed to offer the possibility of easing many immediate material problems facing working-class families in the mid-nineteenth century. By reestablishing the family, mothers would be freed to care for children and protect them from the horrors of child labour that had existed in the early industrial period. Men would concentrate on work, including overtime if necessary, to earn sufficient funds to support the family. Women could engage in domestic labour, improving life for family members and possibly earning extra money by supplementary activities such as taking boarders into the family home. Nevertheless, these theorists argue that the consequence of this process was to more firmly lodge women and children within family structures and increase their oppression.

A third group of historians, such as Michelle Barrett and Mary McIntosh, have pointed out that although the family wage demand was central to reestablishing the family and women's inferior position within it, the family wage was rarely achieved by working-class men in practice. For Barrett and McIntosh, the demand failed because women still had to enter paid labour or to combine domestic labour with money-earning activities.

The demand for the family wage and the re-creation of the working-class family in the United States in the late nineteenth century did coincide with a significant reduction in the involvement of children in the labour market. Because of the lack of research into the relationship between the family wage and the role of children in labour in the United Kingdom, we cannot be sure that the same process took place there.

References Barrett, Michelle, and McIntosh, Mary, "The 'Family Wage' Debate: Some Problems for Socialists and Feminists" (1980); German, Lindsay, *Sex, Class, and Socialism* (1989); Hartmann, Heidi, "The Unhappy Marriage of Marxism and Feminism: Towards a More Progressive Union" (1981); Horan, Patrick M., and Hargis, Peggy G., "Children's Work and Schooling in the Late Nineteenth-Century Family Economy" (1991).

Feminism

Feminism is a social theory that argues that women are systematically disadvantaged in all spheres within modern societies. Modern feminism was greatly stimulated in the 1960s by the civil rights movement in the United States. In turn, feminist analyses of society have influenced thinking about the problems of childhood, including child labour. Ethnic minorities, women, and children may all be seen in some sense as oppressed groups in contemporary society. It is not surprising, therefore, that issues relevant to one group, namely women, will be seen as important for another, that is children.

According to feminist analysis, political, social, economic, and cultural activities in the modern world devalue women's roles and actions and assume their main activity to be within the home, as mothers and wives. Feminism questions these assumptions and women's exclusion from public life. At the same time, feminism offers a political approach that can challenge the dominant structures of male power and authority. Feminism is thus both a philosophy and a political ideology.

Like most philosophies and political movements, feminism consists of different strands. It is possible to broadly identify three groupings. The first we will describe as liberal feminism. Liberal feminism has a substantial history. Its main aim is to establish equal rights for women with men in all areas of social life, equal rights to and within education, equal access to all forms of paid employment at all occupational levels, and equal access to positions of authority—political, economic, cultural, and other. The main vehicle for ensuring equality is state activity. Liberal feminists support equal rights legislation, call for the state to outlaw direct and indirect discrimination, and promote monitoring groups and nongovernmental organizations whose purpose is to enhance equality of opportunity. The main concern of liberal feminists, then, is the public sphere and utilizing government action in this area to obtain equality. However, their reliance on the state and on governmental action to promote and defend women's rights has attracted criticism from other feminists, as has their apparent failure to address concretely issues of home and family life.

For socialist feminists, the state is not a neutral arbiter but is tied in with the interests of business and the capitalist economic system. Socialist feminists attempt to place the position of women in society within the context of conventional socialist critiques of capitalism. There are, of course, many variants of socialism. However, a socialist feminist analysis commonly stresses that women's position cannot be understood as a dimension of capitalism alone but rather is a feature of patriarchal capitalism. Socialist feminists argue that women play a particular role in both biological and social reproduction. Their unwaged domestic labour within the home is a subsidy to capitalism because it reduces the cost of reproducing workers—that is, it feeds, clothes, and houses today's workers and raises future generations of workers. But such unpaid labour also directly benefits men within the home, who are serviced by their wives in this unequal relationship. Women's assumed dependence within the family depresses their own earning capacity and restricts their opportunities in the labor market. The low pay they receive as a consequence reinforces their dependency on marriage. Socialist feminists perceive a symbiotic relationship between capitalism and the family.

Radical feminists approach the position of women within society in terms that are critical both of liberal feminists and of socialist feminists. Like socialist feminists, they reject the notion that the state can protect and look after the interests of women. For radical feminists, however, this is not because it is a capitalist state but because it is a patriarchal state, the protector of male power in all its manifestations throughout society. Radical feminists are also critical of socialist feminists who suggest that class differences within society may lead men and women of the same class

to have common interests; instead, they see all women as having a similar social position, being oppressed by all men as a group. The major cleavages in all societies both today and historically have been between men and women, with the constant feature in all societies being women's oppression by men. For radical feminists, the roots of this oppression lie in biology. Radical feminists argue for separatism: for women's self-organization, independence, and liberation from men.

The conclusions of each of these approaches are radically different, although as feminist approaches they do share some things in common—for example, the perception of women's unequal position in modern society, and for many, a rejection of traditional male hierarchies and modes of living, working, and researching. Recently some writers on childhood have suggested that the concerns, mode of analysis, and approach of feminists are appropriate for the study of childhood and children's position in the world. In essence, it is claimed that patriarchal authority, adult male power in all its manifestations, oppresses children as well as women. It defines their roles in relation to, and as subservient to, those of adult men. Thus feminist concerns, approaches, and methodologies are now consciously used to underpin some writing on childhood.

See also Family Wage; Gender Differences; Gender Stereotypes.

References German, Lindsay, *Sex, Class, and Socialism* (1989).

Fishing

In industrialized countries, our impressions of fishing are tied to images of deep-sea vessels and an awareness that fishing is now a high-technology industry. However, in many countries, fishing is more basic, and there is evidence that children are employed within this sector.

The International Labour Organisation (ILO) has recently highlighted the participation of children in deep-sea fishing in

Mary, an eight-year-old oyster shucker in Dunbar County, Louisiana, 1911 (Lewis Hine, Library of Congress)

Asia. In countries such as Burma, Indonesia, Thailand, and the Philippines, children between the ages of 10 and 15 years are employed on fishing ships. Their task is to dive down to the coral reefs and bang upon them to scare the fish into the nets. Such deep-sea diving is made all the more hazardous by the absence of protective equipment. The ILO suggests that each fishing ship employs up to 300 boys at a time. Given that the nets are set a number of times each day, there are numerous dives to be made, and children may spend up to 12 hours per day in the water.

In Indonesia, another form of fishing is found that relies upon child employees. Offshore fishing from fixed platforms is common off the coast of the Indonesian island of North Sumatra and employs approximately 5,400 boys between 10 and 15 years of age. The fishing platforms *(jermal)* are usually 2.5 miles from the shore and measure 15 x 65 yards. Children stay on the platforms for three months at a time, the length of a typical contract, lured by the offer of high wages.

The work on these platforms is extremely hazardous. According to reports, work starts at 4 A.M. with the hauling in of the nets, which are then recast. This can happen up to ten times each day. Once the catch is landed, the fish, a small anchovy, is boiled, salted, and laid out to dry on the platform. Conditions on these platforms are extremely poor, and the diet is extremely basic. Needless to say, the promised high wages never materialize. The conditions on these platforms recently attracted the attention of two local nongovernmental organizations (NGOs), which used the press to attract attention to the level of exploitation. One NGO, the Indonesian Child Advocacy Institute (LAAI), sued two fishing platform owners and the local government in the courts. Although the court action failed, it did draw attention to the issue. Another NGO, the Working Group on Urban Social Problems (KKSP), has developed a project to remove children from this form of work. The outcomes of this project are not yet known. Both initiatives have received support from the International Labour Organisation.

See also International Labour Organisation; Projects.

References White, Ben, Tjandraningsih, Indrasari, and Haryadi, Dedi, *Child Workers in Indonesia* (1997).

Folks, Homer

In 1904, Homer Folks was appointed to the board of trustees for the National Child Labor Committee (NCLC). Folks was an expert in the field of social welfare, with interests in a wide range of issues, from charities to public health. During his time on the board of the NCLC, Folks was an extremely important force. He chaired the 1909 White House conference on dependent children. One of the resolutions passed by this conference was to create a national children's bureau.

Folks was an advocate of federal legislation on child labour in the early 1900s. In this context it is not surprising to discover that Folks was heavily involved in the scrutinizing and drafting of proposed legislation throughout this time.

In 1935 Homer Folks became chairman of the board of trustees for the NCLC. He remained in this position until 1943, when he resigned at the age of seventy-seven.

See also Children's Bureau; National Child Labor Committee; Zimand, Gertrude Folks.

France

The Republic of France lies to the west in continental Europe. It has a population of almost 60 million people. The constitution has changed several times during the past two centuries. Currently, the head of state is an elected president. France's legislature consists of the National Assembly and the Senate.

As in other countries, industrialization in France was associated with increased use of child labour. However, according to a detailed study by historian Colin Heywood, children played a major role only in a limited number of industries, such as textiles. As heavy industry such as iron and steel production developed, the significance of child workers declined, because the workforce in these industries was made up almost entirely of adult males. The first French legislation on child labour dates from 1841. It arose through the efforts of a relatively small group of humanitarians. Campaigning on child labour in France was never as widespread as in Great Britain, partly because of the slower rate of industrialization in the former. Some enlightened mill owners supported moves to control child labour; in some cases, the mill owners had voluntarily improved the working conditions of children prior to the passing of the law. In contrast, working-class organizations tended to oppose the law. French workers tended to operate in family groups, so any limitation on child employment was seen as a potential threat to the family's joint income. In any case, in France as in other countries, the initial laws on child labour were poorly enforced. However, later laws of 1874, 1880, 1882, and 1892 were backed by adult male workers, and perhaps even more significantly, were made more effective by the formation of a factory inspectorate. Hours and types of work available to children were restricted, and limited provision was made for the education of child workers.

In part the change in attitude among working-class males may have been due to the rise in real incomes that took place as the nineteenth century progressed. As more men became able to support their families by their own earnings, it became less common for women and children to work.

In contemporary France, child employment is controlled by legislation similar to that of other countries in western Europe. Although child labour is generally considered in France as being a global rather than a national problem, there is some reason to believe that illegal child labour exists there. Writing in the magazine *Le Monde de l'Education* in 1979, Danielle Rouard declared that there is a taboo in modern France against admitting the existence of child labour. Her investigations found a family of illegal Yugoslav immigrants, including a small boy, sewing clothes in a backstreet workshop, for a fashion house. The family was paid the equivalent of about one U.S. dollar per hour. Rouard also found children in poor areas producing cheap consumer goods and scavenging for rags and scrap metal. She estimated that hundreds of thousand of children are active on the fringes of the French economy.

See also Europe; Family Wage; Industrial Revolution.

References Heywood, Colin, "The Market for Child Labour in Nineteenth-Century France" (1981); Heywood, Colin, *Children in Nineteenth Century France: Work, Health, and Education among the "Classes Populaires"* (1989); Nardinelli, Clark, *Child Labor and the Industrial Revolution* (1990); Rouard, Danielle, "Enfants au Travail" (1979).

Garment Industry

Historically, production in the garment industry is closely associated with "sweatshop" conditions. Employees do piecework, often in cramped, poorly ventilated spaces and unsafe conditions. They are paid according to units completed, and they receive no side benefits. Their legal rights in the workplace are often disregarded. In the United States, as in many countries at the start of the twentieth century, it was common to find children employed in such establishments.

Conditions at the Triangle Shirtwaist Factory were typical of those in garment manufacturing at this time. In 1911, when a fire broke out in the factory, it took the lives of 146 workers—many of them children. The fire galvanized public opinion in favour of more effective legislation of this industry, particularly relating to child workers.

The International Ladies' Garment Workers' Union (ILGWU), founded in 1900, was actively campaigning against the sweatshop conditions under which adults and children worked. Although tragedies like the Triangle Shirtwaist Factory fire drew public attention to the cause, such tragedies were only one factor leading to the reduction of child employment in this sector. According to Jay Mazur, ILGWU president in 1992, other factors—such as the serious enforcement of labour regulations, and new technology—were also important in removing children from such work. New technology allowed economies of scale to be gained as machinery took over many tasks in garment production, and the need for cheap child labour diminished.

Recent concerns have been raised about the extent to which children in the United States are still employed in the garment industry. One report by Marguerite Holloway notes that in New York City there are approximately 1,500 sweatshops in the garment industry and that child labour violations are found extensively within them.

Children as young as 8 years of age have been found working in such premises. In 1987, nineteen establishments were identified as illegally employing children; in 1988, the figure had risen to 122. The employment conditions are dangerous, with waste products lying around creating fire hazards, machines standing unguarded, and frequent problems with electrical wiring.

As with most industries, the garment sector has an international dimension as well. Many garment producers in industrialized countries complain about cheap imports from developing countries. It can be demonstrated that in a number of countries, child labour is common in the garment industry.

A recent report, *Forgotten on the Pyjama Trail*, looked at the situation of young garment workers in the city of Meknes, Morocco, where between 80 to 100 girls of ages from 12 to 15 years were found working in a single factory. Another example, from Thailand, provides insight into the conditions of child employees in this industry. The case study, reported in the *New Internationalist*, tells the story of one 13-year-old girl. Due to her father's illness she was forced to give up school and move to the city of Bangkok, where she obtained work in a family garment business. She was paid $25 per month, with one-fifth of this being deducted for food and lodging. Typically she worked from 8 A.M. to midnight. Such conditions are to be found in many parts of the world.

See also Apparel Industry Task Force; Meknes; Sweated Labour; Triangle Shirtwaist Factory Fire.

References Holloway, Marguerite, "Hard times" (1993); Mazur, Jay, "Remedies to the Problem of Child Labor: The Situation in the Apparel Industry" (1993); Zalami, Fatima Badry, Reddy,

Nandana, Lynch, Margaret A., and Feinstein, Clare, *Forgotten on the Pyjama Trail* (1998).

Gender Differences

Discussions about child labour tend to cast all children into a single, homogeneous category. By doing this, we fail to appreciate the experiences of work that different groups of children have. Instead, we could compare the employment experiences of children of different ages or of different ethnic groups. We should also ask how gender is reflected in any potential comparison of different experiences of employment.

Researchers in the adult labour market have shown the extent to which male and female occupations and rewards differ. However, the question of whether these differences are reflected in the child employment sector has been largely neglected.

In considering the issue of gender differences, a number of alternative points of comparison emerge. Our starting point will be to consider three key questions. First, are there different numbers of male and female children working? Second, do boys and girls do different types of jobs? Third, is there any differentiation in the rewards they get for working?

These questions pose problems for the researcher. Historically, discussions of child employment have tended to focus on the fact that children worked and have paid less attention to detailing the differences between the sexes. There are, fortunately, some exceptions to this pattern. Hugh Cunningham, a British historian, has looked at the differences in the number of boys and girls working in the period 1850–1911. This material allows us to address our first question. For each decade from 1850 through 1891, Cunningham, using census information, showed that more 10- to 14-year-old boys were working than girls. However, we need to be careful in interpreting this data, since census information from this period may not be complete. Taking the figures at face value, one might conclude that more boys than girls were working. However, these census data did not include information on the amount of household work done by children. Traditionally, girls were far more likely than boys to be involved in domestic work and household chores. It may thus be the case that the number of girls showing up in the census as working outside of the home was limited by the fact that their participation in this form of work was preempted by the demands of their domestic labour.

This pattern appears to have persisted at the global level. UNICEF reported in 1997 that "best estimates" show that 56 percent of all 10- to 14-year-olds who worked in the world were male. However, UNICEF acknowledged that these estimates were based on a limited definition of work that did not include domestic duties. It can be argued that such data lead to underestimates of girls' involvement in work.

Research findings from the past 20 years have tended to paint a confusing picture about the numbers of boys and girls currently working in developed countries. Studies in Britain have produced conflicting results. In some cases males were found more likely to be employed than females. In other studies this pattern was reversed. This possibly reflects different job opportunities in different economic regions. At present no consistent pattern has emerged.

The second question of interest to us is whether gender differences exist in the form of participation that exists for males and females. Do girls and boys do different types of jobs? On this question, the data are far less ambiguous. There is clear evidence that from both a historical and a contemporary perspective, males and females are employed in different types of jobs. There is clear historical documentation reflecting the fact that in nineteenth-century mills and mines the type of jobs children did varied depending on the sex of the child. In the twentieth century this pattern has continued. American researchers have analysed census data from 1940 to 1980 for 16- and 17-year-olds and have

Burmese girls haul bricks at a construction site in Rangoon, Burma, 1996 (Richard Vogel, Associated Press)

shown the different patterns of male and female employment in different sectors. For example, in the 1940 returns, agricultural work was male dominated, while the service sector was female dominated. Over the decades we see a shift away from industry toward service sector employment, reflecting changes in the domestic economy. By 1980, the retail trade is the major employer for males and females. Even here, where males and females are working in the same sector, we see gender differentiation. Males are more likely to be employed in gas stations, and females, in eating and drinking establishments.

The research cited adopted a cross-generational stance, comparing the types of jobs undertaken by mothers and daughters and by fathers and sons, respectively. The data support the view that there is considerable gender stereotyping and that this has existed across generations.

Contemporary studies confirm that sex differences still exist in the types of work done by males and females. From studies performed in Britain it is apparent that more females are more likely to be employed in child care, shop work, and hostelry and catering. Males are more likely to be employed in delivery work, agriculture, and other manual forms of employment. Even where males and females are employed in the same sector, contemporary evidence allows us to argue that it is unlikely that they will perform the same duties. For example, in supermarkets, girls are more likely to be involved in serving customers, whereas males stack shelves and deal with stock issues. More research is needed in order for us to obtain a clear picture of this particular form of gender differentiation.

Interesting insights into the different types of jobs that boys and girls do can be gained from studies based on oral histories. This technique involves interviewing individuals about their past and the events they experienced. Lynn Jamieson and Claire Toynbee used this technique in their research in rural Scotland. They were particularly interested in the experience of childhood in rural communities between 1900 and 1930. It is apparent from these studies that gender differentiation existed in the types of employment and domestic duties carried out by male and female children.

It is worth bearing in mind that many of the world's working children today live in rural, agricultural-based communities. Female children still carry the burden of domestic and child care duties in a range of developing economies. This tendency, according to Jo Boyden, a leading commentator on contemporary child labour, is accentuated by the gender divide in education. Although citizens in economically developed countries take for granted ease of access to education for both males and females, in many developing countries families direct only their male offspring into education. The cost of females attending school is too great, given that the family would lose the child's domestic labour.

The third question to be addressed was related to remuneration: Are males and female child workers paid the same amount? From a historical perspective, this question is difficult to answer. The main problem is that males and females traditionally have carried out different tasks, and therefore it could be argued that differential pay has reflected the different tasks done. However, if females were more likely to be employed in tasks that paid less, then indirectly some differentiation of rewards from work exists.

Contemporary research on pay rates for male and female workers is often lacking from research reports. In Britain, a number of researchers have argued that different rates of reward can be identified. Hourly rates of pay for boys tend to be higher than those for girls, with a higher percentage of girls found in the lowest hourly pay categories. However, it must be acknowledged that more research is needed before we can answer this specific question accurately.

In both historical and contemporary experience, differences are apparent in the types of jobs performed by girls and boys who work, but we have yet to fully elucidate the extent and consequences of this differentiation.

See also Domestic Service; Gender Stereotypes.

References Aronson, Pamela J., Mortimer, Jeylan T., Zierman, Carol, and Hacker, Michael, "Generational Differences in Early Work Experiences and Evaluations" (1996); Boyden, Jo, *The Relationship between Education and Child Work* (1994); Desmardis, Serge, and Curtis, James, "Gender Differences in Employment and Income

Experiences among Young People" (1999); Hobbs, Sandy, and McKechnie, Jim, *Child Employment in Britain: A Social and Psychological Analysis* (1997); Jamieson, Lynn, and Toynbee, Claire, *Country Bairns: Growing Up, 1900–1930* (1992); Lavalette, Michael, *Child Employment in the Capitalist Labour Market* (1994).

Gender Stereotypes

Stereotyping has been defined by psychologist Richard Gross as "the general inclination to place a person in categories according to some easily and quickly identifiable characteristic such as age, sex, ethnic membership, nationality or occupation, and then to attribute to him qualities believed to be typical to members of that category."

Psychologists have been interested in stereotyping because our expectations of others will influence our behaviour toward them, and our behaviour may influence the way they behave in such a way that they simply confirm our stereotype.

Many "commonsense" stereotypes exist: For example, fat people are jolly; redheads lose their tempers quickly; and people with their eyes close together are not to be trusted. Not surprisingly, such stereotypes are more mythical than factual, but they serve to demonstrate the concept.

Many stereotypes exist around the topic of gender. Gender role stereotypes are based on beliefs about what males and females are supposed to be like, what are the "natural" differences between them, and what type of behaviour is appropriate to each. Eleanor Maccoby and Carol Jacklin examined many gender stereotypes in *The Psychology of Sex Differences*, and the interested reader may refer to their book for further details.

Here we will examine to what extent gender stereotypes are reflected in the forms of work that males and females do. In the adult labour market, the past three decades have seen some breaking down of the barriers between "men's jobs" and "women's jobs." Such occupational barriers were based in part upon societies' stereotypes of males' and females' pre-

sumed strengths and weaknesses. Academic scholars continue to debate the extent to which changes in the gender mix in particular occupations reflect a shift in societal stereotypes in recent decades.

It can be argued that gender stereotypes exist also in the area of child employment. Historical and contemporary research shows that boys and girls were and are employed in different types of jobs. Such differentiation reflects common, stereotyped assumptions of the particular abilities of males and females. Let us take an example that can be found around the world: child care. In virtually every society, child care is considered a female job. This reflects stereotypical assumptions that females are the more "caring" members of our societies. In the developed economies, many girls' early employment opportunities are in baby-sitting. Research in Britain has shown that this job is usually done exclusively by females. Researchers in the developing economies have argued that child care and domestic duties tend to fall onto the shoulders of girls and that this limits their employment and educational opportunities.

The argument could be extended by looking at other areas of work, such as the service sector—in particular, at waiting on tables in eating establishments, a form of employment that is dominated by females. Employers may be more inclined to employ females in these types of jobs since they believe them to be more sociable than male adolescents or to have better customer skills than males.

Stereotyping can create a number of social problems, including:

(i) overestimation of differences between groups;

(ii) underestimation of the extent of variation among individuals in a group;

(iii) failure to question stereotypes.

In the context of employment, stereotyping can constrain the opportunities offered to individuals. The danger is that the child employment market might introduce children to gender stereotypes in the workplace at an early age, leading them to accept such constraints as "natural," and possibly depressing their future employment aspirations.

See also Domestic Service; Gender Differences.
References Barling, Julian, and Kelloway, E. Kevin (eds.), *Young Workers: Varieties of Experience* (1999); Gross, R. D., *Psychology: The Science of Mind and Behaviour* (1990); Maccoby, Eleanor, and Jacklin, Carol, *The Psychology of Sex Differences* (1974).

General Agreement on Tariffs and Trade (GATT)

See Globalization.

General Federation of Women's Clubs

Formed in 1890, the General Federation of Women's Clubs grew to have a membership of around several thousand in the United States by the turn of the century. Members of the organization often spoke out on public issues. The organization brought the issue of child labour to the fore in 1898, when at its fourth biennial conference a resolution was adopted calling for the end of child labour. It went on to create a Child Labor Committee at the turn of the century that resulted in local groups producing their own child labour committees to continue the fight for lasting child labour laws.

Germany

Contemporary Germany first took shape in 1866 as the North German Confederation, a group of independent states dominated politically and economically by Prussia. In 1871, following Prussia's victory over France in the Franco-Prussian War, the King of Prussia was proclaimed Emperor of Germany. The Empire survived until 1918, when World War I ended in defeat for Germany. Out of a period of political, social, and economic unrest, a powerful right-wing political force developed—the National Socialists, or Nazis, who led the country into World War II.

Following the Nazis' defeat, Germany came under the control of four of the victorious allies—the United Kingdom, France, the United States, and the Soviet Union. When these four allies passed control of the country back to the German people, two separate states emerged: a parliamentary democracy known as the German Federal Republic, and the German Democratic Republic, which allied itself with the communist bloc in Eastern Europe. The country was reunited in 1990. It has a population of more than 80 million.

The industrial revolution in Germany came somewhat later than it had in Britain, Belgium, and France. There was public awareness of large-scale employment of children in the textile industry as early as 1818; but the first Prussian law to restrict child labour was not passed until 1839, because politicians were anxious not to hamper industrial growth. This law had little impact and was followed by a somewhat more effective one in 1853. The law of 1853 was enforced in some areas but not in others, and legislation in other German states lagged behind that in Prussia. Alongside this rather weak legal approach, a strong humanitarian movement emerged that sought to improve the lives of working people by voluntary means. For example, the King of Prussia helped to set up the Central Society for the Welfare of the Working Classes. The German Empire adopted and strengthened the Prussian child labour laws. Enforcement became stricter with the setting up of an Industrial Code in 1891, by which time Germany was the leading industrial power in Europe.

In Germany today, the Kinderschutzbund (an organization dedicated to the protection of children) estimates that about half a million children are currently working. According to the authors of a recent investigation in the federal state of Hessen, about 50 percent of the children work illegally. Children younger than 14 years, and school-age children generally, are not allowed to work under German law, although there are some exceptions: Young people of 13 years and older can do light agricultural work during the day or distribute newspapers, provided that their

Glass factory worker, Alexandria, Virginia, 1911 (Lewis Hine, Library of Congress)

work does not interfere with their performance at school.

See also Europe, Eastern; European Union.

References Nardinelli, Clark, *Child Labor and the Industrial Revolution* (1990); Vuzina, Dialehti, and Schaffer, Heiner, *Kinderarbeit in Europa* (1992).

Glass-Making Industry

This sector of American industry was responsible for some of the worst child employment practices in the United States in the late nineteenth and early twentieth centuries. It is estimated that around 7,500 boys under 16 years of age were employed in glass-making at that time. Often these boys were kept at work after dark. They usually worked in the furnace rooms, performing a variety of jobs such as that of blowers' assistant. Consequently they had to endure particularly high temperatures and glaring light for hours on end. The temperature in glass-making factories typically ranged between 100 and 130 degrees Celsius. There was thus a high level of illness, with conditions such as pneumonia, rheumatism, tuberculosis, sleeplessness, headaches, and exhaustion being widespread. The most common injuries, however, were cuts and burns, many of which were obtained from the broken glass that continually covered the floors. It should be noted that it took 14 years (1905–1919) of consistent effort by the National Child Labor Committee to obtain the release of thousands of misused children from work in glass factories.

Unfortunately, similar conditions still may be found today in other parts of the world, such as India.

See also India.

References Trattner, Walter I., *Crusade for the Children* (1970).

Global March against Child Labor

November 1997 saw the launch of the Global March against Child Labor, an organization involving children and adult ac-

Children from different countries, accompanied by adults, lead the march in Quezon City, Philippines, January 17, 1998 (Pat Roque, Associated Press)

tivists throughout Asia, Europe, Africa, and the Americas. The Global March aimed to establish a worldwide movement to promote the rights of children with respect to education and freedom from exploitative forms of work. The sponsoring bodies identified a number of goals that they hoped the organization would achieve. These included the raising of general awareness about child labour; the lobbying of governments to ratify and enforce existing conventions relating to child labour and education; the mobilization of national and international resources to support education for all children; the mobilization of public opinion to counter the social injustices that contribute to child labour; the immediate elimination of the most exploitative forms of child labour; the promotion of positive actions by employers and consumers; and the rehabilitation and reintegration of child labourers.

The Global March was timed to finish in Geneva at the beginning of June 1998, when the International Labour Organisation (ILO) was to meet to discuss a new convention on child labour. Children who were too young to participate actively in the March were encouraged to show their support in a number of other ways. In the United States, the Massachusetts-based Kids Campaign to Build a School for Iqbal, working in memory of the murdered child workers' leader Iqbal Masih, sponsored the Online March, in which children were encouraged to leave messages of support on the Global March page of the World Wide Web.

The international coordinator for the March was Kailash Satyarthi, of India. The steering committee comprised representatives of the African Network for the Prevention of and Protection against Child Abuse and Neglect (Kenya), Anti-

Slavery International (Britain), Education International (Belgium), FundaHao ABRINQ (Brazil), International Labor Rights Fund (United States), Network against Child Labour (South Africa), Novib (Holland), Robert F. Kennedy Memorial Center for Human Rights (United States), South Asian Coalition on Child Servitude (India), and Terre des Hommes-Suisse (Switzerland).

See also Anti-Slavery International; International Labour Organisation; Masih, Iqbal; Nongovernmental Organizations.

Globalization

In the 1990s, *globalization* emerged as a key word in the business world, in political discourse, and in a number of academic disciplines (cultural studies, economics, politics, and sociology, in particular). Unfortunately, there is no common agreement over what the word means. The term is suggestive of a growing trend for the various countries of the world to resemble each other in their social, political, cultural, and economic life. A number of trends are thought to characterize globalization: the spread of liberal democracy; the dominance of the world economy by market forces; the integration of the global economy; the transformation of production systems and labour markets; the rapid expansion of technological change; and the media and consumer "revolutions."

Linked to these trends are a number of other claims. The first is that nations are breaking up and becoming less significant. The second is that states in the modern world cannot control their economies and must follow the dictates of global capitalism and market forces. The third is that multinational corporations are becoming less tied to any particular nation-state. Fourthly, it is claimed that there has been a rebalancing within the world economy, with newly industrialized countries and even some economically underdeveloped countries managing to take part in global production. Finally, it is suggested that in order to attract business and compete ef-

fectively in the new global era, it is necessary to have flexible labour markets utilizing the most advanced technologies and providing competitive labour costs. These six trends and five subsidiary points form the common ground of ideas of globalization. However, each of these claims is, at the very least, open to question. We can see this from the following examples.

First, when we look at the major economies of the world, we find that the majority of companies from those states invest in their own countries. The majority of American companies' investment is in the United States; the same is true of German and Japanese firms. Furthermore, the next-largest investors in these countries come from the same group of advanced economies. Great Britain remains a very important investor in the United States, for example. These patterns of investment are not new and do not suggest any major rebalancing or integration on a world scale.

Secondly, states remain very important economic actors in their own countries. Various states have tried to develop or promote their "national champions" in various areas to become major world players. For example, the aircraft industry in the United States relies on government contracts, protection, subsidy, and promotion, despite the U.S. government's abstract commitment to free-market principles.

Thirdly, the idea that nations are becoming less important does not fit easily with the growing conflicts across the globe relating to national identity. The aftermath of the breakup of the former Yugoslavia is a clear example. However, the social costs of the idea of globalization have been great. A belief in the notion of globalization has led some governments to argue that they must accept the dominant position of international financial institutions. Accordingly, these governments believe that they must cut welfare and social spending and introduce flexible labour markets in order to reduce state spending. The new Labour Government in Britain, elected in 1997, argued that globalization meant they would have to follow these policies.

Some reporters and academics have suggested that one consequence of such policies has been a growth of child labour across the globe. They argue that the spread of market capitalism and labour flexibility has forced employers, particularly in the newly industrialized and underdeveloped countries, to use children as a cheap source of labour power and families to send their children out to work in order to help meet daily survival costs. Further, for the countries involved, stopping child labour means introducing labour rigidities and increasing local labour costs, making it more likely that the company will uproot to another global location, where there are no such rigidities or costs. The idea of globalization, therefore, can promote government inactivity in the face of social problems and a feeling that such problems cannot be solved within the confines of national state policies.

See also Stabilization and Structural Adjustment Programmes.

References Commission on Social Justice, *Social Justice: Strategies for National Renewal* (1994); United Nations Research Institute for Social Development, *States of Disarray: The Social Effects of Globalization* (1995).

Gompers, Samuel

Samuel Gompers (1850–1924) was an American labour leader and lifelong opponent of child labour who was born in England and emigrated to the United States in 1863. Gompers helped to build the foundations of the modern American labour market. He progressed through the union ranks to become the founder and first president of the American Federation of Labor (AFL) in 1881—a position that he held (except in 1895) until his death in 1924.

Gompers's leadership of the AFL and his opposition to child labour could be perceived as somewhat contradictory in view of the fact that he was a cigar-maker. The cigar industry at the time was reliant on home-based production. In New York, about half of all cigars produced were made in homes by nonunionized labour. Whole families were involved in making cigars, and several thousand children were employed in this way.

Although the AFL under Gompers's leadership was opposed to child labour, their ideas on how to tackle the problem changed over time. Gompers spoke out against the first attempt by Senator Albert Beveridge to introduce federal legislation on this issue. Gompers was apparently concerned that this would open the door to a raft of federal legislation on all labour issues.

By 1922, Gompers's position had changed, and he called a meeting of opponents of child labour at the AFL's Washington headquarters. From this meeting the Permanent Conference for the Abolition of Child Labor emerged as a body representing the views of a number of national groups. Gompers, who was instrumental in the formation of this forum, had changed his views on how to tackle the question of child labour. The Conference decided that the only way to address the problem was by constitutional change, which would involve federal legislation.

See also American Federation of Labor.

Great Depression, The

The stock exchange crash of 1929 heralded the Great Depression in the United States. Although the socioeconomic impact of the Depression has been well documented, it is worth noting here the particular effects of economic depression on child employment.

As with all groups during the Depression, high levels of unemployment were found among children. This proved to be a short-term effect. As the Depression continued and employers had to find ways of cutting costs, they turned to children as a source of cheap labour willing to work long hours. In the early 1930s, therefore, sweatshop conditions prevailed in industries such as garment manufacturing. The

Samuel Gompers, ca. 1908 (Waldon Fawcett, Library of Congress)

poor conditions had a positive effect on campaigns against child labour. Suddenly politicians were acknowledging the problem of child employment. However, it should be noted that in many cases their main motivation was to free up jobs for adults.

The National Recovery Administration was established to tackle the crisis of unemployment. It identified and targeted child employment through a system of "codes of fair competition." For example, the code of fair competition for the cotton industry forbade the use of children younger than 16 years in cotton textile mills. It has been estimated that in the last six months of 1933, such codes removed over 100,000 children from industrial jobs.

See also United States of America.

Greece

Greece is situated in southeastern Europe, on the Mediterranean Sea. Although most of the population of over 10 million live on the mainland, the country contains many islands. More than a third of the population live in the capital of Athens and its suburbs. Greece achieved its independence from the Ottoman Empire and became a kingdom in the early nineteenth century. From 1967 to 1974, a military government was in power, during which time the monarchy was abolished. Democracy was then restored, but a referendum rejected the restoration of the monarchy.

Although Greece has natural mineral resources and a developing industrial section, agriculture has a central role in the economy: The country's primary exports are fruit and vegetables. Greece also has an important and growing tourist trade thanks to its attractive climate and scenery and the remains of its ancient civilization.

The state provides free education to all children between the ages of 5 and 15 years, but the system has several weaknesses. In some areas, educational facilities are so limited that students attend school in morning and afternoon shifts. Overall statistics on dropouts are reasonably satisfactory; but in particular areas, the numbers of dropouts are unacceptably high. Because of the laws on compulsory education, the collection of statistics on working children was suspended in 1987. Unfortunately, neither compulsory education nor the halt in data collection guarantees that child employment has ceased to exist in Greece.

Agricultural work is widely conducted in family units. Official figures of unemployment in rural areas are remarkably low. However, this conceals the fact that many of those employed, including children, are working for very low wages, and in some cases, for no direct payment at all, being employed as members of a family group. Previously collected statistics suggested that agriculture and manufacture were the commonest forms of child labour. Some forms of work by children largely escaped official notice. Owners of small businesses sometimes employ individual children for only short periods of time to avoid recording them as employees. Some children are self-employed as street traders. Children also work unrecorded in family businesses and in the tourist trade.

Street children are a noticeable part of the life of many towns. Research shows that they earn a living in a variety of ways, including cleaning car windshields and selling flowers. These children seem in the main still to function economically as part of the family group, and their parents see work on the streets as an appropriate way of contributing to the family income. Some working children are from ethnic minorities, particularly Gypsies and Albanians. Others are ethnically Greek but belong to particularly disadvantaged groups, such as those who have returned to Greece after living in the former communist countries of southeastern Europe.

References Georgopoulou, Helen Aganthonos, and Stathakopoulos, Athanassia, *Child Labour in Greece* (1995); Mendelievich, Elias (ed.), *Children at Work* (1979).

Greenberger, Ellen

Along with her colleague Laurence Steinberg, Ellen Greenberger can be viewed as a key figure in the reemergence of research and debate about children working in the United States. During the 1980s Greenberger and a number of her coworkers published joint research findings highlighting the nature, extent, and impact of employment on American youth. Their efforts culminated in 1986 with the publication of *When Teenagers Work: The Psychological and Social Costs of Adolescent Employment.*

Greenberger's central argument was that assumptions about the benefits of work for children had to be evaluated in the light of evidence. Greenberger perceived that employment could also result in costs and that there was a need to recognize these in any discussion about teenagers' employment.

In 1982 she testified at hearings of the House Subcommittee on Labor Standards on changes to child labour regulations that had been proposed by the U.S. Department of Labor in order "to increase the job opportunities for 14- and 15-year-olds." Greenberger's testimony highlighted the findings from the research programme she was running with Laurence Steinberg, pointing to the potentially negative consequences of long working hours and poor-quality work experiences on adolescents.

Greenberger's work has catalysed research on teenagers' work in the United States, as many of the questions raised by Greenberger and Steinberg are key to policy formation in this area.

See also Costs and Benefits; Steinberg, Laurence.

References Greenberger, Ellen (1983) "A Researcher in the Policy Arena: The Case of Child Labor" (1983); Greenberger, Ellen, and Steinberg, Laurence, *When Teenagers Work: The Psychological and Social Costs of Adolescent Employment* (1986).

Guatemala

The Republic of Guatemala, which has a population of around 10 million, lies in Central America, south of Mexico. Since it

This young boy is stripping bark in Cinchona, Guatemala (OAS)

gained its independence from Spain in 1821, Guatemala has had an unstable political history, including periods of military rule. Although Spanish is the country's official language, many native languages also are spoken there. Guatemala's main export is coffee.

Child labour is widespread in Guatemala. It is estimated that children's earnings make up around 15 percent of poor families' incomes. Three-quarters of paid workers are to be found in rural areas, most of them being employed in agriculture. Children start work as young as 7 years of age, and around a quarter of recorded workers are 12 years old or younger. Two-thirds of children in paid employment are male; but since girls are expected to work in the home, the estimates probably understate the extent of female work. One study of adolescent working girls found that in addition to averaging 40 hours per week at their paid jobs, they worked on average 21 hours per week in their own homes.

Nonagricultural work by children includes jobs in fireworks factories and cereal producing plants. The former is particular problematic because of the risk of explosions and the exposure of the workers to toxic chemicals.

The Guatemalan government spends proportionally less on education than is the general norm in Latin America. Guatemala has well-established private schools, but public education until recently has had a poor reputation. Only around 40 percent of children complete four years of schooling. Over half of those attending school have to repeat at least one year of their education.

Dropping out of school does not necessarily mean that the child is going into paid employment. A survey in 1994 found only about a quarter of dropouts said that they had left school to start a job. The inferior quality of the education and bad relations with the teachers were more common reasons given. However, school dropouts, particularly girls, probably take on more responsibilities in the family home.

A programme called the New Unitary School has had some success recently in improving teacher-pupil relations and reducing the dropout rate. Four hundred schools are involved in the scheme, which is based on a similar project in Colombia.

See also America, Central.

References Salazar, Maria Cristina, and Glasinovich, Walter Alarcon, *Better Schools, Less Child Work: Child Work and Education in Brazil, Colombia, Ecuador, Guatemala, and Peru* (1996).

Half-time Working

First introduced to Britain as a result of the Factory Act passed in 1833, half-time working was a system that developed as a response to the growing campaign against child labour led by philanthropists like Lord Shaftesbury, Richard Oastler, and Michael Sadler, as well as the workers' short-time committees. The intention was to spare children from the rigours of a full working day of 12 or 15 hours and instead combine limited working with a rudimentary education. The system was never universal throughout Britain; there was significant geographical and industrial variation, with half-time working particularly prevalent within the textile industry in the cities of northern England.

The legislation gave birth to a number of "factory schools" built within factory compounds. This in turn promoted the "relay system" wherein children worked a rotating shift pattern, with three children now employed sequentially to do the work previously performed by two. Over a 24-hour period, therefore, three children would work 8-hour shifts. In addition they attended school for 4 hours. Thus the educational requirements of the legislation did not interfere with the operation of the factories.

Half-time working was open to considerable abuse. Some employers kept children on the premises for 15 hours a day by mixing work with meal times, breaks, and school hours. The small number of factory inspectors, only four to cover the whole country, made enforcement difficult.

The Factory Act passed in 1844 tightened many loopholes: Children's working hours were to be continuous rather than fragmented throughout the day; meal times were to be regularized; working hours were to be reduced to a maximum of 5.5 hours per day; and children between the ages of 8 and 13 years were required to attend school for at least three hours per day. The effect of this legislation was again felt in the textile industry. The control of child labour generally remained very haphazard. During the following 30 years, various pieces of legislation were passed relating to the employment of children, the effects of which were to standardize the educational requirements of the 1844 Act.

Half-time working was gradually phased out by compulsory full-time education. The Education Act of 1870 marked the start of this process, but half-time working remained in the textile industry until 1918 and the Education Act of that year.

See also Factory Acts; Oastler, Richard; Shaftesbury, Lord.

References Frow, Edward, and Frow, Ruth, *The Half-Time System in Education* (1970).

Hammond, J. L., and Hammond, Barbara

English historians John Laurence Le Breton Hammond (1872–1949) and Lucy Barbara Bradby (1873–1961) married in 1901. Together they published several influential books on the social and economic history of England in the eighteenth and nineteenth centuries, starting with *The Village Labourer, 1760–1832* (1911), *The Town Labourer, 1760–1832* (1917), and *The Skilled Labourer 1760–1832* (1919). The employment of children features in all of these works. However, it is given particular prominence in their biography of the campaigning reformer *Lord Shaftesbury*.

See also Shaftesbury, Lord.

References Hammond, J. L., and Hammond, Barbara, *Lord Shaftesbury* (1939); Hammond, J. L., and Hammond, Barbara, *The Village Labourer, 1760–1832* (1967); Hammond, J. L., and Hammond, Barbara, *The Town Labourer, 1760–1932* (1967); Hammond, J. L., and Hammond, Barbara, *The Skilled Labourer, 1760–1832* (1967).

Four children pick cotton near Mound Bayou, Mississippi, 1957 (AP/ Wide World Photos)

Harkin Bill

In the latter years of the twentieth century, a number of attempts were made by individual politicians in the United States to introduce legislation banning the importation of goods that were made by children. In 1994 Senator Tom Harkin proposed the Child Labor Deterrence Bill, generally referred to as the Harkin Bill. The bill would have affected the importation of such goods as rugs, sports shoes, footballs, toys, and trinkets. Although the promoters of this bill were unsuccessful on that occasion, their effort did raise the prospect of using such legislation as a instrument for change. The Harkin Bill has been followed by other proposed legislation of a similar type. For example, Chris Smith of the House of Representatives put forward the International Child Labor Elimination Act. At the time of writing, however, none of these bills had been passed.

See also Legislation.

Harvesting

In many countries, school calendars have been structured historically to include a long summer break. Some educationists have suggested that such breaks have a detrimental effect on children's learning, but there are no educational arguments in favour of long summer breaks. Why do they occur? The reason has nothing to do with schooling but everything to do with child labour. Long summer holidays were established to allow children to take part in harvesting on local, or family, farms.

Children have always played a role in harvesting crops. In agricultural and rural locations, the demand for labour is seasonal. The need to bring in the crop as quickly as possible means that harvesting is a period of peak labour demand. In traditional, peasant villages and on many small family farms, the lack of modern machines means that harvesting is labour intensive. In these family economies, harvesting requires all household members to take part in the work process. The hours of peak demand may be substantial, starting early in the morning at daybreak and finishing only when the sun sets in the evening. Nevertheless, in these circumstances the family can determine when breaks should occur, and work pressure is less constant and less intensive than that on more modern, mechanized farms. On modern or larger farms, mechanization has altered the types of work to be done. Production has become more intensive and yield has risen substantially; but along with these developments, labour also has become more mechanized and intensive. Cropping, for example, will often involve workers sitting on trailers, working at picking machines in the fields. Here the pace of work is much more intensive, determined by the speed of the tractor and the machinery. In these circumstances workers resemble factory hands, whose labour is set and controlled by the pace of the machines at which they are working. Despite popularly idealized pictures of harvest employment, this type of labour is often quite intensive and exploitative. Nevertheless, farms at harvest time draw heavily on the labour of children.

See also Agriculture.
References Taylor, R. B., *Sweat Shops in the Sun* (1973).

Health

In recent years discussions relating to child employment have focused upon strategies to target intolerable forms of such employment. This stance is exemplified by the most recent position adopted by the International Labour Organisation. The argument reflects concerns that children face short- and long-term dangers if they are working in certain forms of employment. These dangers can result in accidental injury or can be cumulatively detrimental to the individual's health over the long term. Prostitution is one obvious example, where health risks associated with sexually transmitted diseases are clearly recognized. However, it is also possible to identify a range of health hazards arising in a variety of other circumstances. Some of these hazards are related to the environment that the child is working in, and others are related to the child's stage of development. Children are susceptible to the same work-related hazards as are adults. However, their developmental stage increases their susceptibility. Children, by definition, are not yet fully mature in terms of their physical, psychological, and biological growth. In these circumstances there is a greater potential that a health hazard faced by an adult would be multiplied in its impact on a child. This would be most apparent in relation to work with toxic substances where "at risk" dosages are calculated in relation to adults, yet children are exposed to them as well.

Studies in Egypt show that children are employed in the leather industry and work with a range of toxic chemicals and glues. Exposure to such solvents and glues has been associated with neurotoxicity.

In agriculture children face health hazards from pesticides and a range of other chemical agents. Throughout the world, children are employed in this sector and can be found mixing, loading, and handling pesticides and fertilizers. In the United States, a study by S. H. Pollack, P. J. Landrigan, and D. L. Mallino noted that 48 percent of migrant child farm workers had worked in fields that were still wet from crop spraying. The same study reported that over a third of their sample had been caught in the path of spraying.

In Africa, Asia, and Latin America children are employed in mining, with all the risks known to be associated with this industry. Although these risks include accidental injury, they also involve exposure to dusts and gases that are linked to respiratory illnesses such as silicosis, emphysema, and asbestosis.

In India children work in ceramic and glass factories exposed to intense heat and high noise levels. The impact on their health can manifest itself in terms of impaired hearing, heat stress, eye injuries, and breathing problems due to exposure to silica dust and lead and toxic fumes arising from the production process.

That children face long-term damage to their health due to hazardous forms of employment is obvious. However, we should not lose sight of the fact that even employment in apparently nonhazardous jobs may have hidden health implications. For example, many of the jobs done by children in the United States involve carrying weights, as in the case of delivery and shop workers, yet we do not know the long-term impact this activity may have on the growth of the skeletal structure of these individuals. Valerie A. Wilk has noted that some children engaged in farm work that involved lifting heavy loads reported ailments that resembled degenerative osteoarthritis. There is obviously a need for greater understanding of the health implications of such employment.

See also Accidents.

References Castillo, Dawn N., "Occupational Safety and Health in Young People" (1999); International Labour Organisation, *Child Labour: Targeting the Intolerable* (1996); Pollack, S. H., Landrigan, P. J. and Mallino, D. L., "Child Labor in 1990: Prevalence and Health Hazards" (1990); Wilk, Valerie A., "Health Hazards to Children in Agriculture" (1993).

Herding

Herding has an almost romantic appeal. It conjures up an image of a young boy (usually) tending a few sheep or goats in hills or mountains, in sunny, carefree settings. The tending of animals in rural locations is often the responsibility of children, but it is far from the idealized picture portrayed. The work is hard, long, and potentially dangerous (the child being isolated and away from the community for a substantial period).

On modern farms, children are still involved in tending and moving farm animals. Mechanization means that often the work of feeding and moving will be done from tractors or other farm machines, neither of which are designed to be operated by children.

See also Agriculture.

Hine, Lewis Wickes

Lewis Wickes Hine (1874–1940) worked as a photographer for the National Child Labor Committee and played a crucial role in providing evidence to support the Committee's campaign against child labour in the early twentieth century. Through his photographs, Hine documented the working conditions of children. Many of his photos depicted the problems faced by immigrant children. From 1908 to 1924, Hine produced images of children working in mills, agriculture, canneries, coal mines, glass factories, and a wide range of miscellaneous activities such as furniture manufacturing, shoe industry, and service work throughout the United States.

Hine's work, featured in many publications produced by the National Child Labor Committee, also serves as an important source of nonpictorial data, since he carefully recorded the ages, names, and work duties of the children in his photographs. Examples of his work can be found in Judith Gutman's *Lewis W. Hine and the American Social Conscience*.

In 1954, Lewis Hine's photographs, along with records of the National Child Labor Committee, were presented to the Library of Congress. The Prints and Photographs Division of the Library has catalogued and arranged the material based on subject matter.

See also Immigrant Children; National Child Labor Committee.

References Freedman, R., *Immigrant Kids* (1980); Gutman, Judith, *Lewis W. Hine and the American Social Conscience* (1967).

Lewis Hine documented working conditions for children in many industries, including these coal breakers, ca. 1910–1920 (Lewis Hine, Library of Congress)

History of Childhood

In 1960 Philippe Aries, a French social historian, published his influential work *Centuries of Childhood*. This book spurred the sociological and historical study of childhood. Aries argued that childhood was a social construct, not a biological fact. Although his methodological approach and some of his claims have been shown to be untenable, this work remains a classic in the area of childhood studies.

As a consequence of the publication of Aries's work, a number of historians turned their attention to studying the worlds of children and published several important "grand narratives" of family life and childhood. These studies compare children's roles and activities either across nations or over considerable time spans, relating childhood practices to the effects and influences of social and historical developments such as socioeconomic advances, changing family practices, and the transformation of religious ideas. The study of childhood is used as a prism through which to assess and analyse sweeping societal and cultural changes. Writers in this tradition include Lloyd DeMause, who edited a collection of essays in 1974 under the title *The History of Childhood*; Edward Shorter, author of *The Making of the Modern Family* (1977); and Laurence Stone, who wrote *Family, Sex, and Marriage in England, 1500–1800* (1977).

These broad narrative histories were subject to a number of criticisms, especially by Linda Pollock in her *Forgotten Children* (1983). Pollock argued that these approaches failed to use a wide enough range of primary sources, ignored what children themselves actually said, set out to prove pre-existing theory rather than examining the evidence thoroughly, and as a consequence, depicted childhood as uniformly harsh, oppressive, and exploitative prior to modern industrial society, and parents as essentially brutal in their dealings with their offspring. Pollock's methodological critique is powerful. However, she also develops a controversial thesis, drawing on sociobiological studies that draw unwarranted conclusions about the stability of the family and its isolation from changes in other areas of social life.

Generally, by the 1980s, it was the academic fashion to attack grand theories. A point of view began to emerge that questioned our ability to understand the various factors shaping social development. It rejected the idea that there may be any kind of pattern within history, and it emphasized the fragmentary and complicated character of reality. Instead of grand theories, it was suggested that all we can ever obtain is partial knowledge about specific events. These trends provided the impetus for a new history of children and childhood.

Previously in historical research, children's own testimony had been dismissed. But the "new history" set out to listen to "children's voices" and adopted what was described as a child's perspective. As part of this process historians took children's stories, diaries, and records seriously. Further, instead of attempting to provide a broad overview of historical developments, the new history focused in depth on children and their lives in particular periods or locations. The key questions motivating this type of research were: What does the world look like to the child? How do they perceive their role within this world? Who do they interact with (parents, teachers, authority sources, and other children, for example)? What is the role of children themselves in these processes? In other words, rather than present adult views and perceptions of children, there is an attempt to reveal the child as a social actor.

Some important studies in this tradition include Barbara Hanawalt's *Growing Up in Medieval London* (1993); David Wiggins's "The Play of Slave Children in the Plantation Communities of the Old South, 1820–1860" (1985); Lester Alston's "Children as Chattel" (1992); and Anna Davin's *Growing Up Poor* (1996). These scholars gave work a much more prominent place than did Aries in their analyses of children's lives.

See also Centuries of Childhood; Social Construction of Childhood.

References Alston, Lester, "Children as Chattel" (1992); Davin, Anna, *Growing Up Poor* (1996); DeMause, Lloyd (ed.), *The History of Childhood* (1974); Hanawalt, Barbara, *Growing Up in Medieval London* (1993); Shorter, Edward, *The Making of the Modern Family* (1977); Stone, Laurence, *Family, Sex, and Marriage in England, 1500–1800* (1977); Wiggins, David, "The Play of Slave Children in the Plantation Communities of the Old South, 1820–1860" (1985).

History of Legislation
See Legislation, Voices of Children.

Homeworking
See Outwork.

Hotel and Catering Industry
The tradition of providing food and lodging for travellers has a long history. The emergence of this service industry is closely linked to the development of trade routes and of specific, localized markets, as well as the practice of religious pilgrimage. In recent times, the "tourist trade" has also been viewed as a catalyst of growth in local economies.

The provision of hospitality originally was a family-based enterprise, with children naturally participating, as they were part of the family labour force. In such circumstances, children's domestic work extended into work in the family enterprise. We do not have to look far to find examples of the innkeeper's daughter helping in the kitchen or the son working in the stables or as a serving boy.

In modern times the hotel and catering sector has become far more sophisticated, with large business enterprises running chains of hotels. In these kind of establishments, the use of child labour has disappeared. However, we should not assume that children no longer work in this sector. There is clear evidence from around the world that many children are still employed in the hotel and catering sector.

In the developed economies, some researchers have argued that the growth of the service sector has led to the increase in job opportunities for young adolescents. This view is put forward by Ellen Greenberger and Laurence Steinberg, who have asserted that in the United States the rapid growth of the service and retail sectors between 1940 and 1973 led to the creation of 15.8 million new jobs—9.3 million of these in the service sector. It is their opinion that such jobs were ideal for combining work with education, due to their flexibility. Greenberger and Steinberg believed that the growth in part-time employment among 16- and 17-year-olds in the United States was linked to this economic change. To support their argument, they cited the research findings of Lewis-Epstein, who in a 1981 study found that 21 percent of employed high school seniors worked in the food service sector.

Studies in other developed countries also have found that children under the age of 16 years are working in the hotel and catering sector. One study in Britain, carried out in 1993, showed that in the well-known tourist area of the Lake District in England, 20 percent of schoolchildren who worked part time worked in the hotel and catering sector.

In the developing countries it is far more common to find children working in a full-time capacity in this sector. It is difficult to estimate exactly how many children work in this sector in the developing countries, due to the lack of attention paid to this form of employment. One of the few writers who have focused their attention on this sector is Maggie Black, who has ar-

gued that the hotel and catering sectors have become ever more important to the economies of many developing economies and that children increasingly have moved from rural family-based work to this type of employment. Although Black emphasizes the lack of reliable research in this area, she does provide some insight into the scale of employment in this sector. In India, young boys—typically, between 8 and 12 years of age—are recruited in the rural areas and brought to Bangalore to work in the cheap hotels and eating places. They are known as "dhaba boys." In India it is estimated that there are 500,000 such boys, but even these figures are speculative. Black suggests that the total child workforce (under 18 years of age) working in this sector could be between 13 million and 19 million. These figures are rough estimates based on information from the International Labour Organisation (ILO), and they are probably understatements, since they exclude children working in the informal economy.

The lack of information about children working in this sector has been partly remedied in recent years by a serious of small-scale studies carried out by the ILO. These studies, or "situation analyses," took place in Kenya, the Philippines, Mexico, and Sri Lanka. Black used findings from this work in her book *In the Twilight Zone*, to highlight the potential hazards and dangers that such employment creates.

The ILO studies showed that many of the children working in this sector were exploited in terms of payment. Many of the children working in Acapulco, Mexico, were between 7 and 12 years of age and were paid only on a commission basis. In Southeas Asia, a tea-shop boy in Kathmandu earns between 4 and 7.50 U.S. dollars per month.

The child employees also suffer in other ways: They are unable to attend school, and they often work in hazardous and tiring conditions. In the Sri Lankan study, one 12-year-old boy employed in a small lodging house typically worked from 5:30 A.M. to 10 P.M., cooking, cleaning, washing, and preparing rooms for guests.

Children working in this sector also face an additional risk of sexual exploitation. Maggie Black argues that this risk is particularly great for young females, and suggests that many jobs in this sector expose young workers to sexual importunity.

Although it is clear that children have been and continue to be widely employed in the hotel and catering industry, it is far more difficult to be precise about the history or the current state of this form of employment. This is a classic example of the invisible nature of child employment. Recently the ILO and nongovernmental organizations have started to investigate this form of employment, and more reliable information on the nature and extent of such work should be forthcoming.

References Black, Maggie, *In the Twilight Zone: Child Workers in the Hotel, Tourism, and Catering Industry* (1995); Greenberger, Ellen, and Steinberg, Laurence (1986) *When Teenagers Work: The Psychological and Social Costs of Adolescent Employment* (1986); Hobbs, Sandy, and McKechnie, Jim, *Child Employment in Britain: A Social and Psychological Analysis* (1997).

Household Labour

It can be argued that the most common form of work that children do is related to their home environment. Children have always been expected to participate in household chores to some extent. The event is so commonplace that we tend to ignore it when looking at the idea of "work." However, a number of sociologists and psychologists have investigated this issue.

Let us start by looking at some historical examples. In the 1880s, families migrated across and settled in the Great Plains of North America. In a recent book on this subject, the author Elliot West relied on diaries from the period to give an insight into children's lives. It was evident that in such an environment all family members contributed to the family's survival. Children not only worked in helping produce food but also helped in the home environment. West argued that this part of the

children's work was more important than their farm work. Typically, household chores such as cooking and cleaning fell to the female children, whereas boys tended to the animals. Both males and females contributed to supplementing the family food supplies.

Other studies point to the domestic role of urban children at the beginning of the twentieth century. Children were expected to carry out many household duties at a time when modern conveniences were unavailable. For example, the laundry was done entirely by hand, from sorting, washing, and wringing out the clothes to ironing, starching, folding, and putting them away. These tasks typically fell to female children. Other household chores carried out by children included cooking, cleaning, and shopping. Remember that there was no refrigeration at this time, which meant that children had to visit the shops every day as part of their chores.

However, the nature and form of children's household work have not been static over time. Sociologist V. Zelizer, who has analysed the patterns of children's household contributions from 1830 to 1930 in the United States, argues that changes took place in children's household work that were in part rooted in a general change in the concepts of children and childhood. This gradual transformation was based on the replacement of the economic valuation of children by a new view of their intrinsic value. As children came to be seen as gifts to be cherished, childhood began to be sentimentalized. Zelizer believes that given these shifts in cultural ideals, the justification for children's work around the house had to change as well. New emphasis was placed on the developmental value of children's performing household chores: By doing so, it was argued, they would develop a stronger character and would learn responsibility.

Other researchers have focused exclusively on the experiences of contemporary children, considering issues such as the level of variation in children's participation in these tasks according to a particular characteristic (age, gender, class). Parents tend to consider the age of a child in deciding how much work he or she should do, what kinds of tasks should be assigned, and what level of support should be given to the child in carrying out the task. One study carried out in Nebraska in the early 1980s showed that by the age of 9 or 10 years, more than 90 percent of children were regularly involved in chores around the house. In the late teen years, there was a slight drop-off in the level of work done; some studies have shown that for adolescents, household chores and domestic duties often are an area of disagreement with parents. This might stem in part from the fact that many adolescents hold down jobs outside the home.

Gender plays an important role in terms of tasks performed in the house. We saw earlier that even on the American Plains in the 1880s, household labour had some degree of gender division. Recent research shows that such divisions continue to exist. Girls tend to spend more time on household duties than do boys, and they carry out a wider range of tasks, including laundry, cleaning bathrooms, cooking, and general kitchen work. Some tasks show no gender divide. These include the cleaning of your own room and picking up after yourself. These tasks were carried out by males and females alike.

Parents tend to differentiate among certain kinds of chores performed by their children in such a way that girls uniformly perform some and boys others, even at an early age. This differentiation becomes more common among parents with the increasing age of their children. Some research suggests that differentiation by parents between male and female children emerges at around 10 to 13 years of age and is even more marked by 14 to 17 years.

Age and gender are not the only variables that influence the form of household labour undertaken. Socioeconomic status, rural and urban environments, and family composition also have been found to relate to housework patterns. Recent studies have considered the impact of the mother's

participation in the labour force in Western countries as an issue of interest. When both parents are working, it appears that children are expected to pick up some of the household duties. However, these additional burdens fall disproportionately on female children.

As noted earlier, children's domestic work nowadays is often justified by the hypothesis that it fosters positive character traits. One line of scholarly inquiry therefore has been to consider the effect of such work on children's social and cognitive development. Although it is widely believed that children's performance of household chores encourages their development of responsibility, the research evidence does not provide uniform support to this claim. The main effect on children appears to be in the realm of their social development, in what is called "prosocial behaviour." Prosocial behaviour is simply action that shows a positive regard for other people—helping them and looking out for their interests. Children involved in chores that made a difference to the well-being of the family were found more likely to be more prosocial than those who simply tidied up their own rooms.

Household chores also can affect intellectual development. Studies have shown that children exposed to some forms of work develop "tricks of the trade" and strategies to deal with problems. One example shows that children who helped their parents in pottery-making had a better understanding of spatial conservation.

However, negative effects of household chores on children's development also have been shown to exist. It appears that the form and structure of the work expected of children is important. Work that is structured and that has a clear goal, and where support systems are present, is more likely to lead to positive outcomes. There is clearly a need for more research to evaluate the impact of household work on child development.

It is important to place any discussion of children's household labour in the wider context of child employment. It can be argued that household chores are a form of work like any other; however, they tend to be unpaid. More importantly, in the developed countries, many children combine full-time education with part-time work outside of the home and domestic duties in the home. In considering the impact of work, we need to look closely at such patterns.

In developing countries, children face similar burdens of combining multiple roles. It has been argued that a disproportionate burden falls on female children in such settings. Female children take on child-care duties and domestic duties to allow their parents to work. Such duties might well play a role in keeping female children out of school. In many cases, however, the child's contribution to domestic work is vital to the survival of the family.

See also Cultural Traditions; Domestic Service; Social Construction of Childhood.

References Corsaro, William A., *The Sociology of Childhood* (1997); Goodnow, Jacqueline J., "Children's Household Work: Its Nature and Functions" (1988); Nasaw, D., *Children of the City* (1985); Price-Williams, D., Gordon, W., and Ramirez, N., "Skill and Conservation: A Study of Pottery-Making Children" (1969); West, Elliot, "Children on the Plains Frontier" (1992); Zelizer, V., *Pricing the Priceless Child: The Changing Social Value of Children* (1985).

Immigrant Children

In the late 1800s and early 1900s, immigration into the United States was in full swing. Between 1880 and 1920, 23 million immigrants and their families arrived from every corner of Europe. Many faced extreme hardship, and lacking education and skill, found work in low-paying jobs. It was common for whole families, including children, to contribute to the family income.

Although legislation mandated that children under 14 years of age be in school, the law was not enforced, and children were commonly found working. Children as young as 8 or 10 years could be found working in factories, warehouses, and shops. In addition, many children worked in the informal sector, selling newspapers, shining shoes, and running errands. Even those children who did attend school had part-time work in the early morning or the evening or on weekends.

Many immigrant children were involved in outwork, or homeworking, wherein families used the home as a workplace. Outwork tasks performed by children alongside their parents included rolling

Immigrant children making artificial flowers in a New York tenement apartment, 1912 (Lewis Hine, Library of Congress)

121

cigars and sewing clothes. Jacob Riis, a New York City journalist in the late 1800s, photographed many such immigrant children at their work.

The circumstances of this period in the United States have been mirrored subsequently in other countries where immigration has taken place on a large scale. Immigrants tend on the whole to be poor and lacking in the skills needed for success in their new country. They thus tend to find themselves, at least initially, in unskilled work for which the pay is poor. Because of their low incomes, the adults might view their children as a necessary additional source of income. This is particularly the case where immigrants come from rural areas where children traditionally participate in agricultural work.

See also Hine, Lewis Wickes.

References Freedman, Russell, *Immigrant Kids* (1980); Riis, Jacob A., *How the Other Half Lives: Studies among the Tenements of New York* (1997).

India

The large part of Asia that juts into the Indian Ocean is referred to as the Indian subcontinent. Beginning in the eighteenth century, much of the area came under the control or influence of European countries, most notably Great Britain. When Britain negotiated to give up control in 1947, two countries were formed: the secular but predominantly Hindu state of India, and the Islamic state of Pakistan. Relations between the two countries have frequently been strained. The area known as Kashmir was affiliated to India by the decision of its traditional ruler, a Hindu, against the wishes of its predominantly Muslim inhabitants. In 1971, with the support of India, East Pakistan declared itself the independent republic of Bangladesh. India had declared itself a Republic in 1950. Despite often violent political clashes and the assassinations of leading politicians, India has remained a parliamentary democracy since gaining its independence.

The official national languages are Hindi and English, but some states also have other officially recognized languages. India's 900 million inhabitants make it the second-largest country in the world in terms of population. The capital, Delhi, has a population of around 9 million, but Bombay and Calcutta both have populations of more than 10 million. More than two-thirds of the people live in rural areas where agriculture is the main economic activity. The main food crops are rice, wheat, and pulses; and the main cash crops are sugarcane, cotton, tea, and jute. The country also exploits mineral resources and has a variety of manufacturing industries.

It has been suggested that India has the largest number of working children anywhere in the world. However, it should be noted that India is a relatively democratic society and has a free press, which permits uncomfortable facts to emerge about its society. China probably also has a very large population of child workers, but in that country the government maintains tight control over information. What is certain is that the amount of child labour in India is high and that it ranks as a major social problem.

Children can be found working in urban areas and in modern industries. However, it would be misleading to consider these in isolation, since in traditional Indian society work has been considered a normal part of growing up for a child. For example, among the Kamar tribe, who live by a mixture of hunting and cultivation, boys of 7 or 8 years of age are given real, miniature bows and arrows with which to practice the hunting skills they will employ as adults. As they begin to succeed in shooting rabbits and small birds, they acquire status. The children are also given tasks such as herding domestic animals and weaving baskets. By the age of 14 years, they are expected to perform a full range of adult work tasks. When a boy in the Jatapu tribe reaches the age of 6, his father obtains one or two goats for him with the financial assistance of a moneylender. The boy is expected to tend the goats, and the products are divided between the father and the moneylender. Girls about the same age are given household tasks and may also graze animals if there are no boys in the household. Gond children start work by guarding the crops, scaring off monkeys and birds that might eat them. They also collect stubble during ploughing; and when they are older, they undertake the simpler kinds of ploughing themselves. These examples show that work is a natural part of childhood.

In urban areas, children can be found playing a prominent role in trade and service, serving in shops, tea stalls, and restaurants. In some cases the children are self-employed at shining shoes, hawking, and running small stalls. Children are also frequently employed as domestic servants in the towns.

Children are also frequently found in small businesses such as cycle and motor repair. However, the working children for whom activists are most concerned are those employed in factory-like conditions, weaving carpets, making matches, rolling cigarettes, and manufacturing other small consumer products. These children often work very long hours in dark, damp, insanitary conditions. These factors, combined with inadequate diet, can lead to severe health problems.

Around 45,000 to 50,000 children work in the fireworks and matchmaking factories around Sivakasi, in the Tamil Nadu region. Some of the children are as young as 5 years, and all the children work 12-hour days. Their wages vary from 2 to 8 rupees per day, depending on their output. Their work is exhausting and detrimental to their general well-being. They inhale toxic fumes, suffer from intense heat, and are under constant threat of being injured in accidental fires.

In the Uttar Pradesh region, children are widely employed in the glass industry. Thousands of children, mainly boys, work in appalling conditions making bangles and blowing glass. Children in the glass industry work one of three shifts: 8 A.M. to 4 P.M., 4 P.M. to midnight, or midnight to 8 A.M. There are commonly no breaks. The children work with red-hot glass stuck to iron rods that they carry around from work site to work site as the job progresses. The constant mingling of children creates a highly dangerous work environment.

In some parts of the country, debt bondage is a serious problem. In certain rural areas, families can earn wages only a small part of the year. Lack of cash leads them to enter into deals with moneylenders. Children are given work by the moneylender to pay off the family debt. However, the terms of the loan may be such that a lifetime of labour will do no more than cover the interest on the debt, which itself remains outstanding. Thus families may be permanently indebted and their children given no alternative but to do the work they are required to. Sometimes a man may negotiate with the lender to be freed of his debt bond, but only by transferring the liability to his son. These practices are so common in some areas that they may be regarded as central features of the economic life of the communities.

The Bal Mazdoor Union and Bhima Sangha are example of organizations set up to express the views of working children and improve their conditions of life. India also has adult groups concerned with the welfare of working children, The Concerned for Working Children being a notable example.

See also Asia; Bal Mazdoor Union; Bhima Sangha; Carpet Manufacture; Concerned for Working Children, The; Unfree Labour.

References Cadman, Eileen, *No Time to Play: Child Workers in the Global Economy* (1996); Concerned for Working Children, The, *Child Labour in India* (1995); Dube, Leela, "The Economic Roles of Children in India: Methodological Issues" (1981); Lee-Wright, Peter, *Child Slaves* (1990); Mendelievich, Elias (ed.), *Children at Work* (1979).

Indonesia

Indonesia comprises a large number of islands lying between Southeast Asia and northern Australia. The territory includes the whole of Java and Sumatra and parts of the islands of Borneo and New Guinea. Much of this land was colonized by the

Dutch in the seventeenth century. The Dutch remained in control until World War II, when the Japanese occupied the area. The development of a strong nationalist movement led to independence for the Dutch East Indies, rechristened Indonesia in 1949. The population today is about 200 million.

In the nineteenth and early twentieth centuries, child labour was not treated as a social problem in Indonesia. Children worked in family-based agriculture and rural craft production and also as waged employees. Evidence suggests that working children in what was then still a Dutch colony were at least as well off as their counterparts in the Netherlands. After World War I, under the influence of the newly founded International Labour Organisation (ILO), moves were made to restrict and control child employment. However, the regulations introduced by the colonial administration were more lenient than ILO recommendations. For example, the minimum age for considering a worker a child was set at 12 years rather than 14, because "Eastern" peoples supposedly matured earlier. In any case, the inspectors found implementation of the regulations difficult. Sometimes children disappeared when the inspectors entered the workplace. On other occasions, employers claimed that the children had appeared to be older than 12, and they had offered rather vague medical certificates in support of such claims.

The minimum working age was raised from 12 years to 14 on the eve of independence, and this standard was incorporated into the laws of the newly formed Indonesian republic. Since independence, two changes have taken place that have affected the character of child labour. First, as more and more children began to attend school, their availability for employment was limited. Secondly, there was a move toward waged work in large concerns rather than family-based work for children. This latter change seems to have been welcomed by the children concerned and has been associated with a change in lifestyle.

Conflicts arise now between the wishes of parents and those of children. Although younger children generally are involved in part-time work and domestic chores, as they become older they often wish to leave school and enter the labour market. The main advantage from the child's perspective is that he or she has an income and can use it as he or she pleases. There is a disadvantage in this preference for independent earnings, however, because children in Indonesia as elsewhere are in a relatively weak and vulnerable position in the workplace. The need to protect children from exploitation is great.

In 1987, the Ministry of Labor introduced a regulation for the protection of working children. This regulation in effect recognized that work by children under 14 years of age was a reality and in some cases an economic necessity. It therefore stipulated strict conditions under which such children should be employed, including minimum wages, and required employers to cooperate with government agencies to ensure that their child employees had adequate educational opportunities. As with legislation in colonial times, implementation was difficult. Six years after the law was introduced, not a single company had been charged with violations—almost certainly because of failure to detect abuses rather than because abuses did not exist.

Since it had clearly failed, the 1987 regulation was replaced in 1997 by a law prohibiting most forms of child employment. This change seems to have arisen not from developments within the country but from international pressure. In the United States, for example, those advocating a ban on the importation of goods produced by child labour had often cited Indonesia as one of the countries that permitted child labour. The need to appear acceptable to the international community made it difficult for Indonesian authorities to adopt realistic measures to improve the conditions of working children.

See also Asia; Fishing; Projects.
References Mendelievich, Elias (ed.), *Children at Work* (1979); White, Ben, "Children, Work, and

Children working in a textile mill in England, ca. 1835 (Corbis/Bettmann)

'Child Labour': Changing Responses to the Employment of Children" (1994); White, Ben, Tjandraningsih, Indrasari, and Haryadi, Dedi, *Child Workers in Indonesia* (1997).

Industrial Revolution

The industrial revolution began first in Britain, where its onset generally is dated to the 1780s. This was a period when the tempo of industrial production dramatically increased, and when, for the first time, human society was freed from many traditional social and economic constraints.

As a consequence, society was capable of continuous, rapid, and apparently endless multiplication of people, goods, and services. In this sense, although the revolution started in the 1780s, it cannot be assigned a closing date. Since that time there has been a constant revolutionizing of the forces and technologies of production.

Many explanations have been offered for the industrial revolution's having started in Britain, some simple and others more complex. The most common explanations feature the following salient points: An agrarian revolution that dramatically increased agricultural yields was under way at the same time. There were simultaneous demographic changes—in particular, a rapidly growing population. Some explanations stress technological innovation, although many of the pertinent innovations were neither new nor exclusively British. Changing methods of transport and other aspects of economic infrastructure are also cited as having been important. Finally, political developments played a significant role: The Act of Union between Scotland and England in 1707 produced the largest free-trade area in the world at that time.

However, according to economic historian Eric Hobsbawm, many of these elements were also present in other European states; and in some areas, developments were in advance of Britain. This was certainly the case with regard to French superiority in potential for scientific and technological innovation. What Britain had, argues Hobsbawm, were the right conditions. More than a century had passed since the first British monarch had been formally tried and executed. Private profit and economic development had become accepted as the supreme objects of government policy. In other words, the domination of the market system within the British social structure created the conditions for the industrial revolution.

The social consequences of the industrial revolution were dramatic. Population growth and rapid urbanization produced overcrowding, squalor, disease, and early death. At work, wage labour became dominant, but wages were pushed down by the development of new technologies of production. As a consequence, entire families—men, women, and children—were forced to work long hours to meet their financial requirements. Furthermore, control over the pace and organization of work was wrested away from craft workers, embedded in the relentless drive of machines, and enforced, often with extreme brutality, by overseers, managers, and foremen. The exploitation of child labour in this period is seen by some (for example, E. P. Thomp-

son) as one of the most shameful episodes in British history. The competitive drive to create greater and greater profit led factory and mill owners to employ the cheapest form of labour they could find that was able to undertake particular tasks and to increase both the intensity and the period of work. This did not mean that children were employed in all tasks. Their lack of stature, strength, and stamina made them unsuitable for some jobs. Nevertheless, they were employed intensively for 10, 12, or even 15 hours a day in many industrial sectors.

For other social historians, such as Ivy Pinchbeck, the terrible plight of working children during the industrial revolution was no more severe than what they had experienced during the proto-industrial period, in the cottage industries. The difference, Pinchbeck has asserted, was that during the industrial revolution the child labour problem became open and obvious. This in turn motivated action by philanthropists, civil servants, and politicians to eradicate the worst examples of abuse.

See also Factory Acts; Nardinelli Thesis, The; Proto-industrialization; Thompson, E. P.

References Hobsbawm E. J., *The Age of Revolution* (1962); Nardinelli, Clark, *Child Labor and the Industrial Revolution* (1990); Pinchbeck, Ivy, *Women Workers and the Industrial Revolution* (1981); Thompson, E. P., *The Making of the English Working Class*, 2d Ed. (1968).

Industrial Society Thesis

The thesis of the industrial society has developed out of the work of a number of authors and writers going back as far as the French utopian socialist, Henri de Saint-Simon. "Industrial society" is not a precise concept, but its advocates share a number of assumptions. The primary argument is that the most significant change to have occurred in the world has been the transition from traditional societies based primarily upon small-scale and relatively simple agricultural production, to "industrial societies" based upon mechanized production and exchange of goods. This transition is characterized generally as a move from traditional to modern societies, or to modernity. Secondly, this move is portrayed as progressive. Although conflicts may still be embedded within industrial societies, these are counterbalanced, advocates suggest, by the advantages of modernity. These are seen as including economic growth and material affluence, and the breakdown of rigid social hierarchies—such as that between peasants and lords, for example—and their replacement by open and accountable structures with equal opportunity for all. Thirdly, although the transitions from traditional to industrial societies were marked by class conflict in the nineteenth and early twentieth centuries, the modern political system has led to the growth of mass political parties, representative democracy, and the institutionalization of class conflicts. What we have witnessed, so the theory suggests, is the growth and acceptance of liberal democracy as the highest form of governance. In short, self-regulating, market-based economies and liberal democratic political systems bring political freedom and affluence.

Such ideas were particularly dominant in American and British academic sociology before and after World War II. Recent assertions that we are witnessing the "end of history" reflect the continuing popularity of such notions.

Adherents to the industrial society thesis would view child labour as essentially an anachronism, a holdover from traditional societies in which children were viewed and treated rather more harshly than would be acceptable in the modern era. Traditional societies were more brutal, according to this argument, and children were viewed as a family economic resource—which explains why children were widely used in the production process prior to industrialization. For a short period these traditional attitudes persisted; but with the full development of modernism, especially the expansion of open and accountable government, child labour was reduced and more acceptable, modern views of childhood were established. The

continuation of child labour in the newly industrializing or underdeveloped economies can be explained by their failure to fully modernize. Child labour is one, among many, traditional activities that will be eradicated by the further development of marketization and liberal democracy.

The industrialization thesis has been subjected to a number of criticisms. Its implicit assumption that class conflicts are containable in modern industrial societies receives little support from the evidence. The claim that markets are self-regulating has similarly little factual support. The thesis also can be criticized for being Eurocentric—that is, based on West European and North American norms, which it treats as general values and goals applicable to all societies—and for its simplistic and idealized depiction of the eradication of child labour from advanced societies. Child labour declined in these countries for many complex reasons. It was not the consequence of a simple, unilinear process of "modernization."

The industrial society thesis, although essentially a product of sociology, bears many similarities to the claims of "optimist" historians who portray the eradication of child labour as one of the benefits of the industrial revolution.

See also Capitalism; Industrial Revolution.

References Dahrendorf, Ralf, *Class and Class Conflict in Industrial Society* (1959); Giddens, Anthony, *Sociology: A Brief But Critical Introduction* (1986).

Industrial Workers of the World

The Industrial Workers of the World (IWW) (or "Wobblies" as they were affectionately known) was founded on 27 June 1905 at a convention held in Chicago. The meeting was chaired by the then secretary of the Western Federation of Miners, William D. ("Big Bill") Haywood, who opened with the words: "Fellow workers, this is the Continental Congress of the working class. We are here to confederate the workers of this country into a working-class movement that shall have for its purpose the emancipation of the working class from the slave bondage of capitalism."

The United States at the time was still an emerging economic power. Life for workers was hard and punctuated with periods of unemployment. The dominant trade union in the country, the American Federation of Labor (AFL), took pride in its craft orientation and excluded many workers as a consequence of their gender, "race," or skill level. Employers across the United States rejected any concession to collective bargaining and reacted violently to strikes and pickets. During industrial confrontations, the loss of strikers' lives was expected as militia, police, and private strike-breaking organizations such as the Pinkertons Company would face pickets with force of arms.

Against this background the IWW was formed with the aim of organizing general unions in all employment sectors under a single umbrella. Its slogan was "One big union." The IWW organized across gender and ethnic divisions and prioritized direct action to bring substantial change to the lives of working people. They led strikes, pickets, and demonstrations; organized in defence of workers' free speech; and fought racism, sexism, and exploitation of children's labour. The IWW was successful in organizing in a number of industries in textiles, mining, lumberjacks, longshoremen, and agriculture. They were at the heart of many of the most significant industrial conflicts that took place in the United States in the first two decades of the twentieth century, and as a result, they were met with the most vicious responses both from the state and from employers. Many of their organizers were beaten, tarred and feathered, or murdered, including activist and songwriter Joe Hill, who was framed for murder and shot in prison in 1915. Hill's last letter to his friend and comrade "Big Bill" Haywood ended with the words "Don't waste time mourning, organize." Many more were arrested and imprisoned on various charges, including treason, and the full weight of U.S. federal and state police and FBI resources were fo-

cused on undermining the organization. By the 1920s, the level of repression had succeeded in marginalizing the Wobblies within the American labour movement.

References Bird, S., Georgakas, D., and Shaffer, D., *Solidarity Forever: An Oral History of the Wobblies* (1985); Zinn, Howard, *A People's History of the United States* (1980).

International Confederation of Free Trade Unions

Founded in 1949, the International Confederation of Free Trade Unions (ICFTU) was originally an anticommunist organization with close links to various U.S. government agencies and a network of officers and trade union affiliates in many global locations. In the post-1989 era, since the collapse of the Soviet bloc, the ICFTU has transformed itself into an international trade union organization that campaigns on a range of moral and political issues affecting workers.

In 1994, the ICFTU launched a global campaign for the elimination of child labour. The campaign aimed to get national trade union organizations and nongovernmental organizations to produce reports and raise awareness of the issue of child labour in the trade union movement internationally and within local communities. The ICFTU also attempted to organize campaigns against child labour exploitation by raising demands for compulsory free education, antipoverty programmes, implementation of International Labour Organisation (ILO) standards on child labour, and teaching children about workers' rights in the school setting.

This commitment has involved ICFTU affiliates in a number of campaigns against child labour and in support of child workers across the globe. For example, ICFTU affiliate unions supported the young textile worker Iqbal Masih in his attempts to organize bonded workers in Pakistan's carpet industry and organized the support campaign after Iqbal's murder. The ICFTU also has been actively involved in various "toycott" campaigns in North America, pressuring consumers to refuse to purchase toys made by child workers. Recently the organization has campaigned for the ILO and the World Trade Organization to invoke "social clauses." That is, the ICFTU holds that on the basis of evidence and recommendations produced by the ILO, the World Trade Organization should inflict penalties on countries that do nothing about child labour and should provide benefits and full trading rights to countries that take basic steps to eliminate child employment.

On 27 June 1996, the ICFTU adopted a Child Labor Charter. The Charter claims that more than 250 million children are being exploited for profit or are forced to work in order to survive. To stop this exploitation it argues that the five principles of the Child Labor Charter need to implemented. The principles are:

Education for all: Child labor deprives children of the chance to go to school. Without an education, children become locked into a lifelong cycle of poverty. At the start of the third millennium, getting all children, particularly girls, into school is still one of the great challenges facing the world. Governments and the international community must meet this challenge.

No more exploitation: Tens of millions of children are exploited for profit every day. Those who gain from child labor must be stopped and must help undo the damage they have done. They must help to pay for the rehabilitation and education of the child workers. National and international laws against child labor must be enforced.

Economic security: Most of these children work because their families are poor. Child labor can only be ended when adults have decent jobs and social support. National governments and the international institutions need to do much more to ensure that adults can go to work and children can go to school. They need to make sure that the global economy brings benefits to all people, not just a privileged few.

Rights for children and rights for adults:

The rights of children and of adults are guaranteed in national laws and international treaties. Child labor is usually found where adults' rights are also violated. Where there is discrimination and repression, where there is corruption, where there is forced labor, where freedom of association and expression are denied, child labor is found. Child labor can only be ended when universal human rights are respected.

Everyone has a part to play: We cannot afford to turn our backs on child laborers. We must listen to them and help them, so we can help build a better world. Governments, consumers, employers, trade unions, nongovernmental organizations, religious groups, teachers, students, and the general public, working together, we can end the scourge of child labor.

See also Advocacy; Exploitation; International Labour Organisation; Masih, Iqbal; Trade Unions.
References Cadman, Eileen, *No Time to Play: Child Workers in the Global Economy* (1996).

International Financial Institutions

Any government, bank, or international banking organization that lends money to countries across the globe may be described as an *international financial institution.* However, in everyday usage the phrase principally applies to three particular institutions: the International Monetary Fund (IMF), the World Bank, and the Organization for Economic Cooperation and Development (OECD) and its various subcommittees. The IMF and World Bank were both created in 1944 as a result of the Bretton Woods Agreement. The OECD was established in 1961 as a consequence of a convention signed in Paris in December 1960 renaming and extending the Organization for European Economic Cooperation. Each organization is committed to economic development on the basis of free market expansion, economic stability, high growth, and stable finance.

An international conference of financial experts from 44 countries was held at Bretton Woods, New Hampshire, in July 1944. The meeting was convened to discuss postwar debt repayment schemes and to develop economic mechanisms to offset the possibility of any return to the slump conditions of the 1930s. In the immediate postwar period, Keynesian demand management economics was the approach followed by governments, banks, and states to control their economies. Governments were encouraged to strive for full employment because working people would wish to purchase goods, and their actions would in turn encourage production. This approach was enshrined in the policies of the two dominant institutions formed as a consequence of the Bretton Woods Agreement: the IMF and the International Bank for Reconstruction and Development (the World Bank). In the postwar world, these two international financial institutions were created to extend loans to countries in need and to provide advice on how they might bring their economies back into line. But ultimate responsibility for economic policy and finding a way out of the crisis rested with the country itself. In effect what occurred was that countries experiencing economic crisis or debt-repayment problems would enter negotiated agreement with the lending institutions or "advanced" states for a loan. Often loans would be tied to strategic or military interests and other concerns as well as to some form of policy reform in the debtor country—that is, to a stabilization programme.

However, by the end of the 1960s there was a growing crisis in Keynesian economics, and by the late 1970s, economic crisis and debt repayment problems dogged many economically underdeveloped countries. In response to the crisis, a new strand of economics, commonly known as monetarism or neoliberalism, emerged. The development of this new economic outlook coincided with the election of Margaret Thatcher to the post of prime minister in the United Kingdom and Ronald Reagan to that of president of the United States. Both Thatcher and Reagan were committed to the neoliberal agenda, and their positions of power were crucial in reshaping

the loan structures operated by the IMF and World Bank. Now, as well as following the lenders' recommendations for stabilization, debtor countries had to submit to a structural readjustment plan. The phrase may sound innocuous, but such plans involved the wholesale adoption of neoliberal economic objectives such as cutting welfare spending, denationalizing industry, reducing trade barriers, cutting price controls and subsidies, encouraging foreign investment, undermining trade unions' and workers' rights, and restructuring internal banking operations.

The social costs have been dramatic. Poverty and inequality have risen sharply; the cutting of welfare, price subsidies, and wage reductions has left large numbers of people in desperate circumstances. In these circumstances, families have had to utilize the labour power of all their members, with many resorting to a variety of marginal work forms. In many circumstances, children have been drawn out of schooling and the family to take part in wage labour. Many commentators firmly believe that such programmes have substantially increased the level of child labour exploitation throughout the world.

See also International Monetary Fund; World Bank.

References United Nations Research Institute for Social Development, *States of Disarray: The Social Effects of Globalization* (1995).

International Labour Organisation

The International Labour Organisation (ILO) was founded in 1919 to promote social justice in the area of employment. The organization is unique among affiliates of the United Nations in that its governing body includes representatives not only of governments but also of workers' and employers' organizations. The ILO's secretariat and publishing arm is at the International Labour Office, situated in Geneva, Switzerland. The ILO has over the years produced conventions and recommendations concerning conditions of employment, many of which refer specifically to

The International Labour Conference (International Labour Office)

children. For example, Convention No. 5, 1919, prohibited the work of children under the age of 14 in industrial establishments. In 1973, Convention No. 138 and Recommendation No. 146 consolidated the principles that had been developed concerning the economic activity of children. Convention No. 138 sets a general minimum working age of 15 years but acknowledges that where the economy and educational facilities are poorly developed, 14 years may be an acceptable age. The convention distinguishes between types of work: For example, light work may be undertaken by children as young as 13, whereas hazardous work should not be undertaken until the age of 18. In 1992, with financial support from several governments in Europe and North America, the ILO founded the International Program for the Elimination of Child Labor (IPEC). IPEC places primary emphasis on the children who are at greatest risk. Each participating government signs a memo-randum of understanding with the ILO, under which a national steering committee is set up, which receives support from IPEC in developing a programme appropriate to that country's situation. In June 1999, delegates at the annual meeting of the ILO unanimously passed a new convention, "Worst Forms of Child Labour." Its aim is to protect young people from conditions such as slavery, forced labour, debt bondage, using dangerous machinery and substances, and work in prostitution and pornography. The meeting also urged countries to make it a criminal offence to engage in these forms of child exploitation.

See also Legislation, International; Projects.
References International Labour Organisation, *Child Labour: Targeting the Intolerable* (1996).

International Meeting of Working Children

The first international meeting of working

children took place in Kundapur, in India, at the end of 1996. Representatives from Asia, Latin America, and Africa came together to discuss their positions and develop policies.

The meeting was facilitated by the International Working Group on Child Labour (IWGCL) and a number of other nongovernmental organizations. The working children's representatives produced the "Kundapur Ten Points" in the following declaration:

We, working children and adolescents, propose:
1. We want recognition of our problems, initiatives, proposals and our process of organisation.
2. We are against the boycott of products made by children.
3. We want respect and security for ourselves and the work that we do.
4. We want an education system with methods and contents adapted to our reality.
5. We want professional training adapted to our reality and capabilities.
6. We want access to good health care for working children.
7. We want to be consulted on all decisions concerning us, at the local, national and international levels.
8. We want that the root causes of our situation, primarily poverty, to be addressed and tackled.
9. We want more activity in rural areas so that children do not have to migrate to the cities.
10. We are against exploitation at work, but we are in favour of work with dignity and appropriate hours, so that we have time for education and leisure.

Concerning the conferences that will be taking place, we want representation on an equal footing (e.g., if there are twenty ministers, there should be twenty working children). We will have discussions with our ministers, but we do not want them to represent us.

The above proposals are addressed to Heads of State, decision-makers, nongovernmental organizations, and the working children and adolescents the world over.

The Kundapur meeting ended with the representatives presenting their proposals to a number of leading international actors in the field of child labour, including the International Labour Organisation and UNICEF.

See also International Working Group on Child Labour; Voices of Children.

International Monetary Fund

Founded at the Bretton Woods Conference in 1944, the International Monetary Fund (IMF) came into being in March 1947. The IMF is a bank of last resort for countries facing bankruptcy or debt repayment problems. Traditionally loans given by the IMF have been linked to the introduction of economic programmes aimed at reviving debtor countries' prosperity.

In the immediate postwar era, the dominant economic model in operation within the IMF was broadly Keynesian. It was assumed that some form of government expenditure and investment would be necessary to create employment, which would in turn stimulate the economy. In other words, people in jobs would purchase goods, creating more employment; hence, there would be more people with disposable income to buy yet more goods. The downside of this programme was the tendency toward inflation. When inflation rose beyond acceptable levels, the government would take action (disinvestment, for example) aimed at controlling inflation by increasing unemployment, and the economy would slow down. In this scenario, government control of industry, government planning, and investment in some forms of welfare were viewed as acceptable.

By the late 1960s, however, a number of problems had become apparent in the Keynesian model. In response to these problems, a new trend in economics—monetarism, or neoliberalism—emerged. According to this approach, the control of inflation was absolutely essential to regulating the economy. Proponents of monetarism argued that it was necessary for states to control their money supply, reduce their expenditures, open up their economies to the world market, privatize nationalized industries, and allow market forces to play a primary role in regulating economic activity.

Countries wishing to receive an IMF loan have had to submit to a rigorous Stabilization and Structural Adjustment Program (SSAP) involving economic deregulation, denationalization of state-controlled industry, and the pegging of their currency to the U.S. dollar. The aim has been to entice multinational corporations into the particular national economy with guarantees of a stable currency and an open and deregulated economy—especially a deregulated labour market.

SSAPs generally have undermined welfare programmes, and there is increasing evidence that the deregulation of labour markets has led to greater numbers of temporary and casual workers and to the spread of child employment. Some of the worst examples of child labour exploitation in the world today occur in economies where SSAPs have been implemented.

See also International Monetary Fund; Organization for Economic Cooperation and Development; Stabilization and Structural Adjustment Programmes; World Bank.

International Program for the Elimination of Child Labor
See Projects.

International Working Group on Child Labour

In 1994, the International Society for the Prevention of Child Abuse and Neglect and Defence for Children International took joint action to establish the International Working Group on Child Labour (IWGCL), with a secretariat in Amsterdam, the Netherlands. The IWGCL prepared a global report (edited by Jim McKechnie and Sandy Hobbs) based on the experiences of groups developing strategies with or for working children in Africa, Asia, Europe, Latin America, the Middle East, and North America. Based on this report, a plan of action was developed, with two main components: first, a campaign to enable the participation of children and nongovernmental organizations in a worldwide movement on child labour; and secondly, the formulation of a global strategy for the elimination of child labour, allowing for national and regional differences. One of the most distinctive features of the IWGCL was its advocacy of a policy of listening to the voices of working children rather than simply imposing policy decisions upon them.

See also Defence for Children International.

References McKechnie, Jim, and Hobbs, Sandy (eds.), *Working Children: Reconsidering the Debates* (1998); Zalami, Fatima Badry, Reddy, Nandana, Lynch, Margaret A., and Feinstein, Clare, *Forgotten on the Pyjama Trail* (1998).

International Year of the Child

An International Year of the Child was declared in 1979, with the aim of drawing attention to children's issues in economic and social policy across the international community. One of the consequences of the Year of the Child was an agreement, on the initiative of the Polish government, to establish a United Nations Convention on the Rights of the Child, a document that would clearly set out the minimum rights that should obtain to any child anywhere in the world. The Convention eventually was adopted by the United Nations General Assembly in 1989. That same year, a number of investigations of child labour were undertaken. The International Labour Organisation (ILO) in particular was active in raising awareness of the continuing problem of child labour. It undertook a number of studies of working children in various countries and published them in an edited collection called simply *Children at Work*. Reports were included from various geographical regions, among them Latin America (represented by Mexico and Argentina); the Asian subcontinent (India and Pakistan); Southeast Asia (Thailand

and Indonesia); Europe (Italy and Greece); and Africa (Nigeria). As a whole, these studies confirmed that child labour is a global issue, with children working in underdeveloped economic sectors throughout the world. The collection was used by the ILO to highlight child labour exploitation and to obtain ratification of the child labour employment standards contained in ILO Recommendation No. 146 and Convention No. 138.

See also Convention on the Rights of the Child; International Labour Organisation.

References Mendelievich, Elias, (ed.), *Children at Work* (1979).

Islam
See Religion.

Italy
The Italian republic is situated on a peninsula of land extending from Europe into the Mediterranean Sea and on a number of adjacent islands, of which Sicily and Sardinia are the largest. Italy was united as a single state in the nineteenth century. It went through a period of fascist rule from the 1920s until the end of World War II. It has been a republic and a parliamentary democracy since 1947. Contemporary Italy has a population of nearly 60 million and a varied economy ranging from heavy industry to the production of consumer goods, to agriculture. Broadly speaking, the north of the country is more economically developed than the south.

Child labour in Italy is found mostly in three types of economic activity: small industrial units; commercial units giving service to the public, such as shops, restaurants, and bars; and agriculture, where much of the work is seasonal, being connected with harvesting.

Child labour in Italy appears to be long-standing and deeply embedded in the Italian economy. For many families in agricultural areas and in the poorer quarters of towns, it is taken for granted that children will contribute to the family income as soon as they are capable of doing so. Some evidence suggests that child labour is at its highest extent in Sicily, in the far south. Child employment is also widespread in Naples, the largest city in the south of mainland Italy. It is generally believed that in some areas the mafia encourages businesses over which it has influence to take on child workers.

Although a number of official reports have been made public that clearly indicate that child labour is widespread, they have not led to any substantial changes. This may be in part because few Italians are unequivocally opposed to child labour. Caroline Moorehead reports the case of a judge who happily accepts his morning coffee from a boy he knows to be working illegally.

For some children, particularly boys, work is seen as a way of hastening entry into adulthood. Many working children contribute to their family income, and some may not even be paid directly, their earnings being passed from the employer directly to their parents. However, some boys manage to keep control of their own earnings and thereby manage to free themselves from parental control.

The most telling evidence of harmful effects of child employment comes from studies of industrial accidents and health risks. Marina Valcarenghi has presented a number of cases of children—one as young as 8 years—who were injured, maimed, or killed in industrial accidents. In several industries, including agriculture, it appears that increased mechanization has not led to a decline in the employment of children. The risk to many young workers is made greater by their having to operate machinery that they do not have sufficient skill or training in handling.

References Goddard, Victoria, "Child Labour in Naples" (1985); Mendelievich, Elias, (ed.), *Children at Work* (1979); Moorehead, Caroline, (ed.), *Betrayal: Child Exploitation in Today's World* (1989); Valcarenghi, Marina, *Child Labour in Italy: A General Review* (1981).

Jamaica

See Caribbean.

Japan

Japan consists of four large islands and many smaller ones that lie in the north Pacific Ocean off the coast of mainland Asia. It has a population of more than 120 million. After the surrender of the Japanese in 1945 at the end of World War II, the country was occupied by the United States and other allied forces. Following the signing of a peace treaty, Japan became recognized as an independent state again in 1952. Japan's state constitution is a combination of the traditional and the modern: The head of state is the Emperor, but there is a bicameral parliament consisting of the House of Representatives and the House of Councillors. Japan's economic recovery after the war was spectacular, and it is now one of the most highly industrialized countries in the world, with a wide range of both heavy and light industries.

The modern era of Japanese history is generally dated from the 1850s, when after a long period of deliberate isolation from the outside world the Japanese began to move toward becoming a modern industrial economy. Because Japanese industrialization took place later than similar developments in Europe and the United States, enlightened Japanese were aware of some of the social problems that had accompanied the development of the factory system elsewhere. Investigations were conducted early on that give us a clear picture of the nature and extent of child labour in Japan.

A government survey of larger factories in 1900 indicated that the largest numbers of children under 14 years of age were working in silk reeling (more than 100,000) and cotton spinning (more than 50,000). However, in both industries, children made up only around a tenth of the total workforce. In some other industries, particularly matchmaking, rug weaving, rope braiding, and glass-making, children accounted for between one-fifth and one-third of all workers. These figures probably understate the extent of children's involvement in manufacture, because smaller factories and outworking were not included. There is also evidence that children from orphanages and foundling hospitals entered the workforce earlier than other children.

The development of factories led to concern for regulating the conditions under which children worked. However, another consideration weighed heavily with political leaders: the fear that legislation might hamper the growth of the emerging industries. It was not until 1911 that a Factory Law covering child labour was passed and not until 1916 that it came into force. It applied only to larger factories, forbidding night work and limiting hours of work per day to 12 for those under 16 years of age. However, by this time, child labour was in sharp decline and almost all children under 14 years of age were attending school full time.

Today Japan has clear laws restricting the employment of children, similar to those in North America and Western Europe. However, official information on how effectively the laws are enforced is not available.

See also Asia.

References Nardinelli, Clark, *Child Labor and the Industrial Revolution* (1990); Saito, Osamu, "Children's Work, Industrialism and the Family Economy in Japan, 1872–1926" (1996).

Jordan

The Hashemite kingdom of Jordan, which has a population of more than 4 million, is situated in the Middle East between Syria,

Israel, Saudi Arabia, and Iraq. It became an independent kingdom after World War II. Its political and economic life is greatly influenced by the dispute between Israel and the Palestinians. About one million Palestinians currently live in Jordan, some of them in refugee camps.

According to a report prepared in 1995 by the International Working Group on Child Labour, proportionally more Palestinian children work than do Jordanian children; but precise figures are not available. Prior to the development of public schooling, many children started work at an early age. The law now requires children to attend school, but it is not rigorously enforced. Girls in nomadic communities are particularly likely to work rather than attend school. They tend sheep and goats as well as undertaking duties in the home. Both boys and girls work in rural areas, but in towns more boys than girls are found working.

See also Middle East.

References Sawalha, Aseel, *Child Labour in Jordan* (1995).

Keating-Owen Bill

The first federal child labour law in the United States, this bill was signed by President Woodrow Wilson on 1 September 1916. It is named after the two individuals who sponsored it through the respective houses of the U.S. Congress. Although the Keating-Owen bill became law, it was never implemented: The executive committee of the Southern Cotton Manufacturers challenged the law's validity, and the court ruled it unconstitutional.

See also Harkin Bill; Legislation; National Child Labor Committee; United States of America.

Kelley, Florence

See National Consumers League.

Kenya

Kenya is situated in eastern Africa, on the Indian Ocean, and partly north and partly south of the equator. Kenya gained its independence from British rule in 1963. It has a population of more than 25 million, about 80 percent of which live in rural areas. Almost two out of three Kenyans are younger than 20 years. Nairobi, the capital, is by far the largest city. Mombasa is the second-largest city and the main sea-

President Wilson signing the child labour bill, known as the Keating-Owen bill, 2 September 1916 (International News Photos, Inc.)

port. Kiswahili is emerging as the effective national language, although English is the language of official documents and the medium for teaching in the schools.

Until the 1980s, there was little public awareness of child labour as a problem in Kenya. The first issue to be debated publicly was the use of children as maids and ayahs (baby-sitters). Some initial reports were written from a point of view sympathetic to that of employers. The employers were seen as suffering because of the lack of education and motivation of the school dropouts they took into their homes. Subsequently it became clear that many of the children employed in households were ill-treated, and the "maid-beating syndrome" emerged as a focus of public concern. In 1991 it was estimated that there were around 50,000 maids in Kenya, the overwhelming majority of domestic servants being female. Many of the employers are themselves on low incomes and require domestic assistance because they are single women working to bring up children. Some of the maids are actually distant relatives from poor rural areas. However, the bond of kinship does not necessarily mean that the girls will be treated well.

Children in town are frequently engaged in street selling, cleaning, dishwashing, and as "parking boys." In rural areas, children work on sisal, coffee, and tea plantations as well as at logging operations. Children are typically regarded as ready to work at these sites at the age of 9 years, although sometimes they start even younger. When market conditions are good and production targets are raised, children are often seen as the most readily available source of additional labour.

A third situation in which many children are found working is the small family farm enterprise. Here the tasks vary from child-minding, kitchen chores, and running errands to weeding, harvesting, and cereal grinding. The parents of these children see it as inevitable that they assist the family in this way.

See also Africa; Domestic Service.

References Onyango, Philista, and Bader-Jaffer, Zinnat, *International Working Group on Child Labour in-depth Country Report: Kenya* (1995).

Kielburger, Craig

Craig Kielburger (born 1983) is a young Canadian who, since the age of 12 years, has been involved in campaigning against the exploitation of working children. He has provided testimony to U.S. congressional committees, influenced the Canadian government's policy on this issue, and heads an international nongovernmental organization. He was motivated by the death of Iqbal Masih to become involved in the issue.

Kielburger heads an organization called Free the Children, which he and a number of his classmates founded in Toronto in 1995. There are now groups in Canada, the United States, Australia, and Brazil. Free the Children is unusual in that it was formed and run by young people who were not themselves the victims of exploitation in the workplace.

See also Masih, Iqbal; Nongovernmental Organizations; Organizations of Working Children.

Knights of Labor, The Order of

The Knights of Labor was the first significant, general trade union in the United States. There is some evidence of secret assemblies bearing this name operating from the late 1860s in the Philadelphia area, but the group's first open general assembly took place in 1878. They broke with craft organization in favour of general unionism, recruiting any worker regardless of skill, ethnic origin, or gender. Their organizing slogan was "An injury to one is an injury to all." They raised public awareness of issues associated with the extreme exploitation of child labour and linked this problem to their struggle for an 8-hour workday. The Knights played an important role in the strikes of 1886 for the 8-hour day.

References Guerin, D., *100 Years of Labor in the USA* (1979).

Labour Codes and Policy of the U.S.S.R.

The Russian Revolution of October 1917 ushered in a new form of government based on soviets, or councils, of workers' and peasants' deputies. The leaders of the early Soviet state, under Vladimir Lenin and Leon Trotsky, believed they were establishing the first socialist republic, which would soon be joined by other republics as the proletarian revolution swept the globe. This vision was not to be fulfilled, however; by 1928, a counterrevolution was under way, spearheaded of Joseph Stalin, in which the majority of those who had played a leading role in the October Revolution were jailed or murdered by Stalin's supporters.

Nevertheless, between 1917 and 1928, the Soviet government had addressed a number of pressing issues relating to working conditions, including pay, health and safety, and unemployment insurance. After years of suffering caused by World War I, the Revolution, and the Civil War (touched off by the intervention by the major world powers against the new regime), the government tried to bring significant reforms to labour practices. Central among these were restrictions on the employment of children. However, it is of interest to note the change in emphasis that took place over time in the decrees and codes. Initially the decrees presented what could be termed a policy blueprint, similar to many of those passed in countries and by transnational agencies today. But quickly the realization grew that abstract policies were unlikely to resolve the situation, and that alternatives, including financial inducements, would have to be provided, to encourage children out of employment.

The first decree, announced on 29 October 1917, banned children and juveniles (under the age of 18) from night work and work underground. Children younger than 14 years were banned from working altogether. The decree stated, however, that the government's near-term goal was to raise the minimum working age to 15 years on 1 January 1919, and to 16 beginning 1 January 1920. On 28 October 1918, a second decree on child and juvenile labour noted the failure of organizations to adhere to the 1917 decree. It cited a number of possible reasons for this failure—poverty, lack of educational facilities, parental pressure, the large number of orphans—and gave local factory committees and trade unions the power to investigate and identify local solutions to particular cases. In June 1919, the Commissariats of Labor, of Social Welfare, and of Education were invited to combine their efforts to find a solution. What they put forward was novel, especially for its day and in the prevailing conditions: They completely banned the employment of children of 14 years and younger; gave these children financial assistance in order to replace their loss of earnings; and enrolled them all in educational or training establishments. Young people aged 14 to 16 years who were working at the time could continue to work, but no more than 4 hours a day. Where possible, assistance was to be made available to encourage them out of work and into education. Those aged 16 to 18 years were prohibited from working more than 6 hours a day. These measures were formally enshrined in the Labor Code on 9 November 1922 and were quite effective in reducing the cases of child labour.

See also Russia.

References Dewar, M., *Labour Policy in the USSR, 1917–1928* (1979).

Militia members guard the approach to the textile mills during the famous strike, Lawrence, Massachusetts, 1912 (Library of Congress)

Lathrop, Julia
See Children's Bureau.

Lawrence Mill Workers' Strike

The Lawrence strike is one of the most famous confrontations between workers and management in the United States. In 1912 the state of Massachusetts reduced the work week from a maximum of 56 hours to 54 hours. In the textile industry, employers responded by speeding up production and cutting wages. Working conditions in the mills were very bad. A physician in Lawrence, Dr Elizabeth Shapleigh, wrote at the time:

"A considerable number of the boys and girls die within the first two or three years after beginning work. . . . Thirty-six out of every hundred of all the men and women who work in the mill die before or by the time they are twenty-five years of age."

The main company in the town of Lawrence was the American Woolen Company, which owned four mills. Around 60,000 residents were dependent on the mills for their livelihood, and the changes in working conditions had a serious effect. In response, the workforce—mainly women and children, from a variety of nationalities and backgrounds—went on strike.

The strike is notable for the involvement of the Industrial Workers of the World, or "Wobblies," the militant trade union that played a significant role in a number of industrial disputes in the early twentieth century. IWW Local 20 had been active in Lawrence for a number of years prior to the strike. But the makeup of the textile industry provided some unusual problems to labour organizers, particularly due to the fact that the strike involved workers speaking 22 different languages. The IWW resolved this issue by having a large strike committee of almost 300 strikers representing all nationalities and languages. All decisions were voted on and adopted at mass meetings.

Famous IWW leaders, such as "Big Bill" Haywood and Elizabeth Gurley Flynn, were active in the dispute. In one of his speeches during the strike, Big Bill Haywood denounced child labour, saying of the textile owners: "The worst thief is the one who steals the playtime of the children."

The dispute is notable also for several other events, among them the death of a 14-year-old Syrian striker, John Ramy, who was bayoneted while on picket duty. The confrontations between police, militia, and pickets around the town were vicious, and on another occasion a pregnant striker delivered a stillborn child after police clubbed her into unconsciousness. In the face of such intimidation, the women strikers raised the slogan "We want bread, but roses too," which later became the title of a poem by James Oppenheim about the dispute and the women's leading role in it. Finally, as the strike wore on and hunger and poverty started to bite, strikers adopted the innovative tactic of sending their young children away from Lawrence to be cared for by supporters in other towns across the United States. City authorities tried to prohibit this activity, labelling it "child neglect."

Eventually, on 1 March 1912, against the backdrop of increasingly brutal attacks on strikers by the police and militia, the strikers triumphed. After government hearings were held, work hours were reduced and the American Woolen Company offered pay increases of between 5 and 11 percent.

See also Industrial Workers of the World; Mother Jones.

References Bird, S., Georgakas, D., and Shaffer, D., *Solidarity Forever: An Oral History of the Wobblies* (1985); Zinn, Howard, *A People's History of the United States* (1980).

Legislation

Legislation directed at child employment has been aimed at controlling the types of jobs that children can do, the age at which they can start work, and the hours they can work—in some cases, including earliest starting and latest finishing times. Examples of this type of legislation are most evident in the developed countries such as Britain and the United States.

In the United States, in the early twentieth century, child labour legislation was passed and implemented at the state level. It was not until the Fair Labor Standards Act of 1938 that federal legislation was put in place. The historical development of this legislation parallels the history of changing attitudes and vested interests. The historical relationship between the North and South created friction around attempts to implement federal laws, and the Southern states perceived child labour legislation as interference from the North.

Within the developed countries there is a perception that child employment is a "nonissue" and that the real child employment problems lie in the economically less developed countries. Underlying this view is a belief that legislation in developed countries has successfully controlled the evils of child labour and that poorer countries need only to put effective legislation in place in order to control child employment.

Although such an analysis is appealing, it is also fundamentally flawed. Investigation of child employment in Europe and the United States clearly demonstrates that child labour laws in these countries are often broken and are largely ineffective. In the United States, the main form of control is through the use of a permit system. Work permits are issued to children and can be revoked if the school perceives academic work to be suffering as a result of wage labor. Evidence suggests that the permit system is rarely implemented, and when it is, the additional burden it places on schools means that permits are rarely rescinded. Similarly, most children working in Britain have been found to be doing so without the required work permits.

Economically underdeveloped countries

have by and large put legislative packages in place. One example is India, where the Supreme Court in December 1996 implemented new laws to remove children from work. However, as in more developed countries, in India the plethora of laws governing child labour are all flouted with impunity.

Although it is apparent that national legislation is largely ineffective in controlling child employment, this has not stopped some countries from trying to create new legislation that is intended to have an international impact. In the United States, a number of bills (such as the Harkin Bill) have been proposed to stop the importation of goods made in other countries by children. Whether such legislation could be implemented or whether it could be effective is open to debate.

Attempts to influence legislation have also been made at the international level. The International Labor Office and UNICEF have spearheaded a campaign to establish global standards for child employment and for children's rights. Having devised a set of standards that they believe are uniformly applicable, these bodies are campaigning to get countries to sign on to the standards. Implementation remains a problem. A wide range of countries, developed and underdeveloped, have passed laws and regulations that are meant to protect children; yet in the majority of cases, these efforts have been ineffective. Clearly, appropriate legislation is only part of the answer. Governments must also have the will to implement legislation, and the support of the population, if their efforts are to be effective. Popular attitudes must be in tune with legislation.

See also Factory Acts; Harkin Bill; Legislation, International.

References Greenberger, Ellen, and Steinberg, Laurence D., *When Teenagers Work: The Psychological and Social Costs of Adolescent Employment* (1986); Hobbs, Sandy, and McKechnie, Jim, *Child Employment in Britain: A Social and Psychological Analysis* (1997); Pollack, S. H., Landrigan, P. J., and Mallino, D. L., "Child Labor in 1990: Prevalence and Health Hazards" (1990).

Legislation, International

National legislation on child employment exists in many countries. There is also a small body of international laws and regulations that many countries have acknowledged as applicable. Most international legislation stems from the work of the International Labour Organisation (ILO), and more recently, from that of the United Nations (UN).

International legislation on child labour has a relatively short history, but several key documents are worth noting. The first international child labour convention was held in 1919 and passed the first Minimum Age (Industry) Convention No. 5. This convention, which specified that the minimum age for children to be employed in industry was 14 years, was ratified by 72 countries.

This first attempt to regulate internationally children's participation in the workplace was followed by other ILO initiatives. In 1930, the ILO Forced Labour Convention No. 29 aimed to outlaw all forms of "forced or compulsory labour." To date, 139 countries have ratified this convention. The main implication for child employment is that all forms of child slavery and bonded labour are outlawed.

The United Nations General Assembly adopted the International Covenant of Civil and Political Rights in 1966, but it did not come into force until 1976. This covenant reaffirms the 1948 Declaration of Human Rights, which outlined individuals' civil and political rights. Its relevance to child employment stems from one specific article (Article 8) that states that no person should be kept in slavery or servitude, or forced into compulsory labour.

The United Nations also adopted the International Covenant on Economic, Social, and Cultural Rights in 1966. Article 10 of this covenant directs countries to protect young people from economic exploitation and from work that might hamper or prevent their normal development.

It could be argued that what many think of as the landmark international legislation dates from 1973. The ILO Minimum Age

Convention No. 138 was to supersede all existing ILO conventions in this area. The crux of this convention is that countries are obliged to put in place national policies that will lead to the effective abolishment of child labour. Unfortunately, only 49 countries have ratified this convention to date. At the same time the ILO proposed that the minimum age for employment be raised to 16 years.

Although many view Convention No. 138 as the central international legislation on this issue, some consider it to have been superseded by the 1989 Convention on the Rights of the Child (CRC). The latter pulls together civil, political, economic, social, and cultural rights of the child under one banner, highlighting the interrelationships between these elements. Article 32 of the convention adopts a traditional, protectionist stance regarding the exploitation of children in work. This legislation is believed to be particularly important because 187 countries have ratified it.

International legislation has a relatively short history, and as with national legislation, it has had a debatable impact on the exploitation of children at work. Part of the difficulty relates to the fact that not all countries sign up or ratify such legislation. In cases where a significant number of countries do ratify a specific piece of legislation, such as the CRC, other problems emerge. In particular, the monitoring processes and the enforcement of standards in individual countries are sometimes weak and ineffective.

With such caveats, international legislation has played an important role in setting international standards, even despite questions about cultural diversity. That international efforts will continue in this area is without question. In July 1998, the ILO proposed an "updating" of its Convention No. 138 to target intolerable forms of child labour.

See also Convention on the Rights of the Child; International Labour Organisation; Rights Discourse.

References Bellamy, Carol, *The State of the World's Children, 1997* (1997); International Labour Organisation, *Child Labour: Targeting the Intolerable* (1996).

Leisure

One of the many arguments used against children's working is that it deprives them of the opportunity for leisure. It is easy to see the basis of the case the critics make. Play is widely observed to be a natural activity of children from an early age. When not required to eat, sleep, attend school, or work, children engage in a variety of pursuits that give them pleasure.

It seems to be a serious deprivation if, as is sometimes the case, a working child has little time to do anything other than eat or sleep. Most legislation and most international bodies concerned with child labour see restriction on the hours worked by children as a central goal. However, it is not necessarily envisaged that all hours taken from the working day will necessarily be spent in leisure. For example, it would frequently be assumed that schooling would fill part of the gap.

Leisure is usually conceived of as something that is undertaken voluntarily and without outside pressure. However, it is not always clear that what is referred to as leisure activity is actually free of outside pressure. One example that has been considered by psychologists is the involvement of children in competitive sports such as Little League baseball. It has been noted that it is common for parents to exert a high level of pressure on their children to be successful in the games. The pleasure of success when achieved is supplemented by strong parental approval; but feelings of failure, which are inevitably experienced by some players in a competitive game, may also be magnified by parental disappointment. Some psychologists have referred to parental influence of this sort as turning play into work.

See also Definition of Child Labour; Sports.

References Hobbs, Sandy, and Cornwell, David, "Child Labour: An Underdeveloped Topic in Psychology" (1986); Iso-Ahola, Seppo E., *The Social Psychology of Leisure and Recreation* (1980).

Liberationism

Liberationism is a philosophical position that argues that childhood is a socially constructed variable that oppresses children. Proponents of liberationism argue that childhood restricts children from the full range of human experiences that adults take for granted and limits them to a narrow range of legitimate activities and roles. Liberationists argue that the experiences of children during childhood are not determined by their biological or psychological immaturity or needs but rather reflect social and political expectations regarding what they are capable of and expected to do. These expectations, however, have little to do with children's abilities. Instead, they reflect attempts to socialize children into particular modes of living and behaving. In the process, children become socially excluded, noncitizens with no say over the direction of their lives—the powerless victims of adults, parents, institutions, and state agencies. To redress this situation, liberationists argue, children should be freed from the constraints of childhood and the authority of adults (including parents) and state institutions, and allowed to take a full and active role in both shaping and determining their lives, their environments, and their activities.

In his book *Escape from Childhood*, John Holt asserts that children possess the competencies necessary to make decisions about important matters in their lives and should be free to participate in making those decisions. He argues that this involves giving children the same full citizenship rights that adults have. They should have the right to vote, to work, to own property, to enter into sexual relations, and to dispose of their income as they see fit. In *The Handbook of Children's Rights*, liberationist Bob Franklin states that children should have civil, political, and social rights of citizenship—rights that adults in liberal democracies take for granted. Among the social rights of citizenship Franklin enumerates basic standards of welfare such as the right to good health and freedom from poverty, and to

education and a basic income—rights that protect all of us from the naked workings of the market—predicated on the state's commitment to at least a minimal standard of living. Franklin believes that both adults and children should be guaranteed at least these minimal social rights of protection. However, adults have additional rights, what he terms "liberty rights," such as the freedoms of association and speech, the freedom to enter into sexual relations with whomever one chooses, the right to vote and take part in the political process, and the right to have one's voice heard in a range of social and welfare settings that directly affect one's life. Franklin argues that there is no good or rational reason for denying children these additional "liberty rights."

Liberationists like Holt and Franklin conclude that children should, therefore, have the right to go to school, where they should take an active part in determining the educational curriculum; but if they wish, they should also have the right to work. Adults have this right. Moreover, activists within the women's movement have argued that restrictions on women that limit their access to the world of paid employment are a central feature in maintaining their unequal, oppressed position. The argument of child liberationists is that if it is oppressive for women to be forced to stay at home and service the family, then it is equally oppressive to restrict children to the family setting and deny them access to the social contacts and opportunities that are available through paid employment.

See also Children's Rights.
References Franklin, Bob (ed.), *The Handbook of Children's Rights* (1995); Holt, John, *Escape from Childhood* (1975).

Lindsay, Samuel McCune

Samuel McCune Lindsay became the first permanent secretary general of the National Child Labor Committee (NCLC) in 1904. He was a professor of sociology from the University of Pennsylvania and clearly saw the role of the NCLC as reformist. Lindsay played a key role in establishing the organization.

In 1905, Lindsay undertook an investigation of the working conditions facing children in the cotton-producing states of Alabama, Georgia, North Carolina, and South Carolina. Although his aim was to gather information on the conditions of children working in cotton mills, he was also concerned with finding out what the NCLC could do to improve these children's lot.

In 1912, Lindsay was offered the post of head of the new Children's Bureau. However, he turned down this offer to continue his work with the NCLC.

See also Children's Bureau; National Child Labor Committee.

Livingstone, David

David Livingstone (1813–1873) is best known as the Scottish missionary and physician who spent most of his life exploring central and southern Africa. Livingstone's early childhood gives us some insight into child labour at the time.

Livingstone was born in Blantyre, Scotland, in 1813. His parents were not rich, and the family lived in a one-room apartment in a tenement that had been built to house cotton mill workers, on the banks of the river Clyde. By the age of 10, Livingstone was put to work in the mills, where a typical working day was from six o'clock in the morning until eight at night. His first job in the factory was as a piecer. This job entailed piecing together the broken parts of thread on the spinning frames. He gave most of his earnings to his mother, to help with the cost of running the home; but with part of his first wage, he bought a textbook of Latin.

After work, between eight and ten o'clock in the evening, Livingstone would attend night school with the other children. Most of the students would inevitably fall asleep, and it is a testament to Livingstone's motivation that he kept up his study for many years. He would carry on reading either until midnight or until his mother forced him to go to bed, as he had to begin work at six in the morning on the following day. He would continue his reading at breakfast and dinner breaks. According to his autobiography, "Everything I could lay my hands on was devoured, except novels." Classical literature, scientific works, and travel books were his favourite reading.

Livingstone even succeeded in reading books while he was working: "My reading while at work was carried on by placing the book on a portion of the spinning jenny, so that I could catch sentence after sentence as I passed at my work; I thus kept up a pretty constant study undisturbed by the roar of the machinery. To this part of my education I owe my present power of completely abstracting the mind from surrounding noises."

Livingstone was promoted to cotton-spinner at the age of 19 and used his earnings to obtain the university education he needed in order to undertake missionary work.

References Livingstone, David, *Travels and Researches in South Africa* (1905).

Lorimer, George

See Saturday Evening Post.

Lovejoy, Owen R.

Owen Lovejoy was born in 1866 and grew up in the United States, in the state of Michigan. After his education he entered the ministry, where his main concerns were with human rights and dignity. These concerns extended beyond religious affairs and took him into the realms of social work. He became known as the "children's statesman" and as an important advocate of reform in relation to child labour.

In 1902 he witnessed the anthracite coal strike in Pennsylvania and the conditions that miners and their families had to live in. The experience left an indelible mark on him, and within months of returning from his visit, he left the ministry and took up a post as assistant secretary of the newly formed National Child Labor Committee (NCLC). By 1907 he was the NCLC's chief executive, and he remained in this post until 1926.

Lovejoy himself had worked as a child and had firsthand experience of the conditions and dangers that working children were exposed to: He had sustained an injury to his arm while working in a Michigan factory. Such experiences gave him a high degree of emotional involvement in his work. This is reflected in the text of a report he completed after another visit to Pennsylvania coal mines, during the 1904 breakers' strike: "After I had seen those little boys day after day carrying their lunch pails to the breakers every morning like grown men, bending all day over dusty coal chutes, and finally dragging themselves home in the dark at night, I couldn't think of anything else. Sights like that cling to you. I dreamed about those boys."

During his time with the NCLC, Lovejoy made a number of visits to observe at firsthand the conditions of working families. In 1910, along with Alexander McKelway, he went to the mountain regions of North Carolina to study the conditions of the "poor whites" who were migrating to the cotton mills.

Lovejoy's main goal as NCLC executive was to get child labour reform on the statute books. Part of his strategy was linked to the Progressive Party's platform during the 1912 election campaign. Lovejoy had chaired a party committee that laid out minimum social standards for industry, including the prohibition of child labour. The Progressive Party did not win this election, but Lovejoy's work had placed the issue of child labour on the political map.

Lovejoy continued to advocate federal legislation to tackle the issue and became involved in drafting bills toward this end. One such effort became the Palmer-Owen bill, which was introduced to Congress and was passed by 233 to 43 votes in February 1915. However, the political session came to an end before the bill could be taken through its final stages, and it never became law.

In addition to attempting to introduce federal legislation, Lovejoy also managed the internal politics of the NCLC. Lovejoy, along with other NCLC members, believed that the Committee should be involved in a wider range of activities concerning child welfare. The NCLC's evolution in the direction they desired led to an eventual name change, to the National Child Conservation Board. Between 1918 and 1920, arguments raged over the general direction of the NCLC and its name change. Lovejoy initially favoured widening the agenda of the group to include child welfare issues but later changed his mind. The issue came to a head in 1920, and Lovejoy supported the idea of keeping the original name and maintaining its focus on child labour. In the end, his position won the day, but the episode clearly shows the problems he faced in managing the NCLC.

Under Lovejoy's leadership the Committee faced other problems as well. Their failure to obtain federal legislation by 1925 left Lovejoy and other members with the view that the NCLC should refocus its effort on state-level legislation, though without abandoning the aim of eventual federal legislation. The change of direction caused dissent within the NCLC and other organizations.

In 1926, Lovejoy retired from his post as executive of the NCLC. In the 22 years that he had worked for the Committee, Lovejoy had left an indelible imprint. His travels around the country as an advocate of children had contributed to an increase in the public's awareness of child labour as a major social and political issue. By the time of his retirement, the NCLC had done much to publicize the state of child labourers; but Lovejoy was unable to achieve his goal of ending child labour and introducing federal legislation.

See also McKelway, Alexander J.; National Child Labor Committee.

References Trattner, Walter I., *Crusade for the Children* (1970).

Low Pay Network

Refers to a network of independent research units that has been set up in different parts of the United Kingdom to study and publicize the problems of British people earning low pay. The units are independent, nongovernmental organizations, funded by donations from local government, trade unions, and other bodies. The Low Pay Unit based in London is the contemporary body that has had the most consistent record of interest in child labour as a social problem in modern Britain.

In the 1980s, when there was little public debate on the issue, the London Low Pay Unit published two reports by Emma MacLennan. The increased interest in child labour in Britain in the 1990s is in part due to the simultaneous publication in 1991 by the London and Scottish Low Pay Units of two research reports, *The Hidden Army* and *The Forgotten Workforce*.

Chris Pond, the director of the London Low Pay Unit, became a member of the British Parliament in 1997. He introduced a bill on child employment but later withdrew it when the government indicated its intent to give greater priority to child labour as a social issue.

See also United Kingdom.

References Lavalette, Michael, McKechnie, Jim, and Hobbs, Sandy, *The Forgotten Workforce: Scottish Children at Work* (1991); MacLennan, Emma, *Child Labour in London* (1982); MacLennan, Emma, Fitz, John, and Sullivan, Jill, *Working Children* (1985); Pond, Chris, and Searle, Anne, *The Hidden Army: Children at Work in the 1990s* (1991).

Malawi

Malawi is situated in southeastern Africa, bordering Mozambique, Tanzania, and Zambia. Formerly a British colony called Nyasaland, it became independent in 1963 and declared itself a republic in 1966. The population today numbers around 9 million. The capital is Lilongwe (population over 200,000), and the main commercial centre is Blantyre (population over 300,000).

The economy in Malawi is predominantly agricultural. Maize is the main subsistence crop, and tobacco, sugar, tea, and peanuts are grown for export. As in most agricultural societies, children undertake substantial amounts of work. The patterns of work are influenced both by precolonial community practices and by the capitalist farming introduced under the colonial regime. Accounts by travellers strongly suggest that children were involved in food production prior to British rule. The missionary David Livingstone, reported that it was common to see men, women, and children working side by side in the fields. Girls took on a full range of women's jobs around the age of 10. Boys weeded, which was hard work, and scared birds from the crops, which was less hard. They also fished and hunted for small animals. Children also took part in the work of those communities that lived by herding.

When Europeans introduced large-scale plantations in Malawi, they recruited labour among the local, native population, including children, who by Malawian custom worked alongside adults. However, the European planters also from time to time recruited gangs of men and boys from other areas. These boys were regarded as a useful part of the workforce. However, they were now employed as wage earners and not as members of a family group. Much of the work was seasonal. In the early days, payment was not usually in cash but in goods such as blankets and hoes. Christian missionaries were also active in Malawi, and they too employed children as workers, sometimes finding themselves in competition for labour with the local plantation owners.

As the twentieth century progressed, distinctive ways of life emerged among those who lived as tenants on plantations. Although not formally part of any agreement, it came to be taken for granted that the tenant would not only work for the landlord himself but also would make available the work of his family. Boys who grew up on plantations were the most likely to become wage labourers.

The Nyasaland economy suffered several crises in the 1920s and 1930s. Plantation owners had to switch from cotton to tobacco to tea in response to changes in the world markets. Tobacco and tea plants require a lot of care, and children and youths were employed in large numbers on a casual basis to hoe, weed, water, and prune, as well as harvest. Anxieties were expressed by medical authorities that the conditions under which the young people worked, including the long hours, were harmful to their health and physical development. After much debate a law on child labour was passed in 1939. However, when World War II started, labour shortages made the government more concerned with ensuring that work was done than with examining the working conditions of those who did it.

At the end of the war, the number of plantations decreased. With a fall in tea prices internationally, planters looked for ways of cutting costs. Some found immigrant workers from Portuguese East Africa cheaper to employ than the local population. Although both adults and children were recruited, children were particularly common in this workforce.

When the country achieved political independence, the widespread use of child labour was deeply embedded in the economy. Thus children continue to work on a large scale in Malawi today.

See also Africa; Agriculture; Tanzania.

References Chirwa, Wiseman Chijere, "Child and Youth Labour on the Nyasaland Plantations, 1890–1953" (1993).

Malaysia

Malaysia is a federation of thirteen states, some on the mainland of southwest Asia and some on nearby islands. Some of the states received their independence from Britain in 1957 under the name Malaya. In 1983 other states joined the federation, and the name was changed to Malaysia. Singapore, which joined at that time, seceded two years later, but maintains strong economic links. The population of Malaysia is around 20 million, of whom one million live in the capital, Kuala Lumpur. The two largest ethnic groups are Malay and Chinese.

During the colonial era, Malaysia was predominantly an agricultural economy. Rubber had major significance as an export. Industrialization has since taken place, and manufactured goods now make up about three quarters of the country's exports.

The Institute for Social Analysis has published a number of accounts of children working in very bad conditions on plantations and in land development sites. Children on plantations frequently work alongside their mothers but receive no pay. More than half of the children working on rubber plantations are estimated to be between the ages of 10 and 12 years. On palm oil plantations most child workers are younger than 10.

A number of nongovernmental organizations in Malaysia have formed a National Task Force on Working Children. They claim that the Children and Young Persons Employment Act of 1966 is widely ignored. It permits children under the age of 14 years to undertake only light work, or to perform in public entertainment or serve as apprentices. The Task Force's estimation is that between 100,000 and 200,000 children are working in a variety of places—restaurants, markets, construction sites, and small industrial sites. In large urban areas, children earn a precarious living recycling goods from garbage dumps.

References Jomo, K. S. (ed.) *Child Labour in Malaysia* (1986); Jomo, K. S., Zami, Josie, Ramasamy, P., and Suppial, Sumathy, *Early Labour: Children at Work on Malaysian Plantations* (1984); Lee-Wright, Peter, *Child Slaves* (1990).

Malta

Malta is an island in the Mediterranean Sea between Italy and North Africa. Formerly part of the British Empire, since 1974 it has been a republic within the British Commonwealth. It has a population of around 400,000. The 1974 Education Act, which established free and compulsory education up to age 16, also gave the Ministry of Education the power to prohibit school-age children from working. However, Ronald G. Sultana has noted a number of features of the Maltese society and economy that encourage child labour. One is the availability of seasonal employment in the growing tourist industry. A second is the preponderance of small firms—for example, those in manufacturing and quarrying—which remain competitive through employing cheap and casual labour. In part because of high tax rates, Malta has a well developed "black" economy, in which work is paid for in cash. A competitive work ethic is well established in Malta, as is demonstrated by the high proportion of schoolchildren who take private lessons outside school hours. Sultana's research shows that boys studying in trade schools are particularly likely to have part-time work experience.

See also Europe; International Labour Organisation.

References Sultana, Ronald G. "Practices and Policies in Child Labour: Lessons from Malta" (1993).

Malthusianism

Rev. Thomas Malthus (1766–1834) is famous for his book *Essay on the Principle of Population*, originally published in 1798. In this book Malthus argued that rapid population expansion would soon lead to a situation wherein there would be inadequate means of subsistence to support the entire population. He suggested that food production increases arithmetically but population increases geometrically; thus, without population checks, famine and social disaster were inevitable. Malthus's suggested solution was to abolish all benefits paid in cash or kind to families whose wages were insufficient to meet their daily survival needs. Such benefits, he argued, encouraged people to have children when they could not afford them and bred a culture of dependency. To solve this perceived crisis, he advocated moral restraint and later marriage, with fewer children born into families that could fully support them. Despite the fact that Malthus's fears have proven unfounded and the world today easily produces enough food to feed the population globally, Malthusianism remains a powerful philosophy in developmentalist circles. The problems of poverty in places such as India or Bangladesh are often blamed on overpopulation rather than on inequality and exploitation.

The "modern" Malthusian argument suggests that overpopulation brings hardship, want, and starvation. To counter this, poor families have large numbers of children both as an immediate economic resource and as a future safety net for support during parental old age. The fact that families in these circumstances send their children out to work hinders the latter's educational attainment, which forces the children into less skilled, poorer paying jobs as they grow older. This restricts the ability of society to develop a fully educated and trained workforce and thus hinders social development. It imprisons families in a vicious cycle of poverty. The solutions put forward by Malthus's new adherents are not significantly different from those advocated in the late eighteenth century. The essential "cure" is to reduce population, the problem of poverty being based on the activities of the victims themselves. Later marriage, abstention from sexual relations, birth control, and forced abortion have all been advocated at different times and places as means of reducing population size.

References Zinn, Howard, *A People's History of the United States* (1980).

Market Economics

The phrase refers broadly to a strand of economic theory that argues that the allocation of resources should be determined solely by supply and demand in a marketplace. At its heart is a belief that the market is the best institution yet created by human agency for the conduct of economic activity. Individuals bring their preferences to markets, and the aggregate weight of consumer preference can compel suppliers of all kinds of commodities to comply with consumers' demands. Failure to comply will guarantee the failure of any company foolish enough to behave in such a way. Given freedom of entry into the market, other potential suppliers are always available who will recognize the fact of consumer sovereignty. These characteristics make markets efficient, sensitive, and speedy signaling mechanisms, doing spontaneously that which is impossible for the planning structures of command economies.

Modern industrial societies are such vast and complex entities that the idea of government taking responsibility for the myriad decisions necessarily involved in the allocation of resources is foolish. It is beyond the capacity of governments to do what markets do. There should not be interference in markets, for example, by state action, because any such interference will introduce disequilibrium and inefficiencies that will undermine the long-term effectiveness of the productive system. In other words, markets are, or should be, sacrosanct.

The linked processes of deregulation,

privatization, competition, and managerialism that have taken place in former state-run companies and state-provided welfare institutions in various countries in recent years are referred to as *marketization*. Over the last few years, marketization has opened up economies and state welfare institutions to market competition from a range of service providers. In order to provide services, companies have entered into cost-cutting competitions within which the reduction of labour costs has been central. Deregulated labour markets have been exploited to the full, and many marginal workers (including children) have been recruited within these industries.

Belief in the power of the market has led some philosophical supporters of these positions to defend the use of child labour. If children want to work and if there are employers who wish to employ them, then the labour market should decide the question. For example, in Britain, neoliberal politician Digby Anderson stated in 1996 that we must put children to work. He cited the difficulty of finding help in the house or with routine gardening jobs. Retailers especially cannot find suitable low-grade help. He advocates the revival of the practice of a young mate or assistant for self-employed, skilled tradesmen.

See also Capitalism; Globalization; International Financial Institutions; Pro-employment Arguments.

References King, D. S., *The New Right: Politics, Markets and Citizenship* (1987); Self, P., *Government by the Market? The Politics of Public Choice* (1993).

Karl Marx, father of communism (Library of Congress)

Marxism

Karl Marx died in 1883, yet he remains one of the most powerful and influential thinkers the modern world has produced. He was born in 1818 in Germany and educated there, before migrating to Paris in 1843, where he met his friend and collaborator Frederick Engels. In 1845, when he was expelled from France, he moved to Belgium for a short period before settling in London in 1849. He was a prolific writer and theorist. His analysis of world history, known as historical materialism, presents a view of the world as divided into discrete and contending social classes and all social, political, and cultural phenomena as emerging naturally from the dominant mode of production.

In the course of his life, Marx gradually developed a critique of capitalist societies that argued that the source of all wealth in capitalist societies is derived from the labour of workers. This wealth is expropriated from the vast majority in society because the majority of the population in capitalist societies have to sell their labour power to employers to obtain a wage. The vast majority of the wealth created, therefore, goes to the minority within society who own or control the means of production. Marx was aware that within this general picture there could be more extreme forms of labour exploitation, and he identified child labour as one such form.

Marxism differs from liberal political philosophies, which tend to start with the assumption that humans are necessarily selfish pursuers of their own particular ends. Marxists would refer to earlier times and different cultures in which cooperation, not competition, was the norm and the basis for social living.

For Marx, the starting point for analysing any society is how production is organized. His perspective was not purely economic, however. Marx assumed that interwoven with any economic relations of production were a set of political, ideological, social, and cultural practices. Central to Marx's analysis was his identification of social class divisions. Throughout history there have been a number of different types of societies, in which production is organized in different ways, and in which different relationships of exploitation exist between the dominant class and those who actually create the wealth of society. From this point, Marx goes on to argue that, first, generally, history has witnessed a gradual expansion of the forces of human productive potential; this has meant that it has been possible to fulfil more than minimal survival requirements. However, in class-divided societies, such potential has been severely restricted. Secondly, class societies are by their very nature inclined to produce conflict. Thirdly, the form of exploitation changes historically in each mode of production. Finally, each mode of production contains political, social, and economic contradictions and conflicts, which lead to social disharmony, class conflict, and the possibility of revolutionary change.

These general parameters guide Marxist analyses through a whole series of social questions and problems. The first point to note, therefore, is that Marxists view societies as socially integrated wholes. This means, for example, that we cannot separate issues like women's oppression, racism, or child labour from their location within modern capitalist societies.

From the beginning, Marxists clearly recognized child labour as a particularly exploitative labour relationship in which employers have utilized child workers as a cheap source of labour power. Low wages reflect the fact that these workers are children, who it is assumed do not have to fully

support themselves—an assumption embodied in the social construction of childhood. Employers are not giving children work because it is beneficial to their health or well-being but because it increases profits or allows the employers to provide services cheaply that otherwise would cost substantially more.

Marxists promoted education as a solution to the exploitation of children's labour, for a variety of reasons. Working-class activists who sought to establish some form of education for working-class children sometimes were motivated by intense hostility toward state and church interference in schooling. Some in the middle class also considered education necessary in order to impart new skills that industry needed. For others, education was necessary for the purpose of social control, to remove working-class children from the streets and impart useful knowledge. Thus, there were conflicting motives behind demands for expanded education; but educational expansion and the school system created both an activity and a location that was deemed essential for working-class children.

See also Capitalism; Engels, Friedrich; Social Construction of Childhood.

References Engels, Friedrich, *The Condition of the Working Class in England* (1987); Marx, Karl, and Engels, Friedrich, *The German Ideology* (1846).

Masih, Iqbal

Iqbal Masih, who was born in Pakistan in 1982, is probably the most famous child worker in the modern world. At the age of four, Iqbal Masih's father sold him to carpet manufacturers for the sum of 13,000 rupees (around 120 U.S. dollars). For six years he worked around 16 hours per day at a carpet loom. He received no education, and his physical growth was impaired. In 1992, this type of work having been declared illegal by the Supreme Court of Pakistan, Iqbal Masih participated in demonstrations against the carpet makers. With the help of the Bonded Labour Liberation Front, he was freed from his job and taken to Lahore. An appearance on

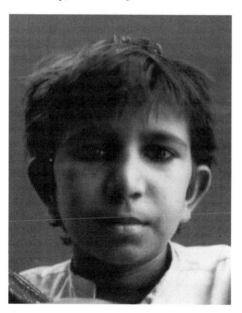

Iqbal Masih, 1994 (Reebok International)

American television networks in 1994 made him a symbol of the struggle against child bonded labour. His progress at school in Pakistan was so rapid that the International Bonded Labour Foundation presented him with the Reebok Prize for outstanding performance.

On 16 April 1995, during a visit to his home village, 25 kilometres from Lahore, Iqbal Masih was shot dead. Disputes arose about the circumstances of his murder. One claim was that he had been shot by a farm labourer after a petty dispute. However, given his prominence, it is not surprising that some commentators suggested that Masih's death was a political assassination. The Carpet Manufacturers' Association of Lahore denied any involvement. However, whatever the truth of the matter, Iqbal Masih's death brought substantial publicity to the cause with which he had been associated.

See also Pakistan; Unfree Labour.

References Kuklin, Susan, *Iqbal Masih and the Crusade against Child Slavery* (1998); Reddy, Nandana, "Iqbal and the Kiss of Judas" (1996).

McKelway, Alexander J.

Alexander J. McKelway (1866–1918) and Owen Lovejoy were the first full-time assistant secretaries of the National Child Labor Committee (NCLC). Lovejoy was appointed to act in this capacity in the northern United States, and McKelway, in the South. McKelway was born in Pennsylvania, but had Southern ancestors and had been raised in the South.

McKelway's family wanted him to follow in his forefathers' footsteps by entering the ministry, and his education was directed toward this end. He became an ordained Presbyterian minister in 1891 and served as a home missionary and as a pastor in a Southern church. Over time, he became close to the adults and children who lived and worked in the mill towns of the South.

McKelway took over the editorship of the *Presbyterian Standard*, a religious weekly paper, in 1887, and quickly turned it into a paper that advocated labour reform. One of the earliest issues raised by the paper was the unquestioning acceptance of child labour in the mills. It is important to note that during this time McKelway made a number of enemies, and this created difficulties for him within the NCLC later on.

McKelway came to his NCLC job with a wealth of experience and firsthand knowledge of the South and the working conditions in mill towns. He shared many Southerners' views and prejudices. For example, McKelway was a defender of white supremacy and a nativist. As Walter Trattner notes, being a nativist at that time was the same as being a racist. Nativists believed that differences between blacks and whites could be explained in terms of hereditary characteristics.

McKelway was concerned about child labour because he saw it as something that would harm the Anglo-Saxon racial strain, since it was white children that were working in the mills. Thus, McKelway's racist views might have helped him in his efforts to regulate child labour. These views allowed him to express his concerns in a way that resonated with Southerners at that time.

McKelway played a key role in developing U.S. legislation to tackle the issue of child labour in America. One of the first battles that he faced was in North Carolina in 1905. A bill drafted by McKelway aimed to raise the minimum age for girl workers from 12 to 14 years. Initially the bill received support and picked up on the changing public opinion at that time on this issue.

However, a number of manufacturers, led by one R. M. Miller of Charlotte, opposed the North Carolina bill. The thrust of the argument against such legislation was that it would have a dramatic effect on their business. The manufacturers accused McKelway and the NCLC of acting as the mouthpiece of New England mill owners who were out to destroy their Southern competitors. In effect, they drew on the long history of North-South animosity to defeat the bill. Against these types of arguments McKelway drew upon his nativist views to mount counterarguments highlighting the dangers of white children working in the mills.

In arguing for legislation against child labour, McKelway antagonized many Southern manufacturers. His critics, coupled with the enemies he had made in his days as an editor of the *Presbyterian Standard* and the *Charlotte News*, mounted attacks on McKelway. The personal nature of the attacks began to worry NCLC members, who by association with McKelway were targets of this antagonism. The situation worsened to the extent that the board of the NCLC started to question the effectiveness of McKelway's position in the South. The end result was that the board appointed Owen Lovejoy, the NCLC secretary in the North, to determine whether McKelway's leadership in the South was in fact acting as a barrier to success.

Lovejoy's report vindicated McKelway. The report highlighted the impact McKelway had had in pushing the NCLC's agenda forward. Lovejoy was also able to establish that the antagonism and personal attacks against his colleague emanated from those manufacturers who opposed all forms of regulation on child labour.

However, even though McKelway was cleared by the report, these events may have had an impact on McKelway's role in the NCLC. It was at this time that he started to spend more time in Washington. His role there was to push forward the NCLC's belief that federal legislation was needed to tackle this issue.

McKelway went on to play a major role in the development of federal legislation. He was involved in the political battle to get the Palmer-Owen and the Keating-Owen bills passed. Although the Palmer-Owen bill failed, the Keating-Owen bill was signed into legislation by President Wilson on 1 September 1916.

President Wilson reaped the political rewards of this outcome; however, the NCLC believed that the true credit for this victory belonged to Alexander McKelway.

In actuality, it mattered little who received the acclaim, because the Keating-Owen Bill was challenged in court, and the presiding judge, James E. Boyd, ruled that the Bill was unconstitutional. Although Judge Boyd presented no written judgment, he ruled that Congress did not have the right to regulate local employment conditions. The case was appealed.

The appeal decision was reported on 3 June 1918. By a 5 to 4 majority, the court upheld the earlier ruling that the Keating-Owen Bill was unconstitutional. The NCLC's hopes of obtaining federal legislation were dashed by this ruling, and McKelway's triumph evaporated.

It is perhaps fitting that Alexander McKelway never knew the outcome of the appeals court ruling. He died in April 1918 of a heart attack. He had spent 14 years of his life working toward the abolition of child labour. Although federal legislation was still some way off, McKelway had played a crucial role within the NCLC and had been an important catalyst influencing public opinion and the position of many state legislatures.

See also Fair Labor Standards Act; Lovejoy, Owen R.; National Child Labor Committee.

References Trattner, Walter, *Crusade for the Children* (1970).

Meknes

The employment of girls in the town of Meknes in Morocco became the focus of international interest as a result of television documentaries in the series *World in Action* shown in Britain in 1995. These programs claimed that some clothes labelled as made in Britain and sold in the shops of a large British retail chain were actually manufactured in Morocco. The retail company admitted that this was the case and attributed it to an administrative error. However, a second claim by the makers of the documentaries—that the retailer was aware that the factory in Meknes was employing child labour—was contested. Granada Television, the company responsible for the programmes, withdrew the claim and paid compensation to the retailer, Marks and Spencer. This aspect of the story attracted considerable media attention.

However, the International Working Group on Child Labour decided the claim might have merit, and it therefore sponsored an inquiry into the situation in Meknes. The IWGCL's report listed four main findings. The first was that girls between 12 and 15 years of age indeed had been working in the factory. Some of the girls were official apprentices, with contracts registered with the Moroccan Ministry of Labor, as is provided for by Moroccan law. However, the report found that these "apprentices" did not actually receive any training and were working under bad conditions for poor pay.

The second finding was that many girls were dismissed from the factory after their working conditions became public knowledge internationally. The third finding was that those dismissed workers who could be traced were now less well off than they had been when working. Some had poorer paying and less prestigious jobs. One had turned to prostitution. When working in the factory, their wages, although low, had made an important contribution to the incomes of their families. Thus, not only were the girls now suffering, but their families were also. The fourth finding of the IWGCL was that the activities of the investigative journalists, however well intentioned, had had a negative outcome, because no action had been planned or implemented in order to deal with the repercussions of the investigations.

Finally, it is worth noting that the television company that sponsored these documentaries also has produced broadcasts of fashion shows staged in Britain by the clothing company under investigation, Marks and Spencer. Children have been featured prominently in these shows as models, but the makers of the programme have made no comment on this.

See also Garment Industry; Modelling; Morocco.

References Zalami, Fatima Badrym, Reddy, Nandana, Lynch, Margaret A., and Feinstein, Clare, *Forgotten on the Pyjama Trail* (1998).

Mexico

Mexico is situated in North America, directly south of the United States. It was conquered by Spain in the sixteenth century and achieved independence in 1821. Throughout much of the nineteenth century, Mexico had an unstable political history, including an attempt by France to impose the rule of Emperor Maximilian, and border disputes with the United States. As a result of the latter, Mexico lost large tracts of territory. The current Mexican constitution dates from 1917. For much of the twentieth century, Mexico has been ruled by the Party of Institutional Revolution.

The population of around 90 million is largely Spanish speaking. Around 15 million people live in the capital, Mexico City, and its suburbs. Mexico has rich mineral resources and an extensive agricultural industry, and exports a wide range of manufactured goods. Its main trading partner is the United States.

Official figures on child employment are believed to greatly underestimate its true extent, because most children's work is informal. However, those statistics that are available suggest that child employment is increasing.

A Mexican girl sweeps the baseball stadium in Mazatlan, Mexico, 1989 (Jorge Nuñez, Reuters/Corbis-Bettmann)

The largest sector employing children is agriculture. Children in peasant communities generally start taking part in work on the family plot from around the age of 6 years. This is partly work, partly learning, and is of course unpaid. As children get older, they begin to accompany family members performing other work. Usually payment is for the work done, so the individual child does not receive direct payment. Mexico earns large sums by exporting fresh fruits and vegetables to the United States. Many of the workers engaged to pick this produce in the fields are older children who are paid low wages.

Mexican children also work in manufacturing industries, generally in relatively small production units with small labour forces. Larger companies are more at risk of being caught breaking the law by employing children, whereas smaller ones may hope to escape detection. Children make up a high proportion of the workforce in brick manufacturing. Children engaged in making carpets and pottery are in many cases not breaking the law because they are working in family enterprises, which are exempt from child labour laws. Many children work in illegal and unregulated workshops manufacturing clothes, some of which are smuggled into the United States.

In urban areas, many children are employed in the service industry—for example, as shop cleaners, rubbish collectors, market porters, and in the case of girls, domestic cleaners. In centres of tourism, such as Acapulco on the Pacific coast, child labour is very obvious. The children are primarily engaged in various types of selling, offering goods and services to the many tourists. In Mexico City, many children try to earn a living as street performers.

For many poor Mexicans, the prospect of moving to the United States seems the best hope of earning a decent living. Much of the migration across the border is illegal. Children are involved in this migration, not only by moving into the United States themselves but also by acting as guides along the illegal crossing routes.

See also America, Central.

References Lee-Wright, Peter, *Child Slaves* (1990); Mendelievich, Elias (ed.), *Children at Work* (1979).

Middle East

This rather vague phrase applies to certain countries in western Asia and northern Africa. The activities of the International Working Group on Child Labour (IWGCL) illustrate some of the difficulties with the phrase. The IWGCL divided its reports into regions, including one called "Middle East" that covered Morocco even though the latter country is in the far west of North Africa. In addition, the IWGCL commissioned a report on Turkey, which was not included in the Middle East. Although most of that country is situated in Asia and only a small part is in Europe, the writers of the Turkish report asked to be treated as part of Europe. A significant but seldom mentioned fact is that "Middle East" is generally thought of as referring to countries where the predominant religion is Islam. This accounts for the area being covered including Morocco. The clear exception is Israel, which is acknowledged as being geographically in the Middle East but culturally very different from its predominantly Islamic neighbours. Turkey is the most secular of the predominantly Islamic countries in this region, a fact that is connected with the tendency of some Turks to see their country's economic and political future in Europe. The government of Turkey is probably more aware of the problems of child labour than are its neighbors. Although the more serious problems of child labour are to be found in other countries of the Middle East, child labour does exist in Turkey on a substantial scale.

See also Algeria; Egypt; International Working Group on Child Labour; Jordan; Morocco; Turkey; United Arab Emirates.

Migrant Workers

This phrase describes workers who move around the country in search of employment. An alternative phrase that also is often used is *itinerant worker.*

There are many examples of children moving to gain employment. Perhaps the clearest example relates to the early factories and the industrial revolution. Due to the introduction of new technologies and alternative forms of power, factories were located in different parts of the country, and workers, including children, had to move to gain employment.

Taking the textile industry as an example: The early production of textiles was reliant on hand-power, and was largely home based. The physical requirements of machinery such as the spinning frame were beyond the capacity of the human hand, and alternative forms of power were needed. Richard Arkwright, a key figure in the British industrial revolution, devised a way in which this machine could be worked by water-wheel. The water-wheel method required a steady supply of flowing water, so in 1771, Arkwright built a large factory beside the river Derwent in Derbyshire.

In the rural setting, however, there was an insufficient pool of labour to service the factory. Arkwright's solution was to build a large number of cottages and to bring employees from all over Derbyshire to work there. Many children were employed in Arkwright's factory. By 1790 there were over 150 water-powered cotton-spinning factories in Britain.

The move from water power to steam power produces another example of the migration of workers. Richard Arkwright was at the forefront of this movement. Arkwright saw the potential in 1783 of the

A young Mexican boy cutting spinach, La Pryor, Texas, 1939 (Russell Lee, Library of Congress)

rotary steam engine invented by James Watt. Factories relying on this power source were no longer dependent on fast-flowing rivers for power. All that was needed was a good supply of coal. This allowed factories to move to high population centres or to move from rural to urban centres. In these urban centres there was a ready supply of labour that was augmented by families following the factories to their new locations.

Clark Nardinelli, an economic historian, argues that it is possible to show that children were part of the industrial migration labour force. In eighteenth-century Britain, Nardinelli argues, children moved around the country to the textile centres in search of high wages. Many migratory children at this time were pauper apprentices; but by the nineteenth century, the migrant workers were mostly nonapprenticed children, moving either with or without their families.

Some of the most compelling examples of itinerant working children can be found in agriculture. Agriculture is a seasonal industry, and there is clear evidence that children have always been used as part of the labour force when demand for workers is high and time is short. Walter Trattner, a historian and social welfare writer, cites many examples of children working in the fields in the United States. Trattner suggests that the extent of exploitation of children in this industry was ignored in the first federal legislation on child labour in America, the 1938 Fair Labor Standards Act (FLSA).

Since agriculture escaped regulation under the FLSA, the use of child workers continued. Attempts to protect migrant farm workers through legislation were hampered by the outbreak of World War II. However, the plight of migrant workers was by then an issue that had entered the wider public domain through John Steinbeck's novel *The Grapes of Wrath*. A year after this book's publication, the number of migrant workers was estimated at four million.

The National Child Labor Committee (NCLC) agitated for action to investigate the causes of migrancy, and in the 1950s the NCLC helped to set up the National Citizens Council on Migrant Labor. In 1963 the NCLC established the National Committee on the Education of Migrant Children. The establishment of this latter group demonstrated that the NCLC felt that there was still a need to protect itinerant workers. The aim of the Committee was to ensure that the children of itinerant farm workers received adequate education, since they felt that this was the only way in which the cycle of poverty could be broken.

Migrant workers, including child workers, are not simply a historical phenomenon. In developing countries there is continuing concern about the migration of the rural population to the urban centres. In many cases, children leave their families behind to seek employment in the cities. However, migrant workers also have continued to be a part of the developed countries' workforces as well. For example, in one research study, Mexican American migrant farm worker children were found to be working in New York state. The study not only exposed the reality that young migrant children were working in agriculture but also highlighted the potential health risks they faced. It was reported that 48 percent of the children had worked in fields still wet with pesticides and that 36 percent had been sprayed, directly or indirectly, while working in the fields. This 1990 study also showed that children under the age of 16 years had mixed and applied pesticides, a clear violation of prohibitions relating to hazardous work for children.

See also Agriculture; Health; Industrial Revolution.

References Trattner, Walter I., *Crusade for the Children* (1970); Wilk, Valerie, "Health Hazards to Children in Agriculture" (1993).

Mining

The history of mining provides myriad examples of the exploitation of children in harrowing work conditions. In Britain, until the Mines Act of 1842, the employment of children was common in the mining industry. Miners were normally paid according to piece rates—that is, a set price was paid in return for a certain weight of coal, tin, or other mineral that was dug out of the ground and transported to the surface.

Mining involves an array of tasks, and it was common for miners to operate in a ganging system whereby a group of workers would perform individually assigned tasks in order to maximize their output. The skilled miner would receive payment for the minerals dug, and he would then distribute wages to those in his gang—to those he had subcontracted work to. It was in the miners' interests to employ direct family members, thus keeping as much of the earned income as possible within the family. All family members, including quite young children, would be involved in the work process. When this was not possible, the cheapest available labour would be hired—that of unrelated children and women. This form of working created many jobs for children in mining communities.

There was a fairly strict age hierarchy attached to different types of jobs. Very young children, often as young as 6 or 7 years (and occasionally even younger), would be taken on as trappers. Their job was to work the trapdoor ventilation system in the mine. They would sit next to trapdoors and open and shut the doors to let workers and trucks pass in or out of the mine. The young workers spent much of the working day alone at the doors, isolated in the dark and damp surroundings. Their working day was very long. The fact that the doors were central to the ventilation of the mines meant that the children were required to be at work before anyone else and could not leave until everyone else had finished work.

At about the age of 8, the children would progress to other types of jobs.

A "greaser" in a coal mine carrying two pails of grease, Bessie Mine, Alabama, 1910 (Lewis Hine, Library of Congress)

Modelling

Most young people and women were involved in "hurrying" or "putting." This was the process of putting the cut coal, or other mineral, into the transportation truck and hauling it to the bottom of the shaft, or to the areas where the pit ponies would take over. This was extremely arduous work. The children would have to push the heavy trucks along narrow seams for hours at a time. Occasionally, they would pull the trucks, which involved them placing a harness around their waists, heads, or shoulders, and with a candlestick in their caps, crawling on all fours to get to their destinations. In some mines the seams were so narrow (as little as 16 inches high) that very young, small children were required to undertake such work. A British government commissioner commented in 1842 that the children were "chained, belted, harnessed, like dogs in a go-cart."

Only at the age of 21 did young men graduate to become miners—or "hewers" or "getters"—digging out the minerals at the face. Then they would set themselves up as independent subcontract gangers, hiring local young people and women to carry out the necessary subsidiary work tasks.

Although these examples are drawn from British history, a similar picture could be painted of mining children across the globe in the nineteenth century. But child miners are not only a historical problem. Numerous reports have made it clear that children continue to work in mines in many countries today. Piece-rate payment, the labour subcontract system, the need to keep labour costs down, and the lack of investment in technologically advanced machinery and equipment all increase the pressure to utilize children within the mining industry.

The International Confederation of Free Trade Unions (ICFTU) recently reported that children are working in tin mines in Brazil, gold mines in Peru, and coal mines in Zimbabwe and Colombia. The ICFTU found evidence of children as young as 6 years working underground, carrying water to family members at the coal face, leading mules carrying the coal, and loading the cut coal into sacks. Given the nature of mines, the work environment is exceptionally dangerous. Potential hazards in most mines include landslides, floods, fires, explosions, and poisonous gases, all risks that can be minimized but not eliminated entirely by appropriate safety regimes. Because the mines operate on low profit margins and are relatively unimportant to the national economy, safety is devalued. The report concludes by noting that many of the children suffer from overexertion, hernias, lack of oxygen, and bone deformation. The blackened faces and exhausted frames of child miners are still a relatively common sight in many countries at the start of the twenty-first century.

See also Coal Breakers.

References Cadman, Eileen, *No Time to Play: Child Workers in the Global Economy* (1996); Page Arnot, R., *A History of the Scottish Miners* (1955); Pinchbeck, Ivy, *Women Workers and the Industrial Revolution* (1981).

Modelling

The use of children as models for press and television advertising is widespread. When the purpose is to display children's toys or clothes, the need for child models is widely understood. Many advertising agencies accept the presence of parents at photographic sessions. Many countries require that special steps be taken to safeguard the child's education.

However, controversy surrounds the use of teenage girls in advertisements that emphasize sexuality. Girls as young as 12 or 13 years are often found posing in sexually suggestive ways virtually identical to the poses of adult models. The international organization Action Against Child Exploitation campaigns against the use of teenagers in advertising if they wear clothes and makeup of an inappropriate, adult type. A number of particular objections have been voiced. One is that girls legally below an age when they may engage in sexual activity are presented in a way that emphasizes their sexuality. A second objection is that this type of advertisement seems to condone adult sexual interest in children. Thirdly, to take part in photographic sessions or fashion shows where there is a strong sexual atmosphere may have a harmful effect on the girls' social and emotional development.

See also Cinema; Entertainment Industry; Meknes.

Morocco

Morocco, a former French colony in northwestern Africa, achieved effective independence as a constitutional monarchy in 1956, following agreements with France and Spain. The population at the census of 1994 was 26 million; a rapidly increasing proportion live in towns. The economy is based on agriculture, mining, and manufacture, with tourism growing in importance.

Children are to be found working in both rural and urban areas. Traditional areas of child labour have included agriculture, textiles, handicrafts, and domestic service. More recently, children have been working as tourist guides, street vendors, porters, and beggars.

The Moroccan carpet industry is world famous and a source of national pride. Traditionally, women dominated the industry; most employers now are men, and most workers are women or girls. Girls as young as 6 years are recruited to work long hours for little pay. When the Anti-Slavery Society investigated working conditions in the industry in the late 1970s, it found children as young as 5 years of age in the workplace, some putting in 12 hours per day in very bad conditions. Technically, these children were not employed by the factory owners but by an adult intermediary who was paid per carpet produced. These intermediaries supervised the children's work and were keen to maximize production.

The girls in the carpet factories come mainly from rural backgrounds, as do those who work as maids. Girls' working as domestic servants is a long established feature of Moroccan society. There are bro-

kers who find potential maids for a fee. Their recruits are seeking an escape from the grinding poverty of their homes; however, wages are typically only 20 U.S. dollars a month, and the girls are often harshly treated. According to the report of the International Working Group on Child Labour, sporadic efforts to reduce the worst forms of exploitation of children in Morocco have been ineffectual.

See also Africa; International Labour Organisation; Meknes.

References Anti-Slavery Society, *Child Labour in Morocco's Carpet Industry* (1978); Zalami, Fatima Badry, *Child Labour in Morocco* (1996); Zalami, Fatima Badry, Reddy, Nandana, Lynch, Margaret A., and Feinstein, Clare, *Forgotten on the Pyjama Trail* (1998).

Mother Jones

Mary Harris Jones (1830–1930), better known as Mother Jones, was a leading figure in the Industrial Workers of the World (IWW) and a militant labour activist in the United States. She was born in Cork, Ireland, and later moved with her family to Toronto, Canada. Her early working life was divided between teaching and dressmaking. In 1861 she married, but six years later tragedy struck when her husband and four children died of yellow fever. She moved to Chicago, where she set up a dressmaking business, but she lost her business and all her possessions in the Chicago Fire of 1871. Around this time she started to attend meetings organized by the Knights of Labor. This gave focus to her increasing concern for the plight of the poor, for employment conditions in general, and for working children.

In spring 1903 she organized a children's march to Washington, D.C., to demand the end of child labour. At this time there was a major strike taking place in the textile industry in Kensington, Pennsylvania, involving 75,000 workers (of which 10,000 were children). Jones organized the children and took them on a ten-day march through New Jersey and New York and down to Oyster Bay, where they attempted to see President Theodore Roosevelt (but he refused to meet with them). Nevertheless, Mother Jones claimed the march was a great success: "Our march had done its work. We had drawn the attention of the nation to the crime of child labor," she said.

Over the next 50 years Mother Jones was involved in organizing working people into trade unions, denouncing and campaigning against the abuse of child labour, and working in support of strikers. Sometimes several of these issues came together, as happened when she became involved in raising support for children on strike against the Philadelphia mills, who had been putting in 60 hours a week before they declared their strike. The striking children carried placards reading "We want to go to school" and "55 hours or nothing."

In 1905 Mother Jones was one of the leading labour leaders to support the establishment of the IWW, and she worked for this organization until her death.

See also Industrial Workers of the World; Lawrence Mill Workers' Strike.

Movement of Working Children and Adolescents from Working-Class Christian Families

Formed in Peru in 1978 by young workers with the support of adult members of volunteer organizations, this organization, known by its Spanish acronym as MANTHOC, has defended the interests of child workers. MANTHOC has branches in a number of districts of Lima and in many other cities of Peru. It has organized three conventions of working children in Latin America (held in the Peruvian capital, Lima, in 1988; in Buenos Aires, Argentina, in 1990; and in Guatemala in 1992). The movement's stated principles are that work should be recognized as a central, formative experience of working-class children in Latin America and that children should lead their own representative organizations, becoming active agents in social processes rather than passive onlookers subject to the whims and the political ac-

tivity of others. These concerns are reflected in MANTHOC's publications, which are devoted to discussing working children's experience of labour and its role in forging their identity. The organization is committed, therefore, to challenging the Western ideal of childhood as a time of life free from worldly concerns. Instead MANTHOC advocates a liberationist position, where the child is liberated from his or her subordinate role within society and is viewed as a fully active participant in social life.

See also America, South; Liberationism; Organizations of Working Children; Peru.

References Schibbotto, G., and Cussianovich, A., *Working Children: Building an Identity* (1990).

Multinational Companies

Multinational corporations are businesses that have operations in more than one country, though they normally retain a strong presence in their original home base. At first the phrase described production-based companies such as car manufacturers. However, banks and financial service companies were also multinational in their lending, investment, and trading activities. Since the late 1970s other types of companies have taken on transnational activities. These include service sector companies, accountancy, legal and advertising agencies, and waste disposal companies. The activities of multinationals have given rise to a number of concerns among economists and other citizens about the healthy development of poorer countries.

The investments multinationals make in various regions or countries are often aimed at gaining access to cheap raw materials or cheap local labour markets. In times of social, political, or economic crisis, multinationals are likely to move on to another location where labour and resources are cheaper and the environment more stable. They are viewed as rootless and opportunistic—able to go anywhere at any time. This characterization of multinationals can be overstated. The long-distance moving of company operations can be complicated and immensely risky. The new site may not have appropriate infrastructure; the company will have to establish new relations with the local state; and a new industrial complex of subsidiary and component manufacturers will have to be created.

A second criticism is that multinationals channel the economies of host countries into narrow specializations that limit the diversity and flexibility of developing economies. This argument too can be overstated, since multinationals exist in most countries, and given that most multinational operations occur between and among the economically more advanced countries.

Finally, it is claimed that multinationals use their powerful position in developing economies to force component manufacturers to utilize cheap labour in order to keep their own prices down. It is also suggested that traditional local producers of goods have to turn to the informal sector to maintain their activities or to compete with the multinationals. In these cases, they will use marginal workers—often children—because of their cheap labour. This is one of the more substantial criticisms made of multinational businesses.

See also Consumerism; Globalization; International Financial Institutions; Market Economics.

Murphy, Edgar G.

Episcopal clergyman, amateur astronomer, and author Edgar G. Murphy is often regarded as the main force against child labour in the southern United States of America at the turn of the century. He conducted a vigorous campaign against child labour within the state of Alabama, which resulted in the introduction of a bill in 1903 that gave Alabama the highest child labour standards of any industrial southern state. Murphy founded the National Child Labor Committee with Felix Adler in 1904.

See also National Child Labor Committee.

Myanmar

Myanmar is situated in Asia, west of Indochina. It has a population of more than 40 million people. Formerly known as Burma, it officially adopted the name Union of Myanmar in 1989. The current government is led by members of the national armed forces. It has come under international condemnation for civil rights violations, and there is a strong opposition campaigning for a parliamentary democracy. The United Nations Commission on Human Rights has frequently condemned the recurring suppression of freedom of expression and the use of forced labour in Myanmar.

According to a report published in 1997 by the United States–based organization Human Rights Watch Asia, the military government has forced thousands of children to work without pay as porters and labourers in the construction of bridges, roads, and railways. Many die from beatings or from exhaustion. Commenting on the report, opposition leader Aung Sang Suu Kyi, who was awarded the Nobel peace prize in 1991, said that everyone in Burma knew that forced labour was a fact. Mon state, where a railway is being built with forced labour, is officially closed to foreigners. However, some foreign journalists have secretly entered the area and have given eyewitness accounts of children undertaking exceedingly arduous work in extremely hazardous conditions.

See also Asia; Unfree Labour.
References Pilger, John, "In a Land of Fear" (1996).

Nardinelli Thesis, The

The traditional interpretation of the industrial revolution in Britain is that it was a time when children were exploited by being drawn into the labour force. In particular, the "evils" of factory and mill work are usually highlighted. These views are reflected in the work of historians such as E. P. Thompson and J. L. and Barbara Hammond.

Clark Nardinelli, in his book *Child Labor and the Industrial Revolution*, challenges many of the assumptions that underpin this traditional interpretation. He argues that the historical evidence on child employment should be reconsidered within an economic history framework and that economic theory can also lend greater insight to analyses of child employment today. In particular, greater attention should be given to the economic role of children within the family.

Applying this theoretical approach to child employment involves looking at children both as producers and as consumers within the family unit. This leads to an acknowledgment that children play a role in contributing to the family at the same time as they use part of the resources available to the family.

The most important idea is that from an economic perspective, children's work is not necessarily harmful. It can reflect rational decisions to improve the overall well-being of the family, including the children. Such an approach also draws attention to the fact that child employment did not begin with the industrial revolution. Children always worked, whether in agriculture or in the domestic environment. Industrialization merely created a new area of employment for children who were already workers. If we accept these statements as true, then the most important question about child labour becomes: Which of these employment alternatives is preferable?

Nardinelli argues that the employment of children in the new factories was not a reflection of changing attitudes toward children. Instead, changing technology created other, more rewarding forms of work that children could do. It became more profitable for children to work in factories than in other kinds of employment, such as domestic work. Children's contributions to the family increased, as did family income.

In Nardinelli's model, children continue to work as long as their income outweighs the costs of their employment, such as loss of domestic work. Nardinelli therefore must explain why children moved out of such employment over time. His argument is that changing technology led to a demand for increasingly skilled labour. This meant that education would have a long-term benefit in moving the individual from unskilled to skilled employment. The long-term economic advantages of education began to outweigh the short-term benefits of wages from working. Families' ability to choose education rather than work for their children came, according to Nardinelli, from increasing real income levels for adults, which allowed the family to maintain its consumption levels when children moved from work to education.

Nardinelli acknowledges that this application of economic theory does not fully address the standard historical interpretation that children were "exploited" in the workforce. He points out that much historical writing about this period uses the word *exploitation* without clearly defining it. Nardinelli considers a number of alternative definitions of this term and concludes that children on the whole were not exploited. This does not mean that no exploitation took place: Nardinelli draws attention to the use of pauper apprentices as an example of the exploitation of children in the workplace. However, the majority of working children were not exploited in this way. Factories and mills were not nice places to work, but given the range of employment opportunities available at that time, they were among the most profitable for the child and the family. Nardinelli argues that it was not the industrial revolution and its factories that exploited children but the poverty faced by many families, which made such employment a rational choice in the circumstances.

Nardinelli takes his argument further in proposing that rather than exploiting children the factory system improved the position of children. This improvement was reflected in the fact that children could earn a wage that allowed them to leave the family home if parents were harsh or mistreated them. In these circumstances parents would start to value their children for their contribution to the family and would therefore view them differently.

Nardinelli's ideas are of value because they have encouraged a second look at traditional interpretations of this period in Britain's history. Placing debates about children's employment in the appropriate historical and socioeconomic context, Nardinelli has directed our attention away from a purely quantitative analysis, toward a consideration of qualitative changes—that is, of the forms of work performed by children, and their effects on those children.

Nardinelli's ideas have not gone unchallenged. Two economic historians at Cambridge University, Sara Horrell and Jane Humphries, have questioned his assertion that child employment did not decline because of legislation but rather because of the rising real incomes of adult males. Their data showed that from the middle of the 1830s onward, children's involvement in the labour market did not decline even when male real earnings were increasing. Such evidence tends to undermine Nardinelli's emphasis of the role of changing real income as an explanation for the general decline in children's factory work in the nineteenth century.

Horrell and Humphries also argued that children were exploited during industrialization. They cited as evidence data showing that children during the periods between 1787 and 1816 and between 1817 and 1839 were working at younger ages. During the 1820s and 1830s, higher proportions of 5- to 9-year-olds and 10- to 14-year-olds were working in factories and mines. Horrell and Humphries therefore believe that historians are correct to suggest that industrialization led to a form of exploitation of young children.

They further suggested that the different interpretations that historians have of this period may in part reflect the fact that industrialization had differing degrees of impact across Britain. Regional variations, particularly between rural and urban areas, would have led to geographic variations in the intensity of industrialization's effects on the employment of children. Conclusions about the impact of the industrial revolution would be coloured by the geographic sources of the data being used.

Although Horrell and Humphries challenged Nardinelli's conclusion, they agreed with him that the industrial revolution was not a watershed in the employment of children. Children had always worked. What was open to debate was the specific character of industrialization's effects on the experience of children's employment.

See also Hammond, J. L., and Hammond, Barbara; Industrial Revolution; Pauper Apprentices; Thompson, E. P.

References Horrell, S., and Humphries, J., "'The Exploitation of Little Children': Child Labor and the Family Economy in the Industrial Revolution" (1995); Nardinelli, Clark, *Child Labor and the Industrial Revolution* (1990); Thompson, E. P., *The Making of the English Working Class* (1968).

National Child Labor Committee

One of the first pressure groups formed to combat the problems of child labour in the United States, the National Child Labor Committee (NCLC) was established in 1904 and is still in existence today. The roots of this Committee are in the New

THE NATIONAL CHILD LABOR
COMMITTEE
WHY?

TWO MILLION CHILD WORKERS
UNDER SIXTEEN YEARS TODAY

WE WANT THEM TO BE
NORMAL MEN AND WOMEN

YOU WANT THIS TOO

JOIN

The National Child Labor
Committee

*A National Child Labor Committee poster, 1915
(Lewis Hine, Library of Congress)*

York Child Labor Committee, which was founded in 1902.

The history of the NCLC charts the changing patterns of child employment in the United States. Walter Trattner provides an analysis of the role of NCLC in the development of and influencing of legislation in the early part of the twentieth century. By the mid-1950s, the organization's primary aims as defined in 1904 had been achieved, and it is possible to identify a change in the organization's interests. For example, the NCLC commissioned studies into work-study programmes, factors influencing school dropout rates, and the wider issues of adolescents' making the transition into adult work. Currently the NCLC is still active in child employment issues. For example, it is a member of the Child Labor Coalition.

The Committee has a web site and is probably one of the main sources of historical record on the changing pattern of child employment in the United States.

References Trattner, Walter I., *Crusade for the Children* (1970).

National Committee for the Rights of the Child

The National Committee for the Rights of the Child (NCRC) is a coalition of organizations promoting a children's rights agenda in the United States. Member organizations have a diverse range of interests and goals, but NCRC's main purpose is to inform and educate the American public about children's rights in general and the United Nations Convention on the Rights of the Child in particular. The NCRC supports children who are undertaking legal cases that will affect the constitutional position of children. For example, the NCRC was heavily involved with the case of "Gregory K.," who successfully divorced his parents.

Although the United States played an instrumental role in drafting the Convention on the Rights of the Child, it has yet to become a signatory. In part this is because rights in America tend to be clarified via judicial process; hence, in time, children's rights may become clearer as a consequence of U.S. Supreme Court decisions. It is also due to the fact that the Convention embodies not only civil and political rights that can be relatively easily squared with the Constitution but also economic, cultural, and social rights that may require a constitutional amendment. Finally, although some Supreme Court decisions have recognized that the child has a right to be treated as an independent, rational individual, others seem to uphold the principle that the rights of parents are superior to those of children.

The NCRC holds forums and conventions with elected representatives at federal, state, and local levels, to advocate the signing of the Convention. It also produces regular briefings and newsletters on children's rights, based on data collected by myriad local organizations working under the NCRC umbrella, which have set up monitoring and research programmes using the Convention on the Rights of the Child as their framework.

See also Children's Rights; Convention on the Rights of the Child.

References Cohen, Cynthia Price. "Children's Rights: An American Perspective" (1995).

National Consumers League

The 1870 United States census was the first to include the number of working children in its returns and to provide some picture of the nature and extent of child employment. It had the effect of arousing new interest in the subject at a time when there was a growing number of groups forming around various social issues: Labor unionization, the growth of socialism, and the spread of women's clubs created a network of bodies interested in child labour. One example of this is to be found in the General Federation of Women's Clubs, which in 1898 passed a series of resolutions on employment including one calling for an end to child labour. The Federation had even set up a committee devoted entirely to combating child labour.

Although all of these groups played a part in raising public awareness, the most important body at this time was the National Consumers League (NCL). The League was founded in 1890, in New York, and from the outset it had the working conditions of adults and children on its agenda.

The drive of the NCL is reflected in its general secretary, Florence Kelley. Kelley was a licensed attorney, a socialist, and the chief factory inspector in the state of Illinois. Her work in Illinois and her reports on the working conditions of children in glass manufacturing, the garment industry, and other sweatshops played a key role in the introduction of the Illinois Factory Act of 1893. In 1899, Kelley took over the leadership of the NCL. She remained in that position until her death in 1932.

The NCL played a major role in supporting the formation of the National Child Labor Committee (NCLC). The League provided the NCLC with its first office space free of charge and the League's existing network of contacts were used by Alexander J. McKelway and Owen R. Lovejoy, the NCLC assistant secretaries, when they travelled around the country.

The League also undertook its own direct action in promoting legislation on child labour. In 1902 the NCL circulated the Massachusetts labour statute around the country, suggesting that it should act as a model for all states developing legislation on this issue. The NCL referred to the Massachusetts statute as the "Standard Child Labor Law."

Although the League was supportive of the NCLC, it did not always agree with the latter's methods. In 1927 Florence Kelley, the leader of the NCL, was incensed by the behaviour of the then secretary of the NCLC, one Wiley Smith. She accused Smith—and by implication, the NCLC—of selling out to manufacturers on the issue of child labour.

The National Association of Manufacturers (NAM) had been staunchly opposed to all child labour legislation but apparently changed its position in 1926. It was at this time that NAM introduced a National Education and Employment Program. According to NAM, the programme was aimed at evaluating the minimum age for work and the role of education in children's lives. NAM went on to propose a minimum work week of 48 hours; the banning of dangerous work and of work between 9 P.M. and 7 A.M.; and a minimum age of 14 years for employment.

Although many of the NAM's proposals fell short of the NCLC's aims, Swift welcomed them and went so far as to recommend that the NCLC should cooperate with the NAM. Kelley and the NCL believed the NAM proposals were a sham, and they vociferously condemned the NAM. They believed that Swift and the NCLC were betraying the interests of working children. The League's view of the NAM programme was subsequently borne out by the NAM's failure to support any legislative moves toward the achievement of its "education program," in any state, in the period leading up to 1929.

See also American Federation of Labor; Lovejoy, Owen R.; McKelway, Alexander J.; National Child Labor Committee.

References Trattner, Walter I., *Crusade for the Children* (1970).

National Movement of Street Children

The National Movement of Street Children is based in Brazil and has been working for street children's rights for over a decade. This group has received a large amount of attention for adopting a strong emphasis on children's participation in the running and organization of its activities.

One of the Movement's major achievements was to organize the Fourth National Meeting of Street Children in 1995. Approximately 900 street children attended, with delegates from 24 states within Brazil. Representatives from government and nongovernmental agencies were present.

See also Brazil; Organizations of Working Children.

Navy

It was long the custom of navies and merchant navies throughout the world to recruit boys to serve on board ships. The life was generally hard and dangerous. However, the case of Sir John Theophilus Lee, who served in the British navy from the age of 5 years, demonstrates that on some occasions these boy sailors matured into happy and successful adults.

Lee's father was a naval lieutenant. In his memoirs, Lee remarks proudly that from the time of his enlistment in 1793, he was completely self-supporting: His annual pay and the daily provisions he received covered the costs of food, clothing, and education. At first, Lee spent days on board ship and returned home in the evening. After two years, however, he joined the frigate *Eurydice*, which was sent to join the British

fleet in the Mediterranean Sea. On that voyage he took part in the Battle of Cape St. Vincent.

Corporal punishment was common. Lee gives an account of a boy being flogged for untidiness and lying. Other boys were made to inflict the punishment, under the threat that if they tried to soften the blows, they would receive the same punishment themselves. At the age of 10, Lee witnessed the hanging of a mutineer. A year later, he was involved in another major naval battle, at Aboukir Bay. When he was 12 years old, his service was discontinued so that he could attend the Royal Naval Academy on shore. When he returned to sea at the age of 16, he was already a veteran of naval warfare.

Lee was remarkable for going to sea at a particularly young age and surviving: Many boys only a year or two older had similar experiences but did not live long enough to tell their stories.

See also Boy Soldiers.

References Garfield, Leon, and Proctor, David, *Child O' War* (1972).

NCH-Action for Children

NCH-Action for Children (originally known as the Children's Home and Orphanage, and after 1908, as the National Children's Homes) was founded in 1869 under the leadership of Thomas Bowman Stephenson. Stephenson was a Methodist minister and set up the homes to provide shelter and spiritual guidance to homeless children. The homes also provided training in appropriate work so they could lead independent lives on reaching adulthood.

In 1872 Stephenson visited Canada and set up a network facilitating child migration from Britain to North America. On 23 May 1873, the first 49 children arrived in Canada for a life of work on Canadian farms.

The child emigrations to Canada stopped in 1934, when the NCH began to send homeless children to Australia. Young children between the ages of 4 and 10 years were selected and transported to farms and

Rajesh Sahani sleeps standing after 12 hours of road-building in Pokhara, Nepal, 1996 (John Moore, Associated Press)

other work outlets in Australia, a policy that continued until the mid-1950s.

In 1994 the organization adopted its present name. It concentrates its work on an array of social work activities, mediation services for families that are breaking up, and support for young children in trouble.

See also Child Migrants Trust.

Nepal

The kingdom of Nepal is an independent Asian state lying between India and China. The population of over 20 million lives mainly in the flat and hilly regions to the south and the centre of the country. The north is made up of part of the Himalayan mountain range, including Mount Everest, the highest mountain in the world. Nepal earns foreign currency through exporting goods such as carpets, clothing, and handicrafts, and agricultural products such as herbs and tea. It also has a growing tourist industry, based in the capital, Kathmandu. Most of the population adhere to the Hindu religion. A caste system exists that has a profound effect on the lives and prospects of children. Although slavery was abolished in Nepal in 1924, observers believe that many adults and children live in conditions that are little different from slavery.

Parents are expected to contribute a part of the cost of a child's education, which means that most children in poorer families do not enrol in school. There is a high level of migration from poor rural areas to cities, one consequence of which is the existence of a large body of poor children in urban areas, some of whom live on the street.

The employment of children in Nepal is legally restricted by provisions of the Labor Act of 1992 and the Children's Act of the same year. However, evidence collected by nongovernmental organizations concerned with child labour shows that children are to be found in a very wide variety of jobs, including domestic service, agriculture, handicrafts, selling, and the tourist trade. A survey by the Nepal Rastra Bank in 1988 found that girls are more likely to be expected to work than boys, and that they start domestic labour as young as 5 or 6 years of age.

A survey of carpet factories in the Kathmandu valley carried out by the organization Child Workers in Nepal found more than 3,000 children at work. They were predominantly between 11 and 14 years of age, but 8 percent were between 8 and 10 years. Almost all of the child workers were members of low castes who had come from poor rural areas. Factory owners generally belong to higher castes. Some children were placed in the factory by their parents, but many were introduced to the work by brokers. In some cases the activities of the brokers amount to kidnapping. Most children worked between 10 and 16 hours per day. Rates of pay equivalent to 7 or 8 U.S. dollars per month were typical. However, in most cases the workers themselves did not receive even these small sums, since the wages were passed to their parents or brokers, or retained by the factory owners.

A survey of the tea growing industry found that 10 percent of workers were children. However, this is probably a severe underestimate because additional children are brought in to help at harvest time. More than 20 percent of child tea workers were the main wage earners in their families. Only three of the twenty-three tea-growing estates surveyed made any provision for the working children's education.

See also Child Workers in Nepal.

References Concerned for Working Children, The, *Child Labour in Nepal* (1995); Sattaur, Omar, *Child Labour in Nepal* (1993).

Netherlands

Situated in northeastern Europe, bordered by Germany and Belgium, this country is often referred to as Holland, although that name properly applies to only one of its regions. The Netherlands is a parliamentary democracy, with a monarch as head of state—currently Queen Beatrix. The Netherlands has a population of more than 15 million and is one of the most densely populated countries in the world. More than half of its territory is below sea level and is kept dry by an elaborate system of dykes and drainage pumps. Two-thirds of the land area is devoted to agriculture, but only 10 percent of the workforce is engaged in agricultural production. Most of the population lives in cities or towns and is engaged in manufacturing or trade. More than one million people live in the capital, Amsterdam, and its suburbs.

The history of the Netherlands is closely linked to that of its neighbour, Belgium. The two countries were united for a time in the early nineteenth century. Belgium led the way in the industrial revolution, the Netherlands being a more agricultural area. Children had traditionally worked in agricultural communities and they also worked in the mills and factories that sprang up in the nineteenth century. From the middle of that century until 1920, child labour and schooling were central topics of political debate in the Netherlands. Starting with Van Houten's "little law" on child employment, a series of laws were passed that led eventually to increasing periods of compulsory education and decreasing work hours. Educational provision and the tightening of child labour laws has continued until the present day. Legislation permits light work in family businesses and work in the entertainment industry by young children. However, other sorts of work by children of school age does continue.

Research carried out in 1988 found that three-fourths of high school pupils between 12 and 19 years of age had had at least one job in the previous year. The most common jobs were in agriculture, shopwork, newspaper delivery, baby-sitting, and occasional services, such as washing cars. More than half of the jobs undertaken were illegal. This was not an isolated finding. A study in 1994 found that more than one in five pupils under 15 years of age had a job, despite the fact that there are severe legal restrictions. A survey of morning and evening newspaper delivery workers by the National Federation of Christian Trade Unions showed that in terms of age and of work hours, the law was widely ignored. In addition, a number of those surveyed said that they suffered from work-related stress.

Most problems of working children in the Netherlands are probably much less serious than those experienced today by working children in other countries. Nevertheless, the Dutch government, trade unions, and welfare bodies see a need for the child labour laws to be more effectively enforced.

See also Belgium; Van Houten, Samuel.
References Meuwese, Stan, *Child Labour in the Netherlands* (1995).

New England Association of Farmers, Mechanics, and Other Working Men

An early labour organization in the United States that condemned child labour. The programme at its convention in 1832 stated that "children should not be allowed to labor in the factories from morning till night, without any time for healthy recreation and mental culture." The members argued that some form of legislation was required.

New Zealand

New Zealand is an island state in the southwest Pacific Ocean, first colonized by the ancestors of the present-day Maori people more than a thousand years ago and later by Great Britain. The country is now an independent democracy within the British commonwealth. During British rule in the nineteenth century, extensive immigration took place. Today the islands of New Zealand have a combined population of more than 3.5 million.

The two main islands are North Island and South Island. Agriculture is particu-larly important to the economy, and hydroelectricity is a significant power source. Although child employment is common in New Zealand, the country has not yet ratified ILO Conventions Nos. 5 and 138.

Surveying three North Island schools, Ronald Sultana found that most school students had had a job at some time. He found that a wide range of jobs were undertaken and that gender, class, and ethnic origin influenced what job a particular school student might have. Girls were more likely to be involved in home-based activities such as cleaning and baby-sitting. Children from middle-class backgrounds tended to be found assisting adult professionals such as photographers or veterinary surgeons. Maoris had greater difficulty finding jobs, and the work they did obtain, such as picking and freezing fruit, reflected what Sultana terms the "job apartheid of New Zealand."

Many school students stated that because the national rate of unemployment was high, they thought that their working before graduation from school was a useful way of maximizing their later competitiveness in the adult job market. Although the conditions of employment and rates of pay of school-age workers are in many cases governed by national agreements between employers and trade unions, school-age workers often complained that they were "ripped off"—in other words, not fairly treated. Most jobs performed by school students involve repetitive and fragmented tasks and provide few opportunities for acquiring or practicing skills that will help the students compete later in the adult workplace.

See also International Labour Organisation.
References Sultana, Ronald G. "Breaking Them In? School Kids in the Twilight Economy" (1990).

Newsies

The transition from the nineteenth to the twentieth century in the United States brought increasing reliance on industrial forms of production. Many children in urban settings lost their jobs as a result of

"Newsies," or boys hawking newspapers, in front of South Station, Boston, Massachusetts, 1917 (Lewis Hine, Library of Congress)

new technology. For example, the introduction of the pneumatic tube in retail shops meant that there was no longer a need to employ children to carry messages and money from counter to counter.

However, children moved into other forms of work. One of the most famous child occupations was that of the "newsies." These were newspaper sellers, or in the eyes of some people, newspaper hustlers, who hawked their papers on the street. Throughout the last two decades of the nineteenth century, newspaper circulation and production were expanding. Newspapers that previously had appeared only in morning editions began to be offered in afternoon editions, too. The newsies were sustained by this expanding market. Children moved into this form of part-time work in place of their previous full-time jobs, as selling newspapers fits more conveniently with attending school. This pattern was established by the beginning of the twentieth century.

Newsies were self-employed, buying their papers from circulation managers, and they had to sell their papers in order to stay in business. They were a recognized group of workers important to the newspaper industry. This is clearly demonstrated by the 1899 New York strike. The New York newsies had organized themselves into a union and came out in strike against the rise in newspaper prices brought in by two eminent New York publishers, Joseph Pulitzer and Randolph Hearst. The strike was successful, with the publishers offering to settle with the newsies.

Some observers, such as Nasaw, believe that this shows children playing an active role in their own socialization. The newsies were behaving in a way that they believed adult workers would and thus were socializing themselves into appropriate adult roles by their actions.

See also Delivery, Newspaper; *Saturday Evening Post*; Socialization.

References Nasaw, D. *Children of the City* (1985).

Nicaragua

The Republic of Nicaragua is the largest state on the isthmus that connects North and South America. It borders both the Pacific Ocean and the Caribbean Sea. The official language is Spanish, but a substantial number of Nicaraguans speak English. Most of the population of 4 million are Roman Catholics. Nicaragua achieved independence from Spanish rule in 1821. Its economy is mainly agricultural, with coffee, sugar, cotton, tobacco, bananas, peanuts, and other crops contributing to the country's export earnings.

In recent times the country has been plagued by political instability: From the 1930s until 1979, a right-wing regime run by the Somoza family was in power. They were overthrown by a left-wing guerrilla group, the Sandinistas. The Sandinista government was in turn opposed by rightist guerrillas called Contras. The civil war officially ended in 1992 when the Sandinistas were defeated in parliamentary elections, but small bands of guerrillas continued to fight for a few more years.

Children make up a substantial part of the population of Nicaragua, and children were prominent among victims and participants in the civil war that overthrew the Somoza family. In 1973 the Somoza government introduced an Immediate Action Plan for Education. Despite its name, this plan was aimed at promoting child labour rather than education. The school week was cut from 30 hours per week to 20 hours, and school terms were reorganized so that children could more readily participate in the harvesting of export crops. Throughout the period of Somoza's government, educational provision was poor and attendance was low. Even children who were not themselves working would absent themselves from school in order to look after younger children while their parents went out to work.

In early 1979, the Somoza regime started what its opponents called a "Herod Policy" of killing older boys in urban slum areas, in the belief that they were a major cause of political unrest. One effect of this was that boys in poor families, believing themselves soon to be murdered, fled to areas controlled by the Sandinista guerrillas. Children of both sexes fought in the civil war.

After 1979, standards of schooling improved significantly, but the economic circumstances of most Nicaraguan children remain poor.

See also America, Central.

References Ennew, Judith, and Milne, Brian, *The Next Generation: Lives of Third World Children* (1989).

Nigeria

The Federal Republic of Nigeria lies on the west coast of Africa. Its population is estimated to be around 120 million. The principal languages are English, Hausa, Yoruba, and Ibo, the last three being spoken by the three main ethnic groups in the country. Islam is the predominant religion in the north of the country; elsewhere, Christianity is widespread. In some rural areas, traditional religions are practiced.

Nigeria achieved independence from British rule in 1963. Since then it has experienced political, economic, and ethnic tension and has undergone periods of military rule. Its economy was based on agriculture until the 1970s, when oil was discovered. Export of oil has not brought as much economic benefit as was hoped. Three quarters of the population lived in rural areas in the early 1980s. That fell to around two-thirds in the 1990s. Thus, urbanization is taking place, but not at a particularly rapid rate.

As in many other societies, work by children is a long-standing practice. Enid Schildkrout's anthropological study of children in Kano City, northern Nigeria, where the population is Muslim, shows clearly the links between traditional values and children's work. Married women in Kano live in *purdah*, a state of religiously ordained seclusion. In normal circumstances, they do not leave their homes. In order to carry out some of the functions of running the home and to engage in economic activity such as selling cooked food or craft goods they have made, the married women have to rely on their children. Much of this work can be classified as being sent out on errands. In addition to requiring their children to work directly for them, the parents are traditionally seen as having the right to direct their children to work for other people. Parents may also choose to send their children to Quranic schools.

Another milieu in which traditional lifestyles give rise to child labour is the nomadic family. Nomadic groups are primarily engaged in herding animals or fishing, and children are assigned part of the family's work load—for example, guarding the livestock. The children of nomadic families have been identified by the government as being in particular need of help, and a National Commission for Nomadic Education has been set up to oversee their elementary education.

Two of the main forms of child labour outside the home are street vending and weaving. Children as young as 6 years may be found in street trading, but most are between 9 and 14 years old. Venders are predominantly boys. Children often start very casually, by accompanying their parents or older children, and then gradually start to trade independently. Authorities have tried since the colonial era to restrict or eliminate street trading, especially by children, but with little long-term success. In the late 1980s, special tribunals were set up to deal with children arrested under edicts forbidding street trading. Hundreds of children were convicted and held in custody until their fines were paid. However, there is little obvious long-term change in the extent of street selling.

Traditionally it has been common for boys to be apprenticed to master craftsmen. This has involved the boys' moving into their master's home and living as part of the family. The values of the apprentice's family and those of the master would usually be similar, so the child would not usually experience this shift as a painful one. However, as urbanization has increased, master-apprentice relations have changed. The dangers to the apprentice of being exploited by the master are greater when the parents and the craftsman are not members of the same small community.

As Nigeria becomes more urbanized, an influx of poorly educated children into the towns from urban areas will lead to more street begging and more children being employed in small businesses in the informal sector of the economy. Nigerian welfare organizations foresee increasing problems. So far, organizations of working children have been weak and short lived.

See also Africa; Burkina Faso.

References Mendelievich, Elias (ed.), *Children at Work* (1979); Oloko, Sarah Beatrice Adenike, *International Working Group on Child Labour in-depth Country Report: Nigeria* (1995); Schildkrout, Enid, "The Employment of Children in Kano (Nigeria)" (1981).

Nongovernmental Organizations

There are many such organizations functioning in the area of child labour. These organizations, usually referred to as "NGOs," are independent from government and normally have a clearly defined aim. For example, one such NGO in India is the Concerned for Working Children group and their specific aim of eliminating child labour. However, it should be recognized that NGOs have existed for a long time: One might reasonably argue that the National Child Labor Committee was an early form of NGO.

Although NGOs are functionally independent from government, many rely on government grants for part of their financial support. NGOs may have specific agendas and aims, but they are also involved in a great deal of general fieldwork, trying to help and improve the situation of working children. This might be achieved by setting up a drop-in centre or an education programme.

Contemporary discussions of child labour inevitably draw upon the views and experiences of workers in NGOs. However, there is a potential problem in countries like India and Africa, where there are large numbers of NGOs. The problem in such situations is one of coordination and effective communication between and among the myriad organizations.

See also Anti-Slavery International; Concerned for Working Children, The; Confederacao Nacional de Accao sobre Trabalho Infantil; Defence for Children International; Low Pay Network; National Child Labor Committee; National Consumers League; Permanent Conference for the Abolition of Child Labor; Save the Children Fund.

Oastler, Richard

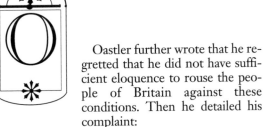

A dedicated Christian and a supporter of English Toryism, Richard Oastler (1789–1861) was a flamboyant campaigner who is said to have dedicated himself to the cause of child workers at the request of a reforming factory owner, John Wood. He began on 16 October 1830, by publishing a letter entitled "Yorkshire Slavery" in the English newspaper *Leeds Mercury*. He wrote:

Let truth speak out, appalling as the statement may appear. The fact is true. Thousands of our fellow creatures and fellow subjects, both male and female, the miserable inhabitants of a Yorkshire town (Yorkshire now represented in Parliament by the giant of antislavery principles) are this very moment existing in a state of slavery, more horrid than are the victims of that hellish system "colonial slavery." These innocent creatures draw out, unpitied, their short but miserable existence, in a place famed for its profession of religious zeal, whose inhabitants are ever foremost in professing "temperance" and "reformation," and are striving to outrun their neighbors in missionary exertions, and would fain send the Bible to the farthest corner of the globe—aye, in the very place where the antislavery fever rages most furiously, her apparent charity is not more admired on earth, than her real cruelty is abhorred in Heaven. The very streets that receive droppings of an "Anti-Slavery Society" are every morning wet by the tears of innocent victims at the accursed shrine of avarice, who are compelled (not by the cart whip of the negro slave driver) but by the dread of the equally appalling thong or strap of the overlooker, to hasten, half-dressed, but not half-fed, to those magazines of British infantile slavery—the worsted mills in the town and neighbourhood of Bradford!!!

Oastler further wrote that he regretted that he did not have sufficient eloquence to rouse the people of Britain against these conditions. Then he detailed his complaint:

Thousands of little children, both male and female, but principally female, from 7 to 14 years of age, are daily compelled to labor from six o'clock in the morning to seven in the evening, with only—Britons blush while you read it!—with only thirty minutes allowed for eating and recreation. Poor infants! Ye are indeed sacrificed at the shrine of avarice, without even the solace of the negro slave; ye are no more than he is, free agents; ye are compelled to work as long as the necessity of your needy parents may require, or the cold-blooded avarice of your worst and barbarian masters may demand! Ye live in the boasted land of freedom, and feel and mourn that ye are slaves, and slaves without the only comfort that the negro has. He knows it is his sordid, mercenary master's interest that he should live, be strong and healthy. Not so with you. Ye are doomed to labour from morning to night for one who cares not how soon your weak and tender frames are stretched to breaking! You are not mercifully valued at so much per head; this would assure you at least (even with the worst and most cruel masters) of the mercy shown to their labouring beasts. No, no! your soft and delicate limbs are tired and fagged, and jaded, at only so much per week, and when your joints can act no longer, your emaciated frames are instantly supplied with other victims, who in this boasted land of liberty are *hired*—not sold—as slaves and daily forced to hear that they are free.

In 1833, Oastler addressed the first meeting on the plight of factory children held in London, the capital city. His opponents, who nicknamed him the "factory king," became particularly incensed when he appeared to threaten that he would teach children to use their grandmothers' knitting needles to sabotage factory machinery. Imprisoned for debt, he was released through the money-raising efforts of "Oastler committees" set up around England.

According to Friedrich Engels, Oastler was a particular favourite of workingmen, who assigned him honorary titles such as "king of the factory children." Oastler was equally well known and respected by factory children, who would flock to see him when he visited their towns.

See also Engels, Friedrich; Shaftesbury, Lord.
References Engels, Friedrich, *The Condition of the Working Class in England* (1987); Hammond, J. L., and Hammond, Barbara, *Lord Shaftesbury* (1939).

Operation Child Watch

Initiated by the United States Labor Department in early 1990 under Labor Secretary Elizabeth Dole, Operation Child Watch was one of the most publicized attempts by the federal authorities to confront employers who for decades had ignored legal restrictions on child labour. Nationwide sweeps were carried out by 1,000 wage and labour inspectors. The first sweep took place in March and was followed by a number of others. Figures released by the Labor Department show that the initiative found 25,886 minors working illegally in more than 2,200 business establishments. These included sweatshops, fast food outlets, neighbourhood shops, car washes, and farms. Minors were also found in homeworking, performing tasks such as the assembly of cheap jewellery.

The effect of this initiative appears to have been to heighten public awareness of the issue of child labour and to increase employers' realization of the possibility of being caught. How successful such approaches are in the long run is open to debate: One might reasonably argue that occasional initiatives cannot substitute for a consistent monitoring force.

References Butterfield, Bruce D. "Business as Usual Despite Federal Crackdown: Child Labor Violations Continue Much as Before in Sweatshops and Fields across the Nation" (1990).

Organisation for Economic Cooperation and Development

Formed in 1961 out of a renamed and expanded Organisation for European Economic Cooperation, the Organisation for Economic Cooperation and Development (OECD) has two main aims. The first is to encourage economic growth and high employment with financial stability, and the second is to promote multilateral trade.

The OECD operates through several committees that undertake investigations of particular subjects. The organization's concern with promoting economic growth and multilateral trade has led its members to voice concerns about the spread of marginal labour activities, or the employment of casual and marginal workforces. Children frequently constitute a substantial part of such worker groups.

See also Globalization; International Financial Institutions.

Organizations of Working Children

In recent years, a debate has sprung up about the role of working children in policy and decisionmaking processes. Nongovernmental organizations (NGOs) have been in the vanguard of those who advocate the inclusion of working children in decisions relating to their lives; and the recent International Working Group on Child Labor (IWGCL) report *Working Children: Reconsidering the Debates* explicitly argues for this position. Such groups point to the United Nations Convention on the Rights of the Child to justify their arguments. The NGOs and the IWGCL point to the growing number of children's organizations that reflect the views of working children as evidence of the fact that children can and should have a voice in issues affecting them.

Historically, working children have shown that they have the capacity to organize and take effective action to protect themselves. In 1902, in the United States, child workers participated in the anthracite coal strike, drawing attention to the conditions of child employees in the mines and to the low wages received by all employees. In 1899, New York newspaper boys provided another historical example of working children organizing themselves into a union: They united to combat wage cuts proposed by the press barons of the time, and succeeded in staving off the cuts.

In the early 1990s, girls working in the garment industry in Bangladesh formed a group to actively fight the potential loss of their jobs. They were at risk of losing their jobs because of international sanctions against products made by children. The girls circulated a petition and gained press coverage for their situation. Although they were unsuccessful in saving their jobs, their example provides clear evidence of working children's ability to organize and take action.

At the international level, there are now numerous examples of working children's organizations. Most of these examples are found in Latin America, Africa, and Asia. The Movement of Adolescents and Children of Christian Workers (MANTHOC) was formed in 1976. In 1996, this organization of working children, along with other NGOs, organized the Sixth National Meeting of Working Children. This meeting brought together 800 children between the ages of 9 and 16 years to discuss problems and develop strategies for resolving them.

Organizations representing working children can be found in a number of other countries. In 1985, the Movimento Nacional de Meninos y Meninas da Rua (MNMMR) was formed to represent street children in Brazil. In India the Bal Mazdoor Union (BMU) and the Bhima Sangha were formed to represent working children. The BMU was founded in 1991 as a direct result of working children's awareness that they were not being recognized as workers.

The growing awareness that working children's voices need to be included in discussions about child labour issues has led to the inclusion of children in a number of forums. For example at the 1997 International Conference on Child Labor in Oslo representatives of three working children's organizations were invited. These were Bhima Sangha, the West African Movement of Working Children and Youth and the Latin American Movement of Working Children and Adolescents. Although such participation is to be encouraged issues such as the level of participation still need to be addressed.

Although working children are beginning to participate in the political arena there are a number of issues surrounding the question of organizations of working children. If working children's organizations are to be taken seriously then appropriate forums need to exist for their views to be heard. At the same time we need to ensure that such organizations are representative of working children as a whole.

Many of the organizations of working children that currently exist were aided by adults in NGOs. In helping to establish such groups adults need to ensure that they adopt the role of facilitators and there is a need to build in systems that protect such organizations from the claim that they merely reflect the views of adult organizers.

There is a growing awareness that organizations of child workers can play an important role in tackling many issues relating to child labour at the international level. There is clear evidence that such groups can be effective and that the emphasis should now be on ways of enhancing representative participation in a way that avoids the trap of tokenism.

See also Advocacy; Anthracite Coal Strike; Bal Mazdoor Union; Bhima Sangha; Convention on the Rights of the Child; Global March against Child Labor; International Working Group on Child Labour; Movement of Working Children and Adolescents from Working-Class Christian Families; National Movement of Street Children; Nongovernmental Organizations.

References McKechnie, Jim, and Hobbs, Sandy (eds.), *Working Children: Reconsidering the Debates* (1998); Swift, Anthony, "Let Us Work!" (1997).

See also Garment Industry; Sweated Labour.
References Bythell, Duncan, *The Sweated Trades: Outwork in Nineteenth-Century Britain* (1978).

Outwork

Outwork, or homeworking, is a form of subcontracting of part of a production process to workers in their home settings. The tasks involved vary enormously. They can be monotonous and require little skill (for example, stuffing envelopes), or they might require high levels of skill (for example, finishing jobs in the textile industry). The workers are contracted to complete a set number of tasks, and they are paid on completion and after quality assurance checks have been made.

Outwork practices are exceptionally exploitative. The pay is normally very poor, and many of the overhead costs (for space, heat, and light) are borne by workers rather than employers. Workers usually are classified as self-employed and thus do not obtain access to any employer-based health or pension insurance plans. They must pay their own state taxes and bear complete responsibility for their personal health and safety.

Outworkers are rarely members of trade unions, and therefore are isolated and vulnerable. As a consequence, outworkers tend to be drawn from among the most oppressed groups within the community: women, migrants, and children fill the ranks of the homeworking labour force.

Owen, Robert

Having established a reputation as a man of shrewd financial and managerial skills, the Welshman Robert Owen (1771–1858) dedicated his later years to philanthropy, trade unionism, and socialism. When he took charge of the New Lanark mills in Scotland, he found that the workforce included almost 500 pauper "apprentices" between the ages of 5 and 10 years. Owen gradually replaced them with older children who worked as free labourers, and for whom he provided educational and recreational facilities in the so-called Institution for the Formation of Character.

Owen began to campaign publicly for children younger than 10 years to be excluded from factory work and for restrictions on the hours worked by older children. In 1818, as part of this effort, he published *On the Employment of Children in Manufactories.* Owen regarded the Cotton Factories Regulation Act (also known as Peel's Act) passed by Parliament in 1819 as inadequate because it applied only to cotton mills and included no provision for inspection.

See also Factory Acts; Pauper Apprentices.
References Hammond, J. L., and Hammond, Barbara, *The Town Labourer, 1760–1832* (1967); Owen, Robert, *A New View of Society* (1967).

Pakistan

When Britain gave up control of much of the Indian subcontinent in 1947, two states were formed—India and Pakistan. The latter comprised two parts entirely separated from each other by the larger country, India. In 1971, East Pakistan broke away and became the independent state of Bangladesh. The current Pakistan dates from that period. It has a population of around 120 million, of whom the overwhelming majority are Muslims. Karachi (8 million) and Lahore (4 million) are the largest cities. Since then there has been considerable political instability, including periods of military rule.

The economy is predominantly agricultural, with an extensive irrigation system. Cotton and rice are among the major crops. Pakistan exports these as well as carpets, textiles, and petroleum products.

Child labour in Pakistan has been described as of epidemic proportions. The Human Rights Commission of Pakistan in 1995 estimated that there were around 11 or 12 million working children in the country, at least half of whom were younger than 10 years. Much of what goes on is illegal under the Employment of Children Act of 1991 and the Bonded Labor Act of 1992. Unfortunately, the machinery to enforce these laws is not strong enough to have any substantial effect. The International Labour Organisation has criticized the Pakistani government for its lack of effective action.

Abdul Rasheed, a young carpet weaver, works in Muridke, Pakistan, 1998 (B. K. Bangash, Associated Press)

Many children work in carpet manufacture under a system called *pesghi*. This is a form of bonded labour based on a contract between a parent and a carpet manufacturer. For an agreed sum of money, typically equivalent to 150 or 200 U.S. dollars, the child is required to work for the factory owner for, say, five years. The deal is presented to the parents as an apprenticeship whereby the child will learn useful skills. In practice, the work is hard and the conditions unhealthy. Payment is in instalments and subject to deductions for food and training, so the family may gain little more than relief from the need to feed that child for the five-year period.

Carpet manufacture is only one of many forms of arduous work undertaken by Pakistani children. Some manufacture soccer balls for a wage of around 1 U.S. dollar per day. They also work in brick kilns, shoe factories, on farms, and in service industries.

Employers claim that child labour is traditional in Pakistan and argue that by giving children work, they help to raise the children's standard of living and that of their families. Local groups working on behalf of child workers claim that much of the country's economy is driven by child labour. Cheap labour costs have led many businesses to relocate to Pakistan. The availability of cheap child labour also discourages investment in machinery that could make the work less taxing. Thus, economic advantage is bought at the children's expense, since many have profound health problems by the time they reach adulthood.

See also Asia; Bangladesh; Bonded Labour Liberation Front; India; Masih, Iqbal; Unfree Labour.

References Anti-Slavery International, *"This Menace of Bonded Labour": Debt Bondage in Pakistan* (1996); Cadman, Eileen, *No Time to Play: Child Workers in the Global Economy* (1996); Mendelievich, Elias (ed.), *Children at Work* (1979).

Palmer-Owen Bill

Although a number of individual states in the early 1900s had instituted child labour regulations, there was a growing awareness in the United States that federal legislation was needed. The Palmer-Owen bill was introduced in 1914 with little overt opposition, since public sentiment supported the control of child labour.

Opposition to the bill did exist among those with interests in industries that employed large numbers of children, especially in southern states. The editor of the *Southern Textile Bulletin*, David Clark, went so far as to characterize the bill as an attack on the South. Even with opposition mobilized, the bill proceeded through all stages of the legislative process. It did not become law, however. The session of the House was coming to an end, and attempts to bring the final bill to the floor for a vote required unanimous consent. A senator from North Carolina objected, and the bill foundered.

See also Legislation; United States of America.

Parents

The dominant view of the role of parents is that of protectors of their children. Within this framework it is difficult to understand why parents allowed their children to work during the industrial revolution and continue to allow them to work in developing countries today.

Historians such as J. L. and Barbara Hammond, have argued that the industrial revolution in Britain was a time when parents could be accused of exploiting their children. The industrial revolution, and in particular the factory system of production, increased the earning potential of children to such an extent that parents ignored their "natural" concern for the children's health and welfare and sent them off to work.

Michael Sadler went so far as to describe parents as "monsters" who reversed the natural order in forcing their children to provide for them. Sadler suggests that children worked while their parents were idle and that this was a conscious decision made by parents.

Some independent evidence appears to support this view. The Factories Inspection Commission reported in 1833 that some parents decided where their children would work simply on the basis of the wages paid and gave little attention to the conditions of employment.

However, the assumption that all parents treated their children in this way is questionable. Economic historian Clark Nardinelli suggests that we need to place the claims of Sadler and the Hammonds in context. Nardinelli does not doubt that some parents during the industrial revolution did exploit their children. However, he believes such cases were the exception rather than the rule.

Nardinelli believes that poverty, and not the industrial revolution, was the main force encouraging parents to let their children work. A number of studies in nineteenth-century England showed the extent to which children's earning were needed simply to keep the family income above the poverty line. In one study undertaken by Frances Collier in Lancashire, it was found that the earnings of children helped the family rise above basic subsistence levels.

Nardinelli also suggests that autobiographies from the time show that parents were not exploiters of their children. The autobiographical studies show that on the whole, warm and positive relations existed between parents and their children. Even though they had to work, children did not blame their parents for this and instead viewed their work as a necessity. In fact, they gained a sense of pride from being able to help their family and contribute to its well-being.

This view is supported by interview evidence from the Children's Employment Commission in Britain dating from 1842 and 1843. Part of the Commission's mandate was to gather information from working children. In these interviews there is little evidence that children saw their parents as exploiting them.

Nardinelli also challenges a number of other traditional assumptions about child labour during the industrial revolution. He believes that children actually gained some degree of independence and autonomy from their parents because they could work. This view, however, is contradicted by other scholars.

Nardinelli's writings have great relevance for current debates about child labour. Two points are particularly noteworthy: First, Nardinelli argues that poverty was the main motivator in drawing children into the labour force. In discussions of child labour in contemporary society, poverty continues to be the dominant explanation for the levels of child labour in developing countries. The recent report form the International Working Group on Child Labour draws attention to the fact that changing economic circumstances can draw children into the workforce. The IWGCL cites changes in the post-Soviet Russian economy as an example.

Secondly, Nardinelli suggests that working allowed children to gain independence from their parents. By implication, this means that working changes the nature and form of family relationships. Such changes can have a positive or a negative outcome. Current research has tended to pick up this last idea and has spent some time studying the impact of work on family relations.

Recent research carried out in countries with developed economies also has cast light on how contemporary parents view adolescents' work. S. Phillips and K. L. Sandstrom have suggested that parents typically have a positive view of modern-day adolescents' work. In particular, parents believed that paid work increased their child's level of independence. (It should be borne in mind that they were generally referring to part-time employment.)

These conclusions have recently been supported by the work of Pamela Aronson and her colleagues. Their research concluded that most parents viewed adolescents' work positively, believing that it led to the development of good work attitudes and that it gave their children an opportunity to learn skills that could not be gained from formal schooling.

When considering the impact of parents on child labour, we also need to acknowledge that they will have an indirect effect. Parents are the main influences on a child's socialization, and they transmit a wide range of values and attitudes to their offspring, including attitudes toward work. Whether we view work as simply a means of providing money or as an experience that should provide other rewards will shape our attitudes toward work.

See also Family Relations; Hammond, J. L., and Hammond, Barbara; Industrial Revolution; Nardinelli, Clark; Work Ethic.

References Aronson, Pamela, Mortimer, Jeylan T., Zierman, Carol, and Hacker, Michael, "Generational Differences in Early Work Experiences and Evaluations" (1996); Nardinelli Thesis, The; Child Labor and the Industrial Revolution (1990); Phillips, S., and Sandstrom, K., "Parental Attitudes Toward Youth Work" (1990).

Parliamentary Committees and Commissions

Britain has a long history of legislative reform that has resulted in the removal of children from a range of hazardous jobs and from full-time work. Much of this legislation was passed in the nineteenth and early twentieth centuries, due in part to evidence gathered about the working conditions of children throughout the nineteenth century. Parliamentary committees and commissions were a means by which the British legislature could collect information on a range of topics. Such commissions are still used at present. However, their role in the nineteenth century was particularly important for children.

Two examples of these commissions were the Sadler Committee and Lord Ashley's Mine Commission. (Lord Ashley later became Lord Shaftesbury, the name by which he is known to historians today.) The Sadler Committee collected evidence about conditions in the textile factories in the early 1830s. Evidence was collected from mill owners and from employees. The latter evidence graphically described the conditions under which children worked. For example, one 23-year-old female, in response to questioning by the commission, explained that she had started

working in the mills at 6 years of age. She usually worked from 6 A.M. to 7 P.M., with one forty-minute break for lunch. Given that the young woman in question lived two miles from the mill, she was often awakened by her mother at 3 or 4 o'clock to start walking to her place of work. Children in the mills were physically punished for not working hard enough or for being late for work. Evidence showed that such practices were widespread. The Sadler Committee Report contributed to the passing of a Parliamentary Act in 1833 that limited the number of hours per day that children and women could be employed in the textile mills.

Lord Ashley's Mine Commission was established in 1842. The evidence given to this commission demonstrated that girls as young as 8 years of age worked underground in the mines. One 12-year-old testified to the commission that she worked as a "coal bearer," carrying coal away from the coal face. She estimated that she carried 1.25 cwt on her back and made 25 to 30 trips on her shift. None of the children working in the mines attended school.

The report from Ashley's Commission played a role in the passing of the Mines Act of 1842, which prohibited the employment of all females in mines and excluded boys younger than 13 years from mining.

See also Factory Acts; Legislation; Shaftesbury, Lord.

References Hammond, J. L., and Hammond, Barbara, Lord Shaftesbury (1939).

Paterson 10-Hour Mill Strikes

In 1845, the Female Labor Reform Association (FLRA) was formed to campaign for the introduction of a 10-hour day and improved working conditions in mills. In response to the association's petitions, the Massachusetts legislature held a public hearing to investigate working conditions (the first such public hearing anywhere in the United States). The investigative committee then visited the mills, which had been especially cleaned for the occasion.

Following the inspection, the state legislature decided that conditions in the mills were acceptable. The FLRA denounced this decision, but their reform effort was stymied.

Gradually there was a migration out of the mills, with the workforce being replaced by a new wave of Irish immigrants. Company towns grew up around the mills on the eastern seaboard. Newcomers had to sign contracts committing their families to working for the company for at least a year. The workers lived in slums that belonged to the mill owners; they were paid in company slips that were redeemable only at company shops; and they were evicted from both job and home if their work was deemed unacceptable.

Against this background, in the late 1840s, the mill company in Paterson suddenly altered the lunch break of the child workers (pushing it back from noon to 1 P.M.). The children immediately walked off the job, with their parents cheering them on. The strike quickly spread, and other workers from the town joined in a general struggle for the 10-hour day. After a week, the company threatened to bring in the militia against the children, and they decided to return to work. Although the ringleaders were sacked and the demand for a 10-hour day went unmet, the company was forced to restore the children's lunch hour to its previous time.

References Zinn, Howard, *A People's History of the United States* (1980).

Pauper Apprentices

Pauper apprentices were orphaned or abandoned children of the poor who were indentured to mill or factory owners under the authority of the local parishes where they were born. In the early days of the British industrial revolution, the water-powered mills were located in rural areas, near running water. For the mill owners, obtaining an adequate supply of labour was difficult, as families were often unwilling to uproot and move to what were often desolate and isolated sites. In these circum-stances, some mill and factory owners turned to the use of pauper apprentices in their mills.

The availability of pauper children was a consequence of the operation of the Poor Laws in Britain. The Poor Laws had a long history dating back to the second half of the fourteenth century, when laws were enacted to restrict labour mobility in the aftermath of the Black Death, the plague that had devastated Europe. However, the main piece of legislation shaping poor relief at this juncture was the so-called 43rd of Elizabeth (meaning the 43rd enactment during the reign of Elizabeth I), dating from 1601. The Poor Laws required parishes (essentially an early unit of non-elected local government in England) to be responsible for the relief of want and hardship of individuals born in their district. The costs of meeting such relief were covered through local taxes on property. Those in charge of overseeing rates and relief within the parishes were known as Poor Law guardians.

The 43rd of Elizabeth identified three groups among the poor who should be dealt with in different and specific ways. First, the "impotent poor" (the elderly, the sick, and those with various physical or mental disabilities) were to be given "institutional relief" (that is, they were to be placed in poorhouses). Second, the "able-bodied poor" were to be put to work (that is, they were required to work at a nonresidential workhouse in order to obtain any money or food for their "relief"). Finally, the "able-bodied idler" or migrant was to be placed in a "house of correction" and put to work. Various acts of Parliament from the eighteenth century enabled parishes to operate workhouses for a profit; allowed them to merge in parish unions covering wider geographical areas; and increasingly saw the establishment of a simplified system whereby relief was given in return for labour. This could be either outdoor relief (in other words, nonresidential) or indoor relief (within the residential workhouse).

The original Poor Laws were designed

to meet the needs of a relatively stable and static population in an economy dominated by peasant production. However, with the development of capitalism in Britain and the related process of land enclosure during which peasants were driven off the land and forced to migrate to the developing towns and cities, the problem of poverty became substantially worse. The number of individuals facing destitution increased, and the costs of providing relief rose. In these circumstances, many parishes looked for ways of reducing their expenditures on poor relief. The system of pauper apprenticeship was one way of reducing parish costs by sending pauper children to work in workplaces beyond the parish district. The system not only met the needs of parish councils but also aided employers in different parts of the country.

Guardians entered into agreements with industrialists to send a specific number of pauper children under their care to work in the mills and factories. The children would be sent at a young age, often only 6 or 7 years, and were normally indentured until the age of 21 years. Throughout this period the children were legally bound to their "masters." The conditions in which the children lived and worked were horrendous. Work days of 12 to 15 hours were not uncommon, and breaks were few and short. When their work was finished, the children would move to another part of the factory, where they would sleep in the "prentice house." Overworked and underfed, their bodies would often be crippled by the work demands.

Regulations on the conditions of pauper apprentices were very slow to develop. The Health and Morals of Apprentices Act, passed in 1802, formally restricted apprentices to 12 hours' work a day; but the Act was rarely enforced, as its promoter, Sir Robert Peel, admitted. The decline of the phenomenon of the pauper apprentices in the first half of the nineteenth century was in general terms a result of the move to factory production within larger towns and cities, itself a consequence of the develop-

ment of steam production. The congregation of workplaces and labourers within the expanding urban settings reduced the need for long-term indentured labour, and the system gradually disappeared.

See also Capitalism; Half-time Working; Industrial Revolution; Owen, Robert; Poverty.

References Hammond, J. L., and Hammond, Barbara, *The Town Labourer, 1760–1832* (1967); Pinchbeck, Ivy, and Hewitt, Margaret, *Children in English Society*, vol. 1 (1969); Pinchbeck, Ivy, and Hewitt, Margaret, *Children in English Society*, vol. 2 (1973).

Permanent Conference for the Abolition of Child Labor

An organization in the United States representing around 25 national groups of varying social and political persuasions, the Permanent Conference for the Abolition of Child Labor was formed in 1922. The organization was founded during a meeting organized by Samuel Gompers, based on the attendees' mutual agreement that an amendment to the constitution was required if child labour was to be extinguished.

The Permanent Conference was instrumental in producing a draft child labour amendment to the Constitution in 1922, which it developed with input from the National Child Labor Committee. The amendment was eventually passed in 1924, after going through various permutations. It should be noted that this amendment merely enabled Congress to enact child labour legislation; it did not mandate the regulation or prohibition of child labour.

See also National Child Labor Committee.

Peru

The Republic of Peru lies on the Pacific coast of South America. Colonized by Spain in the sixteenth century, Peru achieved independence in 1821. There are three official languages: Spanish, Quechua, and Aymara. The population of Peru numbers more than 22 million, around half of whom are children or adolescents. The chief exports of the country are minerals, fish meal, sugar, and cotton. The government's recent attempts to reduce its foreign debt by economic restructuring have created large-scale unemployment and limited the funds available for social purposes.

It is estimated that more than 3 million children work in Peru, predominantly in the rural areas. In the capital, Lima, around a quarter of a million children are believed to be employed in occupations such as shoe shining, loading, selling newspapers, begging, and scavenging at municipal rubbish dumps. Research has shown that about 10 percent of poor families' income in Lima comes from child labour. Many children, predominantly girls, are employed as domestic servants. They sleep at the homes of their employers and receive little or no pay. Because of their isolation from families and friends, they are vulnerable to ill treatment and exploitation. Children as young as 8 years work in small brick-making concerns.

Children in rural areas start to work for their families around the age of 6 years. Boys herd sheep, draw water, sow and reap, and girls cook, spin, and look after younger children. Child labour in the Peruvian gold mining industry is largely unregulated. Two aspects of gold mining are particularly hazardous for children. One is exposure to mercury, and the other is inhalation of volcanic dust.

Two-thirds of child workers do not attend school or any other type of educational centre. Child workers who do attend school are more likely to fall behind in their schoolwork than are nonworkers of the same age. Researchers in Peru see the need for the educational system to be overhauled so that schools become "magnets for children."

See also America, South; Movement of Working Children and Adolescents from Working-Class Christian Families.

References Cadman, Eileen, *No Time to Play: Child Workers in the Global Economy* (1996); Mendelievich, Elias (ed.), *Children at Work* (1979); Salazar, Maria Cristina, and Glasinovich, Walter Alarcon, *Better Schools, Less Child Work: Child Work and Education in Brazil, Colombia, Ecuador, Guatemala, and Peru* (1996).

Pesticides
See Health.

Philippines
The Republic of the Philippines consists of a long string of islands lying southeast of continental Asia. Discovered by Europeans in the sixteenth century, the islands were under the successive control of Spain, Britain, Spain, and eventually, the United States. The country proclaimed its independence in 1946. Its current population is almost 70 million.

Although the government of the Philippines has not ratified International Labour Organisation conventions on child labour, it has signed an agreement with the ILO to develop a programme to deal with child labour's worst features. The national plan gives high priority to dealing with children who are victims of trafficking and working in prostitution and to those working in mines and quarries or on sugarcane plantations and vegetable farms.

Children also work in unhealthy conditions aboard fishing boats and as deep-sea divers. In Manila, the capital, many children earn their living on the streets. The growing city of Cebu is seen as an economic miracle, but child labour plays a large part there also. Large firms subcontract work with small firms, which in turn farm work out to households, in which everyone, including children, is involved in production.

In 1993 a group of child workers were found imprisoned in a fish processing factory in the Philippines. They had been offered jobs as domestics, but on their arrival at the factory they were told that they owed their employer money because he had paid for their travel to the job. To pay the debt, they would be forced to work in the factory. The owner provided their accommodation and food for the week, but a high charge for these benefits was deducted from their wages: Each child was paid 23 pesos a week but had debts totaling

Robert Mehia makes handmade shoes in Marikina, Philippines, 1969 (Corbis-Bettmann)

25 pesos. Hence the debt was never paid off. The children worked on a production line, filling cans with sardine pieces. They started work at 7 A.M. and worked on into the night. By the time their plight was discovered, the children had lived in the factory for a year without being allowed to leave the premises or to write to their parents and tell them where they were.

Campaigners for children's rights in the Philippines see the machinery for the control of child labour as ineffective. For example, in 1994, Senator Nikki Coseteng, Chair of the Filipino Senate Committee on Women and Family Relations, accused the government of "incoherent and ineffective policies" on child labour. Gina Dolorfino, of Save the Children Fund, said Filipino government child labour programmes were underfunded.

See also Asia; International Labour Organisation.

References Cadman, Eileen, *No Time to Play: Child Workers in the Global Economy* (1996); Camacho, Agnes Zenaida V. "Family, Child Labour, and Migration: Child Domestic Workers in Metro Manila" (1999); Forbes, Cameron, and Moorehead, Caroline, "The Sexual Exploitation of Children: The Philippines" (1989); International Labour Organisation, *Child Labour: Targeting the Intolerable* (1996); Lee-Wright, Peter, *Child Slaves* (1990); Sancho-Liao, Nelia "Child Labour in the Philippines: Exploitation in the Process of Globalization of the Economy" (1994).

Pinchbeck, Ivy

Ivy Pinchbeck (1898–1982) was a distinguished social historian of the British industrial revolution. She pioneered the study of working-class women and children in the nineteenth century, a time when most traditional historians were concerned with the activities of the "great men" of the age. Her two most influential studies were *Women Workers and the Industrial Revolution*, originally published in 1930, and (coauthored with her colleague Margaret Hewitt) a two-volume study, *Children in English Society*. Her books draw on a wide range of contemporary materials—for example, literary works, newspapers, and parliamentary reports—to provide a detailed insight into the lives of working children in a range of occupations. Despite the horrors the industrial revolution brought, Pinchbeck concludes that it also brought long-term benefits to women and children in Britain.

References Pinchbeck, Ivy, *Women Workers and the Industrial Revolution* (1969); Pinchbeck, Ivy, and Hewitt, Margaret, *Children in English Society*, vol. 1 (1969); Pinchbeck, Ivy, and Hewitt, Margaret, *Children in English Society*, vol. 2 (1973).

Pornography

People may be sexually aroused and sexually satisfied by words or images. Sometimes the sexual response may be largely unrelated to the intentions of those who created the picture or book. For example, a man may be sexually aroused by pictures of female models that were produced for a catalogue intended to sell the clothes the models are wearing. However, some words and images are made and circulated with the sole or main aim of evoking a sexual response. Such material is referred to as pornography. There is no commonly agreed definition of what constitutes pornography.

The United Nations Convention on the Rights of the Child, Article 34, requires states to take appropriate measures to prevent the exploitative use of children in pornographic performances and materials. Most countries regulate the sale of pornography by law. However, the difficulty of agreeing on a precise definition of what is permissible and what is not means that law enforcement agencies must rely on convention and respond to changing public opinion. Most countries in western Europe and north America permit mild or "soft" pornography and seek to ban "hard" pornography.

Since pornographers are often breaking the law and are subject to moral criticism, they tend to be secretive in their activities. It is often difficult to differentiate fact and myth. For example, with respect to pornographic images involving children, some

believe that this is a widespread and growing business. Others suspect that the involvement of children in the production of such material may be less extensive than is thought. They cite as evidence the fact that some pictures are frequently recycled and some appear to be at least 50 years old. However, whatever the scale, child pornography is a social issue that gives rise to strong and proper concerns.

To what extent does child pornography involve child labour? Again, the secretiveness of pornographers makes it difficult to give a precise answer. Certainly pornographers sell their work, so any child used to create the pictures is involved in economic activity. It appears that in some cases the child models are paid. However, there is also reason to believe that in many cases no payment is involved. The child may be frightened into cooperating by the use of threats. Alternatively, the pornographer may first win the confidence and friendship of a child, who may then be led slowly and gradually into posing in more and more sexually explicit ways.

That the children involved in the production of pornography are at risk emotionally and physically is clear. Compared to these dangers, their economic exploitation may be regarded as of secondary significance.

See also Modelling; Prostitution.

References Ennew, Judith, *The Sexual Exploitation of Children* (1986).

Portugal

Portugal, which has a population of around 10 million, is situated along on the southwestern coast of Europe, bordered by Spain and the Atlantic Ocean. Following political unrest in the 1960s and 1970s due to an illiberal regime and to unsuccessful colonial wars, Portugal since 1976 has been a relatively stable parliamentary democracy. Agriculture, manufacture, and tourism all play a part in an economy that has modernized under the new political regime.

Portugal is believed to have the highest

levels of child labour in western Europe. Many children leave school early to work in a wide variety of occupations. Although there are laws restricting child employment, they are widely regarded as ineffectual. A labour inspectorate exists, but there is reason to believe that it is not particularly effective. There are reports that inspectors notify the managers of factories of their impending visits, after which children who work there are hidden out of sight in locations such as canteens and outlying sheds that the inspectors will not visit.

Shoe manufacture contributes significantly to Portugal's earnings from exports. The industry is centred around Porto, in the north of the country. The industry includes many large factories but also innumerable small establishments employing as few as five people. In addition, a part of the process of shoe manufacture is undertaken by workers in their own homes. Official statistics show that some workers in large factories are of school age. However, there is reason to believe that the smaller concerns are more likely to employ children, who frequently start as part-time, after-school workers but gradually work longer hours, attend school less frequently, and eventually drop out entirely.

Portugal is one of the world's largest exporters of granite, marble, and slate. The industry is located primarily in the north of the country. Many children are involved in the industry as stone breakers. The work is hard and unhealthy, particularly because neither adults or children have any protection against the dust produced. Some of the work is organized on a family basis, with one adult male contracting the work, and family members, including boys, taking part in it. This places the activity outside the jurisdiction of the labour inspectorate.

In the Algarve, a major tourist area in the south, there is concern about the high proportion of children who give up their schooling in order to work in restaurants and hotels. A nationwide survey of hotels by the labour inspectorate found that 15 percent of employees were under 14 years of age. Casual observation shows that there are many children at work in street markets and at fish auctions. This work, which is irregular, casual, and informal, is largely overlooked in official records.

See also Confederacao Nacional de Accao sobre Trabalho Infantil; Europe.

References Lee-Wright, Peter, *Child Slaves* (1990); Williams, Suzanne, *Child Workers in Portugal* (no date).

Post-Fordism

A number of sociologists have used this word to describe changes to productivity and labour market practices in the global economy at the end of the twentieth century. The prefix *post-* emphasizes that the concept is different from the earlier era of Fordism. What are the characteristics attributed to each era? In terms of productivity and labour markets, Fordism was said to be an epoch dominated by mass production of consumer goods. These goods were produced at plants where workers found their jobs de-skilled and reduced to repetitive tasks in an assembly line. Workers were employed in large numbers at plant sites. They were often organized into trade unions. They were relatively well paid. The work was regulated. The demands of the work tasks meant that adults, both men and women, were employed. Assembly line tasks were generally thought unsuitable for children, who would find such work exhausting and would be less productive as a consequence. The archetype of this type of employment regime was the Ford motor company, hence *Fordism*.

Post-Fordism is apparently the antithesis of all of this. The development of computer technology has meant that rather than being forced to create mass-produced goods, companies can be much more flexible. They can respond much more quickly to consumer-led demand and can concentrate on "niche" production for particular groups of consumers. Under these new conditions it is suggested that there have been radical changes to dominant employment regimes. Flexible companies, it is argued, operate dual labour systems. They employ a small number of multiskilled core workers. These workers are highly trained and paid permanent employees. Short-term demands are met by employing a peripheral group of workers on short-term contracts. These workers are less skilled and enjoy fewer work benefits. Many subsidiary tasks are outsourced to a range of small suppliers, these contracts likewise involving short-term agreements. According to a number of analysts, many workers are employed in this marginal, subsidiary sector. The resulting intense competition at this level forces wages and conditions down, as poorer workers, such as migrants, women, and children, become attractive sources of labour power.

See also Globalization; Multinational Companies.

Poverty

A simple view of the connection between poverty and child labour would be as follows:

Childhood is a time for education and leisure. Work is an adult activity. Many children engage in work when they should be at school or at play. Child labour arises because the children, or their families, would have insufficient resources to live if the children did not earn an income through working.

A great deal of evidence could be cited to fit such a model. We know that in many communities throughout the world, the child is the main or sole earner in a family. We also know that in other cases, parents "sell" children to employers, in part to obtain a small, direct monetary gain and in part to relieve themselves of the economic burden of raising the child.

We know too that in some cases children are abandoned by their families and therefore have to work in order to survive.

If we focus on such cases, we are naturally led to explore the causes of poverty, since these in turn could be regarded as the indirect causes of child labour. Two main types of explanation are put forward. On the one hand there are worldwide economic developments, including globalization and the imposition of structural adjustment programmes. On the other hand, we may note specific economic circumstances shaping poverty in particular areas or countries.

First, there is employer demand. A fundamental point to be made about the economics of child labour is that many employers see children as a particularly cheap and docile labour force. It is sometimes claimed that children are employed in particular industries because they are especially suited physically to parts of the production process. Thus, children are needed in carpet manufacture because of their "nimble fingers."

Secondly, there are family needs. When parents come under particular economic stress, children may be perceived as an immediately available way of alleviating their financial problems.

Thirdly, there are politically induced economic problems. In some cases, countries that have undergone large-scale political upheavals have economic problems of the sort that encourage child labour. This appears to be the case in former Soviet-bloc countries such as Russia and Romania.

Fourthly, geographical factors contribute to poverty—for example, the flooding that takes place frequently in Bangladesh and parts of India.

In addition, many causes of child labour other than poverty are acknowledged. The first sort may be referred to as traditional social values. The second is education, or rather the failure of education as an alternative pursuit for children. The third category are the factors associated with children's own values—in particular, their desire to "grow up," to be treated like adults, and to exert control over their own destinies.

See also Carpet Manufacture; Causes of Child Labour; Cultural Traditions; Globalization; Stabilization and Structural Adjustment Programmes.

References McKechnie, Jim, and Hobbs, Sandy (eds.), *Working Children: Reconsidering the Debates* (1998).

Prison

In many countries, children are held in prisons. Most authorities on childhood believe that even children found guilty of serious crimes should not be sent to adult prisons but to special institutions for young people where they may receive appropriate education, therapy, and training. However, this principle has not yet been widely accepted by policymakers.

The prison conditions are often very bad, and contact with adult criminals is likely to increase the chances that a child will become an adult criminal too. In many cases, the children concerned have not even been found guilty of any crime but are in custody supposedly for their own protection, or are awaiting trial, a process that may take a very long time.

The imprisonment of children is relevant to child labour in two ways. First, the many children around the world who earn their living on the streets are among the most likely to be imprisoned, both because they are liable to engage in illegal activity in order to survive and because the city authorities may find it convenient to clear the streets from time to time by arresting street children and accusing them of committing offences. When charged with a crime, these children are unlikely to be able to obtain the quality of legal advice that might allow them to defend themselves successfully.

The second link between imprisonment and child labour is the work done by the children in prison. Once in prison, children may be expected to perform certain tasks either officially, as part of their supposed reeducation, or unofficially, in order to buy favours from the guards or from other prisoners.

See also Street Children; Workhouses.
References Chisholm, Anne, and Moorehead, Caroline, "Children in Prison: India" (1989).

Product Labelling

Since the late 1980s, international attention to the issue of child labour has been growing. Increasing interest in the subject has led international agencies and industries to develop new ways of demonstrating that children are not exploited in the manufacture of products made in developing countries. One such system has been product labelling.

In applying a label to any product, one is supplying the consumer with information that will allow them to make informed purchasing choices. For example, a product label may guarantee to the purchaser that no children were involved in the production of the goods being bought. Alternatively, product labels may tell the buyer that in purchasing the labelled item they will contribute to the welfare of child workers in the country where the item was produced.

We can see product labelling at work in the carpet manufacturing sector. The most well-known example of labelling in this sector is Rugmark. Rugmark provides us with an example of labelling guaranteeing that the product was made without exploitative child labour. However, Rugmark is not the only labelling system in this sector.

For example, in 1995, the STEP label was created by a number of Swiss nongovernmental organizations and carpet traders. STEP differs from Rugmark in that individual carpets are not labelled. Rather, companies carrying the STEP label aim to improve conditions for carpet producers and workers.

Other labelling systems exist in the carpet sector as well. In Germany the importers and dealers in carpets have developed the Care & Fair label. Founded in 1994, the aim of this labelling system is to improve the conditions for children working in the carpet industry, particularly in India and Nepal. All members of Care & Fair make an annual contribution, and this provides funds for schooling and rehabilitation programmes for children in this sector. Care & Fair provides us with an example of the second type of labelling system. In this case, by buying the labelled product, consumers know, they are contributing to programmes aimed at improving the conditions and welfare of child workers.

Although product labelling has become common in carpet manufacturing, this is not the only sector where it is used. Product labelling initiatives have been used in a number of other industries including tea, footwear, and footballs (soccer balls).

Product labelling is a relatively new initiative in the area of child labour and has not yet been fully evaluated. For those labelling systems that guarantee child labour–free products, it has to be shown that credible monitoring systems are in place. Labels guaranteeing improved welfare conditions need to show that the fees generated are sufficient to make a difference to the lives of child employees.

Yet another issue must be considered: The fundamental assumption underlying product labelling is that consumers will be influenced in their purchasing decisions by this system. This raises questions about the level of awareness of product labelling and about consumers' attitudes toward labels.

See also Carpet Manufacture; Fair Trade; Rugmark.

Pro-Employment Arguments

Although most writers today who concern themselves with child employment treat it to some degree as a social evil, others stress its positive features. In this they are following in the footsteps of Canadian sociologist William N. Stephens, author of the book *Our Children Should Be Working*. Stephens argued that in primitive societies, children's character was shaped through work and that the same should apply in advanced societies. Stephens supported his argument that working children learn helpfulness, enterprise, and mechanical skills with case studies illustrating what he saw as good practice.

Roger Vernon Scruton (born 1944), English-born writer and philosopher, formerly professor of aesthetics at Birkbeck College, London, and professor of philosophy at the University of Boston, is well known for his forceful writing defending conservative causes. Scruton has expressed one of the clearest and most unequivocal statements advocating child employment, arguing that many children would be happier and more productive in work than at school. Another leading conservative thinker in Britain, Sir Alfred Sherman, has attacked the trend toward raising the age limit for compulsory schooling. Drawing in part on his own experience teaching in schools, he has argued that during the final years of compulsory schooling many adolescents become disruptive and rebellious because they can see no value in the education they are offered.

These individuals are part of a long-standing tradition of opposition to the regulation of child employment in Great Britain and the United States. In Britain, even at the time of the passing of the Factory Acts, a number of advocates of child employment could be found.

Andrew Ure (1778–1857) published his book *The Philosophy of Manufactures* in 1835. Although the text was aimed at helping the managers and masters of industry avoid various pitfalls on their path to improving manufacturing, it also defended the use of children in factories. Ure's observations on factory children were remarkably positive: "The children seemed to be always cheerful and alert, taking pleasure in using their muscles. The work of these lively elves seemed to resemble a sport. Conscious of their skill, they were delighted to show it off to any stranger. At the end of the day's work they showed no sign of being exhausted."

Other books of the time expressed similar views. Edward Baines's *History of the Cotton Manufacture in Great Britain*, published in 1835, attacked those who wanted to reform the textile factories, arguing that they had given a false picture of conditions there: "It is not true to represent the work of piecers and scavengers as continually straining. None of the work in which children and young persons are engaged in mills require constant attention. It is scarcely possible for any employment to be lighter."

Such views were echoed by members of

parliament. Henry Thomas Hope (1808–1862) opposed the Factory Acts, seeing them as a threat to the competitive position of British manufacturers. Hope was particularly concerned about competition from America and believed the implementation of legislation would affect the profitability of manufacturers. However, this was not the only reason Hope would not support factory legislation. Hope believed that children's work was an important resource for their parents and benefited the children as well.

Of course, manufacturers and factory owners were also in the pro–child employment camp. Richard Arkwright (1732–1792) was an important figure in textile manufacturing and introduced the spinning frame to the factory. The main impact of this machine was that it was too large to work by hand and thus it led to the introduction of water power. The spinning frame is also known as the water frame.

Arkwright's pro-employment position is demonstrated by his employment practices. He preferred to employ weavers who had large families. Although the weavers worked at home, the women and children in their families worked in the spinning factory. Arkwright waited until children were 6 years old before employing them. Arkwright employed 1,900 workers, two-thirds of whom were children.

See also Factory Acts; Market Economics.

References Hammond, J. L., and Hammond, Barbara, *Lord Shaftesbury* (1939); Stephens, William N., *Our Children Should Be Working* (1979).

Projects

A vast number of nongovernmental organizations (NGOs) are involved in child labour issues, and virtually every NGO pursues at least one project that is aimed at improving working children's lives—whether it be education, safe housing, or retraining.

A number of NGOs in the Philippines belong to the National Project on Street Children. These NGOs develop projects aimed at delivering education in a number of alternative ways. For example, mobile schools and street schools show that educators can reach street children and provide street and working children with alternative forms of education.

In Brazil, education is also at the heart of a number of projects aimed at street children. Project Axe works with children in El Salvador and is based upon "the pedagogy of desire." Children are encouraged to plan and dream of their future, and the project workers then offer concrete ways to make such dreams a reality. This might involve learning to read and write. They also have the opportunity to work and earn money through a number of work projects, such as screen-printing T-shirts.

The largest project is one associated with the International Labour Organisation (ILO), the International Program for the Elimination of Child Labor (IPEC). As an international organization, IPEC coordinates a vast number of projects, many of which are joint ventures with NGOs or governments. At present IPEC's main focus is to eliminate the most intolerable forms of employment. Some idea of the scale of this effort can be gained when it is realized that for the period from 1997 to 2001, IPEC's budget is approximately 20 million U.S. dollars and that it runs approximately 700 action programmes in more than 20 countries in Asia, Latin America, and Africa. Three examples of these projects will provide some indication of the range of issues IPEC tackles.

The first examples are projects aimed at mining communities in Peru, where children as young as 6 years of age can be found working in gold mines. These children face long work shifts and a resultant high risk of injury due to fatigue. In 1998, with IPEC's support, projects were put in place in two regions where child labour was known to exist. The projects are aimed at withdrawing children from this hazardous work and providing them with education and training for alternative employment. It is estimated that 1,000 children between 6 and 18 years of age will benefit from this project. The project also aims to reeducate mining communities and parents about the need to keep children away from the hazards of work in mining.

Secondly, IPEC acknowledges that many countries have child labour legislation but little is done to implement these laws. In one IPEC project in Turkey, 108 labour inspectors were trained in issues related to child labour laws. The inspectors covered a range of industries including footwear, textiles, clothing, light industry, restaurants, and services. They visited more than 2,500 workplaces and identified approximately 5,000 working children. Such projects are aimed at improving the conditions faced by working children and raising awareness of the problem.

Thirdly, the Vale dos Sinos region in Brazil is one of the centres of shoe production in the country. Much of the work is subcontracted to informal or home-based producers, which commonly use child labour. IPEC, along with a local NGO, ASBEM, has been supporting a project aimed at eliminating child labour and finding alternatives for children. The project has been running since 1996, and a number of working children have been rehabilitated and moved toward mainstream education. In addition, project staff hold informal and formal meetings with parents, employers, and local politicians to increase their awareness of the problems of child employment and of how they might be tackled.

These three examples are only a small sample of the range of projects in which IPEC is involved; but they give some indication of the international scope of this organization. These projects also show the complexity of the problem of child labour and that it needs to be tackled at a number of levels simultaneously.

It is imperative that such projects be evaluated, and IPEC recognizes this as a key aspect of its work. Through evaluation it is possible to measure the effectiveness of a project or to discover why that project has failed to have an impact. It may also be possible to consider the extent to which any specific project can be extended to cover child labour situations in other countries. When looking at projects, it is worth considering the alternative role that is believed to be acceptable for children. For example, in many projects the primary alternative is education.

See also Brazil; Education, Universal; International Labour Organisation; Peru; Philippines; Turkey.

Prostitution

Prostitution involves transactions in which one person, the prostitute, provides sexual gratification to another person, the client, in exchange for money or other reward. Although it is generally condemned on moral grounds, prostitution is widespread throughout the world. One argument sometimes employed to defend prostitution is that it has existed for such a long time that it should be accepted as a natural human activity. This claim is not well supported by evidence. Even if true, such an argument would need to be balanced against the many kinds of suffering experienced by prostitutes.

Many governments have sought to control prostitution by legal means. However, one disadvantage of such a policy is that laws are often framed in terms that classify prostitutes as criminals. An alternative view that is gaining ground is that prostitutes should be seen as victims rather than criminals. If criminal law is to be invoked, the clients, particularly the clients of child prostitutes, should be regarded as the criminals.

The Convention for the Suppression of the Traffic in Persons and of the Prostitution of Others was agreed by the United Nations in 1949. The Convention treats procuring prostitutes and profiting from prostitution as crimes, but it does not treat being a prostitute in itself as a crime. In addition, the United Nations Convention on the Rights of the Child, Article 34, requires states to take appropriate measures to prevent: "(a) The inducement or coercion of a child to engage in any unlawful sexual activity; (b) The exploitative use of children in prostitution or other unlawful sexual practices."

Of all forms of child labour, prostitution probably receives the most widespread condemnation. Despite this, it is clear that it is practiced on a large scale throughout the world. This ranges from the almost public existence of brothels in Thailand to the more covert activities of child prostitutes of both sexes in countries such as Britain and the United States. The specific circumstances in which prostitution takes place vary considerably. Being an inmate of a brothel is particularly onerous and exploitative because of the individual's lack of freedom of movement and the opportunities for the management to take most of the profit. Other prostitutes solicit individually or under the control of a "protector," whose relationship with the prostitute is not necessarily benign. Prostitutes are vulnerable to sexually transmitted diseases and abuse by clients. The lifestyle is also often associated with drug abuse.

There are a number of reasons why children and adolescents become prostitutes. In some cases, parents are in such extreme conditions of poverty that they see the sale of the child as the only way of ensuring its survival. This appears to be the case in some economically underdeveloped countries. In Britain, some child prostitutes appear to be runaways, children who have found living in the family home (or in some cases in an institution) so intolerable that they seek escape. In such cases, one reason for running away is that they have been the victims of sexual abuse. Once out of their homes, runaways need to find a means of surviving. The likelihood of their engaging in prostitution may be increased by the people with whom they come into contact.

Although it is important for social workers and others seeking to help individual children to understand the circumstances by which they came to be prostitutes, an understanding of prostitution as an aspect of society needs to go beyond personal life

histories. Prostitution would not exist without the clients who use the services. Some argue that prostitution justifies itself, since it allows sexual impulses to be satisfied that might otherwise be expressed in more harmful ways, such as rape. However, this assumes that sexual behaviour can be interpreted simply as the expression of an urge. Human behaviour is under the control of a variety of complex factors including social norms and assumptions about what is acceptable in relationships with other human beings. Social scientists' understanding of prostitutes' clients is still limited. For example, it is unclear to what extent those who use child prostitutes have a particular sexual attraction to children and to what extent they simply find them accessible and easy to manipulate.

References Ennew, Judith, *The Sexual Exploitation of Children* (1986); Lee, Mark, and O'Brien, Rachel, *The Game's Up: Redefining Child Prostitution* (1995); Rosemberg, Fulvia, and Andrade, Leandro Feitosa, "Ruthless Rhetoric: Child and Youth Prostitution in Brazil" (1999).

Protectionism

In the context of child labour, this term refers loosely to a particular child care philosophy found among a range of voluntary agencies, political organizations, state (and suprastate) organizations and institutions, and committed individuals and activists. Essentially, a protectionist position is one that promotes the view that children should enjoy a childhood free from as many of the concerns and stresses of adult life as possible. Children should be nurtured within appropriate caring institutions, such as family and school, and only gradually introduced into the adult world containing the responsibilities (and rights) associated with citizenship. Protectionist philosophies can be combined with a range of political positions on both the right and left of the political spectrum.

Those on the left seek to protect children from the ravages of exploitation and oppression inherent in capitalism. Many in the early socialist movement advocated protectionist positions as a way of stopping child labour exploitation in mines, mills, and factories. German socialist Clara Zetkin (1857–1933) reflected this view when, in an essay entitled "Protect Our Children," she wrote:

> Among the many serious crimes of capitalism about which history will one day sit in judgement, none is more brutal, horrible, disastrous, insane—in one word, outrageous—than the exploitation of proletarian children. Exploitation . . . by capitalism means the deprivation of health, vitality, childhood and education as well as the destruction of the body and the soul of future generations. . . . Capitalism . . . drives the child into the factory, the workshop, the brick kiln, street peddling, beet planting, animal care, pinsetting in bowling alleys, deliveries and the murderous cottage industry. Wherever the child goes, capitalism puts it through the profit mill.

Leftist protectionists believed the only alternative was to provide adequately funded nurseries, day care facilities, schools, and welfare services to enable children to grow to full maturation without being subjected to the rigours of labour. Similar arguments can be found today with regard to the exploitation of child labour in the newly industrialized and underdeveloped countries, or where children are found working at adult jobs in factories, mills, or agriculture in the advanced economies.

For right-wing protectionists, childhood is a particularly special time that should be spent obtaining an education in school, undertaking appropriate sports and leisure activities, and mixing with friends and family—all of which should be supervised by, or at least controlled by, parents, especially mothers. Rightists view childhood as a time when children grow biologically and psychologically to become well adjusted and responsible citizens, gradually being socialized into cultural norms and values. Within this conception, work or labour is illegitimate. It is portrayed as an adult activity. This conception of childhood is based on a commitment to strong family values. Note, however, that commitment to these values is also used to justify children's working in family businesses, or working to earn money for the family; opposition to welfare policies promoted by the United States Children's Bureau often has been phrased in these terms. This view is also based on what might be termed a middle-class norm, reflecting a particular type of family life and childhood that does not easily match the experiences of most children.

Protectionists from the political right and left argue for restrictions on, or the abolition of, child labour. They would certainly unite to call for action to eradicate the worst abuses of child labour in mills, mines, factories, building sites, warehouses, and garages, and on farms. Some protectionists, but not all, would argue that children should be allowed to perform a limited range of light work tasks after school, such as newspaper delivery. When dealing with the question of how child labour should be eradicated, there is some divergence depending on the protectionist's general political perspective. Both right and left would advocate national and international laws and declarations. For those on the left, trade unions and the collective action of children would also be stressed; for those on the right, parents have ultimate responsibility.

Broadly protectionist organizations include the International Labor Office, Anti-Slavery International, CNASTI, Child Workers in Asia Support Group, Defence for Children International, the Low Pay Network in Britain, and the National Child Labor Committee in the United States. Some notable protectionist reformers have included Lord Shaftesbury, Richard Oastler, Samuel Van Houten, Jane Addams, and Grace Abbott.

See also Abbott, Grace; Addams, Grace; Anti-Slavery International; Confederacao Nacional de Accao sobre Trabalho Infantil; Defence for Children International; History of Childhood; Low Pay Network; National Child Labor Committee; Oastler, Richard; Shaftesbury, Lord; Van Houten, Samuel; Zetkin, Clara.

References Zetkin, Clara, *Selected Writings* (1984).

Proto-industrialization

A controversial term used to refer to the period between the end of the seventeenth century and the beginning of the nineteenth century, primarily in England. The term relates to the period of political instability that lasted from the beginning of the English Civil War until the Glorious Revolution (that is, from 1640 until 1688) as well as the more rapid technological developments associated with the industrial revolution (1750–1850). With the Revolution of 1688, English society became increasingly dominated by market principles and methods and by a social and political system shaped by commitment to an expanding capitalist economic system. The term *proto-industrialization* is used to signify the growth and increasing influence of the market, the development of more complex trading patterns, and the increasing privatization of the tools and machinery of production in the hands of the manufacturing class.

At the start of the period, the English economy was still overwhelmingly agrarian. Industry sprang up within the agricultural sector, in the form of the cottage industry system. The expansion of the market and the economy and the pressures this brought, however, increasingly forced skilled workers in the cottage industries to specialize. Two dominant models of production developed: In the first model, the household functioned as a self-contained unit, differentiated internally in such a way that each member of the family, including the children, had a specific task in the production of a complete commodity. An example of this was textile manufacturing, in which different members of the weaver's family carded wool, spun the yarn, and wove the cloth. The second model involved differentiation among households specializing in particular tasks, be it combing, spinning, weaving. Here the article was passed by the merchant capitalist or his agent from one stage of the production process to the next. The crucial feature of the proto-industrial period, then, is the increasing role played by merchant capital.

Although the cottages, machines, and tools were often owned by the craft workers, merchant capitalists controlled the process and provided access to market and distribution systems.

Social historian Ivy Pinchbeck has argued that the cottage industries of the proto-industrial period produced some of the worst examples of child labour exploitation in British history. She claims that children as young as 3 and 4 years could be found working in damp, dark, and overcrowded cottages. They were made to work long hours by their parents in order to meet output quotas and deadlines. As they grew older, children gradually were introduced to more complex tasks, eventually allowing the family to maximize its output.

Criticisms of the concept include claims that it is chronologically vague and that it gives the impression of a static period of industrial development at a time when techniques of production actually developed significantly. It also has been suggested that the concept ignores developments in other industrial spheres at this time (such as in mining and iron foundry) as well as the vast geographical variation in the forms and techniques of production.

See also Industrial Revolution.

References Levine, David, *Family Formation in an Age of Nascent Capitalism* (1977); Pinchbeck, Ivy, *Women Workers and the Industrial Revolution* (1981).

Psychology, Developmental

Psychology as a discipline is concerned with the scientific study of behaviour. Within the discipline, there are many distinct branches of study. Developmental psychology, as its name implies, is concerned with understanding the physical, intellectual, social, and emotional changes that occur in the individual over time.

The early history of this branch of psychology was dominated in part by attempts to identify the milestones of early human development—the age at which a child is able to grasp, crawl, walk, and talk. Even today, it is not uncommon to find textbooks in this subdiscipline dealing with development up to the teenage years and no further.

This emphasis on the early years is not surprising when we look at the issues this branch of psychology typically has focused on. Interest in the development of perceptual, linguistic, and cognitive abilities has predominated, with particular emphasis on their emergence. Historically, this area of psychology has been influenced by figures such as Charles Darwin and by his *Origin of Species,* published in 1859, in which the child is considered as a source of information about the human species in general.

In recent years there has been a growth in lifespan development perspectives. In this case the focus moves from childhood to include the development of the individual during adulthood as well. Louis Sugarman's 1986 text *Lifespan Development: Concepts, Theories, and Interventions* reflects this particular perspective.

Given the interests of those working in developmental psychology, the field would appear an obvious source of information for understanding the role of work in the child's development. However, if we turned to standard textbooks in this field, we would be disappointed, as "work" is largely ignored. That it is not totally ignored is due to the fact that discussion about development through adolescence usually involves some evaluation of the transition from school to the world of work.

The lack of attention to work in the context of childhood is all the more surprising when we consider the number of children who work across the world. The reality is that work of various kinds plays a part in the everyday experiences of most children, whether it be paid employment or domestic chores, caring for siblings, or caring for ailing parents.

One explanation for the failure to attend to children's employment is that textbooks tend to reflect an idealized notion of childhood. Within this idealized period, play, school, the family, and one's peers are thought of as more worthy of study than is

work. It is worth noting that within developmental psychology the dominant research and texts are based upon European and American perspectives and research; they represent a culturally biased interpretation of childhood. As long as we recognize that bias, we can use the products of research in beneficial ways. However, when policies, including international ones, are built unknowingly upon what is essentially a Western notion of child development, they are at risk of failure. That such erroneously founded policies exist is demonstrated by the language in which a number of international policy statements have been formulated. The International Labour Organisation's Conventions and the United Nations Convention on the Rights of the Child make reference to the development of the child, and in some cases the phrase "normal development" appears. Such statements are based on the notion that there is some universal norm of development that pertains to all children.

This assumption is understandable. Some of the most influential figures in developmental psychology have proposed theories that are believed to be universally applicable. One of the most influential figures, Jean Piaget (1896–1980), developed a theory to explain the developmental changes in the way that children think and reason as they develop. For many years, researchers have replicated his work and echoed his findings. Piaget is not alone in proposing universal theories of development. Kohlberg proposed a stage theory of moral development that is also thought to have universal application.

However, for the past 20 years, critics have been pointing out the degree to which such theories are culturally bound. For example, Piaget's theory appears to reflect skills that are attained within European education systems. Children who do not experience the European form of schooling do not perform as well on Piagetian tasks.

In the search for universal explanations, developmental psychology has failed to pay enough attention to cultural and contextual factors and their role in development. That this is now changing is attributable to a number of factors. First, the emergence of lifespan developmental theories such as Sugarman's has led to the argument that social context needs to be considered if we are to understand development. By stressing the social context, researchers are acknowledging that our development is influenced by the society and the culture around us. Researchers such as British psychologist Erica Burman have been challenging traditional assumptions about universal theories of child development.

The second pressure for a reassessment of universal theories has emerged from the attention being given to alternative theories within developmental psychology. In recent years, considerable attention has been paid to the work of the Russian psychologist Lev Vygotsky (1896–1934). Vygotsky's theory emphasizes the importance of the cultural context in constructing our understanding of the world around us and influencing our development. The institutions within any culture—for example, schools—influence our development. However, these institutions are not the same in every culture. Hence there is no "universal" theory of childhood development; individuals are born into specific sociohistorical contexts that in part define their development. Thus, there is no single concept or model of childhood development, but instead, a number of different concepts.

If we adopt such a stance, then we must acknowledge that Western developmental psychology has focused on development within specific contexts. It is conceivable that in some contexts children may work and that this activity may be a central part in the development of the child. It may be that the way the society controls and monitors children's work provides the means by which societal values are transmitted to future generations. We need to be careful that such a view is not misinterpreted as an excuse for exploiting children in some countries because of "traditional cultural values." Within this framework it is still possible to apply criteria judging the appropriateness of particular experiences for children.

See also Adolescence.

References Burman, Erica, *Deconstructing Developmental Psychology* (1994); Sugarman, Louis, *Lifespan Development: Concepts, Theories, and Interventions* (1986).

Religion

The relationship between religious beliefs and practices on the one hand and child labour on the other is not a simple one. Strong religious conviction has lain behind the efforts of campaigners against child labour both in the past and today. For example, Lord Shaftesbury, who led the efforts to reform the laws governing the employment of children in Britain, saw himself as acting on Protestant Christian principles. Similarly, in contemporary Portugal, one finds dedicated Catholics playing a central role in the organization Confederacao Nacional de Accao sobre Trabalho Infantil. In both cases, the emphasis has been on the elimination of what these particular Christian activists have seen as harmful forms of child labour. Like many other Christians, the activists would have found certain forms of employment by children compatible with their religious faith. Christian missionaries to Africa in the nineteenth century employed children as labourers. Many other employers of children during the industrial revolution also saw themselves as dedicated Christians. The definition of a truly Christian position on working children was and is disputed.

In certain circumstances, religious belief actually requires children to work. The most obvious examples include the assignment of children by their parents to a place of worship or of religious education, where the children are given duties in return for their upkeep and instruction. This is the case, for example, with some of the Quranic schools run by adherents of Islam. In parts of India, parents send their children to schools run by holy men where no fees are charged for attendance but the children are expected to work for their instruction.

See also Burkina Faso; Confederacao Nacional de Accao sobre Trabalho Infantil; Malawi; Shaftesbury, Lord.

Retail Trade

The retail sector of any economy is the part that deals with the buying and selling of goods. Retail employment includes people working for superstores, in large shopping malls, and in warehouse work but also those employed in small shops and market stalls. Children can be found working in each of these areas across the globe. Although warehouse work and shelf stacking are often viewed as "boys'" work, retail jobs tend to be filled by girls.

Children work at market stalls across the globe. They are involved from early in the morning till late at night: setting up the stalls, selling the goods, and packing up the leftovers at the end of the day. Market stalls are often marginal outlets, under competitive pressure from larger retail outlets on permanent sites. In these circumstances children are employed because they are cheap and flexible.

In larger retail stores and permanent shop outlets, children work at selling, stocking, and pricing goods. In general terms, wages and employment conditions in this sector are not particularly good, but children are employed because of their cheapness. The fact that shop work is often viewed as women's work means that when children are employed, they are in direct competition with women—yet another poorly paid group within the labour force.

See also Service Sector.

Rights Discourse

Political philosophies based on "rights" have a long history in most Western liberal democratic societies. It is possible to trace their history back to social contract theorists such as seventeenth-century English

Children engaged in retail trade on the street in Togo, 1987 (International Labour Office)

philosopher John Locke. The political and civil rights enshrined in the United States Constitution reflect these liberal concerns. In part the struggles of the early women's and black movements in the United States were attempts to establish the equal rights of women and the black population to these constitutional rights. However, it became clear in practice that civil and political rights legislation cannot alone overcome oppression and inequality.

Partly as a consequence of this awareness, many within the new social movements of the 1960s rejected constitutional rights–based politics for failing to take adequate account of power structures in society, structured inequalities, and the role of the state in maintaining oppression. Activists chose instead to pursue a more contentious, collectivist politics of the streets. By the late 1970s and early 1980s, however, the confrontational nature of these

new social movements had dissipated somewhat, leading some supporters again to look at "rights politics."

Proponents of the "new" politics of rights advocated the recognition of particular groups' social, economic, and cultural rights, as well as the more traditional civil and political rights. However, in so doing, they opened the door to conflicting demands by other groups. For example, the right of racist groups to freedom of expression and assembly in black areas of towns and cities conflicts with the right of the ethnic minority community to be protected, and to protect themselves, from violence and intimidation.

Rights discourse describes the language of the politics of rights. It refers to the language used to articulate, advocate, and justify certain group demands. Those using the phrase do not always assign it the same meaning and do not always deal with the same topic in the same way. The phrase refers to diverse and specific political formulations, including principles and slogans, items of legislation, and various institutional practices.

Because of the variety of forms rights discourse may take and because of the different estimates of its value in achieving significant social change, its relevance to attempts to improve the lives of working children is open to debate.

See also Children's Rights.

Romania

Romania is a republic in southeastern Europe. From 1947 until 1989 when dictator Nicolae Ceausescu was overthrown, Romania was part of the Soviet bloc of communist countries. It is now a parliamentary democracy. In the 1992 census, the population numbered around 23 million.

Although the country has substantial mineral and agricultural resources, its postcommunist governments have faced severe economic problems. Under the communist regime, children younger than 16 years were forbidden to work, except when helping parents in agricultural work. Officially, at least, child labour did not exist. There has been no formal shift in the law concerning work by children since 1989, but some changes seem to have occurred in practice because of the increase in private enterprises. It is believed that substantial numbers of children work both in rural and in urban communities. The International Working Group on Child Labour in 1995 estimated that there were around 5,000 street children living in Romania's larger towns.

See also Europe, Eastern; International Labour Organisation; Street Children.

References Salvati Copiii, *Child Labour in Romania* (1995).

Rugmark

The Rugmark carpet label, in the form of a smiling face, signifies that a particular carpet has been made without the use of il-

legal child labour. The carpet manufacturing sector traditionally has been viewed as an area of rampant exploitation of child labour. This has partly been associated with the "nimble fingers" hypothesis—that children's small fingers aid in the intricate work and in knotting small threads.

It has been estimated that the number of children weaving carpets in India rose from 100,000 in 1975 to 300,000 in 1990. In response to this increase, a number of nongovernmental organizations formed the South Asian Coalition on Child Servitude (SACCS) in 1989. With support from UNICEF and several other sources, this group introduced the Rugmark label.

The Rugmark foundation provides a voluntary licensing system to carpet exporters whereby particular manufacturers are allowed to use the Rugmark label if they certify that children's labour is not used in the carpet manufacturing process. The manufacturers must agree to allow Rugmark access to their premises for surprise inspections.

In addition to its monitoring and labelling efforts, Rugmark is also involved in the rehabilitation of children and in their education. The first Rugmark school was opened in India in 1996. Rugmark-India has been deemed a success by some, since it has led to over 100 carpet exporters registering with the system, with more than 270,000 carpets carrying the Rugmark label. There are plans to extend the scheme into Nepal.

Critics of the system have questioned the effectiveness of the surprise factory inspection system. However, it must be acknowledged that the Rugmark system at the very least has created an awareness of the extent of children's involvement in the carpet industry.

See also Carpet Manufacture; Fair Trade; Product Labelling.

Runaways

Children of school age who leave their parents' home or another institution in which they have been living, without permission. Children tend to run away when they feel that the circumstances in which they are living are intolerable. Some are victims of abuse by parents, other family members, or institutional staff. In other cases, the reasons for leaving may seem trivial to an outside observer; but clearly the fact of running away means that the reason was subjectively important to the child involved.

If the absence extends beyond a few hours or days, then the child must find means of supporting himself or herself. Many runaways are attracted to large towns and cities, in part because they may believe it is easier to hide in a crowd, in part because they may believe the life of cities is more attractive, and in part because they may believe that there are greater employment opportunities there. However, since they are under the appropriate age limit for many jobs, and since they lack the documentation that many employers would expect to see, they are likely to end up doing casual work and engaging in activities at or beyond the margins of legality. Runaways are likely to be homeless, and the lack of a home address is a disadvantage when seeking regular employment. In the circumstances, it is not surprising that some turn to begging or stealing. Those who live off the earnings of prostitutes often see runaways as a likely source of income: Since such children are likely to be alone and without friends, they may be drawn into a life of prostitution by an initially friendly approach.

Welfare authorities treat runaways as seriously at risk, and the phenomenon is regarded as a substantial social problem. The nature of the runaway's lifestyle is such that it is difficult for authorities to have firm evidence of the extent of the problem.

See also Prostitution; Street Children.

Russia

The Russian Federation dates from the collapse of the communist regime in the Soviet Union in the early 1990s. Russia today occupies around three-quarters of the land space of the former Soviet Union; and although it no longer serves as a superpower counterweight to the United States, it has inherited some of the Soviet Union's world role (for example, it retains a permanent seat on the Security Council of the United Nations). Russia now comprises almost 90 territorial divisions and has a total population of around 150 million.

Because Russia has undergone constant and severe economic and social upheaval since the collapse of the Soviet government, it is probably not possible to describe adequately the state of child labour there at present. However, in a study conducted by Valery Mansurov for the International Labour Organisation in 1993, one-fifth of parents surveyed acknowledged that their own children were working. Some children reportedly started work as young as 9 years of age. The work reported included a wide range of jobs, with street trading being particularly common. Most of the working children did not come from particularly impoverished families.

See also Europe, Eastern; International Labour Organisation.

References Mansourov, Valery A., *Child Work in Russia* (1993); Mansourov, Valery A., *International Working Group on Child Labour Supplementary Country Report: Russia* (1995).

Saturday Evening Post

Under the editorship of George Horace Lorimer, from 1899 to 1937, the *Saturday Evening Post* expressed its dedication to business values in a distinctive way. Lorimer had a special interest in youth, and he ran a scheme aimed at increasing the magazine's circulation by hiring boys to sell it. The *Post* boys, some of whom were as young as 8 years, became a crucial part of the magazine's system of distribution. The *Post* encouraged them through advertisements and circulars. Prizes on offer included cash, trips, and college scholarships.

The paper also publicized their work as training in the ways of American business. The *Saturday Evening Post* tried to combine two distinct goals. The first was to establish a sound circulation for itself. The other was to train boys in sound business methods: to sell a product on its merits; to keep good accounts; and to be honest, energetic, and thrifty. Lorimer hoped that the *Post* boys would become adults who were deeply committed to the business ethic.

As Jan Cohn has shown, it is clear that the *Post* aimed to recruit middle-class boys whom it exhorted to sell to "every person with whom you and your family do business." It was believed that these boys not only would have suitable sales opportunities but also the ambition to try to increase sales. Some boys were granted "exclusive agency"—sole rights to a territory, within which, if necessary, they could employ other boys to assist them. At one point in the 1930s, the *Post* was dealing with almost 50,000 boy agents in towns throughout the United States.

See also Business Ethic; Newsies; Work Ethic.

References Cohn, Jan, "The Business Ethic for Boys: *The Saturday Evening Post* and the *Post* Boys" (1987).

Save the Children Fund

The Save the Children Fund, also known as SCF or as Save the Children, is a nongovernmental organization dedicated to children's rights. Its aim is to turn the goals stated in the United Nations Convention on the Rights of the Child into reality. This has involved SCF in supporting programmes over a number of years, aimed at ameliorating the conditions of working children. Although SCF has concentrated on countries that are relatively underdeveloped economically, such as Bangladesh, Nepal, Honduras, Brazil, Lebanon, and the Philippines, it has acknowledged problems of child labour also in more economically developed countries—as, for example, in its programme in Northern Ireland.

SCF's safe water supply projects in central and southern Africa show that technical and social developments are very closely related. In areas where girls have traditionally carried water long distances, new water supplies have helped greatly to reduce the time and energy they have to expend. Sometimes SCF projects demonstrate the substantial scale of the problem of child labour. For example, a programme in Tharparkar, Pakistan, was set up that focused on developing income-generating projects for adults. It was hoped initially that this would lead families to rely less on the earnings of their working children younger than 14 years. However, the adult incomes generated by the programme were not sufficient to offer a viable alternative to the children's wages from carpet weaving. Radda Barnen and Redd Barna, respectively the Swedish and Norwegian branches of Save the Children, have been particularly active in programmes concerned with children's labour, including that performed in armed conflict.

See also Boy Soldiers; Convention on the Rights of the Child; Nongovernnmental Organizations; Projects.

References Marcus, Rachel, and Harper, Caroline, *Small Hands: Children in the Working World* (1996); Pettitt, Bridget (ed.) *Children and Work in the UK: Reassessing the Issues* (1998).

Scandinavia

Name applying to three countries that lie near each other in northern Europe: Denmark, Norway, and Sweden. A looser definition includes the neighbouring country of Finland. However, whereas the Danish, Norwegian, and Swedish languages all are Germanic in origin, the Finnish language has different roots. In terms of population, these four countries are small. Sweden, with more than 8 million inhabitants, is the largest, and Norway, with more than 4 million, is the smallest.

All of these countries traditionally have been admired for their stable democratic governments; healthy economies; strong education, health, and social welfare systems; and relatively limited social problems. Their positive reputations are at least partly grounded in fact. All of the countries have strict laws controlling child employment, and it is the official position of the governments that child labour is not a major social problem. However, the belief that there is no substantial problem has meant that little has been done to explore the actual situation, and the reality might not be quite as satisfactory as is claimed. The case of Denmark illustrates the point: Independent research on the extent of child employment has been carried out there, and the findings suggest that the government greatly underestimates the number of children working.

In contrast to the relative lack of interest in child labour at home, Scandinavian bodies such as the Norwegian Agency for Development Cooperation, the Swedish International Development Cooperation Agency, and the Norwegian and Swedish branches of the Save the Children Fund have a good record assisting international efforts to deal with problems of child labour.

See also Denmark; Save the Children Fund.
References Vuzina, Dialehti, and Schaffer, Heiner (eds.), *Kinderarbeit in Europa* (1992).

Scavenging

In the large cities of Africa, Asia, and Latin America, it is common for children to earn money by collecting and selling items they find in rubbish dumps. Discarded car parts, bottles, plastic bags, and scrap paper all have a small resale value. A few hours' scavenging at a dump may earn a child enough to buy food—not only for himself or herself but in many cases also for the other members of his or her family.

The work is unhealthy because of the risk of skin infections and other diseases, but for many families it may be the only practical alternative to starvation. In addition, the sense that the work is demeaning is often felt by the children themselves, who place it on a par with prostitution. This sense arises because to scavenge in a rubbish dump is, in essence, to attribute value to objects that other, more affluent members of society have discarded as of little or no value. The activity emphasizes the scavengers' position at the lowest level of society.

See also Street Children.
References Lee-Wright, Peter, *Child Slaves* (1990).

Scotland

See United Kingdom.

Self-employment

Many children around the world work as self-employed labourers. Children often set themselves up as car cleaners, garden workers, street shoe shiners, or in other informal jobs in towns and cities across the globe. These jobs have different social meanings in various countries. In advanced economies, such activities are often said to show initiative and a commitment to work. They are thought to be useful short-term means of obtaining money for luxury goods or social activities. All children's jobs are viewed in this idealistic way in these so-

A child polishes shoes while others look on in Cairo, Egypt, ca. 1910–1920 (Matson Photo Service)

cieties, but self-employment even more so. In developing economies, however, such activities are often the last resort of the poverty-stricken, a desperate means of obtaining essential funds, in the most marginal and informal employment sectors within national economies.

Children involved in these activities will have to purchase many of their tools before they can start working, and this may result in initial debt. Furthermore, the children may have to buy rounds or plots from workers who themselves are moving on to other jobs or areas. Employment in these types of jobs is unpredictable. The children do not know how much they will earn or how long they are going to have to work.

Street trading can be dangerous. In some countries street children are often abused and attacked by vigilante groups and harassed and imprisoned by the authorities. The line between street rogue and street worker is often vague. Children often drift into and out of employment, depending on their immediate needs.

In many regions, self-employment is tied in with forms of subcontracting in which children will be given goods to sell on a sale-and-return basis. The quantity of goods sold will affect the child's return. As a result, children have unpredictable hours and conditions: They might be lucky and sell their goods quickly, or sales might be slow and hence hours long. In many countries newspapers, matches, flowers, and other, cheaper goods are sold on this basis.

See also Street Children.

Service Sector

Bus, truck, and train drivers; water, sewage, and waste disposal workers; and those involved in fast-food service and delivery and sports and leisure services all are employed in the service sector. Given the hybrid nature of this employment sector, it is not surprising that children tend to be located in particular areas of the sector rather than across the sector as a whole. Children tend to be employed in personal services: formal fast-food outlets; selling tea, coffee, and snacks at roadsides or railway sidings; waiting on tables at cafes, bars, and restaurants; and serving tourists with a range of legal, semilegal, and illegal tasks.

Children work in fast-food outlets almost everywhere, making and serving hamburgers, pizza, french fries, and various drinks and sweets. These types of outlets tend to structure their employment regimes around peak times of the day and the week. Very often employees will be on "zero-hour" contracts, with no guaranteed employment and no set hours but expected to be available at relatively short notice to meet labour demand. Such flexible work contracts are exceptionally difficult for adult workers: There is no regular income, and the irregular hours make it almost impossible to balance the demands of home and family against those of work. The flexibility, however, can be adapted to the school or college hours of older children; or alternatively, the irregularity of employment is perhaps less dramatic and problematic for children if they live in their family home. In such cases, other, older members of the family may be in a position to give appropriate support and free the working child from some of the obligations of family life that he or she might otherwise have to meet.

In many developing countries, children have informally set themselves up as fast food and drink sellers. Placing themselves with tea, coffee, and snacks at the side of roads or in railway stations, these children sell their goods for small sums. They are often harassed by the authorities, who check their papers or force them to set up shop elsewhere because their presence is considered unsightly. These children exist on the streets, and their lives and working conditions are substantially worse than those in formal fast-food outlets. Their hours are exceptionally long and returns often pitiful.

See also Prostitution; Street Children.

Shaftesbury, Lord

A member of the English aristocracy, Anthony Ashley Cooper (1801–1885) became Lord Ashley in 1811, and the seventh Earl of Shaftesbury in 1851. He is now generally referred to as "Lord Shaftesbury." A lifelong dedication to evangelical Christianity lay behind his many campaigns for social reform. Shaftesbury's home life as a child was unhappy, his father being severe. He was comforted by a servant, Maria Millis, who died when Shaftesbury was still young, but not before impressing on him the religious principles that guided him through later life.

Shaftesbury worked on the care of the mentally ill, the housing of the poor, education, animal welfare, and the care of young delinquents. However, it is with the cause of child workers that his name is probably most closely connected. The unhappy aristocratic child grew up to be an adult who devoted much of his life to the unhappy children of the poor. He played a prominent part in formulating laws restricting work performed by children in factories, mills, and mines. Shaftesbury fought a long battle to end the practice of boys' climbing up chimneys to clean them, culminating in the passage in 1875 of the Chimney Sweep Act.

See also Chimney Sweeping; Factory Acts.

References Hammond, J. L., and Hammond, Barbara, *Lord Shaftesbury* (1939).

Slave Labour

See Unfree Labour.

Social Class

The concept of social class is one of the most important in modern politics, sociology, social theory, and history. It is also frequently referred to in a range of other academic disciplines. Yet while it is often evoked, there is no shared agreement on what the concept means. Class is often used to locate people within a range of occupational strata, to identify consumption patterns, or to describe particular lifestyles. In contrast, it is also used to identify irreconcilable and opposing interests. When writers refer to class, they rarely do so in a dispassionate way. Rather, they are often, consciously or unconsciously, revealing their own social values.

The two dominant definitions of class are those offered by Max Weber and by Karl Marx. Each approach is distinctively relevant to understanding child labour. Weber portrays numerous layers of people in different social classes reflecting their economic, social, and political situation. His definition of "class" consists of both objective and subjective elements. Class partly reflects one's property, skills, and educational background. It is also partly a matter of what interests individuals have in common as a result of sharing the same market situation, partly a result of what we think society is like and how we perceive our position within it.

Weberian sociology also utilizes another concept to explain the divisions of modern society—the concept of status. According to Weber, status is a "quality of social honor or a lack of it." The argument is that one's market situation and life chances can be affected by one's status, which is the social, as opposed to the economic, determinant of life chances.

Marx's definition of class has five distinctive elements. First, Marx views class as essentially a relationship of competing groups within society, groups that have different positions within the system of social production. Second, individuals' class position is determined by their location within the process of production. Whether you describe yourself as "working-class" or not is, at this level, immaterial.

Third, the relationship between classes is necessarily antagonistic. The ruling class always tries to extract more surplus product, and the exploited always want to retain more of their product for their own use and consumption. The interests of each group, therefore, are always opposed. Fourth, as a result, class conflict is inevitable. Such conflict can take many forms: Strikes, riots, rebellions, and revolutions are the most obvious and visible manifestations. Finally, various classes have existed in various societies at different times. The bourgeoisie and the working class have not always existed. They exist, according to the Marxist view, as an aspect of capitalism.

The Marxist conception of class has greatly influenced some who have attempted to understand the emergence of child labour as a feature of capitalist production in the industrial revolution, most notably E. P. Thompson. The Marxist approach to class also underlies the activities of some who oppose child employment in the contemporary world—most obviously, members of the organization Stop Child Labour.

The Marxist notion of class is probably most convincing today if one focuses on the relationship between workers (including child workers) in the poorer countries of the world and those who run the multinational companies and international financial institutions. It is not difficult to see the interests of the contrasting groups as being in conflict.

However, the approach more commonly adopted among sociologists and others attempting to collect and interpret information on the current state of child labour in economically advanced countries such as the United States and Great Britain is closer to Weber's ideas of class and status.

In their discussions of recent trends in child and youth employment in the United States, Ellen Greenberger and Laurence Steinberg have made use of the concept of socioeconomic status. They note that at the beginning of the twentieth century, many poorer families relied on the earnings of children, and hence these children were excluded from school. Gradually, full-time education was extended across society until in general terms it could be said that all children, irrespective of the economic status of their families, attended school. However, that did not mean that no children were employed: In the second half of the twentieth century, they have noted a rising tendency among children of the better-off parents to take jobs. Teenage employment thus has become a phenomenon that cut across classes. Obviously, children in different economic circumstances may work for different reasons. The poorer may be contributing to the household income, and the richer, buying consumer goods.

As attempts are made to study child labour in closer detail worldwide, it seems likely that some notion of class or status or both will be helpful to our understanding of the patterns of child employment that emerge.

See also Consumerism; Marxism; Poverty; Stop Child Labour.

References Greenberger, Ellen, and Steinberg, Laurence, *When Teenagers Work: The Psychological and Social Costs of Adolescent Employment* (1986); Marx, Karl, and Engels, Friedrich, *The German Ideology* (1846); Weber, Max, *Economy and Society* (1968).

Social Construction of Childhood

In recent decades, a new paradigm for the sociological study of children and childhood has emerged. This paradigm challenges notions of a universal or "natural" childhood, developing insights first suggested by Philippe Aries to argue that childhood is a social construct that will vary across time and space. The sociological perspective is one that challenges the dominant commonsense picture of childhood as a time of unrestricted leisure, protected from the cares and concerns of the outside world, where children's best interests are served by their encasement in what Holt has described as a "walled garden" of purely childish concerns. The walled garden represents an idealized world, free of oppression and exploitation—a world that numerous studies have shown does not exist for most children. The metaphor also implies a barrier to the outside world where children, because they are children, are denied access to activities that adults take for granted. The fact of biological immaturity is utilized to determine a presumed social, political, and economic incompetence, as a result of which children find themselves excluded from decision-making at all levels of society; subjected to various forms of punishment (including physical chastisement) to control their behaviour; and represented by parents and a range of welfare professionals who, it is assumed, know what is best for them.

The socially inferior position of children is assumed to be natural. The problem, however, is that young people have not always been treated in this way. Numerous historical and cross-cultural studies portray societies in which children were not encased within the "walled garden" but were much more active participants in family, productive, and social life. Within the sociological literature, it is now recognized that children's experiences are affected and shaped by a range of interacting social divisions and social institutions put in place to control, direct, or meet the perceived needs of young people (as well as their responses, individually and collectively, to these institutional interventions). The result is that childhood has been revealed as a period of flux and development shaped by social and political factors as much as by biological and psychological ones. In reality, there is no single experience of childhood but instead there are various "childhoods" experienced by children in different social situations.

Historically, labour has been an important experience shaping the lives of working-class children. In the area of labour, the experience of children from bourgeois backgrounds was, and remains, radically different from that of working-class children. Looking at the eighteenth and nineteenth centuries, Anna Davin has noted that for bourgeois children in Britain, life experiences were highly gendered. For boys, childhood was shaped by a life trajectory that took them through nursery school, preparatory school, boarding school, university, army, and church or business. For their female counterparts life was far more restrictive. The nursery was gradually replaced by education within the home and preparation for coming out as a debutante. An offer of marriage enabled girls to exchange the confines of the parental home for those of their husband's.

The lives of working-class children in the seventeenth, eighteenth, and early nineteenth centuries were completely different. Their experiences were shaped by poverty and the struggle for survival; domestic labour and paid work in a variety of locations, including family work in cottage and factory, and daily care of younger siblings. Working-class children had a much quicker integration into the adult world.

Yet by the end of the nineteenth century the life stage we call childhood had been imposed on working-class children, and their life experiences had been radically altered. Thus, for working-class children the dominant form of childhood was constructed as a consequence of the interaction of social institutions on the shifting terrain of nineteenth-century industrial capitalism with the responses of children, individually and collectively, to this new way of living. To paraphrase E. P. Thompson, in the latter half of the nineteenth century we can witness the making of a working-class childhood.

Although a working-class childhood may have been constructed during the later part of the nineteenth century, it has not been static since this period. What children do—that is, what they are allowed to, expected to, want to, and actually do—constantly has changed. The experiences of working-class children are radically different today from what they were 20, 30, 50, or 100 years ago. In this sense childhoods are constantly being reconstructed.

This should not be taken to mean that childhoods necessarily become liberalized or better but merely that they alter overtime. This process is not unidirectional. There have been numerous attempts by sections of society to reimpose a mythical "lost" childhood on today's children. For example, there have been attempts to ban children from obtaining access to certain comics or videos and to reimpose discipline in the home and school. For others within society, the child has become an important customer in the drive to sell more goods. Marketing and sales strategists try to persuade children to buy, or get their parents to buy, this good or that. Sudden and recurrent shortages of specific goods suggest that marketing bodies often lag behind this astute group of consumers.

Many academics, child welfare practitioners, and lawyers recently have been emphasizing children's rights to be heard in a range of circumstances. This trend clearly challenges children's traditionally subservient position with regard to legal and welfare professionals. However, it is developing at a time when there has been retrenchment on matters of the age of criminal responsibility and of the treatment of children who have committed crimes.

Although children and young people reinterpret and re-create their surroundings in new and innovative ways, it is important to emphasize that even in the process of its reconstruction, childhood is not an independent social variable but one that is intimately connected to, and affected by, the totality of social relations within society. The consequence is that childhood is a moving feast, an arena over which, and about which, there is constant conflict, debate, and reinterpretation; where the expectations of, and on, children change. That debate shapes the terrain and tenor of childhood's reconstruction.

See also Centuries of Childhood; Children's Rights.

References Aries, Philippe, *Centuries of Childhood* (1973); Corsaro, William A., *The Sociology of Childhood* (1997); Davin, Anna, "When Is a Child Not a Child?" (1990); Davin, Anna, *Growing Up Poor* (1996); Holt, John, *Escape from Childhood* (1975).

Socialization

Some people view childhood work experience in a positive light. Their positive attitude reflects certain commonsense assumptions about employment and its benefits to the individual's early development. It is possible to argue that society too may benefit from children's employment as children grow up and adopt the adult roles they have observed within their culture, including the occupational role. According to this point of view, gaining experience of work will aid the transition from childhood to adulthood by teaching the child about the "world of work." Such views can be found among policymakers, researchers, parents, and children who work. The underlying argument is based on the concept of socialization.

Any society, in order to maintain itself, must replicate itself. Socialization refers to the process by which the current members of society introduce the next generation to the values, beliefs, and behaviour that are central to the maintenance of that culture. Social scientists have always been interested in understanding the way that cultures achieve this end.

Some researchers have focused on cross-cultural comparisons. The differences between developed and underdeveloped countries might be interpreted in terms of the timing of events such as the introduction of children to work. It is also possible

to investigate the main socializing forces—the role of parents, the education system, and other significant bodies, such as the church—in the child's life.

However, the main focus of social scientists has been to explain the process of socialization and the role of the child in that process. Given the importance of this concept to social scientists, it is not surprising to find that psychology and sociology have been preoccupied with this notion. Both of these disciplines talk about socialization, although they use different terminology.

Psychologists have proposed a number of different models to explain socialization and the child's role in the process. Schaffer, a developmental psychologist, has suggested that four models are discernable. They differ in terms of the role proposed for the child in the process, with some emphasizing a passive and others an active role. The passive role of the child is best seen in what Schaffer calls the "clay molding" model. This model views the child as a lump of clay that the significant forces around the child (such as parents) can mould into the appropriate shape, reflecting the wishes of society.

In contrast, the "laissez-faire" model, based on the ideas of eighteenth-century French philosopher Jean-Jacques Rousseau, views the child as neither active nor passive. Instead the child comes into the world preformed, and everything will unfold correctly with the passage of time. The role of society is simply to provide the sustenance necessary for survival and to avoid corrupting what nature has created. In a sense, socialization in this model is equivalent to maturation.

In the third model children are viewed as active agents in their own socialization but also as essentially antisocial, driven by primal desires. Socialization is the process by which society teaches the child to control impulses and adopt acceptable behaviour. This process is not trouble free, and Schaffer therefore refers to this as the "conflict" model.

The final model that Schaffer identifies is the one that is currently thought to be the most apt explanation of socialization. The "mutuality" model draws upon research findings that show that children are active participants in the world around them and that they come into the world preadapted to social interaction According to this view, they cannot be thought of as antisocial. Schaffer argues that children should be viewed as active participants in the socialization process.

This latter view of socialization also predominates in sociology. Sociologist William A. Corsaro has identified two types of models within his discipline: determinist and constructivist. The determinist model views the child as passive in the same way as psychologists' "clay molding" model: The emphasis is on the role of training and directing the child toward appropriate actions, values, and behaviour. The constructivist models that Corsaro refers to draw heavily upon the work of Piaget and Vygotsky. Both of these historically important psychologists highlighted in different ways children's active role in their own development. Although Piaget and Vygotsky agreed about children's active role in constructing their own knowledge and understanding of the world, the two disagreed about the process of socialization. There is an obvious parallel between this model and what Schaffer calls the "mutuality model" in psychology.

There is general agreement in both disciplines that children are active agents in the process of their own socialization. However, the ongoing debate at present revolves around how one conceptualizes the child's role. Corsaro believes that there is an overreliance on linear models of development in which socialization is conceived of as an incremental "building" process. The process, he suggests, is far more complex.

See also Costs and Benefits; Work Ethic.

References Corsaro, William A., *The Sociology of Childhood* (1997); Schaffer, H. Rudolph, *Social Development* (1996).

Soldiers

See Boy Soldiers.

Somalia

Somalia lies in northeastern Africa. It has a long coastline on the Indian Ocean, the Gulf of Aden, and the Red Sea. It is difficult to obtain an accurate estimate of the population because so many of the inhabitants of the country are nomads. One estimate puts the national population at around 8 million, of whom around one million live in the capital, Mogadishu. The nomadic people live by raising sheep, goats, cattle, and camels. There are few natural mineral resources. Less than 10 percent of the population are believed to be literate.

Different parts of the country were for long periods under the control of Britain and Italy. Independence was achieved in 1960, but it has proved impossible to establish an effective, stable, centralized government. Military action is virtually continuous at one or another location, with a number of breakaway regional governments proclaiming their independence. Power lies with the leaders of local clans. Because of civil warfare, famine has been a regular occurrence, leading to intervention by relief agencies and the United Nations.

Nomadic children start work early in their lives, guarding small herds of livestock. It is difficult to arrange education for these children. In some cases teachers travel with the family groups. However, this service is seen by some as wasteful because of the low number of pupils receiving education from each teacher.

Despite the widespread poverty, Mogadishu has a thriving commercial and tourist area. Here urban children can be found working in street trading and similar jobs. Some live with their families, but others are street children in the fullest sense.

In addition to its own economic problems, Somalia has to deal with large influxes of refugees from neighbouring countries. There are very large numbers of people, many of them children, living in refugee camps. Other refugees have moved into towns, attempting to make the difficult transition from their nomadic lifestyle to the settled patterns of urban life. Many refugee children undertake adult work, collecting fuel and water and preparing food, especially if the adults in the family are too weak or ill to perform these duties.

References Ennew, Judith, and Milne, Brian, *The Next Generation: Lives of Third World Children* (1989); Shaw, John, and Moorehead, Caroline, "Refugee Children: Somalia" (1989).

South Africa

The Republic of South Africa occupies the most southerly part of the African continent. The British and Dutch governments at various times controlled the area, and tensions between colonists from these two countries led to the so-called Boer Wars, "Boer" being the name applied to the descendants of Dutch settlers. The whole area was united as part of the British Empire in 1910. Political control lay in the hands of descendants of European settlers, although the great majority of the population were native black Africans. The government in 1948 initiated a formal policy of apartheid, or racial segregation.

Rising militant opposition to this policy made it harder and harder to sustain, and in 1990 the government began a process of dismantling the apartheid system, leading to the country's first multiracial general election in 1994. The African National Congress, a group that had been at the forefront of the struggle against apartheid, won an overwhelming majority of votes.

The current population of South Africa is around 40 million. About three quarters are black, and the remainder are white, Asian, or "coloured" (of mixed ethnic origin). Agriculture, gold mining, manufacturing, and tourism all play a major role in South Africa's economy. Because South Africa is relatively advanced industrially compared with its neighbours, it has many migrant workers, some of whom are illegal.

Child labour has existed in South Africa on a large scale since colonial times. The children of slaves were required to work in exchange for their maintenance. There are accounts of settlers kidnapping and selling children as slaves. Although it is widely acknowledged that child labour is still common today, there is a shortage of accurate figures. One estimate puts the number of children working at almost 800,000.

Most child workers are believed to come from the black and coloured communities. In rural areas, the children of agricultural workers are expect to do housework and farm work from an early age. The farm schools that many attend are poorly equipped and offer inadequate preparation for any further education or training. Many children leave for what they see as better prospects in town. However, they can eke out only a precarious living on the urban streets. A Network against Child Labour (NACL) was formed in South Africa in 1990.

See also Africa; Malawi; Tanzania; Zimbabwe.

References Dube, Linde, *Child Labour in South Africa* (1995).

Spain

Spain is situated in southwestern Europe, with coastlines on both the Mediterranean Sea and the Atlantic Ocean and frontiers with Portugal and France. It has a population of around 40 million. It was a monarchy until 1931, when a republic was proclaimed. Civil war (1936–1939) resulted in the coming to power of General Francisco Franco, who ruled until his death in 1975. Spain then became a parliamentary democracy with a monarch as head of state. Considerable power has been placed in the hands of the 17 autonomous regions that make up the country. In some regions local languages, such as Basque and Catalan, are spoken in addition to Spanish.

Spain's economy has grown during the democratic regime. It produces a wide range of agricultural products, including wine. It has rich mineral resources, including coal, and a diverse manufacturing sector. Tourism also flourishes in Spain, particularly on the Mediterranean coast and many offshore islands.

The General Workers' Union claimed in 1991 that around 11 percent of children between the ages of 12 and 15 were officially recognized to be working, despite laws passed in 1976. The economic sectors where these children were acknowledged to be employed were services (38 percent of children's jobs), agriculture (31 percent of children's jobs), manufacturing (18 percent of children's jobs), and construction (7 percent of children's jobs). These proportions are almost certainly underestimates, for a number of reasons. First, some children started working before the age of 12 but were not included in the survey. Secondly, domestic service was not included. Thirdly, children are also engaged in many forms of work in the informal sector of the economy, including small businesses in rural areas. In larger towns, they are engaged in begging and prostitution. Neither category was included in the survey.

The large proportion of children whose work is in services—for example, in hotels and restaurants—is in part explained by the extensive tourist industry. Most children work in small concerns that employ fewer than five people. Girls tend to be found working in the kitchens; boys are more likely to be serving the clients directly. Children are particularly heavily employed in agriculture during the harvest—for example, in picking tomatoes in the Canary Islands. Some Spanish children migrate to France to take part in harvesting. They also herd goats and cattle. The Spanish branch of the nongovernmental organization Defence for Children International has been active in attempts to increase public awareness of child labour.

Some observers have suggested that child labour problems are particularly serious among the Gypsy community. There are an estimated 300,000 Gypsies in Spain, around half of whom are under 16 years of age. Only a small proportion of Gypsies follow the traditional nomadic style of life. However, other aspects of their traditional culture remain strong. This includes a tendency for children to take up adult pursuits earlier than is common in other ethnic groups.

See also Defence for Children International.

References Cadman, Eileen, *No Time to Play: Child Workers in the Global Economy* (1996); Defensa de Niños y Niñas Internacional, *El Trabajo Infantil en Espana* (1995); Searight, Susan, *Child Labour in Spain* (1980).

Sports

Sports and child labour are linked in two ways: Children are involved in the manufacture of sports equipment and clothing, and some are employed as performers in spectator sports.

One of the major issues concerning child labour in the world today is that many goods bought by consumers in relatively wealthy countries are produced at least in part by children in poor countries, working in bad conditions for poor wages. To some critics, the moral case against this state of affairs is heightened when the goods being produced are associated with sports. It is objectionable, from this point of view, for a well-known figure in sports to profit by endorsing products made with child labour. Even if no sports personality is individually involved, the question is raised of whether leisure activities, such as playing or watching sports, should be bought at prices that are lower than they would be if the child workers had better pay and conditions.

The Soccer World Cup is one of the biggest sporting events in the world. The competition is organized by FIFA (the world governing body of soccer) and is held every four years in a different country. Thirty-two countries compete in the finals, which last four weeks. In 1998 the competition was held in France, but controversy raged before play had even begun when it became known that the balls being used in the competition were made by poorly paid young children working in factories in various locations in the developing countries.

Professional sports are a worldwide industry, partly because large audiences can be created through the medium of television. Success in a sport with a mass audience may bring individuals great financial rewards. It is clearly to the benefit of those who run sports enterprises to seek out talented individuals, and in many cases, to identify young people who are potentially successful future performers. There are two dangers in this. One is that young athletes might be encouraged to concentrate on a single activity too early in life. The other is that they will be required to sign a contract that leads them to anticipate success but that offers them no security if the employer decides later that they are not as talented and as likely to succeed as they had appeared.

Some sports—for example, swimming and gymnastics—have developed in such a way that it is common for leading international participants to be of school age. Since success in international events such as the Olympic Games almost always demands many hours of rigorous training, it is reasonable to argue that the lives of these young people must be seen as a form of child labour. Of course, almost invariably, successful performers will state in interview that they are happy that the hard work has brought them success. However, it should be noted that unsuccessful performers are less likely to have their views spread publicly than are successful ones. Although children and young people in most sports are treated far better than are camel jockeys, there is still good reason to remain vigilant and critically scrutinize the treatment of young athletes.

See also Camel Jockeys; Entertainment Industry; Leisure; Product Labelling.

References Cottingham, M., *A Sporting Chance* (1997).

Stabilization and Structural Adjustment Programmes

Prior to the early 1980s, the phrase held little meaning for policymakers, social scientists, and the newly industrializing countries (NICs) and underdeveloped countries (UDCs). By the end of the decade, however, structural adjustment programmes had become the main method for promoting neoliberal development in poor countries with large debts. The promotion of such policies has had the general tendency to encourage the growth of child labour.

In a sense, of course, economies have always adjusted to changes in production regimes and fluctuating prices and exchange and interest rates as well as to inflation and various man-made economic disasters and crises. Countries have had to find ways to deal with a negative balance of payments. The adjustment programme undertaken in any one country can have an effect throughout the world economy. For example, in the 1920s and 1930s, countries tried to deal with the problem by undertaking protectionist policies (aiming to block imports coming into the country); but this approach created a crisis for the supplying countries, which lost their market, which in turn pushed up prices at home. Both inflation and unemployment resulted.

To counter protectionism in the postwar era, the governments of the advanced economies signed the Bretton Woods Agreement in 1944. This agreement was an attempt to solve the balance of payments problems of indebted countries, especially developing countries, by making available, and extending, loans. The international financial institutions (IFIs) would offer advice on how economies could be brought into line, but it was essentially left to governments to decide how they would meet their repayment obligations.

In the three decades following World War II, NICs and UDCs with internal economic crises and balance of payments problems sought loans with governments of the advanced economies or various IFIs. In return, these institutions tended to demand some form of stabilization programme, primarily concerned with cutting budget deficits. This could involve (1) either reducing spending or increasing public revenue; (2) limiting the money supply to reduce inflation; (3) developing export sectors to solve balance of trade weaknesses; (4) reducing imports and inflation, which might be achieved by wage reduction; and (5) setting exchange rates at an appropriate level, which might involve currency devaluation. The consequence of these policies was economic contraction, and the resultant burden was most severely felt by the country's rural and working classes. However, until the early 1980s, governments had some degree of leeway in meeting these policy requirements; state intervention and action was viewed as a legitimate response.

With the onset of world economic crises from the early 1970s, NICs and UDCs with massive debts became particularly vulnerable. By the early 1980s several countries were having severe problems meeting their debt repayments. Politically, at this time, Britain and the United States were being governed by administrations committed to free-market principles, and neoliberal thinking predominated in the IFIs. Gradually, as a consequence, debtor nations came under intense pressure to follow radical, neoliberal programmes known as stabilization and structural adjustment programmes (SSAPs). This resulted in increased poverty for much of the population in these countries and an increased demand for cheap child labour.

Debtor nations were being forced to sign up for an experiment in economic development. As well as following the "stabilization" measures listed above, loan conditions required structural adjustment in the form of the following: (1) the lowering of trade barriers, exposing local producers to foreign competition and increasing bankruptcy and unemployment; (2) the abolishment of subsidies and price controls, and hence, the removal of "price distortions" in the market, and the raising of prices of many staple goods for impoverished populations; (3) the restructuring of financial systems to allow the free movement of capital, making economies vulnerable to price and share fluctuations and governments susceptible to pressure from international finance capital; (4) the priva-

tization of state-owned organizations and acceptance of private foreign investment. Although state intervention was supposed to be drastically cut in terms of economic management and provision of social services and welfare benefits, paradoxically, in many countries this package would be achieved by authoritarian state activities, including military intervention in political and social life.

The economic successes of SSAPs have been limited, even on their own terms, and their social consequences have been traumatic. Unemployment; poverty; declining wages; rising prices, especially of food and transport; and cuts in social, educational, and welfare spending all have resulted from SSAPs. Unemployment for some has brought a transition from skilled work to "flexible" work in the informal sector. For many families the struggle for survival has meant that family members must take whatever work can be found, no matter what the conditions.

The International Labour Organisation (ILO) has plotted a rising curve of child labour, with the worst exploitation and abuses taking place in small, undercapitalized firms at the margins of the market, which use the cheapest labour available in order to compete with larger and more efficient companies. By undermining social, welfare, and educational spending and forcing deregulation on national economies and labour markets, SSAPs have increased the pressure on employers and families to engage in flexible, marginal employment. Child labour has increased as a result.

See also Globalization; International Labour Organisation.

References United Nations Research Institute for Social Development, *States of Disarray: The Social Effects of Globalization* (1995).

Steinberg, Laurence

In 1986, Laurence Steinberg coauthored a groundbreaking book on adolescent employment in the United States. *When Teenagers Work: The Psychological and Social*

Costs of Adolescent Employment still serves as a basis for current research in this area.

Steinberg, a professor of psychology at Temple University, has been researching and publishing on the impact of adolescent employment throughout the 1980s and 1990s. In the 1980s, along with his colleague Ellen Greenberger, Steinberg argued that the issue of adolescent employment had been neglected in the United States.

For Steinberg one of the fundamental changes in American society in the latter part of the twentieth century was the extent to which American youth combined education and work. He attributed much of this change to the growth of the service sector, particularly of fast food outlets.

Steinberg's main concern has been to evaluate the impact of such work experience on adolescents' lives. Of particular interest to him is the impact of work on educational outcomes. In this context, he has long argued that the number of hours worked must be viewed as a key variable in looking at the balance between the costs and benefits of work.

Steinberg has also published textbooks on the broader subject of adolescent development. Within such texts he has highlighted the issue of employment. Steinberg is still highly involved in examining issues connected with child labour, and he is currently a member of the National Research Council Institute of Medicine's Committee on the Health and Safety Implications of Child Labor.

See also Educational Achievement; Greenberger, Ellen.

References Greenberger, Ellen, and Steinberg, Laurence, *When Teenagers Work: The Psychological and Social Costs of Adolescent Employment* (1986); Steinberg, Laurence, and Dornbusch, Sanford M. "Negative Correlates of Part-Time Employment during Adolescence: Replication and Elaboration" (1991); Steinberg, Laurence, Fegley, Suzanne, and Dornbusch, Sanford M. "Negative Impact of Part-Time Work on Adolescent Adjustment: Evidence from a Longitudinal Study" (1993); Steinberg, Laurence, *Adolescence* (1993).

Stop Child Labour

In January 1995, an International Confer-ence against Child Labor and Forced Labor took place in Dhaka, Bangladesh. Although delegates attended only from India, France, Nepal, New Zealand, and Thailand, the organizers of the conference received support from individuals and organizations in 16 other countries including the United States and the United Kingdom. A committee of support set up in Britain served as the catalyst for the formation of a group called Stop Child Labour. Although still small, Stop Child Labour has the advantage of receiving active support from a number of members of the British Parliament, the most vocal of whom is Jeremy Corbyn.

One of the most distinctive features of the Dhaka conference and the Stop Child Labour Group is that although not all of the supporters would call themselves Marxists, it is the most prominent body concerned with child labour that adopts a Marxist standpoint. The final declaration of the Dhaka conference criticized structural adjustment programmes because of their impact on child labour; but that in itself is not a position confined to Marxists. More unusual was the claim that the European Union directive on the protection of young people at work was actually intended to encourage child labour. The conference called for the establishment of an international tribunal on child labour, independent from all states and governments as well as from other international bodies, such as the United Nations. In Britain, Labour members of parliament supporting the Stop Child Labour group have put pressure on the government to take more decisive action against child labour, with little apparent success as yet.

See also European Union; Marxism; Stabilization and Structural Adjustment Programmes; United Kingdom.

Street Children

This phrase is often found in discussions of child labour, although the fact that it is so widely used does not necessarily mean that

Manuel Rodriguez, a street child who washes cars for a living in Lima, Peru, 1969 (Corbis-Bettmann)

it always refers to the same circumstances. In many large cities throughout the world, children may be found who appear not to go to school and who earn a living at casual jobs, such as street trading, begging, stealing, or prostitution. It is generally assumed that these children are orphans or that they have been abandoned by their families or have run away from home. Investigations show that many street children fall into one of these three categories but others do not.

Some children who work on the streets maintain contact with their families. In some cases, poor families regard the child's being on the streets as a way of earning a living. Some street children also have a relationship with official institutions, perhaps occasionally spending some time living in an orphanage or attending school from time to time. Benno Glauser, who has researched the problems of street children in Paraguay, argues that the children to whom this label may be applied in fact vary so much in several important ways that the category "street children" is unhelpful.

Many street children sleep wherever they can find a suitable place. Most appear to enter into some sort of relationship with children like themselves, forming gangs for mutual assistance and protection. The specific pattern of life may vary depending on what the child sees as the best opportunities for earning. Some work at day and sleep at night; others work all or part of the night, if they can find customers for their services.

Street children are prone to many health risks because of their inadequate diet and lifestyle. Many make recourse to drugs. They tend to be poorly educated and hence have little prospect of improving their conditions of life by finding better forms of employment.

Reactions to street children vary strikingly, depending on the point of view of the observer. Members of organizations concerned with child labour or child welfare often regard street children as being in the greatest need of positive action to improve the circumstances of their lives. In contrast, many ordinary citizens may be most struck by the fact that by sleeping and eating on the streets these children are making improper use of facilities that were put there for other purposes. Since some street children steal, some members of the public regard them primarily as a threat. In some countries, the attitude of people in authority to street children is particularly hostile. They may be regarded as embarrassments to the country's government, especially when the country is seeking to encourage tourism. In several countries street children often are victims of violence by the police or by hostile adults whose actions are condoned by the authorities.

See also Scavenging.
References Glauser, Benno, "Street Children: Deconstructing a Construct" (1997).

Sweated Labour

Originally applied to describe those working in sweatshops of the clothing industry in New York. The *Westminster Gazette*, on 2 November 1895, noted: "All but 15 of the 385 wholesale clothing manufacturers in New York have their goods made in sweatshops." The clothing manufacturers in New York drew their labour supply from among migrants coming to the United States from the old world, many of whom were from rural areas and few of whom could speak English. The work tasks of clothing manufacturing translated quite easily from the rural village to the urban city; so the migrants found that it was the kind of employment they could easily undertake on arrival in their new homeland. For the manufacturers, the advantages were that they had a large supply of cheap and compliant labour, desperate for work. The workers could be employed in a rudimentary factory or given outwork for completion in their home. Outwork had the added advantage of incurring no overhead for the employer. Entire families, men, women, and children, often were put to work in the sweatshops of home and factory, and the plentiful supply of labour kept rates of pay very low. The labourers typically were paid for piecework—that is, payment was based on the number of units produced rather than the hours worked. To make anything approaching a minimal living wage, workers had to put in long shifts in cramped conditions. The physical exertion required of the sweatshop worker was great for little return.

There are thus two defining elements to sweated labour: first, the conditions of employment—the need to sweat long and hard in order to obtain limited financial rewards; and secondly, the work takes place on the edges of the labour market and often plays on social divisions to segregate workers and reinforce their disadvantaged position. Thus, sweatshop workers are very unlikely to be unionized. They tend to be drawn from disadvantaged groups such as migrants, women, and minority communities. The social classification of children as marginal workers has made them vulnerable to sweated labour practices.

Today the phrase *sweated labour* denotes any form of extreme labour exploitation that involves hard work for little financial remuneration. A vast amount of the work performed by children across the world today can be classified as sweated labour.

See also Garment Industry; Immigrant Children.

References Bishton, D., *The Sweat Shop Report* (1984).

Tanzania

The east African country of Tanzania was formed in 1965 by the union of Zanzibar, an island state, and Tanganyika, a former British colony. It has a population of around 30 million. Its economy is largely based on agriculture.

Child labour was a major feature of the farms run by British colonists in Tanganyika. In part this was because adult African workers did not wish to be separated from their families when they travelled long distances for work. However, by far the most important reason was that the use of child labour was greatly to the farmers' advantage financially. Although many children worked almost as productively as adults, they were always paid much less than adults. Cases of children hurt or killed because of farmers' negligence and of children working in unhealthy conditions were largely ignored by colonial officials.

In the late 1930s, the British government pointed out that Tanganyika was the only British colony that had not passed laws restricting child labour in accordance with international agreements that Britain had entered into almost 20 years earlier. Draft regulations were formulated, but the farmers lobbied effectively, and the final versions were so watered down that they had little impact on what actually happened on the farms.

See also Africa; Agriculture; Malawi.

References Shivji, Issa, "Law and Conditions of Child Labour in Colonial Tanganyika, 1920–1940" (1985).

Thailand

This country in southeast Asia, bordering Malaysia, Burma, Cambodia, and Laos, was formerly know as Siam. It has been a constitutional monarchy since 1932. Its population of almost 60 million is overwhelmingly Buddhist. Around two-thirds of the labour force are engaged in agriculture, rice being the principal crop. Fruit, rubber, and timber also are produced.

The Buddhist temple has traditionally played a significant role in Thai society and continues to do so today. An important practice partially surviving from the past is for parents to entrusts their sons to a temple, where they are looked after in return for various services. Many modern schools have been built in the grounds of temples.

The Thai government publishes figures of child employment, but they must be interpreted with caution. For example, one survey in the early 1990s indicated that there were 7,500 children aged 13 to 14 years who were individually engaged in paid employment in agriculture. However, this survey greatly underestimated the role played by children in farming, because in rural areas much of the work is undertaken by a whole family operating as a single labour unit and the survey did not take into account children working in this sector as members of the family.

Public awareness of children employed in manufacturing and construction industries is relatively high, partly because they are based in large urban areas and are thus highly visible to the public. Despite public awareness, it is clear that many of these children work in unhealthy and physically dangerous conditions.

Children also play a prominent part in the Thai fishing industry. Payment depends on the size of the catch, and when it is good, the wages are considered high by local standards. Because of this, child fishermen are often seen taking serious risks while at sea.

In 1991 a Thai television programme, called "Raid on the Hell Factory," included pictures of a raid carried out in Bangkok.

Boy digging ditches in Bangkok, Thailand, 1989 (International Labour Office)

On entering the factory, the cameras found children working intensively at a production line making paper cups. The children were dirty and gaunt. Many had bad burns on their hands as a result of constant contact with the strong glue used in the production process. Many children suffered from deformities as a direct consequence of the long working hours (up to 15 hours a day being the norm), the repetitive motions and bad working position, and inadequate nutrition. Many children also had been beaten by the factory owner to "encourage" them to work harder.

From the point of view of outsiders, the most substantial child labour problem in Thailand is that of child prostitution. A police report in 1991 estimated that of the 200,000 prostitutes in the capital city, Bangkok, 20,000 were children. Other estimates suggest that the numbers of children working in brothels and massage parlours is higher than this. Thailand has the unfortunate reputation of being a major centre of the "sex tourism" industry, particularly because of its child prostitutes.

See also Asia; Fishing; Prostitution; Tourism.
References Cadman, Eileen, *No Time to Play: Child Workers in the Global Economy* (1996); Concerned for Working Children, The, *Child Labour in Thailand* (1995); Ennew, Judith and Milne, Brian, *The Next Generation: Lives of Third World Children* (1989); Lee-Wright, Peter, *Child Slaves* (1990); Mendelievich, Elias (ed.), *Children at Work* (1979).

Thompson, E. P.

Edward Palmer Thompson (1924–1993) was an English historian and political campaigner. His reputation as a historian was primarily based on his book *The Making of the English Working Class* (first published in 1963, with a revised edition appearing in 1968). Writing about the industrial revolution in England, Thompson concluded that "the exploitation of little children, on this scale and with this intensity, was one of the most shameful events in our history." Thompson was arguing against the views of writers such as W. H. Hutt, who had suggested that the evils of factory work for children had been exaggerated. Thompson acknowledged that children previously had worked within the family. However, he believed that as far as children were concerned, the factory system had all of the evils of domestic labour and none of the compensations. Furthermore, factory work was more monotonous and more continuous than the work children had typically undertaken in earlier times.

See also Industrial Revolution; Nardinelli Thesis, The; Pro-employment Arguments.
References Hutt, W. H., "The Factory System of the Early Nineteenth Century" (1954); Nardinelli, Clark, *Child Labor and the Industrial Revolution* (1990); Thompson, E. P., *The Making of the English Working Class* (1968).

Tourism

The growth of the tourist industry is a relatively recent phenomenon. Not until the twentieth century did mass travel become common. International tourism is rooted in the 1960s and 1970s, when increasing disposable income, longer holiday periods, the marketing of "leisure time," cheap oil, and the jet plane allowed the industry to grow.

Although developed countries tended to dominate as prime destinations in the early years of tourist travel, the developing economies have begun to catch up. Countries such as Egypt, Jamaica, Thailand, Sri Lanka, Kenya, the Philippines, and Mexico now earn considerable revenue from tourists. As an employment sector tourism attracts both adult and child employees. In developing countries the growth of tourism has been linked to the migration of workers, both adult and child, to urban centres.

Research into the level of child labour associated with tourism is rare. Where material does exist, it tends to focus upon the links between child prostitution and tourism. In the early 1980s a number of nongovernmental organizations (NGOs) started to draw attention to the use of children in "sex tourism." The NGO Terre des Hommes in 1981 published a report drawing attention to paedophile tourism in

Sri Lanka; and Redd Barna (the Norwegian branch of Save the Children) in 1989 brought out a report entitled "The sexual exploitation of children in developing countries." In Asia concern among NGOs about child prostitution has led to the creation of End Child Prostitution in Asian Tourism, an umbrella group for NGOs working in this area.

In 1990 the European Parliament claimed that one million children worldwide had been forced into the market for sex. However, the reliability of such figures is open to question. Maggie Black, a researcher in the area of child labour, has argued that there is a lack of reliable research from which to derive any accurate estimation of the numbers of children involved. For example, estimates of children working in the sex industry in Thailand range from 2,500 to 800,000. Estimates from other countries, including Sri Lanka, China, Vietnam, Taiwan, and the Philippines, are equally divergent.

Although one cannot put an accurate number on how many are involved, it can be agreed that many children, especially young teenage girls, are kidnapped, bought, or forced into the sex industry. These children face sexual exploitation and a range of other risks to their psychological development. They also face major health risks related to sexually transmitted diseases. In particular, many child sex workers are infected with HIV/AIDS.

The example of children being pulled into prostitution is a powerful example of the worst excesses of tourism. Tourists have been prosecuted for hiring child prostitutes in Thailand and the Philippines, and other governments (for example, those of Norway, Sweden, and Germany) have introduced legislation allowing for the similar prosecution of tourists in their own countries. However, Maggie Black argues that the current focus on combating child prostitution through legislation has resulted in two problems.

First, this approach implies that tourism is the primary causal factor in the growth of the number of children involved in the sex industry. Black suggests that tourism is not the only factor and might not even be the primary cause. She bases this assertion in part on a study in Thailand showing that underage prostitutes mainly served the local population and that Western tourists mainly dealt with women over the age of 18 years. Black does not deny that tourists contribute to the problem but reminds us that we cannot assume they are its sole cause.

Secondly, the focus on prostitution detracts from a more thoroughgoing analysis of the full range of children's employment in tourism. Many children earn their living from work other than prostitution—for example, those working in hotels and catering concerns.

In addition, Black highlights the extent to which children who are not employed in any regular work may also survive on the back of the tourist industry. Black calls attention to children working in the "open air" economy, often referred to by others as "street children" (Black finds this a problematic description). Many earn money from street vending, shoe-shining, and hawking, and therefore are directly or indirectly dependent upon the tourist industry. What we lack at present is a clear picture of the nature and extent of such employment at the national and international levels.

See also Hotel and Catering Industry; Nongovernmental Organizations; Prostitution; Street Children.

References Black, Maggie, *In the Twilight Zone: Child Workers in the Hotel, Tourism, and Catering Industry* (1995).

Trade Unions

Trade unions are organizations of workers who join together in order to improve their pay and conditions of employment, generally through collective action and common representation.

There are two basic types of unions: Craft unions organize workers on the basis of their skill levels and craft training. They tend to be exclusive and have an overarching aim in maintaining their members' rights and conditions irrespective of any effect this might have on other workers. General unions attempt to organize workers at all skill levels within particular industries. The craft unions tend to be older and have longer traditions; the general unions are more recent creations dating from the late nineteenth century and after.

Trade unions have had an active interest in controlling and eradicating child labour throughout their history, for two reasons. First, as organizations of working people, they have reflected concern that working children should not have to suffer exploitation and abuse in the workplace and that children should be free of the need to work. Secondly, the extensive employment of children occasionally has undermined the position and employment conditions of certain categories of adult workers.

Since child labour is seen today as a global issue, trade unions involve themselves with the issue not only within particular countries but also through their own international organizations. The International Confederation of Free Trade Unions (ICFTU) campaigns for what its members refer to as a "social clause" in international trade agreements. Such a clause would make working conditions an element in any agreement between countries. The aspects of work that the ICFTU seeks to have taken into consideration include the right to belong to a trade union; abolition of forced labour; no discrimination in pay on grounds of sex; and a minimum age for employment. The ICFTU's campaign pursues a step-by-step approach to the abolition of child labour, targeting one industry at a time and concentrating on the most severe abuses.

Trade unions are also engaged in combating the evils of child employment through their membership in the International Labour Organisation.

See also American Federation of Labor; Industrial Workers of the World; International Confederation of Free Trade Unions; International Labour Organisation; Knights of Labor; The Order of.

References Cadman, Eileen, *No Time to Play: Child Workers in the Global Economy* (1996). Fyfe, Alec, and Jankanish, M., *Trade Unions and Child Labour: A Guide to Action* (1997); International Labour Organisation, *Trade Unions and Child Labour* (1996).

Traditional Societies

Traditional societies—sometimes referred to as "primitive societies" in anthropological accounts—are preindustrial, land-based societies. In historical and sociological writing, they are often juxtaposed to industrial, urban, and modern societies.

The phrase *primitive societies* is not often used nowadays because of its connotations of inferiority and its racist overtones. Although *traditional societies* is preferred, many of the negative and judgmental implications are often still present. Furthermore, both phrases suggest that for thousands of years prior to the onset of the modern industrial world, human societies were relatively homogeneous and static. Yet this position is hard to justify: There is as much that differentiates ancient Greek societies from African communities, Inca tribal societies, and feudal European societies as there is that unites them all in commonality.

See also Cultural Traditions; Industrial Society Thesis.

Training

Everyone goes through a process of training at work. This may be a formal process organized by a company, an employers' organization, a government agency, or a trade union body. At the end of formal training, the trainee is expected to show competency or mastery of certain skills, and in return will receive a formal qualification. Alternatively, training may be an informal process involving the worker's absorption of knowledge and acquisition of skills while on the job.

Training allows us to master tasks, to perform them more quickly, and perhaps to learn a few "tricks of the trade." Training is ongoing throughout our working lives. However, the most intensive period of training takes place when individuals first enter the labour market or when they are preparing to do so. Thus, training is most intensively directed at young workers.

The notion that training is something new workers require has led some people to think of child labour as an acceptable learning activity rather than a form of unfair exploitation. This concept is relatively common, especially in the advanced economies. It leads people to suggest that child work in these societies is part of a process that provides young people with work-based skills and knowledge and thus gives them certain advantages when they have to enter the labour market full time.

See also Apprenticeship; Career; Costs and Benefits; Pro-employment Arguments; Transition Debate.

Transition Debate

Whenever child employment in modern Western society is being discussed, it is common to find some reference to the role of work in the child's development. Whether it is parents or professionals talking, one hears phrases extolling the value of employment, such as "it teaches them about the value of money"; "it teaches responsibility"; or that employment is important since "they have to learn about the real world." Such views have a common thread to them—namely the assumption that work experiences have a role to play in helping children move from childhood to adulthood.

Work plays a central role in the lives of adults. A dominant view in society is that the sooner children learn about the world of work, the better off they will be in the long run. Historically, however, the move from adolescence to adulthood through work was perhaps more gradual. Work within the family unit was the most common starting point, followed by some form of apprenticeship. Adult status was attained by demonstrating the capacity to fulfil a range of tasks and social roles.

Such interpretations appear to have played a significant role in influencing a number of government reports in the 1960s and 1970s. In the United States, the National Commission on Youth (1980), the National Panel on High School and Adolescent Education (1976), and the President's Science Advisory Committee (1973) were all influenced by such views. In Britain, the Central Advisory Council on Education's 1963 report reflected a similar interpretation of the value of work. Many of these reports called for the early integration of adolescents into the labour force.

All of these bodies believed that children's work should be organized within planned work experience programmes. The reality, however, is that most adolescents will have their own experience of employment through naturally occurring paid employment. Does this form of work facilitate the transition into adulthood?

Some researchers are very skeptical. Ellen Greenberger and Laurence Steinberg, in particular, argue that those who propose the transition value of work fail to attend to the real world of adolescent employment. The position of Greenberger and Steinberg is influenced by the fact that they believe that the transition is not simply about adopting the social roles of adults but must also be about the psychological transition from adolescence to adulthood. It is their opinion that employment may harm the individual's transition to adulthood.

For example, they argue that the amount of time adolescents commit to work, if excessive, can limit their time for other important interactions with peers, families, and other social groupings. However, limited time also hampers individuals' ability to discover the full range of their skills and abilities. An additional danger of excessive involvement in work is that it limits experimentation in other roles and can interfere with mental exploration, which according to some psychologists plays a role in psychological development.

For Greenberger and Steinberg, the

danger is that adolescents achieve a pseudomaturity from their work experiences. They gain access to money, independence, new social roles, and new work roles that they may be socially mature enough to deal with but not psychologically mature enough to handle well. The rush to take on adult roles can lead to the individual's "playing at" the roles without fully understanding them or being fully committed to them.

This view resonates with a number of writers, such as David Elind and Marie Winn, who have argued that children and adolescents are growing up too quickly. Work may be accelerating this process. Simply carrying out adult tasks does not make you an adult unless these activities are accompanied by a level of psychological maturity or perception.

Let us look at one example: Adolescents at work are supposed to gain an understanding of the value of money and the skill to manage it. One American researcher questions whether this is true. Jerald Bachman has argued that instead of learning the true value of money, working adolescents who freely dispose of their earned income might be led astray by this "premature affluence" and use their money to purchase items that they want. Because their parents provide food, shelter, and other basic needs, working adolescents tend not to have any other demands on their income. Thus, they often move into adult employment with the expectation of high levels of discretionary income. The reality of mortgages, bills, and living expenses comes as a shock because they have not learned the adult responsibilities of budgeting, saving, and delaying satisfaction of consumer desires.

In Western countries the debate about the role of work in facilitating transitions also has been linked to the move from compulsory education to the workplace. Under the heading of "adolescence," a number of psychologists and sociologists have considered this transition and the problems inherent in it. In recent times the questions have been as much about adolescents moving from school to unemployment as from school to work. As with the idea that work aids the move to adult roles, there is considerable debate about the extent to which experience of work while at school aids or hinders the move to adult employment.

Scholars have tended to look at the idea of transition only within Western societies. However, one of the earliest explanations of the role of work as a facilitator of children's development into adults came from another cultural context. Margaret Mead, an anthropologist, wrote about Samoans in a 1928 book called *Coming of Age in Samoa*. In it she explained that children within this culture did not attend compulsory education; instead, their education was part of their socialization into work roles. Children were assigned real work tasks suitable to their age and skill level. These tasks were adjusted over time, and the child was slowly brought into the adult work roles of the culture.

Anthropologist Jo Boyden reviewed the work of a number of researchers in 1994 and showed the extent to which cultural differences exist in the transition to work. Boyden highlighted the importance of work as a transition rite, allowing individuals to move from the status of children to that of adults. Working affects children's status within family and societal relationships and can provide children with a sense of self-worth. This emerges from their ability to contribute to family incomes, which changes the structure of the relationship between the child and other family members.

Boyden's discussion suggests that different institutions confer different forms of status on children. For example, work may allow adolescents to think of themselves as adults because they are earning money and are working alongside adults. In contrast, school reinforces adolescents' social status as children. Such discrepancies may play a part in the relative value children ascribe to school and to work.

See also Adolescence; Costs and Benefits; Greenberger, Ellen; Steinberg, Laurence.

References Boyden, Jo, *The Relationship between Education and Child Work* (1994); Coleman, John C., and Hendry, Leo, *The Nature of Adolescence* (1990); Furlong, Andy, *Growing Up in a Classless Society? School to Work Transitions* (1992); Greenberger, Ellen, and Steinberg, Laurence, *When Teenagers Work: The Psychological and Social Costs of Adolescent Employment* (1986).

Triangle Shirtwaist Factory Fire

At the end of the nineteenth century and the beginning of the twentieth, the United States passed the first legislation targeting child employment. This early legislation varied from state to state, and its primary focus appears to have been to move children from work to school. For example, New York state in the latter part of the nineteenth century passed legislation making education compulsory for children who were between the ages of 8 and 14 years.

However, the ineffectiveness of this legislation became evident in the aftermath of a fire that took place in 1911. The event became known as the Triangle Shirtwaist Fire, named after the garment factory in New York where the blaze broke out, killing a large number of women and children who had been working in sweatshop conditions. Many of the children were working illegally at the time of the fire, since they should have been in school, in accordance with the law.

See also Garment Industry; Legislation; Sweated Labour.

Turkey

Geographically, Turkey lies in both Asia and Europe. Its population is estimated to be over 60 million. The largest city, Istanbul, has more than 7 million inhabitants, and the capital, Ankara, has more than 3 million. Modern Turkey dates from 1923, when Kemal Ataturk declared the nation a republic. Since then there have been periods of democracy and periods of military rule.

About half of the country's workforce are engaged in agriculture. Turkey also has large mineral deposits. Children are to be found working on farms, in factories, and in the tourist industry. Turkish cities have shantytowns known as *gecekondu*, inhabited in the main by families who have come from rural areas, seeking work and a better quality of life. Most of these families live precariously. Many of them rely on their children for subsistence.

A valuable insight into their way of life is provided by a study conducted by Erol Kahveci and his colleagues in Izmir. This team set out to interview shoe-shine boys—highly visible members of the child labour force in Izmir and other cities. They found that the shoe-shine boys stayed mainly with their families in a *gecekondu* district. Most of their parents had come from rural areas of eastern Turkey, and the boys usually had several brothers and sisters. About a third of the fathers worked in the construction industry. About as many fathers were dead, disabled, retired, or unemployed.

Some of the boys attended school as well as working; some had dropped out of school; and some had never been to school. Those who attended school had lower average weekly earnings than those who did not, presumably because they worked fewer hours. Those who did not attend school gave mainly economic reasons when asked to explain. The money they earned shining shoes was almost always given over entirely to the parents for family expenses. Typically, a shoe-shine boy's earnings made up 30 or 40 percent of his family's income.

Most of the boys had had other jobs before becoming shoe-shine boys. Those who were born in villages had looked after sheep and harvested cotton. In the cities, they had worked in places such as garages, restaurants, shops, and factories. They also sold goods in markets and on the streets. Many of the shoe-shine boys combined sales activities with other jobs. One ran an illegal gambling game on the streets. Another was a leather worker who shined shoes when the leather trade was slack. Some worked in cafes in the evening. Oth-

154 KILLED IN SKYSCRAPER FACTORY FIRE; SCORES BURN, OTHERS LEAP TO DEATH.

700 WORKERS, MOSTLY GIRLS, TRAPPED; BODIES OF DEAD HEAP THE STREETS; ONLY ONE FIRE ESCAPE FOR ALL.

Front page of the New York World *newspaper showing three images of the Triangle Shirtwaist fire, March 16, 1911 (Library of Congress)*

ers washed cars or sold flowers and bird-seed. Those who combined jobs tended to have long work weeks. Many of the shoe-shine boys told stories about being cheated by customers and harassed by police and city inspectors. Nearly all of them claimed they would do other work if they could.

The city authorities of Ankara have attempted to reduce the problems faced by child workers by creating a local centre where they receive sympathetic coun-selling as well as medical and educational aid. Some children have been provided with vocational training. Shoe-shine boys who normally would be working on the open streets have been provided with more

233

protected locations, such as public buildings. The local police were consulted for their input, and this involvement has led to their adopting a more cooperative approach. The programme, supported by the International Labour Organisation, is modest in comparison to the size of the problem, but it may serve as a model to be followed in other areas.

See also Europe; Middle East; Projects; Tourism.

References International Labour Organisation, *Child Labour: Targeting the Intolerable* (1996); Kahveci, Erol, Nichols, Theo, and Sugur, Nadir, "The Shoe Shine Boys of Izmir" (1996); Konanc, Esin, and Zeytinoglu, Sezen, *Child Labour in Turkey* (1995); Lee-Wright, Peter, *Child Slaves* (1990).

Unfree Labour

Capitalism is acknowledged both by its supporters and by its detractors to be a system dominated by free wage labour. This latter phrase is used in a number of senses to distinguish the modern era from previous social structures where labour relations were not free but were structured by political or legal obligations. During the feudal era in Europe, for example, an individual was obliged by political and military pressure to work without pay on a lord's land at certain periods of the year. In the modern era the wage labourer is free from such requirements. Wage labourers are free to work for whomever they choose (provided they have jobs available), and can move to another job. Employers are free to hire whomever they choose. Employer and employee enter into a specific labour contract with each other. It may be noted, of course, that the worker's freedom is limited in practice in many ways, most obviously by the need to have an income in order to survive.

Although the dominant social relationship in the modern world is that centred around free wage labour as described above, there still exist examples of unfree labour. Unfree labour, in contrast to free labour, is work that is forced or structured by political, familial, or legal strictures requiring the worker to labour for a specific employer. The freedom to change employers or conditions of employment has been altered or removed to a significant degree. A number of forms of unfree labour have existed and continue to exist in the present era.

The most obvious example of unfree labour is slavery. The transportation, selling, and owning of African men, women, and children was crucial to the early development of the West Indies and southern states of the United States. The income derived from the slave trade was important in the development of capitalist industry in England and a number of other European states. Yet the formal abolition of slavery in Britain and America did not stop this practice. Slavery continues in many parts of the world today, and many children find themselves enslaved and required to work for their "owner." The children are either forcibly removed from their families or sold by their families to alleviate their poverty.

Debt-bonded labour, or tied labour, also has a very long history. Indeed, before the transatlantic slave trade fully took off, the demand for labour for the plantations in the West Indies was fulfilled by debt-bonded indentured workers. This means that people were transported from Britain, for example, to work on the plantations. However, they were expected to pay for their transportation and their initial living costs. As they did not have the necessary capital, they would enter into agreements with the plantation owners. They would be indentured for seven years and would work on the plantation until they had paid back their transport and living costs.

Bonded labour continues across the globe today. Young children are indentured to landowners, factory owners, craftsmen, hotel owners, and others. To pay off a family debt, or to pay for their transportation to the city from their rural homes, or to pay for their living expenses, children are tied to employers for a specified number of years, until it is deemed that the debt has been paid off. Very often, especially when the child is young, the employer will claim that the costs of supporting the child are greater than the labour he receives, so the debt becomes greater, reducing the prospect of its being paid off, at least in the near future.

Domestic labour, in contrast to the

Children demonstrate against bonded labour on the eve of India's independence day in New Delhi, India, August 14, 1994 (Corbis/Reuters)

above two examples, is viewed as a much less repressive form of unfree labour. In most families children perform some forms of unpaid domestic labour. In rural and peasant economies such work is clearly arduous and extensive due to families' poverty-level existence.

See also Bonded Labour Liberation Front; Domestic Service; India.

References Anti-Slavery International, *"This Menace of Bonded Labour": Debt Bondage in Pakistan* (1996); Rodgers, Gerry, and Standing, Guy, *Child Work, Poverty, and Underdevelopment* (1981).

UNICEF
See United Nations International Children's Emergency Fund.

United Arab Emirates
The United Arab Emirates is a federation

situated on the southeastern Arabian peninsula. The seven emirates, of which Abu Dhabi is the largest, formed a federal union in 1971. The combined population numbers around two and a half million people. The official language is Arabic, and the official religion is Islam.

The discovery and exploitation of huge oil reserves since the late 1960s has been the driving force of the economy here, and has allowed substantial investment in education, health, and social welfare. The most obvious form of child labour to be found in the Emirates is the employment of children as jockeys in the extremely popular local sport of camel racing. Although steps were taken in 1993 to curtail abuses of children in this sport, there is evidence that the laws are being evaded.

See also Camel Jockeys; Middle East.

United Kingdom
The United Kingdom of Great Britain and Northern Ireland is one of the oldest parliamentary democracies in Europe. It is made up of four distinctive parts: England, Scotland, Wales, and Northern Ireland. The total population is just under 60 million, of which almost 50 million live in England.

Britain played a major role in the industrial revolution and was at that time a major user of child labour. Throughout the nineteenth century, there were many campaigns against child labour, and a succession of acts of Parliament made various types of work and conditions of work illegal. Initially these laws lacked impact because of a failure to set up appropriate ways of monitoring their implementation. Nevertheless, the worst excesses were gradually eliminated, in some cases because changing production techniques required an older or more skilled workforce. Compulsory education was established in Britain in the late nineteenth century, and the required number of years in school was lengthened during the twentieth century. Currently, children and adolescents are expected to attend school from age 5 until age 16.

Adult miners and pit boys waiting to go to work at the Sirland & Alfreton coal mine, Derbyshire, England, ca. 1905 (Corbis-Bettmann)

Compulsory schooling did not lead to the abolishment of child employment. However, children were expected to fit their work around their school attendance. A law of 1933 allowed children to work during school holidays and for limited periods of time on school days. Local authorities were expected to formulate regulations suited to their localities and to ensure that the law was obeyed.

In the second half of the twentieth century, child employment has been a political issue only intermittently in Britain. In 1972, a research report was published suggesting that many schoolchildren had part-time jobs and that this was harmful to their schooling. This led to the speedy passage in 1973 of a law that would have led to stricter

237

control of child employment. However, implementation of the law was delayed because of the costs of enforcement.

In the 1990s, a number of further reports began to appear that established overwhelmingly that child employment exists on a large scale in Britain. Some of the work children perform is light and may be beneficial to them. However, most children who work do so illegally—whether because they are too young, because the jobs they are doing are forbidden by law, or because they have not received the necessary work permit. The jobs British children undertake are varied, the most common being the delivery of milk and newspapers. These tend to be younger children's jobs. Many older children work in shops, restaurants, and hotels. Adolescents are also to be found working in garages and factories and on building sites, almost invariably outside the law.

In 1994, the European Union issued a Directive on the Protection of Young People at Work to come into effect in 1996. Britain under the Conservative government—alone of all the members of the European Union—fought to obtain exemption from some clauses until the year 2000. This stance puzzled those in Britain concerned with child labour because the directive seemed not very different in its requirements from existing British law. The impression was confirmed by the plans the government later circulated for bringing Britain into line with the directive, since they made only minor changes to the law. The Labour government that followed in 1997 seems to take issues of child labour more seriously than had its predecessor. It has issued guidelines to local authorities that have the responsibility of implementing the child employment laws, proposing clearer rules on what jobs children may do. Whether the local authorities respond to this guidance will depend in part on whether they have the necessary financial resources.

See also Factory Acts; Industrial Revolution; Low Pay Network; Parliamentary Committees and Commissions; Stop Child Labour.

References Hobbs, Sandy, and McKechnie, Jim, *Child Employment in Britain: A Social and Psychological Analysis* (1997); Lavalette, Michael, *Child Employment in the Capitalist Labour Market* (1994); Lavalette, Michael, "Thatcher's Working Children: Contemporary Issues of Child Labour" (1996); Lavalette, Michael, Hobbs, Sandy, Lindsay, Sandra, and McKechnie, Jim, "Child Employment in Britain: Policy, Myth, and Reality" (1995); Nardinelli, Clark, *Child Labor and the Industrial Revolution* (1990); Pond, Chris, and Searle, Anne, *The Hidden Army: Children at Work in the 1990s* (1991).

United Nations International Children's Emergency Fund

More commonly known by its acronym UNICEF, this international aid organization was founded on 11 December 1946. Its establishment stemmed from the concern that children were not adequately provided for in the overall relief effort then under way in Europe after World War II.

Later, as developing countries emerged from the colonial era, the need for special attention to children's needs in these countries led to an expansion of UNICEF's mandate. UNICEF's work today focuses on the implementation of the United Nations Convention on the Rights of the Child. To mark its first 50 years of work, UNICEF published *The State of the World's Children, 1997*. The main focus of this report was child labour and its impact on children's development.

See also Convention on the Rights of the Child.

References Bellamy, Carol, *The State of the World's Children, 1997* (1997); Black, Maggie, *Children First: The Story of UNICEF* (1996).

United Nations

See Convention on the Rights of the Child.

United States of America

As is the case in most industrialized countries, people in the United States tend to view child labour as belonging to the historical past. There is certainly evidence that in the early part of the country's his-

Young girl working as a spinner in a textile mill in the early twentieth-century United States (Library of Congress)

tory all family members were viewed as a legitimate part of the labour force. With the industrialization that took place in the nineteenth century, children became a valuable economic resource. By 1820, the *Digest of Manufacturers* was noting that in the textile mills of Massachusetts, Connecticut, and Rhode Island, children made up 43 percent, 47 percent, and 55 percent of the respective labour force.

At the turn of the century, the 1900 census showed that approximately 1,750,178 children between 10 and 15 years of age were employed. Even this figure underestimates the level of child employment, since children as young as 8 and 9 years of age were working. Throughout the twentieth century, the number of children employed declined. This has been partly attributed to the impact of groups such as the National Child Labor Committee and the implementation of the Fair Labor Standards Act. The downward trend has

on occasion been interrupted. For example, during the Depression years and World War II, levels of child employment increased.

By the 1940s, the proper work role of children was beginning to be redefined, with education being viewed as their main task. As Lawrence Steinberg has pointed out, at the start of the twentieth century the majority of children entered the world of work by 15 years of age, and most children left school between the ages of 12 and 15 years. In the 1930s and 1940s it became more common for children to stay on at school. The worlds of work and education became mutually exclusive. According to U.S. Census information, by 1940, 70 percent of 14- to 17-year-olds were enrolled at school, and only 2.4 percent were found to be working as well as attending school.

Is it possible to argue that by the mid-twentieth century childhood had been redefined as a period when education was the primary task of the young? Yes, in part. However, adopting this interpretation would be to ignore an alternative view. Although for the majority of children the excesses of child employment had been eliminated by this time, this does not mean that children no longer worked. A new pattern was emerging that suggests that children had started to combine work and education.

In the period following World War II, the United States' economy witnessed some dramatic changes, including the growth of the service sector and the need for a cheap, flexible workforce. These changes drew children back into the labour market. Data from the Department of Labor and Bureau of Labor Statistics support this interpretation. In 1940, 3 percent of 14- to 15-year-old males and fewer than 1 percent of females were employed. For 16-year-olds the figures were 4 percent for males and 1 percent for females. By 1980 approximately 16 percent of males and 14.5 percent of females aged 14 to 15 years were employed; for 16- to 17-year-olds the figures were 44 percent and 41 percent, respectively.

Steinberg has noted that more recent data from the late 1980s also testify to this trend. Some researchers quote more recent Department of Labor figures indicating that 4 million children (defined as those under 18 years of age) were employed in 1988. Steinberg put the figure at well over 6 million. The discrepancy in figures reflects the different conclusion reached using official statistics that report legal employment but ignore the high level of illegal employment.

Steinberg is of the opinion that children tend to enter the formal employment sector when they are between 14 and 16 years old. However, they will have worked before this in more informal settings, such as baby-sitting, gardening, housecleaning,

and newspaper delivery. There appears to be a progression in employment from informal, "low-level" types of work to more formal employment in a range of jobs that are more likely to be associated with adult forms of employment.

Although the service sector has been identified as a major employer of children, this does not fully represent the range of jobs in which children have been found. Researchers concerned with agricultural injuries have argued that children are often employed on farms. In one study of 614 farmers in central Washington, it was found that 73 percent used child workers under 16 years of age, many of them working 24 hours per week during the school year. The media also have raised the question of the offspring of migrant farm workers working in the fields alongside their parents. The garment industry in New York has been linked to child employment, even though the state has been very active in trying to control this activity.

In considering the issue of child employment in the context of American society, it is evident that economic development and compulsory education do not necessarily remove children from the labour force. However, it can be argued that in industrialized countries like the United States and the United Kingdom, we can identify a qualitative change in children's work over time.

See also Education, Universal; Fair Labor Standards Act; Garment Industry; Great Depression, The; National Child Labor Committee.

References Mortimer, Jeylan T., Finch, Michael D., Dennehy, Katherine, Lee, Chaimum, and Beebe, Timothy, "Work Experience in Adolescence" (1994); Steinberg, Laurence, *Adolescence* (1993); Trattner, Walter I., *Crusade for the Children* (1970).

Upper Volta
See Burkina Faso.

Van Houten, Samuel

Samuel Van Houten (1837–1930) was a Liberal member of the Dutch Parliament. He was responsible for introducing *het kinderwetje*, the "little law," which was the first attempt at statutory control of child labour in the Netherlands. Passed in 1874, this law outlawed most forms of work for children younger than 12 years. Of little practical effect because it contained no provision for an inspectorate, it is nevertheless seen as an important step in social legislation in the Netherlands.

See also Netherlands.

References Stuurman, Siep, "Samuel Van Houten and Dutch Liberalism, 1860–1890" (1989); White, Ben, "Children, Work and 'Child Labour': Changing Responses to the Employment of Children" (1994).

Vietnam

Vietnam is situated in southeast Asia, bordering China, Laos, and Cambodia. Having come under French control in the nineteenth century, Vietnam achieved its independence in the 1950s. However, a long period of instability and violence followed. For a time there was a communist government in North Vietnam seeking to undermine the South Vietnamese government, which was supported first by France and later by the United States. Following the end of the Vietnam War in 1975, North and South Vietnam were united in a single republic. Political power has since resided in the Vietnamese Communist Party. In recent years, the Party has allowed the development of a free market. The population is estimated at more than 70 million

A Vietnamese girl carries a load larger than she is in Hanoi, Vietnam, 1997 (Richard Vogel, Associated Press)

people and is expected to exceed 80 million by the year 2000.

The economy recovered fairly rapidly after the war, but there are many social problems, of which child labour is acknowledged to be one. Because around two-thirds of the population live in agricultural areas, and children in farming communities typically work informally within the family unit, it is difficult to be sure of the extent of child labour. Similarly, it is difficult to be sure about the numbers of girls, some as young as 10 years old, who are engaged in domestic service outside their own families. However, such official statistics as do exist show substantial numbers of 13- and 14-year-olds participating in the labour force. This is particularly true of children in families with the lowest income levels. It has been estimated that there are 50,000 street children in Vietnam, of whom 14,000 are to be found in Ho Chi Minh City (formerly known as Saigon) and 7,000 in Hanoi. They are seen as a growing problem as the country industrializes and more and more of the population are attracted to the cities. In many countries, nongovernmental organizations play a large role in bringing problems of child labour to the public's notice. However, there is no tradition of such bodies in Vietnam, so there is little concerted effort exerted there on behalf of child workers.

References Binh, Vu Ngoc, *Child Labour in Vietnam* (1995).

Voices of Children

During the final decade of the twentieth century there has been a growing realization that for a number of years researchers and policymakers have been discussing child labour with little attention paid to the views of children who work. In the mid-1990s a number of bodies started to argue for the inclusion of "children's voices" in any discussion of working children.

To solicit children's views about their work is not necessarily to support "child power." Rather, it is to acknowledge that children have rights in society and that one of those rights is to be heard on issues relating to their lives. The root of this argument is to be found in the United Nations Convention on the Rights of the Child (CRC). Article 12 of the CRC reads: "State Parties shall assure to the child who is capable of forming his or her own views the right to express those views freely in all matters affecting the child, the views of the child being given due weight in accordance with the age and maturity of the child."

In practice, the idea of listening to children's voices can be looked at from two perspectives, namely the political or research perspective. The political pressure to listen to children on the issue of their work appeared to reach its zenith in the approach to the 1998 International Labour Organisation meeting in Geneva. A number of nongovernmental organizations (NGOs) have been suggesting that any discussion of child labour should include representatives of working children. These NGOs include Save the Children (Britain), Radda Barnen (Sweden), and the International Working Group on Child Labour. Such bodies have highlighted the fact that many working children's organizations already exist and have proposed that it should be policy to include representatives of these groups in any debate. Groups of organized working children are found in Asia, Africa, and Latin America, and include Bal Mazdoor Union, Bhima Sangha, MANTHOC, and CWIN.

That working children do have views on their experiences and on what can be done to constructively help them is evidenced in the reports of the First International Meeting of Working Children. This meeting, held in Kundapur, India, in 1996, consisted of working children discussing their problems and offering solutions.

Partly as a result of this meeting, in 1997 a number of other international meetings took place at which working children's representatives were present. In June 1997, ChildWatch International or-

Nearly 2,000 child labourers protest during election season in New Delhi, India, November 20, 1998 (John Mc-Connico, Associated Press)

ganized the Urban Childhood Conference in Trondheim (Norway). Part of the proceedings focused on working children, and working children's representatives were there to participate alongside adults. The report from the conference notes that the participation of working children "helped to keep the discourse grounded within the realities of young people's working lives and aspirations."

Working children's representatives also participated in the Dutch government's conference on the Most Intolerable Forms of Child Labor, which took place in February 1997. The final example of this form of participation took place in Oslo at the International Conference on Child Labor. At this conference, some NGOs were not satisfied with the level of representation given to children. One of these organizations, Radda Barnen, organized a parallel conference called the Children's Forum, to highlight the lack of representation. Discussions about the level of participation permitted to working children will continue. What has been established is that children can make a valuable contribution to discussions of their experiences.

The second area where the concept of children's voices has been raised is in research on the nature and impact of child labour. Within social science research there has been a tension between quantitative and qualitative forms of investigation. Some researchers have been advocating the use of more qualitative approaches to researching child employment, in order to gain greater insight into children's perceptions and interpretations of this experience. Researchers who have adopted this child-centred approach have used focus groups, essay writing, and picture drawing to allow children to express their views. Martin Woodhead adopted this approach while studying children's work in Bangladesh, Ethiopia, Guatemala, and the Philippines. Similarly, Johnson, Hill, and Ivan-Smith adopted participatory techniques in carrying out research on working children's lives in Nepal.

See also Advocacy; Bal Mazdoor Union; Bhima Sangha; Children's Rights; International Meeting of Working Children; International Working Group on Child Labour; Liberationism; Movement of Working Children and Adolescents from Working-Class Christian Families; Organizations of Working Children.

References Johnson, Victoria, Hill, Joanna, and Ivan-Smith, Edda, *Listening to Smaller Voices: Children in an Environment of Change* (1995); Woodhead, Martin, *Children's Perspectives on Their Working Lives: A Participatory Study in Bangladesh, Ethiopia, the Philippines, Guatemala, El Salvador, and Nicaragua* (1998); Woodhead, Martin, "Combatting Child Labour: Listen to What the Children Say" (1999).

Wages

Wages are the returns people receive for the efforts they expend at work. The level of wages workers receive will be determined by a variety of factors, such as their skill level, the supply and demand of labour power, and pay agreements between employers and trade unions. It does not relate in any direct sense to the value of the goods that their work week may have produced. For example, a car worker may make goods in any week that will sell for a substantial sum; and a car factory manager will take some executive decisions over the same period but will not create anything approaching the value of the cars made on the production line, yet the manager will receive a wage substantially higher than the production worker.

Wage levels also reflect certain social criteria or assumptions. For example, on average, women receive less than men, and

A boy receives 20 cents for a basket of beans he picked for a farmer, Homestead, Florida, 1939 (Corbis-Bettmann/UPI)

workers belonging to ethnic minority groups are paid less than the average wage. Thus, distinctions of ethnicity and gender affect wage rates. So it is with children: When children work, they are paid as children. That is, the wage rate is based on assumptions that the child will be living in a family and his or her wage does not need to cover all of the social costs. It is assumed that the child's wage is extra family income, not essential income. Further, it is assumed that children cannot work as hard as adults and therefore should be paid less.

Yet when children work in factories, mines, and warehouses across the globe, they are driven relentlessly and often work at machines whose pace of operation takes no account of their child status. In the advanced economies it is even sometimes denied that children earn wages. In recent years a number of politicians in Britain have claimed that children who work actually do so for a little extra pocket money (their weekly allowance) rather than for a wage. Such assumptions have little to do with the reality of children's labour or the complexity or arduousness of their work. Instead, they reflect social conventions: Children do not need a wage, because they can rely on someone else in their family to support them. This makes child labour cheap, and it is this cheapness that makes children attractive to employers.

See also Causes of Child Labour; Poverty.

Water Babies, The

The Water Babies is a widely read and frequently reprinted novel that first appeared in *Macmillan's Magazine* in 1862–3 and in book form in 1863. The author, Charles Kingsley (1819–1875), was a Church of England clergyman and a professor of modern history at the University of Cambridge. Kingsley was interested in social issues and had published several novels prior to *The Water Babies*, for which he is best remembered.

In the novel, the hero Tom, while cleaning chimneys in the home of an affluent family, accidentally enters the bedroom of Ellie, a daughter of the household. The contrast between the lives and outlooks of the two children is great. Tom flees from the house and falls into a river, where he is transformed into a water creature. Most of the novel is set in a fantastic underwater world and concerns Tom's spiritual development.

Because the hero is a chimney sweep and because the book was published at the time of the campaign that led to the act of Parliament that helped put a end to the practice of sending children up chimneys, *The Water Babies* is sometimes thought of as a programmatic book. However, Kingsley was not an active campaigner on the issue, and his portrayal of the chimney sweep's life is not particularly unfavourable. The physical dangers of the job are not stressed. What apparently concerned Kingsley more was that working children lacked contact with religion.

See also Chimney Sweeping.

References Kingsley, Charles, *The Water Babies* (1863).

Welfare, Child

The relationship between child welfare and child labour is potentially complex because the two terms are not easily defined. When we talk about a child's welfare, we might be referring to the individual's well-being, happiness, or prosperity. Some believe that the very existence of child labour is a threat to children's welfare. Thus, saving children from this experience protects their welfare. We then face the second problem of defining child labour. Do all forms of work threaten a child's welfare, or only some forms?

Let us take a simple position at present and assume that all child labour is a threat to children's welfare. Can it be demonstrated that decreasing child labour increases children's welfare?

Economic historian Clark Nardinelli has tried to answer this question by analysing a specific historical case. The introduction of the Factory Acts in nineteenth-century Britain was meant to reduce child labour. There is evidence showing that the number of children employed in factories did decline after the acts were passed. However, Nardinelli points out that in the present context, welfare would have been improved only if these children remained out of the labour force. Nardinelli hypothesizes that children who left their factory jobs may simply have moved on to alternative employment. His argument is based on the premise that children worked because of poverty. Therefore, losing one job meant that another had to be found.

No empirical data are available that would allow us to test this hypothesis, but Nardinelli believes that the documentary evidence supports this argument. For example, one of the Factory Inspector's Reports from 1876 comments on the fact that employees had been attracted to types of employment establishments other than factories partly because they could not get into factories any more.

Even if the Factory Acts did not remove children from the world of work, they might have improved children's welfare. Such a view is based on the argument that the alternative forms of work were preferable, or less harmful to children's welfare, than their original jobs. This argument returns us to the issue of how we might define child labour and the relationship between the quality of work and its impact on the child's welfare.

This discussion has contemporary relevance as well. The International Working Group on Child Labour (IWGCL) has argued that any attempts to tackle child labour must consider the alternatives for working children and the implications of removing children from the workplace. In one report, *Forgotten on the Pyjama Trail*, the authors highlight the fact that young garment workers forced out of their jobs in Meknes, Morocco, in the mid-1990s had to seek other employment. In some cases this alternative employment put them at greater risk and therefore reduced their welfare.

This theme also emerges in another recent book. The authors of *What Works for Working Children* argue that policymakers dealing with contemporary child employment issues around the world need to consider the implications of their policies on the child employees themselves. Removing children from work does not necessarily lead to an improvement in their welfare.

See also Definition of Child Labour.

References Boyden, Jo, Ling, Birgitta, and Myers, William, *What Works for Working Children* (1998); Nardinelli, Clark, *Child Labor and the Industrial Revolution* (1990); Zalami, Fatima Badry, Reddy, Nandana, Lynch, Margaret A., and Feinstein, Clare, *Forgotten on the Pyjama Trail* (1998).

Work Ethic

The phrase *work ethic* refers to an individual's beliefs and values relating to the role of work. In some cases the work ethic may be linked to religious value systems. This is the case in the United States, where some Protestant theologies consider work, and more specifically, hard work, the route to salvation. Work takes on moral overtones that are viewed in a positive light because work is believed to be character building.

Historically, this particular value system can be traced back to the Puritans and early settlers. The religious context provided the justification for bringing children into the workforce. By doing so parents and employers were preparing them for adult life and instilling positive work habits that would be beneficial to them in the long run.

Other religious systems contain equivalent beliefs in the virtue of labour. It is important to realize that such views of work continue to influence modern interpretations of work. It could be argued that one reason that parents view their children's employment positively is because adults accept, implicitly, that work is good for young people.

See also Burkina Faso; Business Ethic; Parents; Religion; *Saturday Evening Post*.

Work Values

Psychologists have established that two

clearly different sets of work values can be identified. First, there are extrinsic values, by which work itself does not provide the rewards for the individual. Instead, the income or the status gained from the job provides the rewards for working. Secondly, intrinsic work values exist when the rewards gained from working are built into the job you do. For example, if the form of work allows you to help others or to be creative, and you find these aspects challenging and rewarding, then the work itself can reward you.

It is important that we understand how individuals acquire extrinsic and intrinsic value systems. It can be argued that work value systems will be constructed partly from one's own work experiences; however, it should also be noted that parents also influence the development of these value systems.

This is most clearly seen in the work of researchers looking at the occupational linkage hypothesis. The basis of this hypothesis is that parents' experiences of work will influence their behaviour, which in turn, through socialization, influence their children's work values.

Two researchers who have carried out work in this area are Seongryeol Ryu and Jeylan Mortimer. Their findings provide support for the occupational linkage hypothesis, in that parental work values are related to their own work experiences. This is in turn reflected in the parents' interactions with their children and influences the development of their children's work values. Ryu and Mortimer also found that the link between parents' work and their adolescent children's work values is stronger for males than females.

See also Saturday Evening Post; Socialization; Work Ethic.

References Ryu, Seongryeol, and Mortimer, Jeylan, T. "The 'Occupational Linkage Hypothesis' Applied to Occupational Value Formation in Adolescence" (1996).

Workhouses

Workhouses—also known as poorhouses—have a long history. In Britain

they originated in the old Poor Laws and the state's earliest attempts to control the unemployed. In the two and a half centuries following the Black Death (when England lost approximately one-third of its population to the plague), the provision of relief from poverty became an increasingly important state function.

In the fourteenth and fifteenth centuries, one of the consequences of the plague was a severe labour shortage, which encouraged labour mobility as people moved to obtain better wages or conditions of life. The state's response was to pass a series of acts that fixed wages and prohibited workingmen from moving around. However, the result of these acts was that those workers who could not support themselves had to turn to their local parish for relief. These individuals, known at the time as vagabonds, rogues, or criminals, would not simply be given food or money; they had to work for their relief.

Putting the poor to work, as it was known, took two forms. One was known as "outdoor relief." Here the poor would be expected to work for a day at some task, in local agriculture, for example, or breaking stones. At the end of the day they would be given payment in cash or kind and sent on their way. The following day, if they still could not support themselves or their families, they would have to repeat the process. The second form of relief was "indoor relief," by which the poor became residents in workhouse institutions. The first workhouse was opened in Blackfriars, London, in the sixteenth century, and it set a pattern that was soon to be followed across the country.

As a consequence of the Poor Law Act of 1601, the state began to classify the poor and adopted what were deemed appropriate responses for the needs of different groups of the poor. Those known as the "impotent" poor—the aged, chronically sick, and disabled—were to be accommodated in specific poorhouses where they would undertake suitable work to earn their support. The able-bodied poor were to be put to productive work, working on hemp for example, at a "house of correction." This would not necessarily be residential. Children in this category were to be apprenticed to local artisans so that in the future they would become self-supporting citizens. Lastly, the "persistent idler" or "vagabond" who took to the road was to be incarcerated in a house of correction. Interesting to note is the fact that these were in essence early prisons. To be a pauper was a crime, and pauperism had to be corrected through exposure to work.

The purpose of this law, at least in theory, was to identify three different responses to the needs of the three different groups of paupers. In reality, however, the lines between these classes and the various responses became blurred. Nevertheless, the Act of 1601 embedded workhouses within the state's response to poverty relief.

In the second half of the seventeenth century, the early phase of the industrial revolution, the workhouses became a valuable source of labour. The first mills, for example, had to be located close to running water, so mills were most often built in rural areas. Labour was hard to attract to such areas, so employers frequently entered into contracts with local parishes, recruiting children from their workhouses as apprentices. These young children, known as "pauper apprentices," would be sent from London or other large towns to be indentured until the age of 21 to mill owners working in isolated regions. However, especially after the development of steam-powered mills suited to operation in urban areas, the system of pauper apprentices went into decline.

With the development of a more fully fledged industrial capitalist society, the old Poor Laws, the aim of which was to stop labour mobility, became a hindrance to the needs of the new age in which a national labour market was emerging. The old Poor Laws were anachronistic, and by the early nineteenth century, a number of politicians and writers were heavily criticizing the system and regretting its costs. Malthus wrote that the growth of population was outstripping food production. The cause of this problem was the existing Poor Laws, which encouraged early marriage and large families by offering allowances, in cash or kind, to parents. He and his supporters argued for moral restraint and later marriages with fewer children. To encourage this trend, they advocated abolition of all poor relief. Ricardo, in his *Principles of Political Economy* (1817), argued that there was a strictly limited "wages fund." The more relief was paid, he suggested, the less there was for wages. Hence the Poor Laws were self-defeating and should be abolished. The case for abolishment is best summed up by Joseph Townsend, quoted in the *Edinburgh Review* (1820): "What encouragement have the poor to be industrious and frugal when they know for certain that should they increase their store it will be devoured by drones, or what cause have they to fear when they are assured, that if by their indolence and extravagance, by their drunkenness and vices they should be reduced to want, they be abundantly supplied?"

To those in favour of the abolishment of public relief, putting the poor to work on public works represented unfair competition for free labour in the newly developing labour market.

In the years following Britain's wars with France (1815), the costs of poor relief escalated, with local rate-payers bearing the costs. But the poverty of these years also brought increased working-class discontentment and rebellion. It had become increasingly difficult to maintain order in society, and by the late 1820s and 1830s the unrest had spread to southern agricultural areas. On top of this, the costs of administering the poor laws were rising. In these circumstances complete abolition was rejected as likely to cause increased unrest. In 1832 a report was commissioned on the operations of the poor laws. The report was written by Nassau Senior, a classical economist, and civil servant Edwin Chadwick. The Poor Law Report was published in 1834, and the Poor Law Amendment Act of that year was modelled on its recommendations.

The New Poor Law was a vicious and vindictive piece of legislation. It was based on four principles: uniformity, centralization, limitation of eligibility, and the workhouse test. The justification for these principles remains embedded within much welfare debate today. In essence, the framers of the New Poor Law suggested that life for the "idle poor," as opposed to the respectable working poor, was too easy. The old Poor Laws were too generous, allowing people to opt for life on benefits rather than work. Further, as benefits were paid for children, the system encouraged the idle poor to procreate.

Local control over the existing Poor Laws meant that some areas were more charitable than others, and this encouraged migration to more generous districts. This system allowed unscrupulous employers to pay less than the normal rates for jobs, because the government would make up the difference. In consequence, this system had a demoralizing effect on the working poor, who saw that they could lead a better life on benefits than they could on wage labour.

The solution was to make the life of the idle poor "less eligible" (by which was meant "harsher") than the living that was achievable by performing the poorest paying jobs. The only way to ensure this result was to prohibit outdoor relief (benefits of cash or kind paid in return for work) and to enforce a centralized, uniform system across the country that required the idle poor to submit to the "workhouse test." In other words, to get relief, the poor had to enter the workhouse. In the workhouse, conditions were worse than outside. Families would be separated, work would be hard, uniforms rough and uncomfortable, and food indescribably bad.

The workhouse was to be a deterrent. Its purpose was to instill in the working class the moral principles of laissez-faire capitalism. George Nicholls, a future member of the Poor Law Commission, emphasized the point: "I wish to see the Poor House looked to with dread by our

labouring class, and the reproach for being an inmate of it extended downwards from Fathers to Son, . . . for without this, where is the needful stimulus to industry?"

However, the workhouse system proved unworkable. During economic recession the numbers of people looking for relief was so great that the workhouses could not accommodate them; so outdoor relief continued despite the state's intentions. The workhouses nonetheless remained the feared symbol of a repressive attitude toward poverty and unemployment. They became an institution where the old and sick went "for relief"—or to die—when they could no longer fully support themselves.

See also Pauper Apprentices.
References Fraser, Derek, *The Evolution of the British Welfare State*, 2d ed. (1984).

World Bank

Like the International Monetary Fund (IMF), the World Bank (officially called the International Bank for Reconstruction and Development) was formed as a consequence of the Bretton Woods Agreement signed in 1944. The Bank began its operations in June 1946. In the early years of its operation it followed a path similar to that of the IMF. An initial commitment to Keynesian economic demand management was replaced in the 1970s by a neoliberal agenda.

However, by the middle of the 1990s, the World Bank had adopted a strategy for economic growth significantly different from that of the IMF. The World Bank had realized that the crude neoliberal agenda being forced on debtor nations by stabilization and structural adjustment programmes (SSAPs) was creating short-term social and political problems and long-term economic development difficulties. The Bank suggested that the rapid introduction of SSAPs created widening social inequality and the potential for social conflict. As a consequence, SSAPs were rarely carried out under conditions of liberal democracy but often required strong authoritarian or military governments, prepared to repress their populations in order to introduce the programmes. Across Africa and Latin America, SSAPs were often initially introduced in countries run by military juntas. But such repression created short- and long-term political problems and social discontent.

Secondly, the Bank argued that the economic model was problematic because it hindered investment in human capital—that is, in human beings who would make up the future workforce. In other words, in cutting welfare spending, states often reduced spending on schools and school equipment, teachers, and teacher training; and hence, education levels were affected. Lack of investment in skills, higher education, and training results in a less well-trained workforce. Cutting food subsidies increases family poverty, forcing many families to pull their children out of school and to direct them into low-paying, low-skill jobs in the marginal economy. Taken together, these factors affected the long-term prospects for sustained economic growth.

Instead of imposing SSAPs, the Bank increasingly has argued for the social costs of restructuring to be acknowledged and countered, to some degree, in future pro-grams. Thus the Bank has highlighted some of the social consequences of readjustment. Armeane Choksi, the Bank's vice president for human resources, said in 1995: "It is intolerable that, as the world approaches the twenty-first century, hundreds of millions of people still lack minimally acceptable levels of education, health and nutrition. Investing in people must therefore be the highest priority for developing countries—until human capital limitations no longer restrain growth or keep people in absolute poverty. Investing in people is the core of the World Bank's work."

Of course, in the Bank's practice there may well be significant divergence from these aims; but this statement nevertheless signals a significant move away from neoliberal orthodoxies.

In terms of children, the conclusion is that children are an investment. They should be allowed to develop and grow, take part in education, and obtain appropriate skill training that will help future economic development. The expansion of child labour exploitation, partly as a consequence of SSAPs, is viewed as a major social problem that needs to be addressed.

References Deacon, Bob, *Global Social Policy* (1996).

Young Caregivers

A young caregiver is generally someone under the age of 18 years who has the responsibility of looking after a family member, often a parent, who is disabled, chronically sick, or elderly. Because of the family relationship with the person for whom the caregiver has taken responsibility, it is likely that she or he will feel bound to do the work through feelings of affection or duty or both. Nevertheless, this does not overcome the fact that the demands on the caregiver may be very high. One particular problem is that the young person may start out with relatively minor responsibilities and then gradually be drawn in to doing more and more. In such cases, there is not a moment at which the caregiver decides to take on that role. Therefore the caregiver probably did not ever carry out a review of the circumstances or plan how to deal with the consequences.

The young person may have restricted opportunities for leisure and for mixing with other young people. Educational opportunities may be reduced or cut off, which in turn may limit career opportunities. The caregiver may also be unable to exercise the chances to earn money available to other people of the same age in their communities. The caregiver may thus be paying a high price for showing the dedication, either literally in financial terms, or in many social and psychological ways that are harder to specify. Many caregivers have an urgent need for support that is not met by the welfare authorities of the country in which they live. The support needed may vary from person to person. Sometimes it may be financial. Sometimes it may be simple practical support such as a "sitter" who can allow the caregiver some freedom to take part in some leisure pursuit by spending some time with the person who needs the care. Another common problem is that the caregiver feels isolated and cut off from the outside world. In these cases it is helpful to know that other people are aware of the problems imposed by the caring way of life.

Three demographic changes mean that the problems of caring are likely to increase. One is the fact that throughout the world populations are aging. In the next quarter of a century, the proportion of people living in the European Union who are over 60 years of age is likely to rise to almost a third. The figures for the United States are not predicted to rise to quite that level, but the trend nevertheless exists. It is also estimated that there are more than 500 million disabled people in the world, many of them living in the poorer, economically underdeveloped countries. At the same time, there is a tendency for the birthrate to fall and for families to be small. Thus the prediction in broad terms is that we can expect the number of people in need of care to rise without an equivalent rise in the number of available caregivers.

In most countries the authorities give little or no recognition to the valuable work done by caregivers. Without the caregivers' efforts, the cost of looking after the sick and disabled would fall on the state. However, despite the fact this means that the caregivers are thus not simply benefiting the relatives in their charge but also the state itself, there is little awareness of any need to compensate the caregivers for the work they do.

Where government action is limited, the gap is sometimes filled by charities and other voluntary bodies. One way of helping is by bringing caregivers together to share experiences and perhaps find common solutions to the difficulties they face. The specific circumstances faced by caregivers can show considerable variation, so some projects for young caregivers have a special focus. For example, young caregivers who have to look after people who are mentally handicapped may gain more from meeting with other caregivers who do the same, rather than caregivers with mixed responsibilities. Similarly, caregivers from particular ethnic communities may benefit from sharing experiences with others from the same community.

The Young Carers Research Group, which was set up in Loughborough University, England, in 1992, has taken a lead internationally in raising the issue of young caregivers and increasing understanding of their problems. Members of the group draw attention to the fact that in most countries even simple information about how many young caregivers there are is not available. They favour international discussion of the problems of young caregivers, in the hope that ideas and policies from the more enlightened countries may be spread more rapidly.

References Becker, Saul, Aldridge, Jo, and Dearden, Chris, *Young Carers and Their Families* (1998).

Zetkin, Clara Eissner

Clara Zetkin (1857–1933) was a German socialist and feminist who actively campaigned for the rights of working-class women and children. In two articles published in the newspaper *Die Gleichheit* (Stuttgart) on 21 May and 4 June 1902, she denounced child labour in Germany and argued for increased protective state legislation. She wrote: "Among the many serious crimes of capitalism about which history will one day sit in judgment, none is more brutal, horrible, disastrous, insane—in a word, outrageous—than the exploitation of proletarian children."

Although a decree issued by Emperor Frederick William III in 1827 had attempted to introduce some protection for children working in factories, the law was easily evaded. Various trade regulations from 1869, 1890, and 1891 restricted some aspects of child employment but did not completely ban factory employment for children younger than 12 years or reduce their hours in the factory to a maximum of 6 per day. Against this background, Zetkin argued for the issue of child labour to be taken seriously by the Social Democratic Party and for increased, specific state protection of working children.

See also Germany; Marxism.
References Zetkin, Clara, *Selected Writings* (1984).

Zimand, Gertrude Folks

Gertrude Zimand, daughter of Homer Folks, was a key activist in the area of child labour in her own right in the first half of the twentieth century. She joined the staff of the National Child Labor Committee (NCLC) in 1916 and became its chief executive in 1943.

By the time Zimand came to her new position, the Fair Labor Standards Act had been passed. Zimand began to press for a reformulation of the NCLC's goals. For her, the area of greatest interest was the educational and employment problems of youth—that is, children between the ages of 14 and 18 years.

Zimand convinced the NCLC to undertake two key research projects. The first considered the issue of work-study programmes. These programmes, developed during World War II to combat labour shortages, involved combining work and school according to well-planned schedules. The project considered the efficacy of these programmes and found that they had been successful. The second project focused on understanding the reasons for students' dropping out of high school. This study suggested that one of the main reasons students left school was because of lack of interest. Such findings led to a discussion of the relevancy of curriculum content and of ways in which it might be changed to maintain student interest.

When the NCLC celebrated its 50th anniversary in 1954, Gertrude Zimand was still its secretary-general. She had played a key role in expanding the scope of the NCLC's efforts: The Committee was still monitoring child labour issues and had become increasingly concerned about itinerant workers, but it was also equally committed to monitoring problems of youth employment.

See also Folks, Homer; National Child Labor Committee.

Zimbabwe

The Republic of Zimbabwe is situated in southern Africa, bordering South Africa, Mozambique, and Zambia. Formerly known as Southern Rhodesia, Zimbabwe became an independent republic within the British Commonwealth in 1980. Its population is estimated at more than 10 million. Prior to European colonization in the nineteenth century, children's work was traditional in African society. Most people lived and worked on a homestead under the control of a male head, who had authority over his wives, children, and servants, and in some cases, the wives and children of his sons.

In the late nineteenth and early twentieth centuries, European settlers employed African workers mainly through contracts with heads of homesteads, who undertook to provide the labour of the members of their households. However, after World War II, this system began to break down. Many young men left their family homes to seek individual employment. Employers found them difficult to control: If they did not like the conditions of work, they would leave—something that children working under contracts entered into by their fathers or grandfathers would have found much harder to do.

In the 1920s, the control of unaccompanied boys was a major concern of farmers.

In 1926, the Native Juveniles Employment Act was introduced. Among the measures included were provisions authorizing minors to enter into legally binding contracts; permitting the physical punishment of young workers; and allowing children without parents or guardians to be contracted into service by the authorities, to any appropriate person willing to employ them. There were many objections to this law both locally and in Britain, of which Zimbabwe was a colony at that time.

In the 1970s, an anticolonial struggle took place, involving guerrilla warfare. The use of young people to gather information and to fight was substantial. The use of child labour in agriculture continues to be a common feature of the Zimbabwean economy today.

See also Africa; Agriculture; Malawi; Tanzania.

References Grier, Beverley, "Invisible Hands: The Political Economy of Child Labour in Colonial Zimbabwe, 1890–1930" (1994); Raftopoulos, Brian, and Dube, Linde, *The Problem of Child Labour in Zimbabwe* (1995); Reynolds, P., *Dance, Civet Cat: Child Labour in the Zambesi Valley* (1991).

Appendix: Web Sites

As a resource for considering the issue of child labour, the World Wide Web offers a number of possibilities. A simple key word search will turn up recent reports from nongovernmental organizations or statements on policy related issues. For example, the 1998 Global March against Child Labor advertised itself and informed people of its aims and progress through the Web.

You may also find dedicated Web sites on historical aspects of child labour, though they are rarer. Listed below are a few current sites worth visiting.

Child Rights Information Network
http://www.crin.org

Free the Children International
http://www.freethechildren.org

International Confederation of Free Trade Unions
http://www.icftu.org/

International Labor Affairs Bureau's International Child Labor Study
http://www.ilr.cornell.edu/library/
  e_archive/childlabor/

International Labour Organisation (ILO)/International Programme for the Elimination of Child Labor (IPEC)
http://www.ilo.org/

Iqbal Masih Tribute
http://www.mirrorimage.com/iqbal/
  index.html

National Institute for Occupational Safety and Health
http://www.cdc.gov/niosh/homepage.html
http://www.cdc.gov/niosh/childlab.html

Rugmark Foundation
http://www.rugmark.org/

Street Kids International
http://www.streetkids.org/

United States Department of Labor
http://www.dol.gov/

United Nations International Children's Emergency Fund (UNICEF)
http://www.UNICEF.org/

Glossary

Act
A law that has passed through the appropriate processes of Congress (in the United States) or Parliament (in the United Kingdom). This contrasts with a bill, which is a proposed law under discussion.

Advanced
Referring to a country's level of economic development, indicates a high level of industrialization. See Development.

Age Stratification
A situation where some social feature is divided according to age, as when children of different ages are expected to do different types of work.

Agribusiness
A large farm or other agricultural enterprise run as a capitalist concern, as opposed to a smaller, family-run farm. See Capitalism entry.

Alienation
Literally, separation. With reference to work, *alienation* describes individuals' psychological state when they feel that they have no power over how their work is done and that they are under the control of forces greater than themselves.

Assembly Line
A method of industrial production in which the manufacturing process is divided into a number of small parts. The items being produced—say, cars—are moved step by step along a production line, in which specialized machinery and specialist workers contribute a small part to the manufacturing process. Although devised to increase efficiency, this method is criticized because workers sometimes feel alienated in these working conditions.

Autonomy
Independence. Used by psychologists particularly to refer to the adolescent's relationship with his or her parents. Autonomy implies freedom from parental control and the opportunity to make significant decisions for oneself.

Ayah
Childminder (Kenya and elsewhere).

Bairn
Child (Scottish dialect).

Bill
A proposed law under discussion. See also Act.

Black Economy
Business enterprises that are run without the knowledge of state authorities, the main motive for secrecy being to avoid the payment of taxes. See also Informal.

Glossary

Blacking
A preparation to make objects black. In particular, blacking was employed for shoes and stoves. At one time blacking was very extensively used.

Bonded Labour
Work that results from an agreement to pay off a debt, or the labourers who perform such work. For example, impoverished parents may receive money in return for committing a child to work in repayment of the loan. See Unfree Labour entry.

Chattel
Any movable property. In societies where slavery or bonded labour exists, a slave or bondsman may be referred to as a chattel.

Class Conflict
According to the Marxist view of society, individuals belong to different classes depending on whether they are workers (individuals who sell their labour) or owners of the means of production (who pay the workers' wages). Since the interests of the two groups are irreconcilable, according to Marx, the members of these two classes are in a permanent state of conflict. See Capitalism entry.

Cognitive
A term employed by psychologists to refer to the thinking aspects of the mind as opposed to the emotional ones. Cognitive skills include the ability to reason, to count and manipulate numbers, and to engage in abstract thinking.

Common Law
In addition to laws that have been formally passed, some countries, including the United States and the United Kingdom, have "common law." This means that in law courts, reference may be made not only to the laws passed by Congress or Parliament but also to previous decisions made by the courts. Thus, common law is law based on custom and precedent.

Conservation
A term used by psychologists to refer to the ability to recognize the stability that can exist even when the surface appearance of a thing changes. For example, a piece of clay may be moulded into many different shapes but maintain the same mass. When we are young children we do not appreciate this fact, so the ability to understand conservation must develop with experience.

Constitutional Monarchy
A country with a king or queen as head of state but in which effective political power lies largely in the hands of an elected body such as a parliament. Belgium, the Netherlands, and the United Kingdom are examples.

Deconstruction
When used with reference to an academic discipline, deconstruction is a process of questioning the explicit assumptions made in that discipline and of revealing hidden assumptions.

Demand Management
An attempt by government to regulate the healthy functioning of the economy by influencing the demand for goods. For example, high levels of employment might be encouraged in order to produce large numbers of people with spending power, who will seek goods to buy and thus encourage production. See also Keynes.

Development
This term has a variety of meanings. In discussions of child labour, two meanings are likely to be employed, one from economics and one from psychology.

In economics, *development* refers to the degree to which a country's economy is based on agriculture or on industry. Highly industrialized countries such as the United States are described as "developed." Predominantly agricultural countries are "underdeveloped"; as they go through a process of industrialization, they are "developing." See Capitalism entry.

In psychology, *development* applies to the changes that an individual goes through as he or she gets older, particularly to changes during childhood, adolescence, and early adulthood. See Psychology, Developmental entry.

Differentials
When referring to earnings, *differentials* indicates difference in payment between or among groups of workers. Skilled workers often have struggled to ensure that the difference between their earnings and those of unskilled workers remains proportional.

Ecology
The study of the relationship between individuals and their environment. Used particularly

to refer to the relationship between human society and the natural biological and physical environment.

Economic Growth
Economic growth refers to the amount of economic activity of a country. In the modern world, the natural tendency is for countries to expand economically, at least in the long run. Economic growth is usually estimated in terms of the value of goods and services produced.

English Civil War
Fought in the middle of the seventeenth century between supporters of the king and supporters of the parliament, this conflict ended with the execution of King Charles I and ushered in a period of republican government. Although the monarchy was restored a few years later, the English Civil War was an important step in the building of democracy in Great Britain.

Feudalism
The form of society that existed in Europe in the Middle Ages, based on the ownership of land. Land was owned by lords, who granted it to lesser people, called vassals, in return for the performance of certain duties. The majority of the population were serfs, who worked the land but did not own it. The rising importance of towns as centres of trade and craftsmanship weakened the feudal system, and capitalism eventually displaced it.

Flexible Labour Market
This refers to a condition in a country's economy in which workers move readily and frequently between different types of jobs to meet the changing needs of employers. It contrasts with a situation found in some traditional societies in which workers learn a skill when young and expect to earn a living for the rest of their lives using that skill.

Flue
A passage for conveying air or other gases, as in a chimney. Chimneys for coal fires in British houses can contain complicated arrangements of flues. Children were used to clean these passages and remove blockages. See Chimney Sweeping entry.

Glass Ceiling
Although an organization may have no explicit rules excluding women from its most senior positions, there may be unstated assumptions and biases that prevent women from reaching these positions. These informal obstacles to career development are referred to as "the glass ceiling."

Glorious Revolution
In 1688, King James II of England was deposed and replaced by King William III and Queen Mary, who were seen as more likely to respect political and religious liberties. This event is called the Glorious Revolution because it was an important step toward greater power for Parliament.

Indenture
A formal written agreement, particularly an agreement between a master craftsman and an apprentice or the parents of the apprentice. The apprentice usually agrees to serve the master for a stated number of years in exchange for being taught the master's skilled trade. Such apprentices are described as *indentured*, to distinguish them from other children or young adults who might be simultaneously working and learning without such a formal agreement.

Indigenous
Referring to the population of a country, indigenous means the ethnic group or groups that have lived in that country longest. Examples are Maoris in New Zealand and Native Americans, formerly called Indians, in the United States.

Inflation
A tendency for prices to increase. When inflation is high, workers try to obtain higher wages in order that the actual purchasing power of their earnings will not decline. See also Real Wages.

Informal
When referring to a business enterprise, *informal* indicates that it has one or more of the following characteristics: Written financial records are either not kept or are kept only partially. Workers do not have contracts of employment. Laws concerning business premises are ignored. The existence of the enterprise is not on record with the relevant state authorities. Taxes are not paid, or are paid only partially.

Institutionalization
A process whereby a practice that has emerged over time or has become traditional is given

Glossary

added status by being formalized as a set of rules.

Intellectual Development

It is widely recognized that abilities found in adults, such as the skills of talking, reasoning, and remembering, are not present in newborn babies. The gradual process of acquiring these skills during childhood and adolescence is referred to as intellectual development.

Isthmus

A narrow strip of land that forms a link between two larger blocks of land. Much of Central America is an isthmus between North and South America.

Keynes

John Maynard Keynes (1883–1946), an English economist whose work, particularly the book *The General Theory of Employment, Interest and Money* (1936), had a considerable influence on governments until the 1960s. Before Keynes, most conventional economists believed that by the working of the forces of supply and demand, high unemployment would only occur on a short-term basis. Keynes tried to demonstrate that this was not the case and argued in favour of government intervention to stimulate demand and employment. Monetarism is a rival view to Keynesianism. See also Demand Management and Monetarism.

Labour Flexibility

Many workers develop particular skills and specializations. In some modern enterprises, management prefers that workers move between different jobs rather than specialize. When workers do take on a variety of different jobs, this is referred to as labour flexibility.

Landlocked

A country completely surrounded by other countries and hence with no direct access to the sea.

Left Wing

A term applying to political groups that seek the redistribution of wealth so as to benefit the poorer social classes—for example, socialists and communists. The term derives from the seating arrangements in the National Assembly during the French Revolution.

In most countries of western Europe, the labels *left wing* and *right wing* are still widely accepted and used even by party members; in the United States, in contrast, there is more doubt as to whether the terms can be helpfully applied to the major political parties. However, applying the broadest definitions of these labels, some Democrats might describe their party as left wing, and some Republicans might describe their party as right wing.

Liberal Democracy

A country that has the following characteristics. First, power rests with an elected assembly and governments change on the basis of popular votes rather than armed struggle. Secondly, the press and other media of communications are relatively free of state control, allowing open discussion of controversial political and social issues.

Linguistic

Pertaining to language. Linguistic development forms part of the broader process of intellectual development.

Means of Production

The various things required to be able to produce goods, such as raw materials, machinery, and a location.

Monetarism

Monetarism is the name given to the view that it is the primary duty of government to control the money supply in the country's economy. If the government ensures that the money supply matches production, inflation will be avoided. This approach to economic management became popular with certain governments in the economically advanced countries after weaknesses began to be perceived in the theory of Keynes, which had previously predominated. See also Keynes.

Moslem

Also *Muslim*. A follower of the religion of Islam.

Neoliberalism

The view that governments should adopt the principles of market economics. See Market Economics entry.

North

See South.

Nyasaland

A British colony in southern Africa; now named Malawi. See Malawi entry.

Opportunity Cost
If taking one course of action means that some alternative course of action becomes impossible, that alternative becomes a "cost" of the action taken. For example, if children drop out of school to earn money at a full-time job, their failure to complete their education is counted as an opportunity cost to be placed against the money earned on the job.

Pedagogy
Teaching, or the theory of how to teach.

Psychology
The study of mind and behaviour.

Qualitative
Qualitative assessment or analysis is based on general impressions and not precise measurement.

Quantitative
Based on precise measurement.

Quran
The holy book of the Islamic religion. Also sometimes spelled "Koran." Quranic schools are centres of Islamic religious teaching.

Racism
Racism has two main features: (a) the belief that one race is superior to others; (b) the active favouring of one race over others. Scholarly inquiry has led to the conclusion that the concept of "race" has no scientific foundation. However, racism can still exist insofar as some people believe in the reality of race. See Ethnicity entry.

Real Wages
Wages calculated in terms of what can be bought rather than the face value of the money paid. When comparing incomes received at different times, it is usually preferable to take account of any differences in prices of goods and services bought. Thus, if the face value of the wage increases over a period of time by 50 percent but prices rise during the same time by 100 percent, there is a decrease in real wages.

Right Wing
A term applied rather vaguely to political groups advocating conservative or nationalistic policies. See also Left Wing.

Sector
A term used to refer to all the economic enterprises of a particular sort. Thus, *the garment sector* refers to all companies producing garments, and *the tourist sector* refers to all companies engaged in the tourist business.

Social Contract
An actual or hypothetical agreement among the members of a society, or between a community and a ruler, on which social order and governance are based. The agreement defines and limits the rights and duties of each. Even if the agreement is unwritten and implicit, certain behaviour is commonly regarded as required in particular circumstances. All members of society understand that if society is to work smoothly, they must respect and obey these unwritten rules. Although they are unwritten, the effect of the rules is the same as if members of society had entered into a formal contract with each other.

Social Hierarchy
Describes the division of society into status-differentiated groups or classes that are more or less fixed. See also Feudalism.

Sociology
The study of society.

South
The South sometimes refers to the economically underdeveloped countries of the world, as opposed to the economically advanced countries, which are referred to as *the North*. Geographically this is not particularly accurate, but the North-South distinction is attractive because of its brevity.

Tanganyika
A British colony in southeast Africa, now part of Tanzania.

Tempo
Three-wheeled vehicle widely used as a bus in Bangladesh. See Bangladesh entry.

Third World
When the major economic powers in the world were divided into the Western, capitalist bloc based in North America and Western Europe, and the Eastern, communist bloc based in Eastern Europe and Asia, the phrase *Third World* was coined to refer to the economically underdeveloped countries that were

not aligned with either of these main groups. With the collapse of the communist bloc, the phrase is falling into disuse.

Underdeveloped Country (UDC)

A country where agriculture is the main economic activity.

Union of Soviet Socialist Republics (U.S.S.R.)

Also called the Soviet Union; the name of Russia during the communist regime.

United Nations

The body set up at the end of World War II with the main aim of achieving international understanding and resolving disputes by peaceful means. Most countries of the world are members.

Wedlock

Marriage. The phrase *born out of wedlock* is used as an alternative to *illegitimate*, in reference to children whose parents are not legally married.

West

A rather vague term employed to describe the countries of North America and Western Europe, which share common political objectives and are among the economically most advanced in the world. Since the collapse of the Eastern bloc of communist countries centred around the Soviet Union, the term is less commonly used. See also North and South.

Wobblies

Nickname for members of the Industrial Workers of the World (see entry).

List of Acronyms

AFL	American Federation of Labor
BMU	Bal Mazdoor Union
CNASTI	Confederacao Nacional de Accao sobre Trabalho Infantil
CRC	Convention on the Rights of the Child
CWC	Concerned for Working Children, The
CWIN	Child Workers in Nepal
DCI	Defence for Children International
EU	European Union
FLRA	Female Labor Reform Association
FLSA	Fair Labor Standards Act
GATT	General Agreement on Tariffs and Trade
ICFTU	International Confederation of Free Trade Unions
ILGWU	International Ladies' Garment Workers' Union
ILO	International Labour Organisation
IMF	International Monetary Fund
IPEC	International Program for the Elimination of Child Labor
IWGCL	International Working Group on Child Labour
IWW	Industrial Workers of the World
KKSP	Working Group on Urban Social Problems (Indonesia)
LAAI	Indonesian Child Advocacy Institute
MNMMR	Movemento Nacional de Meninos y Meninas da Rua
NACL	Network against Child Labour
NAM	National Association of Manufacturers
NCL	National Consumer's League
NCLC	National Child Labor Committee
NGO	nongovernmental organization
NIC	newly industrializing country
OECD	Organization for Economic Cooperation and Development
SACCS	South Asian Coalition on Child Servitude
SCF	Save the Children Fund
SSAP	Stabilization and Structural Adjustment Program
UDC	underdeveloped country
UNICEF	United Nations International Children's Emergency Fund

Chronology

1724–
1726 Daniel Defoe included descriptions of children working in his account of a tour through Great Britain.

1771 Richard Arkwright built a large water-powered factory near the River Derwent in England. The location was relatively remote, and many children were brought there to work.

1793 John Theophilus Lees (later an admiral) enlisted in the British Navy at the age of 5 years.

1802 The Health and Morals of Apprentices Act, the first legislation in Britain on child labour, was passed, but it had little impact.

1818 As part of his campaign to restrict child labour, the Welshman Robert Owen published the book *On the Employment of Children in Manufactories.*

1830 The Englishman Richard Oastler began his campaign against child labour when he published a condemnation of it in the newspaper *Leeds Mercury.*

1832 *A Memoir of Robert Blincoe*, an account by John Brown of the life of a pauper apprentice was published. It was used as propaganda against child labour in Britain.

1833 A Factory Act was passed that restricted the hours children could work in British textile mills.

1839 The Anti-Slavery Society for the Protection of Human Rights was formed. Later renamed Anti-Slavery International, it has played a large part in campaigns against child labour throughout the world.

The first legislation on child labour in Prussia (Germany) was passed, but it had little impact.

1841 The first, but relatively ineffective, French laws on child labour were passed.

1842 King Leopold of Belgium announced a bill to protect children working in factories. However, the first Belgian law on child labour was not passed until 1889.

1842
cont. Lord Ashley's Mines Commission collected information on the conditions of women and child workers in the mines to present to the British Parliament. [Lord Ashley is usually known by his later title, Lord Shaftesbury.]

The Mines Act restricted the employment of children in mines in Britain.

1844 A Factory Act established the Half-Time System (part work, part school) for child workers in Britain.

1845 In his book, *The Condition of the Working Class in England*, the German writer Friedrich Engels drew attention to the widespread use of child labour in many industries.

1850 *David Copperfield*, which contains a fictionalized account by Charles Dickens of his years spent working as a child, was published in England.

The anonymous autobiography *Chapters in the Life of a Dundee Factory Boy* was published in Scotland.

1853 The first effective legislation on child labour in Prussia (Germany) was passed.

1863 *The Water Babies*, a novel by Charles Kingsley, was published. It drew attention to the lives of child chimney sweeps.

1870 The United States census for the first time gathered information on children working.

1873 The first laws restricting the employment of children were passed in Denmark.

The first group of children left Britain for Canada under a scheme organized by the National Children's Homes.

1874 The first effective French laws on child labour were passed.

The "little law" was passed in the Netherlands. It was the first legislation on child labour in that country, but did not have much effect.

1875 The Chimney Sweepers Act stopped the practice in Britain of sending children up chimneys to clean them.

1881 At the first annual conference of the American Federation of Labor, a resolution was passed calling on states to pass laws against child labour.

1889 After many years of debate, the first Belgian laws on child labour were passed.

1902 The American Academy of Political and Social Science devoted a session at its conference to the question of child labour.

The Anthracite Coal Strike focused attention on the large numbers of children employed in the mines of Pennsylvania.

The New York Child Labor Committee was formed. Out of it grew the National Child Labor Committee.

1904 The National Child Labor Committee was formed in the United States.

1906 Senator Beveridge of Indiana made the first, but unsuccessful, attempt to introduce federal legislation against child labour in the United States.

1909 The Child Emigration Society was founded with the aim of encouraging the migration of British children to the colonies. The children were expected to work for their living when they arrived.

1911 The fire at the Triangle Shirtwaist Factory that killed many adult and child workers drew public attention to child labour in the American garment industry.

A Factory Law restricting child labour in large factories was passed in Japan, but not enforced until 1916.

1912 The United States Children's Bureau was established.

The strike by a workforce predominantly made up of women and children took place at the American Woolen Company, a mill in Lawrence, Massachusetts.

1914 The Burston School Strike, which arose from a dispute between teachers and farmers on the employment of schoolchildren in agricultural work, took place in England.

1915 The Palmer-Owen Bill on child labour failed to make its way through the U.S. Congress in time to become law.

1916 The Keating-Owen Bill, the first federal child labour law in the United States, was passed by Congress and signed by President Wilson. It was later challenged in court and declared unconstitutional.

1918 A decree was issued in postrevolutionary Russia aimed at banning work by young people at night and underground. This was the first of a number of steps by the new government to reduce child employment.

1919 The International Labour Organisation was founded. Its Convention No. 5, approved that year, sought to prohibit work by children younger than 14 years.

1922 The Labor Code of the Soviet Union was established. It contained a number of prohibitions and restrictions on child labour.

The Permanent Coalition for the Abolition of Child Labor was formed in the United States.

1926 The Native Juveniles Employment Act was passed in the British colony of Southern Rhodesia (now Zimbabwe).

1930 The International Labour Organisation passed Convention No. 29, outlawing forced or compulsory labour.

1938 The Black-Connery Wages and Hours Bill became law as the Fair Labor Standards Act. It was the first successful federal legislation in the United States on child labour.

1939 *Boy Slaves*, probably the only Hollywood feature film to deal with child labour, was released by RKO Radio Pictures.

The California State Assembly passed the so-called Coogan Act, which provided for half of the earnings of child actors to be held in trust.

The British colony of Nyasaland (later Malawi) passed a law restricting child labour, but it had little impact because of the outbreak of World War II.

1941 The Supreme Court of the United States upheld the Fair Labor Standards Act, thus confirming the power of Congress to legislate on the employment of children.

1944 The International Monetary Fund and the World Bank were both founded as a result of an international conference held at Bretton Woods, New Hampshire. The policies of these bodies have had a great influence on child labour in the poorer countries of the world.

1946 The United Nations International Children's Emergency Fund (UNICEF) was founded.

Chronology

1954 The photographs of Lewis W. Hine and the records of the National Child Labor Committee were presented to the Library of Congress.

1960 *Centuries of Childhood*, the influential book by Philippe Aries on the history of childhood, was published in French.

1966 The Children and Young Persons Employment Act was passed in Malaysia. It was not subsequently enforced in any substantial way.

1973 The International Labour Organisation passed Convention No. 138, requiring countries to put in place policies that would lead to the abolition of child labour.

1979 Proclaimed the International Year of the Child.

1985 The nongovernmental organization The Concerned for Working Children was officially registered as a charity in Bangalore, India.

1986 *When Teenagers Work*, by Ellen Greenberger and Laurence Steinberg, was published. It was the first major study of the effects of work on young Americans.

The Compulsory Education Law in China made it nationally illegal to employ children younger than 16 years.

The Child Labor (Prohibition and Regulation) Act was passed in India.

1987 The nongovernmental organization Child Workers in Nepal was founded.

1988 The Bonded Labour Liberation Front, one of the most vigorous bodies fighting child labour, was founded in Pakistan.

1989 The Convention on the Rights of the Child was adopted by the General Assembly of the United Nations.

Bhima Sangha, an independent organization of working children, was founded in India.

1990 Operation Child Watch, a campaign to restrict child labour, was initiated by the United States Labor Department.

1991 The Employment of Children Act was passed in Pakistan but has not proved effective in restricting child labour.

1992 The Bonded Labor Act was passed in Pakistan, but this form of exploitation of adults and children still continues in that country.

1993 Sheik Zayed, president of the United Arab Emirates, decreed that children should not be employed as camel jockeys.

1994 Confederacao Nacional de Accao sobre Trabalho Infantil (CNASTI), a nongovernmental organization opposed to child labour, was founded in Portugal.

The European Union Directive on the Employment of Children and Young People was introduced, to take effect two years later.

U.S. Senator Harkin introduced a bill to ban the import of goods made with the use of child labour.

1995 Iqbal Masih, the 12 year-old Pakistani who had become an internationally known symbol of the struggle against child labour, was killed.

1996 The International Confederation of

Free Trade Unions adopted its Child Labor Charter.

The First International Meeting of Working Children took place in Kundapur, India, bringing together child workers from Asia, Africa, and Latin America.

1997 An international conference on the most intolerable forms of child labour was hosted by the Dutch government in Amsterdam.

UNICEF devoted its fiftieth anniversary report, *The State of the World's Children 1997*, to child labour.

The Global March against Child Labor was launched in November and concluded in June 1998.

1998 The International Labour Organisation met to revise its policy on child labour to emphasize the need to eliminate the most intolerable forms of exploitation.

Bibliography

Abdalla, Ahmed. 1995. *Child Labour in Egypt: An Overview and an Exploratory Study of the Child Labour Triangle of Masr Al-Qadeema Old Cairo*. Amsterdam: Defence for Children International.

Ackroyd, Peter. 1990. *Dickens*. London: Sinclair-Stevenson.

Aghajanian, Akbar. 1979. "Family Income and Economic Contribution of Children in Iran: An Overview." *Journal of South Asian and Middle Eastern Studies* 3:21–30.

Alston, Lester. 1992. "Children as Chattel." In West, E., and Patrick, P., eds. *Small Worlds*. Lawrence: University Press of Kansas.

Amin, Aloysius Ajab. 1994. "The Socio-Economic Impact of Child Labour in Cameroon," *Labour, Capital and Society* 27:234–248.

Anonymous. 1951. *Chapters in the Life of a Dundee Factory Boy*. Dundee, UK: John Scott. [First Published 1850.]

Anti-Slavery International. 1996. *"This Menace of Bonded Labour": Debt Bondage in Pakistan*. London: Anti-Slavery International.

Anti-Slavery Society. 1978. *Child Labour in Morocco's Carpet Industry*. London: Anti-Slavery Society.

Aries, Philippe. 1973. *Centuries of Childhood*. Harmondsworth, UK: Penguin. [First published in French, 1960.]

Aronson, Pamela J., Mortimer, Jeylan T., Zierman, Carol, and Hacker, Michael. 1996. "Generational Differences in Early Work Experiences and Evaluations." In Mortimer, Jeylan T., and Finch, Michael D., eds., *Adolescents, Work, and Family: An Intergenerational Developmental Analysis*. Thousand Oaks, CA: Sage.

Bachman, Jerald G. 1983. "Premature Affluence: Do High School Students Earn Too Much?" *Economic Outlook* 10:64–67.

Bachman, Jerald G., and Schulenberg, John. 1993. "How Part-Time Work Intensity Relates to Drug Use, Problem Behavior, Time Use, and Satisfaction among High School Seniors: Are These Consequences or Merely Correlates?" *Developmental Psychology* 29:220–235.

Barling, Julian, and Kelloway, E. Kevin, eds. 1999. *Young Workers: Varieties of Experience*. Washington, DC: American Psychological Association.

Barrett, Michelle, and McIntosh, Mary. 1980. "The 'Family Wage' Debate: Some Problems for Socialists and Feminists." *Capital and Class* 11:51–72.

Becker, Saul, Aldridge, Jo, and Dearden, Chris. 1998. *Young Carers and Their Families*. Oxford: Blackwell.

Bekombo, Manga. 1981. "The Child in Africa: Socialization, Education, and Work." In Rodgers, Gerry, and Standing,

Bibliography

Guy, eds., *Child Work, Poverty and Underdevelopment*. Geneva: International Labour Office.

Bellamy, Carol. 1997. *The State of the World's Children, 1997*. New York: Oxford University Press for UNICEF.

Binh, Vu Ngoc. 1995. *Child Labour in Vietnam: a Country Report Prepared for the International Working Group on Child Labour*. Amsterdam: Defence for Children International.

Bird, S., Georgakas, D., and Shaffer, D. 1985. *Solidarity Forever: An Oral History of the Wobblies*. London: Lawrence and Wishart.

Black, Maggie. 1995. *In the Twilight Zone: Child Workers in the Hotel, Tourism, and Catering Industry*. Geneva: International Labour Office.

———. 1996. *Children First: The Story of UNICEF*. London: Oxford University Press.

Blagbrough, Jonathan and Glynn, Edmund. 1999. "Child Domestic Workers: Characteristics of the Modern Slave and Approaches to Ending Such Exploitation." *Childhood* 6:51–56.

Bonnet, Michel. 1993. "Child Labour in Africa." *International Labour Review* 132:371–389.

Bowes, Jennifer M., and Goodnow, Jacqueline J. 1996. "Work for Home, School, or Labor Force: The Nature and Source of Changes in Understanding." *Psychological Bulletin* 119:300–321.

Boyd, Rosalind. 1994. "Child Labour within the Globalizing Economy." *Labour, Capital and Society* 27:153–161.

Boyden, Jo. 1994. *The Relationship between Education and Child Work*. Florence, Italy: UNICEF International Child Development Centre.

Boyden, Jo, Ling, Birgitta, and Myers, William. 1998. *What Works for Working Children*. Florence, Italy: UNICEF International Child Development Centre.

Boyden, Jo, and Myers, William. 1995. *Exploring Alternative Approaches to Combating Child Labour: Case Studies from Developing Countries*. Florence, Italy: UNICEF International Child Development Centre.

Branne, Julia, and O'Brien, Margaret. 1996. *Children in Families: Research and Policy*. London: Falmer Press.

Bray, Reginald A. 1980. *Boy Labour and Apprenticeship*. New York: Garland. [First Published 1911.]

Bronfenbrenner, Urie. 1986. "Ecology of the Family as a Context for Human Development: Research Perspectives." *Developmental Psychology* 41:723–742.

Brooks, Daniel R., Davis, Letitia K., and Gallagher, Susan S. 1993. "Work-Related Injuries among Massachusetts Children: A Study Based on Emergency Department Data." *American Journal of Industrial Medicine* 24:313–324.

Brown, John. 1977. *A Memoir of Robert Blincoe*. London: Caliban. [First Published 1832.]

Burman, Erica. 1994. *Deconstructing Developmental Psychology*. London: Routledge.

Burnett, John, Vincent, David, and Mayall, David, eds. 1984. *The Autobiography of the Working Class*, Vol. 1. Brighton, UK: Harvester Press.

Butterfield, Bruce D. 1990. "Business as Usual Despite Federal Crackdown: Child Labor Violations Continue Much as Before in Sweatshops and Fields across the Nation." *Boston Globe* (November 11).

Bythell, Duncan. 1969. *The Handloom Weavers: A Study in the English Cotton Industry During the Industrial Revolution*. Cambridge: Cambridge University Press.

———. 1978. *The Sweated Trades: Outwork in Nineteenth-Century Britain*. London: Batsford.

Cadman, Eileen. 1996. *No Time to Play: Child Workers in the Global Economy*. Brussels: International Confederation of Free Trade Unions.

Cain, Mead, and Khorshed Alam Mozumber, A. B. M. 1981. "Labour Market Structure and Reproductive Behaviour in Rural South Asia." In Rodgers, Gerry, and Standing, Guy, *Child Work, Poverty and Development*. Geneva: International Labour Organisation.

Call, Kathleen Thiede. 1996. "Adolescent Work as an 'Area of Comfort' under Conditions of Family Discomfort." In Mortimer, Jeylan T., and Finch, Michael D., eds. *Adolescents, Work and Family: An Intergenerational Developmental Analysis*. Thousand Oaks, CA: Sage.

Camacho, Agnes Zenaida V. 1999. "Family,

Child Labour, and Migration: Child Domestic Workers in Metro Manila." *Childhood* 6:57–73.

Cameron, D., Bishop, C., and Sibert, J. R. 1992. "Farm Accidents in Children." *British Medical Journal* 305 (4 July):23–25.

Castillo, Dawn N. 1999. "Occupational Safety and Health in Young People." In Barling, Julian, and Kelloway, E. Kevin, eds., *Young Workers: Varieties of Experience*. Washington, DC: American Psychological Association.

Caulton, T. J., ed. 1985. *Children of the Industrial Revolution in Sheffield*. Sheffield, UK: University of Sheffield, Department of Continuing Education.

Cecchetti, Roberta. 1998. *Children Who Work in Europe*. Brussels: European Forum for Child Welfare.

Chirwa, Wiseman Chijere. 1993. "Child and Youth Labour on the Nyasaland Plantations, 1890–1953." *Journal of Southern African Studies* 19:662–680.

Chisholm, Anne, and Moorehead, Caroline. 1989. "Children in Prison: India." In Moorehead, Caroline, ed., *Betrayal: Child Exploitation in Today's World*. London: Barrie and Jenkins.

Clark, Sylvia. 1988. *Paisley: A History*. Edinburgh: Mainstream.

Cockerill, A. W. 1984. *Sons of the Brave: The Story of Boy Soldiers*. London: Leo Cooper.

Cohen, Cynthia Price. 1995. "Children's Rights: an American Perspective." In Franklin, Bob, ed., *The Handbook of Children's Rights*. London: Routledge.

Cohn, Jan. 1987. "The Business Ethic for Boys: The *Saturday Evening Post* and the Post Boys." *Business History Review* 61:185–215.

Cole, Sheila. 1980. "Send Our Children to Work?" *Psychology Today* (July):44–67.

Coleman, John C. 1992. "Current Views of the Adolescent Process." In Coleman, John C., ed. *The School Years: Current Issues in the Socialisation of Young People*. New York: Routledge.

Coleman, John C., and Hendry, Leo. 1990. *The Nature of Adolescence*. New York: Routledge.

Commission on Social Justice. 1994. *Social Justice: Strategies for National Renewal*. London: Vintage.

Concerned for Working Children, The. 1995. *Child Labour in Asia: A Regional Profile*. Amsterdam: Defence for Children International.

———. 1995. *Child Labour in Bangladesh*. Amsterdam: Defence for Children International.

———. 1995. *Child Labour in India*. Amsterdam: Defence for Children International.

———. 1995. *Child Labour in Nepal*. Amsterdam: Defence for Children International.

———. 1995. *Child Labour in Sri Lanka*. Amsterdam: Defence for Children International.

———. 1995. *Child Labour in Thailand*. Amsterdam: Defence for Children International.

Corsaro, William A. 1997. *The Sociology of Childhood*. Thousand Oaks, CA: Pine Forge Press.

Cottingham, M. 1997. *A Sporting Chance*. London: Christian Aid.

Cross, Peter. No Date. *Kashmiri Carpet Children: Exploited Village Weavers*. London: Anti-Slavery International.

Cruickshank, Marjorie. 1981. *Children and Industry: Child Health and Welfare in North-West Textile Towns during the Nineteenth Century*. Manchester, UK: Manchester University Press.

Cunningham, Hugh. 1990. "The Employment and Unemployment of Children in England, c. 1680–1851." *Past and Present* 126:115–150.

———. 1991. *The Children of the Poor: Representations of Childhood since the Seventeenth Century*. Oxford: Blackwell.

Cunningham, Hugh, and Viazzo, Pier Paolo, eds. 1996. *Child Labour in Historical Perspective, 1800–1985: Case Studies from Europe, Japan and Colombia*. Florence, Italy: UNICEF International Child Development Centre.

D'Amico, R. 1984. "Does Employment During High School Impair Academic Progress?" *Sociology of Education* 57:152–164.

Dahrendorf, Ralf. 1959. *Class and Class Conflict in Industrial Society*. London: Routledge and Kegan Paul.

Davies, Emrys. 1972. "Work out of School." *Education* (10 November):i–iv.

Davin, Anna. 1990. "When Is a Child Not a Child?" In Carr, H., and Jamieson, L., eds., *The Politics of Everyday Life*. Basingstoke, UK: Macmillan.

Bibliography

———. 1996. *Growing Up Poor: Home, School and Street in London, 1870–1914*. London: Rivers Oram Press.

De Herdt, Rene. 1996. "Child Labour in Belgium, 1800–1914." In Cunningham, Hugh, and Viazzo, Pier Paolo, eds., *Child Labour in Historical Perspective, 1800–1985: Case Studies from Europe, Japan and Colombia*. Florence, Italy: UNICEF International Child Development Centre.

De la Luz Silva, Maria. 1981. "Urban Poverty and Child Work: Elements for the Analysis of Child Work in Chile." In Rodgers, Gerry, and Standing, Guy, eds., *Child Work, Poverty, and Underdevelopment*. Geneva: International Labour Organisation.

Deacon, Bob. 1996. *Global Social Policy*. London: Sage.

Defensa de Niños y Niñas Internacional. 1995. *El Trabajo Infantil en Espana*. Amsterdam: Defence for Children International.

Defoe, Daniel. 1971. *A Tour through the Whole Island of Great Britain*. Harmondsworth, UK: Penguin. [First Published 1724–1726.]

DeMause, Lloyd, ed. 1974. *The History of Childhood*. New York: Psychohistory Press.

Desmardis, Serge, and Curtis, James. 1999. "Gender Differences in Employment and Income Experiences among Young People." In Barling, Julian, and Kelloway, E. Kevin, eds., *Young Workers: Varieties of Experience*. Washington, DC: American Psychological Association.

Dewar, M. 1979. *Labour Policy in the USSR, 1917–1928*. New York: Octagon.

Di Robilant, Andrea, and Moorehead, Caroline. 1989. "Street Children: Brazil." In Moorehead, Caroline, ed. *Betrayal: Child Exploitation in Today's World*. London: Barrie and Jenkins.

Dickens, Charles. 1850. *David Copperfield*. [Many Editions.]

Dube, Leela. 1981. "The Economic Roles of Children in India: Methodological Issues." In Rodgers, Gerry, and Standing, Guy, eds., *Child Work, Poverty and Underdevelopment*. Geneva: International Labour Office.

Dube, Linde. 1995. *Child Labour in South Africa: A Supplementary Report Prepared for the IWGCL*. Amsterdam: Defence for Children International.

Durai, Jayanti. No Date. *Helping Business to Help Stop Child Labour*. London: Anti-Slavery International.

Eccles, J. S., Midgley, C., Wigfield, A., Buchanan, C. M., Reuman, D., Flanagan, C., and MacIver, D. 1993. "Development during Adolescence: The Impact of Stage-Environment Fit on Young Adolescents' Experiences in Schools and in Families." *American Psychologist* 48:90–101.

Edwards, B. 1974. *The Burston School Strike*. London: Lawrence and Wishart.

Engels, Friedrich. 1987. *The Condition of the Working Class in England*. [First Published in German, 1845.]

Ennew, Judith. 1982. "Family Structure, Unemployment, and Child Labour in Jamaica." *Development and Change* 13:551–563.

———. 1986. *The Sexual Exploitation of Children*. Cambridge: Polity Press.

———. 1995. "Outside Childhood: Street Children's Rights." In Franklin, Bob, ed., *The Handbook of Children's Rights*. London: Routledge.

Ennew, Judith, and Milne, Brian. 1989. *The Next Generation: Lives of Third World Children*. London: Zed Books.

Epstein, Irving. 1993. "Child Labor and Basic Education Provision in China." *International Journal of Educational Development* 13:227–238.

Erikson, Erik H. 1968. *Identity: Youth and Crisis*. New York: Norton.

Finch, Michael D., and Mortimer, Jeylan T. 1985. "Adolescent Work Hours and the Process of Achievement." *Research in the Sociology of Education* 5:171–196.

Finch, Michael D., Shanahan, Michael J., Mortimer, Jeylan T., and Ryu, Seongryeol. 1991. "Work Experience and Control Orientation in Adolescence." *American Sociological Review* 56:597–611.

Forastieri, Valentina. 1997. *Children at Work: Health and Safety Risks*. Geneva: International Labour Office.

Forbes, Cameron, and Moorehead, Caroline. 1989. "The Sexual Exploitation of Children: The Philippines." In Moorehead, Caroline, ed., *Betrayal: Child Exploitation in Today's World*. London: Barrie and Jenkins.

Franklin, Annie, and Franklin, Bob. 1996. "Growing Pains: The Developing Children's Rights Movement in the U.K." In Pilcher, Jane, and Wragg, Stephen, eds., *Thatcher's Children*. London: Falmer Press.

Franklin, Bob, ed. 1995. *The Handbook of Children's Rights.* London: Routledge.

Fraser, Derek. 1984. *The Evolution of the British Welfare State*, 2d ed. London: Macmillan.

Frederiksen, Lisa. 1999. "Child and Youth Employment in Denmark: Comments on Children's Work from Their Own Perspective." *Childhood* 6:101–112.

Freedman, Russell. 1980. *Immigrant Kids.* New York: Penguin.

Freeman, Arnold. 1980. *Boy Life and Labour: The Manufacture of Inefficiency.* New York: Garland. [First Published 1914.]

Frone, Michael R. 1999. "Developmental Consequences of Youth Employment." In Barling, Julian, and Kelloway, E. Kevin, eds., *Young Workers: Varieties of Experience.* Washington, DC: American Psychological Association.

Frow, Edward, and Frow, Ruth. 1970. *The Half-Time System in Education.* Manchester: Moxton.

Fuller, Raymond G. 1930. "Child Labor." In E. R. A. Seligman, ed. *Encyclopaedia of the Social Sciences*, Vol. 3. New York: Macmillan.

Furlong, Andy. 1992. *Growing Up in a Classless Society? School-to-Work Transitions.* Edinburgh: Edinburgh University Press.

Fyfe, Alec. 1989. *Child Labour.* Cambridge: Polity Press.

Fyfe, Alec, and Jankanish, M. 1997. *Trade Unions and Child Labour: A Guide to Action.* Geneva: International Labour Organisation.

Garate, Martin, and Salazar, Maria Cristina. 1996. *International Working Group on Child Labour Regional Report: Latin America.* Amsterdam: Defence for Children International.

Garfield, Leon, and Proctor, David. 1972. *Child O' War: The True Story of a Boy Sailor in Nelson's Navy.* London: Collins.

Georgopoulou, Helen Aganthonos, and Stathakopoulos, Athanassia. 1995. *Child Labour in Greece.* Amsterdam: Defence for Children International.

German, Lindsay. 1989. *Sex, Class, and Socialism.* London: Bookmarks.

Giddens, Anthony. 1986. *Sociology: A Brief but Critical Introduction* (2d ed.). Basingstoke, UK: Macmillan.

Gilmour, David. 1879. *Reminiscences of the Pen' Folk, Paisley Weavers of Other Days, Etc.*, 2d ed. Edinburgh: Alexander Gardner.

Glauser, Benno. 1997. "Street Children: Deconstructing a Construct." In James, Allison, and Prout, Alan, eds., *Constructing and Reconstructing Childhood: Contemporary Issues in the Sociology of Childhood*, 2d ed. London: Falmer Press.

Goddard, Victoria. 1985. "Child Labour in Naples." *Anthropology Today* 6(5):18–21.

Goodnow, Jacqueline J. 1988. "Children's Household Work: Its Nature and Functions." *Psychological Bulletin* 103:5–26.

Green, David L. 1990. "High School Student Employment in Social Context: Adolescents' Perceptions of the Role of Part-Time Work." *Adolescence* 25:425–434.

Greenberger, Ellen. 1983. "A Researcher in the Policy Arena: The Case of Child Labor." *American Psychologist* 38:104–110.

———. 1988. "Working in Teenage America." In Mortimer, Jeylan T., and Borman, K. M., eds., *Work Experience and Psychological Development through the Life Span.* Boulder, CO: Westview Press.

Greenberger, Ellen, and Steinberg, Laurence. 1986. *When Teenagers Work: The Psychological and Social Costs of Adolescent Employment.* New York: Basic Books.

Greenberger, Ellen, Steinberg, Laurence, and Vaux, Alan. 1981. "Adolescents Who Work: Health and Behavioural Consequences of Job Stress." *Developmental Psychology* 17:691–703.

Greenberger, Ellen, Steinberg, Laurence, Vaux, Alan, and McAuliffe, Sharon. 1980. "Adolescents Who Work: Effects of Part-Time Employment on Family and Peer Relations." *Journal of Youth and Adolescence* 9:189–202.

Greene, David, and Lepper, Mark R. 1974. "September How to Turn Play into Work." *Psychology Today* 8(4):49–54.

Greenfield, Lauren. 1997. *Fast Forward: Growing Up in the Shadow of Hollywood.* New York: Alfred A. Knopf.

Grier, Beverly. 1994. "Invisible Hands: The Political Economy of Child Labour in Colonial Zimbabwe, 1890–1930." *Journal of Southern African Studies* 20:27–52.

Gross, Richard D. 1990. *Psychology: The Science of Mind and Behaviour.* London: Hodder and Stoughton.

Guerin, D. 1979. *100 Years of Labor in the USA.* London: Ink Link Press.

Gulrajani, Mohini. 1994. "Child Labour and the Export Sector in the Third World: A

Bibliography

Case Study of the Indian Carpet Industry." *Labour, Capital and Society* 27:192–214.

Gutman, Judith M. 1967. *Lewis W. Hine and the American Social Conscience.* New York: Walker.

Hammond, J. L., and Hammond, Barbara. 1939. *Lord Shaftesbury.* Harmondsworth, UK: Penguin. [First published 1923.]

———. 1967. *The Skilled Labourer, 1760–1832.* New York: August M. Kelley. [First published 1919.]

———. 1967. *The Town Labourer, 1760–1832.* New York: August M. Kelley. [First published 1917.]

———. 1967. *The Village Labourer, 1760–1832.* New York: August M. Kelley. [First published 1911.]

Hanawalt, Barbara. 1993. *Growing Up in Medieval London.* New York: Oxford University Press.

Hartmann, Heidi. 1981. "The Unhappy Marriage of Marxism and Feminism: Towards a More Progressive Union." In Sargent, L., ed., *Women and Revolution.* London: Pluto.

Heaven, Patrick C. L. 1994. *Contemporary Adolescence: A Social Psychological Approach.* South Melbourne, Australia: Macmillan Education.

Heywood, Colin. 1981. "The Market for Child Labour in Nineteenth-Century France." *History* 66:34–49.

———. 1989. *Children in Nineteenth-Century France: Work, Health, and Education among the "Classes Populaires."* Cambridge, UK: Cambridge University Press.

Hibbett, Angelika, and Beatson, Mark. 1995. "Young People at Work." *Employment Gazette* 103:169–177.

Himes, James R., Colbert de Arboleda, Vicky, and Garcia Mendez, Emilio. 1994. *Child Labour and Basic Education in Latin America and the Caribbean: a Proposed UNICEF Initiative.* Florence, Italy: UNICEF International Child Development Centre.

Hobbs, Sandy, and Cornwell, David. 1986. "Child Labour: An Underdeveloped Topic in Psychology." *International Journal of Psychology* 21:225–234.

Hobbs, Sandy, Lindsay, Sandra, and McKechnie, Jim. 1993. "Part-Time Employment and Schooling." *Scottish Educational Review* 25:53–60.

———. 1996. "The Extent of Child Employment in Britain." *British Journal of Education and Work* 9:5–18.

Hobbs, Sandy, and McKechnie, Jim. 1997. *Child Employment in Britain: A Social and Psychological Analysis.* Edinburgh: Stationery Office.

Hobsbawm, Eric J. 1962. *The Age of Revolution.* London: Weidenfeld and Nicolson.

Holloway, Marguerite. 1993. "Hard Times." *Scientific American* (October): 8–9.

Holmes, M., and Croll, P. 1989. "Time Spent on Homework and Academic Achievement." *Educational Research* 31:36–45.

Holt, John. 1975. *Escape from Childhood.* Harmondsworth, UK: Penguin.

Horan, Patrick M., and Hargis, Peggy G. 1991. "Children's Work and Schooling in the Late Nineteenth-Century Family Economy." *American Sociological Review* 56: 583–596.

Horrell, Sara, and Humphries, Jane. 1995. "The Exploitation of Little Children: Child Labor and the Family Economy in the Industrial Revolution." *Explorations in Economic History* 32:485–516.

Howieson, Catherine. 1990. "Beyond the Gate: Work Experience and Part-Time Work among Secondary-School Pupils in Scotland." *British Journal of Education and Work* 3:49–61.

Humphreys, Margaret. 1994. *Empty Cradles.* London: Doubleday.

Hutt, W. H. 1954. "The Factory System of the Early Nineteenth Century." In Hayek, F. A., ed., *Capitalism and the Historians.* Chicago: University of Chicago Press.

International Labour Organisation. 1996. *Child Labour: Targeting the Intolerable.* Geneva: International Labour Office.

———. 1996. *Trade Unions and Child Labour.* Geneva: International Labour Office.

Iso-Ahola, Seppo E. 1980. *The Social Psychology of Leisure and Recreation.* Dubuque, IA: Wm. C. Brown.

James, Allison, and Prout, Alan, eds. *Constructing and Reconstructing Childhood,* 2d ed. London: Falmer Press.

Jamieson, Lynn, and Toynbee, Claire. 1992. *Country Bairns: Growing Up, 1900–1930.* Edinburgh: Edinburgh University Press.

Jefferys, James B. 1954. *Retail Trading in Britain, 1850–1950.* Cambridge: Cambridge University Press.

Jesson, J. 1993. "Understanding Adolescent

Female Prostitution: A Literature Review." *British Journal of Social Work* 23:517–530.

Johnson, Victoria, Hill, Joanna, and Ivan-Smith, Edda. 1995. *Listening to Smaller Voices: Children in an Environment of Change.* London: Actionaid.

Jomo, K. S., ed. 1986. *Child Labour in Malaysia.* Selangor, Malaysia: Forum.

Jomo, K. S., Zami, Josie, Ramasamy, P., and Suppial, Sumathy. 1984. *Early Labour: Children at Work on Malaysian Plantations.* London: Anti-Slavery Society.

Jones, Gavin Steadman. 1976. *Outcast London: A Study of the Relationship between Classes in Victorian Society.* Harmondsworth, UK: Penguin.

Judge, Roy. 1979. *The Jack in the Green.* Cambridge, UK: D. S. Brewer.

Kahveci, Erol, Nichols, Theo, and Sugur, Nadir. 1996. "The Shoe Shine Boys of Izmir." In Kahveci, Erol, Sugur, Nadir, and Nichols, Theo, eds. *Work and Occupation in Modern Turkey.* London: Mansell.

King, Desmond S. 1987. *The New Right: Politics, Markets, and Citizenship.* Basingstoke, UK: Macmillan.

Kingsley, Charles. 1863. *The Water Babies.* [Many editions.]

Knight, Sheilagh. 1995. *Child Labour in Canada: A Look at Our Children.* Amsterdam: Defence for Children International.

Konanc, Esin, and Zeytinoglu, Sezen. 1995. *Child Labour in Turkey.* Amsterdam: Defence for Children International.

Kuklin, Susan. 1998. *Iqbal Masih and the Crusade against Child Slavery.* New York: Holt.

Landsdown, G. 1995. "Children's Right to Participation: A Critique." In Clarke, C., and Davies, M., eds. *Participation and Empowerment in Child Protection.* Chichester, UK: Wiley.

Lavalette, Michael. 1994. *Child Employment in the Capitalist Labour Market.* Aldershot, UK: Avebury.

———. 1996. "Thatcher's Working Children: Contemporary Issues of Child Labour." In Pilcher, Jane, and Wagg, Stephen, eds., *Thatcher's Children.* London: Falmer Press.

Lavalette, Michael, Hobbs, Sandy, Lindsay, Sandra, and McKechnie, Jim. 1995. "Child Employment in Britain: Policy, Myth, and Reality." *Youth and Policy* 47:1–15.

Lavalette, Michael, McKechnie, Jim, and Hobbs, Sandy. 1991. *The Forgotten*

Workforce: Scottish Children at Work. Glasgow: Scottish Low Pay Unit.

Lee, Mark, and O'Brien, Rachel. 1995. *The Game's Up: Redefining Child Prostitution.* London: Children's Society.

Lee-Wright, Peter. 1990. *Child Slaves.* London: Earthscan.

Lepper, M. R., and Greene, D. 1975. "Turning Play into Work: Effects of Adult Surveillance and Extrinsic Rewards on Children's Intrinsic Motivation." *Journal of Personality and Social Psychology* 31:479–486.

Levine, David. 1977. *Family Formation in the Age of Nascent Capitalism.* New York: Academic Press.

Lindenmeyer, K. 1997. *A Right to Childhood: The U.S. Children's Bureau and Child Welfare, 1912–1946.* Urbana: University of Illinois Press.

Livingstone, David. 1905. *Travels and Researches in South Africa.* London: Amalgamated Press. [First Published 1857.]

Maccoby, Eleanor, and Jacklin, Carol. 1974. *The Psychology of Sex Differences.* Palo Alto: Stanford University Press.

MacLennan, Emma. 1982. *Child Labour in London.* London: Low Pay Unit.

MacLennan, Emma, Fitz, John, and Sullivan, Jill. 1985. *Working Children.* London: Low Pay Unit.

Manning, Wendy D. 1990. "Parenting Employed Teenagers." *Youth and Society* 22:184–200.

Mansourov, Valery A. 1993. *Child Work in Russia.* Geneva: International Labour Office.

———. 1995. *International Working Group on Child Labour Supplementary Country Report: Russia.* Amsterdam: Defence for Children International.

Marcus, Rachel, and Harper, Caroline. 1996. *Small Hands: Children in the Working World.* London: Save the Children.

Markel, Karen S., and Frone, Michael R. 1998. "Job Characteristics, Work-School Conflict, and School Outcomes among Adolescents: Testing a Structural Model." *Journal of Applied Psychology* 83:277–287.

Marsh, Herbert W. 1991. "Employment during High School: Character Building or a Subversion of Academic Goals?" *Sociology of Education* 64:172–189.

Marx, Karl, and Engels, Friedrich. 1846. *The German Ideology.* [Many Editions.]

Mazur, Jay. 1993. "Remedies to the Problem

of Child Labor: The Situation in the Apparel Industry." *American Journal of Industrial Medicine* 24:331–334.

McKechnie, Jim, and Hobbs, Sandy, eds. 1998. *Working Children: Reconsidering the Debates—Report of the International Working Group on Child Labour.* Amsterdam: Defence for Children International.

McKechnie, Jim, Hobbs, Sandy, Lindsay, Sandra, and Lynch, Margaret A. 1998. "Working Children: The Health and Safety Issue." *Children and Society* 12: 38–47.

McKechnie, Jim, Lindsay, Sandra, and Hobbs, Sandy. 1994. *Still Forgotten: Child Employment in Dumfries and Galloway.* Glasgow: Scottish Low Pay Unit.

McKechnie, Jim, Lindsay, Sandra, Hobbs, Sandy, and Lavalette, Michael. 1996. "Adolescents' Perceptions of the Role of Part-Time Work." *Adolescence* 31:193–204.

Mead, Margaret. 1975. *Growing Up in New Guinea: A Comparative Study of Primitive Education.* New York: Morrow Quill. [First published 1930.]

Mendelievich, Elias, ed. 1979. *Children at Work.* Geneva: International Labour Office.

Meuwese, Stan. 1995. *Child Labour in the Netherlands.* Amsterdam: Defence for Children International.

Mizen, Paul. 1992. "Learning the Hard Way: The Extent and Significance of Child Working in Britain." *British Journal of Education and Work* 5:5–17.

Moorehead, Caroline, ed. 1989. *Betrayal: Child Exploitation in Today's World.* London: Barrie and Jenkins.

Mortimer, Jeylan T., and Finch, Michael D. 1986. "The Effects of Part-Time Work on Self Concept and Achievement." In Borman, Kathryn, and Reisman, J., eds., *Becoming a Worker.* Norwood, NJ: Ablex.

Mortimer, Jeylan T., and Finch, Michael D., eds. 1996. *Adolescents, Work, and Family: An Intergenerational Developmental Analysis.* Thousand Oaks, CA: Sage.

Mortimer, Jeylan T., Finch, Michael D., Dennehy, Katherine, Lee, Chaimum, and Beebe, Timothy. 1994. "Work Experience in Adolescence." *Journal of Vocational Education* 19:39–70.

Mortimer, Jeylan T., Finch, Michael D., Ryu, S., Shanahan, Michael J., and Call, Kathleen T. 1996. "The Effects of Work Intensity on Adolescent Mental Health, Achievement, and Behavioral Adjustment:

New Evidence from a Prospective Study." *Child Development* 67:1243–1261.

Mortimer, Jeylan T., Finch, Michael, Shanahan, Michael, and Ryu, Seongryeol. 1992 . "Work Experience, Mental Health, and Behavioural Adjustment in Adolescence." *Journal of Research on Adolescence* 2:25–57.

Mortimer, Jeylan, and Johnson, Monica. 1998. "Adolescents' Part-Time Work and Educational Achievement." In Borman, Kathryn, and Schneider, Barbara, eds., *The Adolescent Years: Social Influences and Educational Challenges.* Chicago: University of Chicago Press.

Mortimer, Jeylan T., and Shanahan, Michael J. 1994. "Adolescent Work Experience and Family Relationships." *Work and Occupations* 21:369–384.

Munoz Vila, Cecilia. 1996. "The Working Child in Colombia since 1800." In Cunningham, Hugh, and Viazzo, Pier Paolo, eds., *Child Labour in Historical Perspective, 1900–1985: Case Studies from Europe, Japan, and Colombia.* Florence, Italy: UNICEF International Child Development Centre.

Murray, Norman. 1978. *The Scottish Hand Loom Weavers, 1790–1850: A Social History.* Edinburgh: John Donald.

Myers, William E. 1999. "Considering Child Labour: Changing Terms, Issues, and Actors at the International Level." *Childhood* 6:13–26.

Nardinelli, Clark. 1990. *Child Labor and the Industrial Revolution.* Bloomington: Indiana University Press.

Nasaw, D. 1985. *Children of the City.* New York: Anchor Press.

National Commission on Youth. 1980. *The Transition of Youth to Adulthood: A Bridge Too Long.* Boulder, CO: Westview Press.

National Institute for Occupational Safety and Health. 1997. *Child Labor Research Needs: Recommendations from the NIOSH Child Labor Working Team.* Cincinnati, OH: National Institute for Occupational Safety and Health.

National Panel on High School and Adolescent Education. 1976. *The Education of Adolescents.* Washington, DC: U.S. Government Printing Office.

National Research Council Institute of Medicine. 1998. *Protecting Youth at Work.* New York: National Academy Press.

Newman, Philip, and Newman, Barbara.

1986. *Adolescent Development*. Columbus, OH: Merrill.

Nieuwenhuys, Olga. 1993. "To Read and Not to Eat: South Indian Children between Secondary School and Work." *Childhood* 1:100–109.

———. 1996. "The Paradox of Child Labor and Anthropology." *Annual Review of Anthropology* 25:237–251.

———. 1998. "Global Childhood and the Politics of Contempt." *Alternatives* 23:267–289.

Noller, Patricia, and Callan, Victor. 1991. *The Adolescent in the Family*. New York: Routledge.

Ojwang, J. B. 1996. *Child Labour in Africa*. Amsterdam: Defence for Children International.

Oloko, Sarah Beatrice Adenike. 1995. *International Working Group on Child Labour in-depth Country Report: Nigeria*. Amsterdam: Defence for Children International.

Onyango, Philista P. M., and Bader-Jaffer, Zinnat. 1995. *International Working Group on Child Labour in-depth Country Report: Kenya*. Amsterdam: Defence for Children International.

Owen, Robert. 1967. *A New View of Society*. Harmondsworth, UK: Penguin.

Page Arnot, R. 1955. *A History of the Scottish Miners*. London: George Allen and Unwin.

Pettitt, Bridget, ed. 1998. *Children and Work in the UK: Reassessing the Issues*. London: Save the Children.

Phillips, Sarah, and Sandstrom, Kent L. 1990. "Parental Attitudes toward Youth Work." *Youth and Society* 23:160–183.

Pilger, John. 1996. "In a Land of Fear," *London Observer* (May 4), Weekend Supplement, 12–21.

Pinchbeck, Ivy. 1981. *Women Workers and the Industrial Revolution*, 3d ed. London: Virago.

Pinchbeck, Ivy, and Hewitt, Margaret. 1969. *Children in English Society*, Vol. 1. London: Routledge and Kegan Paul.

———. 1973. *Children in English Society*, Vol. 2. London: Routledge and Kegan Paul.

Pollack, Susan H., Landrigan, Philip J., and Mallino, David L. 1990. "Child Labor in 1990: Prevalence and Health Hazards." *Annual Review of Public Health* 11:359–375.

Pollock, Linda. 1983. *Forgotten Children*. Cambridge: Cambridge University Press.

Pond, Chris, and Searle, Anne. 1991. *The Hidden Army: Children at Work in the 1990s*. London: Low Pay Unit.

President's Science Advisory Committee, Panel on Youth. 1973. *Youth: Transition to Adulthood*. Chicago: University of Chicago Press.

Price-Williams, D., Gordon, W., and Ramirez, N. 1969. "Skill and Conservation: A Study of Pottery-Making Children." *Developmental Psychology* 1:789.

Raftopoulos, Brian, and Dube, Linde. 1995. *The Problem of Child Labour in Zimbabwe: An Overview*. Amsterdam: Defence for Children International.

Reddy, Nandana. 1996. "Iqbal and the Kiss of Judas." *IWGCL Newsletter* 1:15–16.

Reynolds, P. 1991. *Dance, Civet Cat: Child Labour in the Zambesi Valley*. London: Zed Books.

Riis, Jacob A. 1997. *How the Other Half Lives: Studies among the Tenements of New York*. New York: Penguin. [First published 1890.]

Rodgers, Gerry, and Standing, Guy. 1981. *Child Work, Poverty, and Underdevelopment*. Geneva: International Labour Office.

Rosemberg, Fulvia, and Andrade, Leandro Feitosa. 1999. "Ruthless Rhetoric: Child and Youth Prostitution in Brazil." *Childhood* 6:113–131.

Rouard, Danielle. 1979. "Enfants au Travail." *Le Monde de L'education* 53:8–20.

Ryu, Seongryeol, and Mortimer, Jeylan T. 1996. "The 'Occupational Linkage Hypothesis' Applied to Occupational Value Formation in Adolescence." In Mortimer, Jeylan T., and Finch, Michael D., eds., *Adolescents, Work and Family: An Intergenerational Developmental Analysis*. Thousand Oaks, CA: Sage.

Sadeque, Shah Ahmed. 1992. *Tempo Boy: Child Labour on the Buses of Bangladesh*. London: Bangladesh International Action Group.

Saito, Osamu. 1996. "Children's Work, Industrialism, and the Family Economy in Japan, 1872–1926." In Cunningham, Hugh, and Viazzo, Pier Paolo, eds., *Child Labour in Historical Perspective, 1800–1985: Case Studies from Europe, Japan, and Colombia*. Florence, Italy: UNICEF International Child Development Centre.

Salazar, Maria Cristina, and Glasinovich, Walter Alarcon. 1996. *Better Schools, Less Child Work: Child Work and Education in Brazil, Colombia, Ecuador, Guatemala, and*

Peru. Florence, Italy: UNICEF International Child Development Centre.

Salvati Copiii. 1995. *Child Labour in Romania*. Amsterdam: Defence for Children International.

Sancho-Liao, Nelia. 1994. "Child Labour in the Philippines: Exploitation in the Process of Globalization of the Economy." *Labour, Capital and Society* 27:270–281.

Santrock, John W. 1996. *Adolescence*, 6th ed. Dubuque, IA: Brown and Benchmark.

Sattaur, Omar. 1993. *Child Labour in Nepal*. London: Anti-Slavery International.

Saul, Mahir. 1984. "The Quranic School Farm and Child Labour in Upper Volta." *Africa* 54:71–87.

Sawalha, Aseel. 1995. *Child Labour in Jordan*. Amsterdam: Defence for Children International.

Saxe, Geoffrey. 1988. "The Mathematics of Child Street Vendors." *Child Development* 59:1415–1425.

Schaffer, H. Rudolph. 1996. *Social Development*. Oxford: Blackwell.

Schibbotto, G., and Cussianovich, A. 1990. "Working Children: Building an Identity." Lima, Peru: MANTHOC.

Schildkrout, Enid. 1981. "The Employment of Children in Kano (Nigeria)." In Rodgers, Gerry, and Standing, Guy, eds., *Child Work, Poverty, and Underdevelopment*. Geneva: International Labour Office.

Schlemmer, Bernard, ed. 1996. *L'enfant Exploite: Oppression, Mise au Travail, Proletarisation*. Paris: Editions Ostrum.

Searight, Susan. 1980. *Child Labour in Spain*. London: Anti-Slavery Society.

Self, P. 1993. *Government by the Market? The Politics of Public Choice*. London: Macmillan.

Shanahan, Michael J., Elder, G. H., Burchinal, M., and Conger, R. D. 1996. "Adolescent Earnings and Relationships with Parents: The Work-Family Nexus in Urban and Rural Ecologies." *Addition* 15:97–128.

Shanahan, Michael J., Finch, Michael, Mortimer, Jeylan T., and Ryu, Seongryeol. 1991. "Adolescent Work Experience and Depressive Affect." *Social Psychology Quarterly* 54:299–317.

Shaw, John, and Moorehead, Caroline. 1989. "Refugee Children: Somalia." In Moorehead, Caroline, ed., *Betrayal: Child Exploitation in Today's World*. London: Barrie and Jenkins.

Sherington, Geoffrey, and Jeffery, Chris.

1998. *Fairbridge: Empire and Child Migration*. Ilford, UK: Woburn Press.

Shivji, Issa. 1985. "Law and Conditions of Child Labour in Colonial Tanganyika, 1920–1940." *International Journal of the Sociology of Law* 13:221–235.

Shorter, Edward. 1977. *The Making of the Modern Family*. Glasgow: Collins.

Simon, Brian. 1965. *Education and the Labour Movement*. London: Lawrence and Wishart.

Stadum, Beverly. 1995. "The Dilemma in Saving Children from Child Labor: Reform and Casework at Odds with Families' Needs, 1900–1938." *Child Welfare* 74:33–55.

Steinberg, Laurence. 1993. *Adolescence*. New York: Mcgraw-Hill.

Steinberg, Laurence, and Dornbusch, Sanford M. 1991. "Negative Correlates of Part-Time Employment during Adolescence: Replication and Elaboration." *Developmental Psychology* 27:304–313.

Steinberg, Laurence, Fegley, Suzanne, and Dornbusch, Sanford M. 1993. "Negative Impact of Part-Time Work on Adolescent Adjustment: Evidence from a Longitudinal Study." *Developmental Psychology* 29:171–180.

Steinberg, Laurence, Greenberger, Ellen, Garduque, L., Ruggiero, Mary, and Vaux, A. 1982. "Effects of Working on Adolescent Development." *Developmental Psychology* 18:385–395.

Steinberg, Laurence, Greenberger, Ellen, Jacobi, M., and Garduque, L. 1981. "Early Work Experience: A Partial Antidote for Adolescent Egocentrism." *Journal of Youth and Adolescence* 10:141–157.

Steinberg, Laurence, Greenberger, Ellen, and Ruggiero, Mary. 1982. "Assessing Job Characteristics: When 'Perceived' and 'Objective' Measures Don't Converge." *Psychological Reports* 50:771–780.

Steinberg, Laurence, Greenberger, Ellen, Vaux, A., and Ruggiero, Mary. 1981. "Early Work Experience: Effects on Adolescent Occupational Socialization." *Youth and Society* 12:403–422.

Stephens, William N. 1979. *Our Children Should Be Working*. Springfield, IL: Charles C. Thomas.

Stern, David, Stone, James R., III, Hopkins, Charles, and McMillion, Martin. 1990. "Quality of Students' Work Experience and Orientation toward Work." *Youth & Society* 22:263–282.

Stevens, Constance J., Putchell, Laura A., Ryu, Seongryeol, and Mortimer, Jeylan T. 1992. "Adolescent Work and Boys' and Girls' Orientations to the Future." *Sociological Quarterly* 33:153–169.

Stone, Laurence. 1977. *Family, Sex, and Marriage in England, 1500–1800.* London: Weidenfeld and Nicolson.

Stuurman, Siep. 1989. "Samuel van Houten and Dutch Liberalism, 1860–1890." *Journal of the History of Ideas,* 50, 135–152.

Sugarman, Leonie. 1986. *Lifespan Development: Concepts, Theories, and Interventions.* London: Methuen.

Sultana, Ronald G. 1990. "Breaking Them In? School Kids in the Twilight Economy." *New Zealand Journal of Industrial Relations* 15:19–33.

———. 1993. "Practices and Policies in Child Labour: Lessons from Malta." *British Journal of Education and Work* 6:45–59.

Sumner, H. L., and Merritt, E. A. 1915. *Child Labor Legislation in the United States.* Washington, DC: Government Printing Office for the United States Children's Bureau.

Swift, Anthony. 1997. "Let Us Work!" *New Internationalist* (July), 21–23.

Sylva, Kathy, and Lunt, Ingrid. 1985. *Child Development: A First Course.* Oxford: Blackwell.

Taylor, R. B. 1973. *Sweat Shops in the Sun.* Boston: Beacon Press.

Thompson, E. P. 1968. *The Making of the English Working Class,* 2d ed. Harmondsworth, UK: Penguin [1st Ed. 1963].

Trattner, Walter I. 1970. *Crusade for the Children: A History of the National Child Labor Committee and Child Labor Reform in America.* Chicago: Quadrangle Books.

Tucker, R., ed. *The Marx-Engels Reader,* 2d ed. New York: Norton.

Tymms, P. B., and Fitz-Gibbon, C. T. 1992. "The Relationship between Part-Time Employment and A-Level Results." *Educational Research* 34:193–199.

United Nations Research Institute for Social Development. 1995. *States of Disarray: The Social Effects of Globalization.* Geneva: United Nations Research Institute for Social Development.

Valcarenghi, Marina. 1981. *Child Labour in*

Italy: A General Review. London: Anti-Slavery Society.

Vincent, David. 1981. *Bread, Knowledge, and Freedom: A Study of Nineteenth-Century Working Class Autobiography.* London: Europa.

Vuzina, Dialehti, and Schaffer, Heiner. 1992. *Kinderarbeit in Europa.* Düsseldorf: Ministerium für Arbeit, Gesundheit und Soziales des Landes Nordrhein-Westfalen.

Weber, Max. 1968. *Economy and Society.* New York: Bedminster Press.

Wessells, Mike. 1997. "Child Soldiers." *Bulletin of the Atomic Scientists* (November/December):32–39.

West, Elliot. 1992. Children on the Plains Frontier." In West, E., and Petrick, P., eds., *Small Worlds.* Lawrence: University Press of Kansas.

White, Ben. 1994. "Children, Work, and 'Child Labour': Changing Responses to the Employment of Children." *Development and Change* 25:848–878.

White, Ben, Tjandraningsih, Indrasari, and Haryadi, Dedi. 1997. *Child Workers in Indonesia.* Amsterdam: Defence for Children International.

Whittaker, Alan, ed. No Date. *Children in Bondage: Slaves of the Subcontinent.* London: Anti-Slavery International.

Wiggins, David. 1985. "The Play of Slave Children in the Plantation Communities of the Old South, 1820–1860." In Hiner, N., and Hawes, J., eds., *Growing Up in America.*

Wilk, Valerie A. 1993. "Health Hazards to Children in Agriculture." *American Journal of Industrial Medicine* 24:283–290.

Williams, Suzanne. No Date. *Child Workers in Portugal.* London: Anti-Slavery International.

Woodhead, Martin. 1998. *Children's Perspectives on Their Working Lives: A Participatory Study in Bangladesh, Ethiopia, the Philippines, Guatemala, El Salvador, and Nicaragua.* Stockholm: Redda Barnen.

———. 1999. "Combatting Child Labour: Listen to What the Children Say." *Childhood* 6:27–49.

Zalami, Fatima Badry. 1996. *Child Labor in Morocco: A Preliminary Exploration.* Amsterdam: Defence for Children International.

Zalami, Fatima Badry, Reddy, Nandana, Lynch, Margaret A., and Feinstein, Clare. 1998. *Forgotten on the Pyjama Trail: A Case Study of Young Garment Workers in Meknes*

Bibliography

Morocco Dismissed from Their Jobs Following Foreign Media Attention. Amsterdam: Defence for Children International.

Zelizer, V. 1985. *Pricing the Priceless Child: The Changing Social Value of Children.* New York: Basic Books.

Zetkin, Clara. 1984. *Selected Writings.* New York: International Publishers.

Zierold, Norman J. 1965. *The Child Stars.* London: MacDonald.

Zinn, Howard. 1980. *A People's History of the United States.* New York: Longman.

Index

Abbott, Grace, **1**, 36, 199
Accidents, **1–2**, 7, 22, 47, 76–77, 103, 109, 134, 162
Action against Child Exploitation, 75, 162
Addams, Jane, **2**, 199
Addams Family, The, 43
Adler, Felix, **2–3**, 165
Adolescence, **3–4**, 55–56
Advertising, 162
Advocacy, **4**
Africa, **4–5**, 158, 203, 207
Age of the child, xiii, 55, 85–86, 87
Agriculture, 1, **5–7**, 13, 15, 21–22, 24, 52, 72, 108, 109, 112, 113, 114, 134, 149, 157, 159–160, 240, 245
Alabama, 145, 161, 165
Alcohol and drugs, **7**
Algeria, **7–9**
Alston, Lester, 116
America, Central, **9**
America, Latin, **9**. *See also* America, Central; America, South
America, South, **9–10**
American Academy of Political and Social Sciences, 10
American Civil Liberties Union, 2
American Federation of Labor, xix, **10**, 106, 128
Anderson, Digby, 152
Anthracite Coal Strike, **10–11**, 181
Anthropology, xviii, **11**, 231
Anti-Slavery International, 4, **11–12**, 26, 104–105, 163, 179, 199

Apparel Industry Task Force, **12**
Apprenticeship, 5, **12–13**, 26–27, 32–33, 177. *See also* Pauper apprentices
Argentina, **13**
Aries, Philippe, 31–32, 115, 212
Arkwright, Richard, 158–159, 196
Aronson, Pamela, 185
Asia, **13–14**, 93, 158
Australia, 33–34, 171–172

Baby-sitting, 101
Bachman, Jerald, 49, 231
Baines, Edward, 195
Bal Mazdoor Union, **15**, 123, 181, 242
Bangladesh, **15–16**, 25–26, 122, 181, 183, 193, 207, 220
Barrett, Michelle, 91
Becker, Saul, xv
Belgium, **16–17**, 79, 173
Belize, 9
Benefits of child labour, xvii, 50–51, 195–196
Beveridge, Albert J., 2, **17–19**, 106
Bhima Sanga, **19**, 46, 123, 181, 242
Biograph Company, 42
Black, Maggie, 117–118, 228
Black-Connery Wage and Hours Bill, 87
Blincoe, Robert, xvi, **19**
Bonded labour, xvii, 235–236
Bonded Labour Liberation Front, **19**, 153–154
Boy Slaves, **19–20**, 43
Boy soldiers, **20–21**

Index

Boy Soldiers, xv
Boyden, Jo, 69–70, 100, 231
Brazil, xiii, xvi, **21–23**, 52, 171, 196, 197, 207
Bretton Woods Conference, 129–130, 132, 218, 250
Brown, John, 19
Bruce, Rev. Charles Lang, xix, **23**
Buddhism, 225
Burkina Faso, **23**
Burston School Strike, **23–24**
Business ethic, **24**, 206

California, 43
Cambodia, 20
Camel jockeys, **25–26**, 218, 236
Cameroon, **26–27**
Canada, **27**, 33, 54, 138, 171
Capitalism, 4–5, 12, **27–29**, 83, 152–153, 198, 235
Care and Fair labels, 194
Career, **29**
Caribbean, **29–30**, 78
Caring, 253–254
Carpet manufacture, 8, **30–31**, 153–154, 163, 184, 194–195, 205
Catering, 116–118
Causes of child labour, **31**
Central Advisory Council on Education, 230
Centuries of Childhood, **31–32**, 115
Ceramic manufacture, 2
Chadwick, Edwin, 249
Chaplin, Charles, 43
Child Actors Bill, 43
Child Emigration Society, 33–34
Child labour
  causes, 31, 51–54, 193
  chronology, 267–271
  definition, xiii, 55–57
  extent, xvi
  types, xv–xvi
Child Labor Charter, 129
Child Labor Coalition, 169
Child Labor in the Industrial Revolution, xv
Child Labor Legislation in the United States, 36
Child Labour: Targeting the Intolerable, xv, 74
Child markets, **32–33**
Child Migrants Trust, **33–34**
Child migration, 8, 33–34, 95, 171–172
Child Slaves, **34**, 43
Child Workers in Asia Support Group, 199
Child Workers in Nepal, **34–35**, 173, 242
Children's Bureau, 1, 2, **35–36**, 145, 199
Children's rights, xviii, 4, 8, **37–39**, 144
ChildWatch International, 242–243
Chile, **39**
Chimney sweeping, **39–40**, 210–211, 246

China, **40–41**, 122
Christianity, 24, 65, 85, 149, 165, 179, 203, 210, 247
Cigarette smoking, 7
Cinema, xix, 17, **41–43**, 76
Clark, David, 184
Coal breakers, **43–44**
Cockerill, A. W., xv, 20
Cohn, Jan, 207
Cole, Sheila, 50–51, 88
Collier, Francis, 185
Colombia, xvii, 9, 20, **44–46**
Colonialism, 5, 11, 29, 149, 150, 216, 225, 256
Colorado, 6
Columbia, District of, 18, 163
Commission on Children in Wartime, 36
Concerned for Working Children, The, xix, 19, **46**, 123, 177
Condition of the Working Class in England, The, 74–76, 90
Confederacio Nacional de Accao sobre Trabalho Infantil, **46–47**, 199, 203
Congo-Kinshasa, 20
Coninx, Stijn, 17
Construction industry, 2, 16, **47**, 165
Consumerism, **47–49**, 213
Convention on the Rights of the Child, 15, 20, 34, 37–38, **49–50**, 55, 69, 133, 143, 169–170, 180, 191, 197–198, 201, 206, 238, 242
Coogan, Jackie, 41, 43
Coogan Act, 43
Corbyn, Jeremy, 220
Corsaro, William A., 215
Costa Rica, 9
Costs and benefits, xvii, **50–51**, 108
Crime, 58–59, 206
Cross, Peter, xv
Cuba, 29–30
Cultural traditions, **51–54**
Cunningham, Hugh, 58, 78–79, 98

Daens, 17, 43
David Copperfield, 61–62
Davies, Emrys, 70
Davin, Anna, 116, 213
Decleir, Jan, 17
Defence for Children International, 4, **55**, 133, 199, 217
Definition of child labour, xiii, **55–57**
Defoe, Daniel, xviii, **57–58**
Delinquency, **58–59**
Delivery, milk, **59–60**
Delivery, newspaper, **60**, 173–174

DeMause, Lloyd, 115
Denmark, **60–61**
Depression, 106–107
Dickens, Charles, xvi, **61–62**
Dinwiddie, Courtenay, **62**
Division of labour, **62–63**
Dole, Elizabeth, 180
Domestic service, 26, 52, **63–64**, 138, 183, 189
Dornbusch, Sanford, 7, 89
Drawboys, **65**
Drugs, 7, 198
"Dundee factory boy," xvi, 62, **65–67**

Ecuador, 20, 52–54
Education, universal, **69–70**, 79, 111, 153. *See also* School attendance
Educational achievement, 23–24, 27, 50–51, **70–72**
Egypt, xvii, **72**, 113, 209
El Salvador, 9, 196
Elimination of child labour, **72–74**
Encyclopaedia of the Social Sciences, 56
End Child Prostitution in Asian Tourism, 228
Engels, Friedrich, 29, **74–76**, 90, 152, 180
England, 57–58, 117. *See also* United Kingdom
Ennew, Judith, 30, 38
Entertainment industry, **76**
Epstein, Irving, 41
Ergonomics, **76–77**
Erikson, Erik, 3
Escape from Childhood, 144
Ethical Cultural Movement, 2
Ethnicity, 33–34, 52–53, **77–78**, 108, 154–155, 174, 216
Europe, **78–79**, 158
Europe, Council of, **79–81**
Europe, Eastern, xvi, **81**, 108, 205, 206
European Social Charter, 80
European Union, xix, 61, 79, **81–83**, 238, 253
Exploitation, **83**

Factory Acts, xix, 75–76, **85–86**, 86–87, 111, 195–196, 246–247
Factory inspectors, **86–87**, 94, 170, 192
Fair Labor Standards Act, 36, **87–88**, 141, 159, 239, 255
Fair trade, **88**
Fairbridge, Kingsley, 34
Family relations, **88–89**
Family wage, **89–91**, 167–168
Famous Players Company, 42
Female Labor Reform Association, 186–187
Feminism, 90, **91–92**, 255

Finch, Michael, 51, 71
Fireworks manufacture, 123
Fishing, 2, **92–94**, 225
Flynn, Elizabeth Gurley, 141
Folks, Homer, **94**, 255
Forgotten on the Pyjama Trail, 97, 156, 247
France, 7, **94–95**
Franklin, Bob, 38, 144
Free The Children, 138
Frone, Michael R., 71
Fuller, Raymond, 56, 74
Fyfe, Alec, 7, 56

Garment industry, 12, 18, **97–98**, 222–223
Gender differences, 63, **98–101**, 119, 120
Gender stereotypes, 52, **101–102**
General Federation of Women's Clubs, **102**, 170
Georgia, 145
German, Lindsay, 90–91
Germany, **102–103**, 255
Gilmour, David, 65
Glass-making industry, 2, **103**, 123
Glauser, Benno, 222
Global March against Child Labor, **103–105**
Globalization, 28–29, 63, **105–106**, 184–185
Gompers, Samuel, xix, 10, **106**, 107, 188
Granada Television, 156
Grapes of Wrath, The, 159–160
Great Depression, The, **106–107**
Greece, **107–108**
Greenberger, Ellen, xviii, 7, 49, 50–51, 58, 70–72, **108**, 117, 211, 220–221
Gross, Richard, 103
Guatemala, 9, **109–110**
Gulrajani, Mohini, 31
Gypsies, 217

Half-time working, xix, **111**
Hall, Calvin S., 3
Hammond, Barbara, xviii, 40, **111**, 167, 184–185
Hammond, J. L., xviii, 40, **111**, 167, 184–185
Handbook of Children's Rights, 144
Hannawalt, Barbara, 116
Hargis, Peggy G., 80
Harkin Bill, xix, **112**, 142
Hartmann, Heidi, 90
Harvesting, 4, **112–113**, 176
Haywood, "Big Bill," 127–128, 141
Health, xvii, 31, 41, 82, 103, **113–114**, 123, 162, 208, 227
Herding, 4, **114**
Herod Policy, 176
Heywood, Colin, 94
Higdon, Tom, 24

Index

Hill, Joanna, 144
Hill, Joe, 128
Hine, Lewis Wickes, xix, **114**
History of childhood, 31–32, **115–116**
Hobbs, Sandy, 4, 71, 133
Hobsbawm, Eric, 126
Hollway, Marguerite, 97
Holt, John. 144, 212
Homeworking, 182
Honduras, 9, 207
Hope, Henry Thomas, 196
Horan, Patrick M., 90
Horrell, Sara, 168
Hotel and catering industry, **116–118**
Household labour, **118–120**
Hull House, 2
Human Rights Watch Asia, 165
Humphreys, Margaret, 33
Humphries, Jane, 168
Hunting, 122
Hutt, W. H., 227

Illinois, 163, 170
Immigrant children, 27, **121–122**
In the Twilight Zone, 117
India, xiii, xvi, 2, 11, 12, 15, 19, 46, 52–53,
    114, **122–123**, 126, 132, 142, 183, 193,
    203, 205, 236, 243
Indiana, 17
Indonesia, xvii, 2, 93–94, **123–125**
Industrial Revolution, xiii, xviii, 12, 16, 62–63,
    85, 94, 102, **125–126**, 126–127, 190–191,
    227
Industrial society thesis, 29, **126–127**
Industrial Workers of the World, **127–128**,
    140, 164
International Confederation of Free Trade
    Unions, xix, 45, **128–129**, 162, 229
International Conference against Child
    Labour and Forced Labour, 220
International financial institutions, **129–130**,
    218–219
International Labour Organisation, xv, xix,
    1, 29, 31, 55, 89–70, 72, 74, 92–94, 104,
    113, 117–118, 124, 128–129, **130–131**,
    132, 133–134, 142, 142–143, 183, 189,
    199, 201, 206, 219, 229, 234, 242
International Ladies' Garment Workers'
    Union, 97
International Meeting of Working Children,
    19, **131–132**, 142
International Monetary Fund, xviii, 38,
    129–130, **132–133**, 250
International Programme for the Elimination
    of Child Labour, 74, 92, 131, 186–187
International Society for the Prevention of

Child Abuse and Neglect, 55, 133
International Working Group on Child
    Labour, xiv, 4, 49, 55, 56–57, 132, **133**,
    156, 158, 163, 180, 185, 205, 242, 247
International Year of the Child, 37, **133–134**
Islam, 15, 23, 78, 176–177, 183, 203. *See also*
    Quranic schools
Israel, 137–138, 158
Italy, 12, **134**
Ivan-Smith, Edda, 244

Jacklin, Carol, 101
Jamaica, 30
Jamieson, Lynne, 100
Japan, **135**
Johnson, Monica, 72
Johnson, Victoria, 244
Jones, Mary Harris "Mother," xix, **163–164**
Jordan, **135–136**

Kahveci, Erol, 232
*Kashmiri Carpet Children: Exploited Village
    Weavers*, xv
Keating-Owen Bill, 36, **137**, 155
Kelley, Florence, 33, 170–171
Kenya, xvi, **137–138**
Khymer Rouge, 20
Kid, The, 43
Kids Campaign to Build a School for Iqbal,
    104
Kielburger, Craig, **138**
Kingsley, Charles, 246
Knights of Labor, The Order of, 10, **138**, 163
Kundapur Ten Points, 132

Labour codes and policies of the U.S.S.R.,
    139
Landrigan, P. J., 113
Lathrop, Julia, 35–36
Lawrence Mill Workers' Strike, **140–141**
Lebanon, 207
Lee, John Theophilus, 171
Lee-Wright, Peter, 34
Legislation, 16–17, 40, 41, 43, 46, 59, 60–61,
    76, 85–86, 94, 102, 111, 112, 124, 135,
    139, **141–142**, 160, 241, 256
Legislation, international, xix, **142–143**
Leisure, **143**, 218
Leopold, King of Belgium, 17
Liberationism, 4, 37–39, **144**
Liberia, 21
Lindsay, Samuel McCune, **144–145**
Little League baseball, 143
Livingstone, David, xvi, **145**, 149
Lord's Resistance Army, 20
Lorimer, George, 207

Louisiana, 93
Lovejoy, Owen R., **145–146**, 154–155
Low Pay Network, **147**, 199

Maccoby, Eleanor, 101
MacLennan, Emma, 147
Maid-beating syndrome, 138
Making of the English Working Class, The, 227
Malawi, **149–150**
Malaysia, **150**
Mallino, D. L., 113
Malta, **150**
Malthus, Thomas, 151
Malthusianism, **151**
Mansourove, Valery, 206
Markel, Karen S., 71
Market economics, xix, 130, 132–133, **151–152**, 219
Marks and Spencer, 156
Marx, Karl, 27–28, 63, 152, 211
Marxism, xix, 27–28, 40–41, 74, 83, 90–91, **152–153**, 211, 220
Masih, Iqbal, xvi, 104, 128, 138, **153–154**
Massachusetts, 104, 140–141, 170, 175, 186–187, 239
Match manufacture, 123
Mazur, Jay, 97
McIntosh, Mary, 91
McKechnie, Jim, 4, 71, 133
McKelway, Alexander J., 17–18, 146, **154–155**
Mead, Margaret, 3, 231
Meknes, xix, 97, **156**, 247
Mexico, 9, 117, **156–158**, 159, 160
Michigan, 145–146
Middle East, **158**
Migrant workers, 149, 157–158, **158–160**, 217, 222–223
Milkmaids, 59
Mining, 5, 10, 43–44, 46, 75, **160–162**, 186, 189, 237
Minor Consideration, A, 43
Mississippi. 112
Modelling, **162–163**
Moorehead, Caroline, 134
Morocco, xvii, 12, 52, 97, 156, 158, **163**, 247
Mortimer, Jeylan, 7, 51, 71–72, 89, 248
Mother Jones. See Jones, Mary Harris "Mother"
Movement of Working Children and Adolescents from Working-Class Christian Families (MANTHOC), **164**, 181
Multinational companies, **164–165**
Munoz Vila, Cecilia, 44
Murphy, Edgar G., 2, 17, **165**
Myanmar, 2, 21, 48, 72, 99, **165**

Nardinelli, Clark, xv, xviii, 86, 159, 167–168, 185, 246–247
Nardinelli Thesis, The, 86, 159, **167–168**, 185, 246–247
Nasaw, D., 175
National Association of Manufacturers, 2, 170–171
National Child Labor Committee, xix, 10, 17–18, 35–36, 62, 74, 87, 94, 103, 114, 144–146, 154–155, 160, 165, **168–169**, 170, 177, 188, 199, 225, 239
National Civic Federation, 2
National Commission on Youth, 230
National Committee for the Rights of the Child, **169–170**
National Consumers League, **170–171**
National Foundation for Child Welfare, 22–23
National Movement of Street Children, **171**
National Panel on High School and Adolescent Education, 230
National Research Council, 220
Navy, **171**
NCH-Action for Children, xix, 33, **171–172**
Nepal, 34–35, 117, **172–173**, 207
Netherlands, 69, 123–124, **173–174**, 241
New England Association of Farmers, Mechanics, and Other Working Men, **174**
New Jersey, 183
New York, 2, 12, 17–18, 23, 56, 106, 121, 122, 160, 168–169, 170, 175, 222, 232, 233
New York Child Labor Committee, 168–169
New Zealand, 33, **174**
Newman, Barbara, 3
Newman, Philip, 3
Newsies, **174–175**, 181
Nicaragua, 9, **176**
Nicholls, George, 250
Nieuwenhuys, Olga, 11
Nigeria, 52, 54, **176–177**
Nimble Fingers argument, 31
Nobel Peace Prize, 2, 165
Nomads, 136, 177, 215
Nongovernmental organizations, 30, 80, **177–178**, 180–181, 196–197, 227–228
North Carolina, 145, 146, 155, 184
Northern Ireland, 207. *See also* United Kingdom
Norway, 243

Oastler, Robert, xix, 66, 111, **179–180**, 199
On the Employment of Children in Manufactories, 182
Operation Child Watch, **180**
Oppenheim, James, 141

Index

Organization for Economic Development and Cooperation, 129–130, **180**

Organizations of working children, xix–xx, **180–182**

Our Children Should Be Working, xv, 195

Outwork, 121–122, **182**, 222–223

Owen, Robert, **182**

Pakistan, xvii, 2, 19, 153–154, **183–184**, 207

Palestinians, 136

Palmer-Owen Bill, 10, 146, 155, **184**

Panama, 9

Parents, 26, 88–89, 94, **184–186**, 205–206, 222

Parliamentary Committees and Commissions, **186**

Parsons, Herbert, 17–18

Paterson Ten Hour Mill Strikes, **186–187**

Pauper apprentices, 12–13, 19, 167–168, 182, **187–188**, 249

Peel, Sir Robert, 188

Pennsylvania, 10, 44, 144, 145, 154, 163–164

Permanent Conference for the Abolition of Child Labor, 106, **188**

Peru, xvii, 164, **188–189**, 196–197, 221

Pesticides, 113

Petersen, Paul, 43

Philippines, 92, **189–190**, 196, 207

Phillips, S., 185

Physique, 60, 76–77

Piaget, Jean, 201, 215

Pickford, Mary, 41–43

Pinchbeck, Ivy, 126, **190–191**, 200

Pixote, 23, 43

Play, 143

Pollack, S. H., 113

Pollock, Linda, 115–116

Pond, Chris, 147

Poor Laws, 187–188, 248–250

Population trends, 9, 151, 253

Pornography, **191**

Portugal, 9, 12, 46–47, **191–192**

Post-Fordism, **192–193**

Poverty, 31, 47, **193**

President's Science Advisory Committee, 230

Prison, **194**

Product labelling, xix, 31, **194–195**, 205

Pro-employment arguments, **195–196**

Projects, **196–197**, 207, 233–234

Prostitution, 113, **197–198**, 206, 227–228

Protectionism, xviii, 4, 37–39, **198–199**

Proto-industrialization, 32–33, 57–58, 89, **200**

Psychology, developmental, xviii, 29, **200–202**, 214–215, 230–231

Quranic schools, 23, 54, 177, 203

Radda Barnen, 20, 207, 208, 242–243

Ramy, John, 141

Redd Barna, 207, 208, 228

Reebock Prize, 154

Refugees, 136, 215–216

Religion, 54, **203**, 247. *See also* Buddhism; Christianity; Islam

Retail trade, 8, **203**, 210

Rhode Island, 239

Rhodesia, 33–34

Ricardo, David, 249

Rights discourse, 37–39, **203–205**

RKO Radio Pictures, 19

Romania, **205**

Roosevelt, Eleanor, 20

Roosevelt, Franklin D., 87

Roosevelt, Theodore, 2, 18, 35, 163–164

Rouard, Danielle, 95

Rousseau, Jean-Jacques, 214

Rugmark, 31, 194, **205**

Runaways, 198, **205–206**

Russia, 139, 185, **206**

Ryu, Seongryeol, 248

Sadler, Michael, 111, 184–185, 186

Saint-Simon, Henri de, 126

Sandstrom, K. L., 185

Santrock, J. W., 3

Saturday Evening Post, **207**

Satyarthi, Kailsash, 104

Saul, Mahir, 23

Save the Children Fund, xix, 4, 21, 190, **207–208**, 208, 242. *See also* Radda Barnen; Redd Barna

Scandinavia, **208**.*See also* Denmark

Scavenging, **208**

Schaffer, H. Rudolph, 214–215

Schildkrout, Enid, 176

School attendance, 11, 107–108, 109–110, 112, 176, 189

Scotland, 57, 65–57, 100, 145. *See also* United Kingdom

Scruton, Roger Vernon, 195

Self-employment, **208–210**

Senegal, 64

Senior, Nassau, 249

Service sector, **210**

Shaftesbury, Lord, xix, 77, 111, 186, 199, 203, **210–211**

Shanahan, Michael J., 89–90

Shapley, Elizabeth, 140

Sherman, Alfred, 195

Shoe manufacture, 21–22

Shoeshining. *See* Street trading

Shorter, Edward, 115

Slave labour, 235–236

Smith, Adam, 62
Smith, Chris, 112
Smith, Wiley, 170
Soccer, 184, 217
Social class, 15, 28, 63, 153, **211–212**, 213
Social construction of childhood, **212–214**
Socialism, 24, 74, 170, 182, 198–199, 255. *See also* Marxism
Socialization, 58, 175, **214–215**
Soldiers, 20–21
Somalia, **215–216**
South Africa, 52, **216**
South Asia Coalition on Child Servitude, 104–105, 205
South Carolina, 145
Spain, 9, 20, **216–217**
Sports, 143, **217–218**.*See also* Camel jockeys; Soccer
Sri Lanka, 117
Stabilization and structural adjustment programmes, xviii, 130, 133, **218–219**, 250–251
State of the World's Children 1997, The, 238
Steinbeck, John, 159–160
Steinberg, Laurence, xviii, 7, 49, 50–51, 58, 70–72, 89, 108, 117, 211, **219–220**, 230–231, 239–240
Stephens, William N., xv, 195
Stone, Lawrence, 115
Stonebreaking, 192
Stop Child Labour, 4, 211, **220**
Street children, xvi, 5, 9, 21, 27, 108, 171, 175, 181, 194, 196, 205, 215, **220–222**, 228, 232–234
Street trading, 177, 203, 209, 210, 232–234
Sudan, 20, 21
Sugarman, Leonie, 201–202
Sultana, Ronald, 150, 174
Suu Kyi, Aung Sang, 185
Sweat Shops in the Sun, 7
Sweated labour, **222–223**

Tanzania, **225**
Taylor, Elizabeth, 41
Taylor, R. B., 7
Television, 34, 41, 43, 76
Temple, Shirley, 41–42
Tempos, 15–16
Terre des Hommes, 105, 227–228
Texas, 159
Textile manufacture, 33, 65–67, 85–86, 94, 145, 158–159, 182, 195–196, 239
Thailand, 93, 97, 198, **225–227**, 228
Theatre, 76
Thompson, E. P., xviii, 29, 126, 167, 211, 213, **227**

Togo, 204
Tour through the Whole Island of Great Britain, 57–58
Tourism, 30, 116–118, 150, 157, 192, 217, **227–228**
Townsend, Joseph, 249
Toynbee, Claire, 100
Trade unions, xix, 10, 46, 128–129, 138, 192, **228–229**
Traditional societies, 5, 127, 177, **229**, 256
Training, 13, **229–230**
Transition debate, **230–232**
Trattner, Walter, 154, 159, 168
Triangle Shirtwaist Fire, xix, 97, **232**, 233
Turkey, 158, 197, **232–234**
Twentieth Century Fox, 41

Uganda, 20
Unfree labour, xvii, 11–12, 19, 30, 123, 172, 189–190, **235–236**
United Arab Emirates, 25–26, **236**
United Artists Corporation, 43
United Kingdom, xiii, 1, 32–33, 39–40, 50, 69, 70–71, 85–86, 86–87, 125–126, 160–162, 198, 200, 220, **236–238**
United Nations, xix, 37, 49–50, 55–56, 130, 142–143, 238
United Nations Children's Emergency Fund (UNICEF), 4, 20–21, 69–70, 98, 132, 142, 205, **238**
United States of America, xiii, 1, 17, 20, 43–44, 70–72, 88–89, 97, 103, 113, 114, 117, 118–119, 121–122, 138, 198, 204, **238–240**
Ure, Andrew, 195

Valcarenghi, Marina, 134
Van Houten, Samuel, xix, 173, 199, **241**
Vietnam, **241–242**
Virginia, 33, 58, 103
Voices of children, 133, **242–244**
Vygotsky, Lev, 202, 213

Wade, James, 20
Wages, 83, 100, **245–246**
Washington, George, 20
Washington State, 240
Water Babies, The, **246**
Weber, Max, 27, 211–212
Welfare, child, 9, **246–247**
West, Elliot, 118
What Works for Working Children, 247
When Teenagers Work: The Psychological and Social Costs of Adolescent Employment, 108, 219–220
White, Ben, 47-48, 74

Index

Wilk, Valerie A., 114
Wilson, Woodrow, 137
Wolfson, P. J., 20
Woodhead, Martin, 243–244
Work ethic, 34, 150, **247**
Work values, **247–248**
Workhouses, 75, **248–250**
Work-labour distinction, 55–57
World Bank, 38, 129–130, **250–251**
World Trade Organization, 129

Young caregivers, **253–254**
Young Carers and Their Families, xv
Young Carers Research Group, 254

Zelizer, V., 118
Zetkin, Clara Eissner, 29, 199, **255**
Zimand, Gertrude Folks, **255**
Zimbabwe, xvii, 52, **255–256**

Sandy Hobbs has taught psychology in several Scottish universities and is currently a reader in psychology at the University of Paisley, Scotland. He has published many articles on aspects of psychology, education, and popular culture. **Jim McKechnie** is a developmental psychologist and senior lecturer in psychology at the University of Paisley, Scotland. He has undertaken research on various aspects of child labour in Britain and was an adviser to the International Working Group on Child Labour. **Michael Lavalette** is a lecturer in social policy at the University of Liverpool, England. He was one of the first people in Britain to be awarded a Ph.D. for work in the area of child labour. He has also published works on wider aspects of social policy.